SECOND EDITION

# 21st Century C

*Ben Klemens*

Beijing · Cambridge · Farnham · Köln · Sebastopol · Tokyo

**21st Century C, Second Edition**

by Ben Klemens

Copyright © 2015 Ben Klemens. All rights reserved.

Printed in the United States of America.

Published by O'Reilly Media, Inc., 1005 Gravenstein Highway North, Sebastopol, CA 95472.

O'Reilly books may be purchased for educational, business, or sales promotional use. Online editions are also available for most titles (*http://www.safaribooksonline.com*). For more information, contact our corporate/institutional sales department: 800-998-9938 or corporate@oreilly.com.

| | |
|---|---|
| **Editors:** Rachel Roumeliotis and Allyson MacDonald | **Indexer:** Judy McConville |
| **Production Editor:** Nicole Shelby | **Interior Designer:** David Futato |
| **Copyeditor:** Becca Freed | **Cover Designer:** Karen Montgomery |
| **Proofreader:** Amanda Kersey | **Illustrator:** Rebecca Demarest |

September 2014:     Second Edition

**Revision History for the Second Edition**
2014-09-24:    First Release
2015-05-15:    Second Release

See *http://oreilly.com/catalog/errata.csp?isbn=9781491903896* for release details.

978-1-491-90389-6

[LSI]

# Table of Contents

# Preface

*Is it really punk rock*
*Like the party line?*

—Wilco,
*"Too Far Apart"*

## C Is Punk Rock

C has only a handful of keywords and is a bit rough around the edges, and it rocks. You can do anything with it. Like the C, G, and D chords on a guitar, you can learn the basic mechanics quickly, and then spend the rest of your life getting better. The people who don't get it fear its power and think it too edgy to be safe. By all rankings, it is consistently the most popular language that doesn't have a corporation or foundation spending money to promote it.[1]

Also, the language is about 40 years old, which makes it middle-aged. It was written by a few guys basically working against management—the perfect punk rock origins—but that was in the 1970s, and there's been a lot of time for the language to go mainstream.

What did people do when punk rock went mainstream? In the decades since its advent in the 1970s, punk certainly has come in from the fringes: The Clash, The Offspring, Green Day, and The Strokes sold millions of albums worldwide (to name just a few), and I have heard lite instrumental versions of songs from the punk spinoff known as grunge at my local supermarket. The former lead singer of Sleater-Kinney now has a popular sketch comedy show that frequently lampoons punk rockers.[2] One

---

[1] This preface owes an obvious and huge debt to *Punk Rock Languages: A Polemic* (*http://bit.ly/punk-lang*) by Chris Adamson.

[2] With lyrics like "Can't get to heaven with a three-chord song," maybe Sleater-Kinney was post-punk? Unfortunately, there is no ISO punk standard we can look to for precise in-or-out definitions.

reaction to the continuing evolution would be to take the hard line and say that the original wave was punk and everything else is just easy punk pop for the masses. The traditionalists can still play their albums from the '70s, and if the grooves are worn out, they can download a digitally mastered edition. They can buy Ramones hoodies for their toddlers.

Outsiders don't get it. Some of them hear the word *punk* and picture something out of the 1970s—a historic artifact about some kids that were, at the time, really doing something different. The traditionalist punks who still love and play their 1973 Iggy Pop LPs are having their fun, but they bolster the impression that punk is ossified and no longer relevant.

Getting back to the world of C, we have both the traditionalists, waving the banner of ANSI '89, and those who will rock out to whatever works and may not even realize that the code they are writing would not have compiled or run in the 1990s. Outsiders don't get the difference. They see still-in-print books from the 1980s and still-online tutorials from the 1990s, they hear from the hardcore traditionalists who insist on still writing like that today, and they don't even know that the language and the rest of its users continue to evolve. That's a shame, because they're missing out on some great stuff.

This is a book about breaking tradition and keeping C punk rock. I don't care to compare the code in this book to the original C specification in Kernighan & Ritchie's 1978 book. My *telephone* has 512 MB of memory, so why are our C textbooks still spending pages upon pages covering techniques to shave kilobytes off of our executables? I am writing this on a bottom-of-the-line red netbook that can accommodate 3,200,000,000 instructions per second; what do I care about whether an operation requires comparing 8 bits or 16? We should be writing code that we can write quickly and that is readable by our fellow humans. We're still writing in C, so our readable but imperfectly optimized code will still run an order of magnitude faster than if we'd written comparable code in any number of alternative, bloated languages.

# Q & A (Or, the Parameters of the Book)

### Q: How is this C book different from all others?

A: Some are better written, some are even entertaining, but C textbooks are a somewhat uniform bunch (I've read *a lot* of them, including *C for Programmers with an Introduction to C11*; *Head First C*; *The C Programming Language, 1st Edition*; *The C Programming Language 2nd Edition*; *Programming in C*; *Practical C Programming*; *Absolute Beginner's Guide to C*; *The Waite Group's C Primer Plus*; and *C Programming*). Most were written before the C99 standard simplified many aspects of usage, and you can tell that some of those now in their *n*th edition just pasted in a few notes about updates rather than seriously rethinking how to use the language. They all mention that there might be libraries that you could maybe use in writing your own code, but most predate the installation tools and ecosystem we have now, which make using those libraries reliable and reasonably portable. Those textbooks are still valid and still have value, but modern C code just doesn't look like much of the code in many of those textbooks.

This book picks up where they left off, reconsidering the language and the ecosystem in which it lives. The storyline here is about using libraries that provide linked lists and XML parsers, not writing new ones from scratch. It is about writing code that is readable and has a friendly user interface.

**Q: Who is this book for? Do I need to be a coding guru?**

A: You have experience coding in any language, maybe Java or a scripting language such as Perl. I don't have to sell you on why your code shouldn't be one long routine with no subfunctions.

The body of the book assumes basic knowledge of C gained from time spent writing C code. If you are rusty on the details or are starting from zero, Appendix A offers a short tutorial on basic C for readers who are coming from a scripting language like Python or Ruby.

I might as well point out to you that I have also written a textbook on statistical and scientific computing, *Modeling with Data* (Klemens, 2008). Along with lots of details of dealing with numeric data and using statistical models for describing data, it has a longer, more standalone tutorial on C, which I naturally think overcomes many of the failings of older C tutorials.

**Q: I'm an application programmer, not a kernel hacker. Why should I use C instead of a quick-to-write scripting language like Python?**

A: If you are an application programmer, this book is for you. I read people asserting that C is a systems language, which impresses me as so un-punk—who are they to tell us what we're allowed to write?

Statements along the lines of "Our language is almost as fast as C, but is easier to write" are so common that they are almost cliché. Well, C is definitely as fast as C, and the purpose of this book is to show you that C is easier to write than the textbooks from decades past imply that it is. You don't have to call `malloc` and get elbow-deep in memory management half as often as the systems programmers of the 1990s did, we have facilities for easier string handling, and even the core syntax has evolved to make for more legible code.

I started writing C in earnest because I had to speed up a simulation in a scripting language, R. Like so many other scripting languages, R has a C interface and encourages the user to make use of it any time the host language is too slow. Eventually, I had so many functions jumping out from the host script to C code that I just dropped the host language entirely.

**Q: It's nice that application programmers coming from scripting languages will like this book, but I *am* a kernel hacker. I taught myself C in fifth grade and sometimes have dreams that correctly compile. What new material can there be for me?**

A: C has evolved in the last 20 years. As I'll discuss later, the set of things we are guaranteed that all C compilers support has changed with time, thanks to two new C standards since the original ANSI standard that defined the language for so long. Maybe have a look at Chapter 10 and see if anything there surprises you. Some sections of this book, like the chapter clarifying common misconceptions about pointers (Chapter 6), cover material that has changed little since the 1980s.

Also, the environment has advanced. Many of the tools I cover, such as make and the debugger, may already be familiar to you, but I have found that others are not as well known. Autotools has entirely changed how distribution of code happens, and Git has changed how collaborative coding happens.

**Q: I can't help but notice that about a third of this book has almost no C code in it.**

A: This book intends to cover what the other C textbooks don't, and at the top of that list are the tools and environment. If you're not using a debugger (standalone or part of your IDE), you're making your life much more difficult. Textbooks often relegate the debugger to an afterthought, if they mention it at all. Sharing code with others requires another set of tools, including Autotools and Git. Code doesn't live in a vacuum, and I felt that I would be doing a disservice writing yet another textbook that pretends that all the reader needs to be productive is the syntax of the language.

**Q: Out of the many tools available for C development, how did you pick the ones in this book?**

A: More than most, the C community holds itself to a high standard of interoperability. There are a lot of C extensions provided by the GNU environment, IDEs that work only on Windows, and compiler extensions that exist only in LLVM. This is probably why past textbooks shied away from covering tools. But in the present day there are some systems that work on anything we commonly recognize as a computer. Many of them are from the GNU; LLVM and its associated tools are quickly making ground but are still not as prevalent. Whatever you are using, be it a Windows box, a Linux box, or an instance you just pulled up from your cloud computing provider, the tools I cover here should be easy and quick to install. I mention a few platform-specific tools, but will be explicit in those cases.

I do not cover any integrated development environments (IDEs) because few if any reliably work across all platforms (try pulling up an Amazon Elastic Compute Cloud instance and installing Eclipse and its C plug-ins), and the choice of IDE is heavily influenced by personal preference. IDEs typically have a project build system, which is usually incompatible with every other IDE's project build system. IDE project files are therefore unusable for project distribution outside of situations (classrooms, certain offices, some computing platforms) where everybody is mandated to use the same IDE.

**Q: I have the Internet and can look up commands and syntax details in a second or two, so, really, why should I read this book?**

A: It's true: you can get an operator precedence table from a Linux or Mac command prompt with `man operator`, so why am I going to put one here?

I've got the same Internet you've got, and I've spent a lot of time reading it. So I have a good idea of what isn't being talked about, and that's what I stick to here. When introducing a new tool, like `gprof` or `gdb`, I give you what you need to know to get your bearings and ask your search engine coherent questions, and what other textbooks missed (which is a lot).

# Standards: So Many to Choose From

Unless explicitly stated otherwise, everything in this book conforms to the ISO C99 and C11 standards. To make sense of what that means, and give you some historical background, let us go through the list of major C standards (passing over the minor revisions and corrections).

*K & R (circa 1978)*
  Dennis Ritchie, Ken Thompson, and a handful of other contributors came up with C while putting together the Unix operating system. Brian Kernighan and Dennis Ritchie eventually wrote down a description of the language in the first edition of their book, which set the first de facto standard (Kernighan, 1978).

*ANSI C89*
  Bell Labs handed over the stewardship of the language to the American National Standards Institute (ANSI). In 1989 the institute published its standard, which made a few improvements over K & R. The second edition of K & R's book included a full specification of the language, which meant that tens of thousands of programmers had a copy of the ANSI standard on their desks (Kernighan, 1988). The ANSI standard was adopted by the International Organization for Standardization (ISO) in 1990 with no serious changes, but *ANSI '89* seems to be the more common term (and would make a great t-shirt slogan).

A decade passed. C went mainstream, in the sense that the base code for more or less every PC and every Internet server was written in C, which is as mainstream as a human endeavor could possibly become.

During this period, C++ split off and hit it big (although not quite as big). C++ was the best thing to ever happen to C. While every other language was bolting on extra syntax to follow the object-oriented trend and whatever other new tricks came to the authors' minds, C stuck to the standard. The people who wanted stability and portability used C, the people who wanted more and more features so they could wallow in them like moist hundred dollar bills got C++, and everybody was happy.

*ISO C99*

The C standard underwent a major revision a decade later. Additions were made for numeric and scientific computing, with a standard type for complex numbers and some type-generic functions. A few conveniences from C++ got lifted, including one-line comments (which originally came from one of C's predecessor languages, BCPL) and being able to declare variables at the head of for loops. Using structures was made easier thanks to a few additions to the rules for how they can be declared and initialized, plus some notational conveniences. Things were modernized to acknowledge that security matters and that not everybody speaks English.

When you think about just how much of an impact C89 had, and how the entire globe was running on C code, it's hard to imagine the ISO being able to put out anything that wouldn't be widely criticized—even a refusal to make any changes would be reviled. And indeed, this standard was controversial. There are two common ways to express a complex variable (rectangular and polar coordinates) —so where does the ISO get off picking one? Why do we need a mechanism for variable-length macro inputs when all the good code got written without it? In other words, the purists accused the ISO of selling out to the pressure for more features.

As of this writing, most compilers support C99 plus or minus a few caveats. However, there is one notable exception to this broad consensus: Microsoft currently refuses to add C99 support to its Visual Studio C++ compiler. The section "Compiling C with Windows" on page 6 covers some of the many ways to compile C code for Windows, so not using Visual Studio is at most an inconvenience, and having a major establishment player tell us that we can't use ANSI- and ISO-standard C only bolsters the punk rock of it all.

*C11*

Self-conscious about the accusations of selling out, the ISO made few serious changes in the third edition of the standard. We got a means of writing type-generic functions, and things were modernized to further acknowledge that security matters and that not everybody speaks English.

The C11 standard came out in December of 2011, but support for the standard has been implemented by compiler authors at a surprisingly rapid pace, to the point that a number of major compilers already claim near-complete conformance. However, the standard defines behavior for both the compiler and the standard library—and library support, such as for threading and atomics, is complete on some systems but catching up on others.

## The POSIX Standard

That's the state of things as far as C itself goes, but the language coevolved with the Unix operating system, and you will see throughout the book that the interrelationship matters for day-to-day work. If something is easy on the Unix command line, it is probably because it is easy in C; Unix tools are often written to facilitate writing C code.

*Unix*

C and Unix were designed at Bell Labs in the early 1970s. During most of the 20th century, Bell was being investigated for monopolistic practices, and one of its agreements with the US federal government included promises that Bell would not expand its reach into software. So Unix was given away for free for researchers to dissect and rebuild. The name Unix is a trademark, originally owned by Bell Labs and subsequently traded off like a baseball card among a number of companies.

Variants of Unix blossomed as the code was looked over, reimplemented, and improved in different ways by diverse hackers. It just takes one little incompatibility to make a program or script unportable, so the need for some standardization quickly became apparent.

*POSIX (Portable Operating System Interface)*

This standard, first established by the Institute of Electrical and Electronics Engineers (IEEE) in 1988, provided a common basis for Unix-like operating systems. It specifies how the shell should work, what to expect from commands like ls and grep, and a number of C libraries that C authors can expect to have available. For example, the pipes that command-line users use to string together commands are specified in detail here, which means C's popen (pipe open) function is POSIX-standard, not ISO C-standard. The POSIX standard has been revised many times; the version as of this writing is POSIX:2008, and that is what I am referring to when I say that something is POSIX-standard. A POSIX-standard system must have a C compiler available, via the command name c99.

This book will use the POSIX standard, though I'll tell you when.

With the exception of many members of a family of OSes from Microsoft, just about every current operating system you could name is built on a POSIX-compliant base: Linux, Mac OS X, iOS, webOS, Solaris, BSD—even Windows servers offer a POSIX subsystem. And for the hold-out OSes, "Compiling C with Windows" on page 6 will show you how to install a POSIX subsystem.

Finally, there are two more implementations of POSIX worth noting because of their prevalence and influence:

*BSD*

After Unix was made available from Bell Labs for the public to dissect, the researchers at the University of California, Berkeley, made major improvements, eventually rewriting the entire Unix code base to produce the Berkeley Software Distribution. If you are using a computer from Apple, Inc., you are using BSD with an attractive graphical frontend. BSD goes beyond POSIX in several respects, and we'll see some functions that are not part of the POSIX standard but are too useful to pass up (most notably the lifesaver that is `asprintf`).

*GNU*

It stands for GNU's Not Unix, and is the other big success story in independently reimplementing and improving on the Unix environment. The great majority of Linux distributions use GNU tools throughout. There are very good odds that you have the GNU Compiler Collection (`gcc`) on your POSIX box—even BSD uses it. Again, the `gcc` defines a de facto standard that extends C and POSIX in a few ways, and I will be explicit when making use of those extensions.

Legally, the BSD license is slightly more permissive than the GNU license. Because some parties are deeply concerned with the political and business implications of the licenses, one can typically find both GNU and BSD versions of most tools. For example, both the `gcc` and the BSD's `clang` are top-notch C compilers. The authors from both camps closely watch and learn from each other's work, so we can expect that technical differences that currently exist will tend to even out over time.

---

## The Legal Sidebar

US law no longer has a registration system for copyright: with few exceptions, as soon as anybody writes something down, it is copyrighted.

Of course, distribution of a library depends on copying from hard drive to hard drive, and there are a number of common mechanisms for granting the right to copy a copyrighted work with little hassle.

*The GNU Public License (GPL)*

This allows unlimited copying and use of the source code and its executable version. There is one major condition: If you *distribute* a program or library based on the GPLed source code, then you must distribute the source code to your program. Note well that if you use your program in-house and don't distribute it, this condition doesn't hold, and you have no obligation to distribute source. Running a GPLed program, like compiling your code with `gcc`, does not in itself obligate you to distribute source code, because the program output (such

---

as the executable you just compiled) is not considered to be based on or a derivative of gcc. Example: the GNU Scientific Library.

*The Lesser GPL (LGPL)*
The LGPL is much like the GPL, but it explicitly stipulates that if you are linking to an LGPL library as a shared library, then your code doesn't count as a derivative work, and you aren't obligated to distribute source. That is, you can distribute closed-source code that links to an LGPL library. Example: GLib.

*The BSD License*
This license requires that you preserve copyrights and disclaimers for BSD-licensed source code, but it doesn't require that you redistribute source code. Example: Libxml2, under the BSD-like MIT license.

Please note the usual disclaimer: I am not a lawyer, and this is a sidebar summary of several rather long legal documents. Read the documents themselves (*http://open source.org/licenses*) or consult a lawyer if you are unsure about how the details apply to your situation.

# Some Logistics

## The Second Edition

I used to be a cynic and think that people just wrote second editions to disrupt all the people selling used copies of the first edition. But this second edition actually could not have happened without the first being published, and could not have happened sooner (and most of the book's readers are reading electronic copies anyway).

The big addition from the first edition is the chapter on concurrent threads, aka parallelization. It focuses on OpenMP and atomic variables and structs. OpenMP is not part of the C standard, but it is a reliable part of the C ecosystem, so it comfortably fits into this book. Atomic variables were added in the December 2011 revision of the C standard, so when this book came out less than a year later there were no compilers that supported them. We are now far enough along that I could write this chapter based both on the theory presented in the standard and the practice of a real-world implementation and tested code. See Chapter 12.

The first edition was blessed with some wonderfully pedantic readers. They caught everything that could be somehow construed as a bug, from the stupid thing I said about dashes on the command line to sentences whose wording could be misconstrued incorrectly in certain cases. Nothing in this world is bug-free, but the book is much more accurate and useful as a result of so much great reader feedback.

Other additions to this edition:

- Appendix A provides a basic C tutorial for readers coming from another language. I was reluctant to include it in the first edition because there are so many C tutorials out there, but the book is more useful with it than without.

- By popular demand, I expanded the discussion of how to use a debugger significantly. See "Using a Debugger" on page 33.

- The first edition had a segment on how to write functions that take in a list of arbitrary length, so both sum(1, 2.2) and sum(1, 2.2, 3, 8, 16) would be valid. But what if you want to send multiple lists, like writing a dot-product function that multiplies two arbitrary-length vectors, like dot((2, 4), (-1, 1)) and dot((2, 4, 8, 16), (-1, 1, -1, 1))? "Multiple Lists" on page 212 covers this.

- I rewrote Chapter 11, on extending objects with new functions. The primary addition is an implementation of virtual tables.

- I wrote a little more on the preprocessor, with an intro to the morass of test macros and their use in "Test Macros" on page 172, including a passing mention of the _Static_assert keyword.

- I stuck to a promise I made to myself to not include a tutorial on regular expression parsing in this book (because there are hundreds online and in other books). But I did add a demo in "Parsing Regular Expressions" on page 324 on the use of the POSIX regular expression parsing functions, which are in a relatively raw form compared to regex parsers in many other languages.

- The discussion of string handling in the first edition relied heavily on asprintf, a sprintf-like function that autoallocates the required amount of memory before writing a string to the space. There is a version widely distributed by the GNU, but many readers were constrained from using it, so in this edition I added Example 9-3, showing how to write such a function from C-standard parts.

- One of the big themes in Chapter 7 is that micromanaging numeric types can cause trouble, so the first edition made no mention of the dozens of new numeric types introduced in the C99 standard, like int_least32_t, uint_fast64_t, and so on (C99 §7.18; C11 §7.20). Several readers encouraged me to at least mention some of the more useful types, like intptr_t and intmax_t, which I now do where appropriate.

## Conventions Used in This Book

The following typographical conventions are used in this book:

*Italic*
> Indicates new terms, filenames and file paths, URLs, and email addresses. Many new terms are defined in a glossary at the end of this book.

`Constant width`
> Used for program listings, as well as within paragraphs to refer to program elements such as variable or function names, databases, data types, environment variables, statements, and keywords.

`Constant width italic`
> Shows text that should be replaced with user-supplied values or by values determined by context.

> This icon signifies a tip, suggestion, or general note.

> This icon indicates a warning or caution.

## Using Code Examples

This book is here to help you get your job done. In general, you may use the code in this book in your programs and documentation. You do not need to contact us for permission unless you're reproducing a significant portion of the code. For example, writing a program that uses several chunks of code from this book does not require permission. Selling or distributing a CD-ROM of examples from O'Reilly books does require permission. Answering a question by citing this book and quoting example code does not require permission. Incorporating a significant amount of example code from this book into your product's documentation does require permission.

The code examples for this title can be found here: *https://github.com/b-k/21st-Century-Examples.*

We appreciate, but do not require, attribution. An attribution usually includes the title, author, publisher, and ISBN. For example: "*21st Century C, 2nd Edition* by Ben Klemens (O'Reilly). Copyright 2014 Ben Klemens, 978-1-491-90389-6."

If you feel your use of code examples falls outside fair use or the permission given above, feel free to contact us at *permissions@oreilly.com*.

## Safari® Books Online

 Safari Books Online (*www.safaribooksonline.com*) is an on-demand digital library that delivers expert content in both book and video form from the world's leading authors in technology and business.

Technology professionals, software developers, web designers, and business and creative professionals use Safari Books Online as their primary resource for research, problem solving, learning, and certification training.

Safari Books Online offers a range of product mixes and pricing programs for organizations, government agencies, and individuals. Subscribers have access to thousands of books, training videos, and prepublication manuscripts in one fully searchable database from publishers like O'Reilly Media, Prentice Hall Professional, Addison-Wesley Professional, Microsoft Press, Sams, Que, Peachpit Press, Focal Press, Cisco Press, John Wiley & Sons, Syngress, Morgan Kaufmann, IBM Redbooks, Packt, Adobe Press, FT Press, Apress, Manning, New Riders, McGraw-Hill, Jones & Bartlett, Course Technology, and dozens more. For more information about Safari Books Online, please visit us online.

## How to Contact Us

Please address comments and questions concerning this book to the publisher:

O'Reilly Media, Inc.
1005 Gravenstein Highway North
Sebastopol, CA 95472
800-998-9938 (in the United States or Canada)
707-829-0515 (international or local)
707-829-0104 (fax)

We have a web page for this book, where we list errata, examples, and any additional information. You can access this page at *http://bit.ly/21st_century_c_2e*.

To comment or ask technical questions about this book, send email to *bookquestions@oreilly.com*.

For more information about our books, courses, conferences, and news, see our website at *http://www.oreilly.com*.

Find us on Facebook: *http://facebook.com/oreilly*

Follow us on Twitter: *http://twitter.com/oreillymedia*

Watch us on YouTube: *http://www.youtube.com/oreillymedia*

## Acknowledgments

- Nora Albert: general support, guinea pig.
- Jerome Benoit: Autoconf tips.
- Bruce Fields, Dave Kitabjian, Sarah Weissman: extensive and thorough review.
- Patrick Hall: Unicode erudition.
- Nathan Jepson, Allyson MacDonald, Rachel Roumeliotis, and Shawn Wallace: editorial.
- Andreas Klein: pointing out the value of `intptr_t`.
- Rolando Rodríguez: testing, inquisitive use, and exploration.
- Rachel Steely, Nicole Shelby, and Becca Freed: production.
- Ulrik Sverdrup: pointing out that we can use repeated designated initializers to set default values.

# PART I

# The Environment

In the wilds outside the scripting languages' walled gardens, there is an abundance of tools that solve the big annoyances about C, but you have to hunt for them. And I mean *have to*: many of these tools are absolutely necessary to write without pain. If you aren't using a debugger (standalone or within an IDE), then you're imposing arbitrary hardship on yourself.

There is also an abundance of existing libraries waiting to be used in your code, so you can work on the problem at hand instead of wasting time reimplementing linked lists, parsers, or other basics. It needs to be as easy as possible to compile your program using external libraries.

The following is an overview of Part I:

Chapter 1 covers setting up the basic environment, including getting a package manager and getting it to install all the requisite tools. This is all background for the interesting part, where we compile programs using libraries from elsewhere. The process is pretty standardized, involving a small set of environment variables and recipes.

Chapter 2 introduces tools for debugging, documenting, and testing, because what good is code until it's debugged, documented, and tested?

Chapter 3 addresses Autotools, a system for packaging your code for distribution. But the chapter takes the long way, and so also covers more about writing shell scripts and makefiles.

Nothing complicates life like other people. Therefore, Chapter 4 covers Git, a system for keeping track of the slightly different versions of a project on your and your collaborators' hard drives, and making the process of merging all those versions as simple as possible.

Other languages are a key part of the modern C environment, because so many languages advertise a C interface. Chapter 5 will offer some general notes on writing the interface, and give an extended example with Python.

# Set Yourself Up for Easy Compilation

*Look out honey 'cause I'm using technology.*
—Iggy Pop, "Search and Destroy"

The C standard library is just not enough to get serious work done.

Instead, the C ecosystem has expanded outside of the standard, which means that knowing how to easily call functions from common but not-ISO-standard libraries is essential if you want to get past doing textbook exercises. If you want to work with an XML file, a JPEG image, or a TIFF file, then you will need libxml, libjpeg, or libtiff, which are all freely available but not part of the standard. Unfortunately, this is the point where most textbooks taper off and leave you to work it out for yourself, which is why you can find C detractors who will say self-dissonant things like *C is 40 years old, so you have to write everything from scratch in it*—they never worked out how to link to a library.

Here is the agenda for the chapter:

*Set up the requisite tools*
> This is much easier than it was in the dark days when you had to hunt for every component. You can set up a full build system with all the frills in maybe 10 or 15 minutes (plus all the download time to load so much good stuff).

*Compile a C program*
> Yes, you know how to do this, but we need a setup that has hooks for the libraries and their locations; just typing cc *myfile.c* doesn't cut it anymore. *Make* is just about the simplest system to facilitate compiling programs, so it provides a good model for discussion. I'll show you the smallest possible makefile that offers enough room to grow.

*Set up variables and add new libraries*

Whatever system we use will be based on a small set of environment-like variables, so I'll discuss what they do and how to set them. Once we have all that compilation machinery in place, adding new libraries will be an easy question of adjusting the variables we've already set up.

*Set up a compilation system*

As a bonus, we can use everything up to this point to set up a still simpler system for compilation, which will let us cut and paste code onto the command prompt.

A special note to IDE users: you may not be a make user, but this section will nonetheless be relevant to you, because for every recipe that make executes when compiling code, your IDE has an analogous recipe. If you know what make is doing, you'll have an easy time tweaking your IDE.

# Use a Package Manager

If you are not using a package manager, you are missing out.

I bring up package managers for several reasons: first, some of you may not have the basics installed. For you, I put this section first in the book, because you need to get these tools, and fast. A good package manager will have you set up quite rapidly with a full POSIX subsystem, compilers for every language you've ever heard of, a half-decent array of games, the usual office productivity tools, a few hundred C libraries, et cetera.

Second, as C authors, the package manager is a key means by which we can get libraries for folding into our work.

Third, if you are making the jump from being somebody who downloads packages to being somebody producing a package, this book will take you halfway, showing you how to prepare your package for easy autoinstallation, so that when the administrator of a package repository decides to include your code in the repository, he or she will have no problem building the final package.

If you are a Linux user, you set up your computer with a package manager and have already seen how easy the software obtention process can be. For Windows users, I'll cover Cygwin (*http://cygwin.com*) below. Mac users have several options, such as Fink (*http://finkproject.org*), Homebrew (*http://brew.sh*), and Macports (*http://macports.org*). All the Mac options depend on Apple's Xcode package, available for free via (depending on your Mac's vintage) the OS install CD, the directory of installable programs, the Apple App Store, or by registering as a developer with Apple.

What packages will you need? Here's a quick rundown of the C development basics. Because every system has a different organization scheme, some of these may be bundled differently, installed by default in a base package, or oddly named. When in doubt about a package, install it, because we're past the days when installing too many things could somehow cause system instability or slowdown. However, you probably don't have the bandwidth (or maybe even the disk space) to install every package on offer, so some judgment will be required. If you find that you are missing something, you can always go back and get it later. Packages to definitely get:

- A compiler. Definitely install `gcc`; `clang` may be available.
- GDB, a debugger.
- Valgrind, to test for C memory usage errors.
- `gprof`, a profiler.
- `make`, so you never have to call your compiler directly.
- `pkg-config`, for finding libraries.
- Doxygen, for documentation generation.
- A text editor. There are literally hundreds of text editors to choose from. Here are a few subjective recommendations:
  — Emacs and vim are the hardcore geek's favorites. Emacs is very inclusive (the E is for *extensible*); vim is more minimalist and is very friendly to touch typists. If you expect to spend hundreds of hours staring at a text editor, it is worth taking the time to learn one of them.
  — Kate is friendly and attractive, and provides a good subset of the conveniences we expect as programmers, such as syntax highlighting.
  — As a last resort, try nano, which is aggressively simple, and is text-based, and therefore works even when your GUI doesn't.
- If you are a fan of IDEs, get one—or several. Again, there are many to choose from; here are a few recommendations:
  — Anjuta: in the GNOME family. Friendly with Glade, the GNOME GUI builder.
  — KDevelop: in the KDE family.
  — XCode: Apple's IDE for OS X.
  — Code::blocks: relatively simple, works on Windows.
  — Eclipse: the luxury car with lots of cupholders and extra knobs. Also cross-platform.

In later chapters, I'll get to these more heavy-duty tools:

- Autotools: Autoconf, Automake, libtool
- Git

- Alternate shells, such as the Z shell.

And, of course, there are the C libraries that will save you the trouble of reinventing the wheel (or, to be more metaphorically accurate, reinventing the locomotive). You might want more, but here are the libraries that will be used over the course of this book:

- libcURL
- libGLib
- libGSL
- libSQLite3
- libXML2

There is no consensus on library package naming schemes, and you will have to work out how your package manager likes to dissect a single library into subparts. There is typically one package for users and a second for authors who will use the library in their own work, so be sure to select both the base package and the -dev or -devel packages. Some systems separate documentation into yet another package. Some require that you download debugging symbols separately, in which case GDB should lead you through the steps the first time you run it on something lacking debugging symbols.

If you are using a POSIX system, then after you've installed the preceding items, you will have a complete development system and are ready to get coding. For Windows users, we'll take a brief detour to understand how the setup interacts with the main Windows system.

# Compiling C with Windows

On most systems, C is the central, VIP language that all the other tools work to facilitate; on a Windows box, C is strangely ignored.

So I need to take a little time out to discuss how to set up a Windows box for writing code in C. If you aren't writing on a Windows box now, feel free to skip this segment and jump to "Which Way to the Library?" on page 10.

## POSIX for Windows

Because C and Unix coevolved, it's hard to talk about one and not the other. I think it's easier to start with POSIX. Also, those of you who are trying to compile code on a Windows box that you wrote elsewhere will find this to be the most natural route.

As far as I can tell, the world of things with filesystems divides into two slightly overlapping classes:

- POSIX-compliant systems
- The Windows family of operating systems

POSIX compliance doesn't mean that a system has to look and feel like a Unix box. For example, the typical Mac user has no idea that he or she is using a standard BSD system with an attractive frontend, but those in the know can go to the Utilities folder (inside the Applications folder), then open the Terminal program and run `ls`, `grep`, and `make` to their hearts' content.

Further, I doubt that many systems live up to 100% of the standard's requirements (like having a Fortran '77 compiler). For our purposes, we need a shell that can behave like the bare-bones POSIX shell, a handful of utilities (sed, grep, make, etc.), a C99 compiler, and additions to the standard C library such as `fork` and `iconv`. These can be added as a side note to the main system. The package manager's underlying scripts, Autotools, and almost every other attempt at portable coding will rely on these tools to some extent, so even if you don't want to stare at a command prompt all day, these tools will be handy to have for installations.

On server-class OSes and the full-featured editions of Windows 7, Microsoft offers what used to be called INTERIX and is now called the Subsystem for Unix-based Applications (SUA), which provides the usual POSIX system calls, the Korn shell, and gcc. The subsystem is typically not provided by default but can be installed as an add-on component. But the SUA is not available for other current editions of Windows and will not be available for Windows 8, so we can't depend on Microsoft to provide a POSIX subsystem for its operating systems.

And so, Cygwin.

If you were to rebuild Cygwin from scratch, this would be your agenda:

1. Write a C library for Windows that provides all the POSIX functions. This will have to smooth over some Windows/POSIX incongruities, such as how Windows has distinct drives like *C:* while POSIX has one unified filesystem. In this case, alias *C:* as */cygdrive/c*, *D:* as */cygdrive/d*, and so on.

2. Now that you can compile POSIX-standard programs by linking to your library, do so: generate Windows versions of `ls`, `bash`, `grep`, `make`, `gcc`, X, `rxvt`, `libglib`, `perl`, `python`, and so on.

3. Once you have hundreds of programs and libraries built, set up a package manager that allows users to select the elements they want to install.

As a user of Cygwin, all you have to do is download the package manager from the setup link at Cygwin's website (*http://cygwin.com*) and pick packages. You will certainly want the preceding list, plus a decent terminal (try mintty, or install the X subsystem and use the xterm, because both are much friendlier than Windows' cmd.exe), but you will see that virtually all of the luxuries familiar from a development system are there somewhere.

In "Paths" on page 13, I discuss various environment variables that affect compilation, including paths for searching for files. That's not just for POSIX: Windows has environment variables as well, which you can find in the system settings segment of the control panel. Cygwin is much more usable if you add its bin directory (probably c:\cygwin\bin) to the Windows PATH.

Now you can get to compiling C code.

## Compiling C with POSIX

Microsoft provides a C++ compiler, in the form of Visual Studio, which has a C89 compatibility mode (commonly referred to as *ANSI C*, even though C11 is the current ANSI standard). This is the only means of compiling C code currently provided by Microsoft. Many representatives from the company have made it clear that anything beyond support for a few C99 features (let alone C11 support) is not forthcoming. Visual Studio is the only major compiler that is still stuck on C89, so we'll have to find alternative offerings elsewhere.

Of course, Cygwin provides gcc, and if you've followed along and installed Cygwin, then you've already got a full build environment.

By default, programs you compile under Cygwin will depend on its library of POSIX functions, *cygwin1.dll* (whether your code actually includes any POSIX calls or not). If you are running your program on a box with Cygwin installed, then you have no problem. Users will be able to click on the executable and run it as expected, because the system should be able to find the Cygwin DLL. A program compiled under Cygwin can run on boxes that don't have Cygwin installed if you distribute *cygwin1.dll* with your code. On my machine, this is the path to cygwin: */bin/cygwin1.dll*. The *cygwin1.dll* file has a GPL-like license (see "The Legal Sidebar" on page xvi), in the sense that if you distribute the DLL separately from Cygwin as a whole, then you are required to publish the source code for your program.[1]

If this is a problem, then you'll have to find a way to recompile without depending on *cygwin1.dll*, which means dropping any POSIX-specific functions (like fork or popen) from your code and using MinGW, as discussed later. You can use cygcheck to find out which DLLs your program depends on, and thus verify that your executable does or does not link to *cygwin1.dll*.

---

1 Cygwin is a project run by Red Hat, Inc., which will also allow users to purchase the right to not distribute their source code as per the GPL.

To see what other libraries a program or dynamically linked library depends upon:

- Cygwin: cygcheck `libxx`.dll
- Linux: ldd `libxx`.so
- Mac: otool -L `libxx`.dylib

## Compiling C Without POSIX

If your program doesn't need the POSIX functions, then you can use MinGW (Minimalist GNU for Windows), which provides a standard C compiler and some basic associated tools. MSYS is a companion to MinGW that provides a shell and other useful utilities.

MSYS provides a POSIX shell (and you can find the mintty or RXVT terminals to run your shell in), or leave the command prompt behind entirely and try Code::blocks (*http://www.codeblocks.org/*), an IDE that uses MinGW for compilation on Windows. Eclipse is a much more extensive IDE that can also be configured for MinGW, though that requires a bit more setup.

Or if you are more comfortable at a POSIX command prompt, then set up Cygwin anyway, get the packages providing the MinGW versions of gcc, and use those for compilation instead of the POSIX-linking default version of Cygwin gcc.

If you haven't already met the Autotools, you'll meet them soon. The signature of a package built using Autotools is its three-command install: `./configure && make && make install`. MSYS provides sufficient machinery for such packages to stand a good chance of working. Or if you have downloaded the packages to build from Cygwin's command prompt, then you can use the following to set up the package to use Cygwin's Mingw32 compiler for producing POSIX-free code:

```
./configure --host=mingw32
```

Then run `make && make install` as usual.

Once you've compiled under MinGW, via either command-line compilation or Autotools, you've got a native Windows binary. Because MinGW knows nothing of *cygwin1.dll*, and your program makes no POSIX calls anyway, you've now got an executable program that is a bona fide Windows program, that nobody will know you compiled from a POSIX environment.

However, MinGW currently has a paucity of precompiled libraries.[2] If you want to be free of *cygwin1.dll*, then you can't use the version of *libglib.dll* that ships with Cygwin. You'll need to recompile GLib from source to a native Windows DLL—but GLib depends on GNU's `gettext` for internationalization, so you'll have to build that library first. Modern code depends on modern libraries, so you may find yourself spending a lot of time setting up the sort of things that in other systems are a one-line call to the package manager. We're back to the sort of thing that makes people talk about how C is 40 years old, so you need to write everything from scratch.

So, there are the caveats. Microsoft has walked away from the conversation, leaving others to implement a post-grunge C compiler and environment. Cygwin does this and provides a full package manager with enough libraries to do some or all of your work, but it is associated with a POSIX style of writing and Cygwin's DLL. If that is a problem, you will need to do more work to build the environment and the libraries that you'll need to write decent code.

# Which Way to the Library?

OK, so you have a compiler, a POSIX toolchain, and a package manager that will easily install a few hundred libraries. Now we can move on to the problem of using those in compiling our programs.

We have to start with the compiler command line, which will quickly become a mess, but we'll end with three (sometimes three and a half) relatively simple steps:

1. Set a variable listing the compiler flags.
2. Set a variable listing the libraries to link to. The half-step is that you sometimes have to set only one variable for linking while compiling, and sometimes have to set two for linking at compile time and runtime.
3. Set up a system that will use these variables to orchestrate the compilation.

To use a library, you have to tell the compiler that you will be importing functions from the library twice: once for the compilation and once for the linker. For a library in a standard location, the two declarations happen via an `#include` in the text of the program and a `-l` flag on the compiler line.

---

2  Although MinGW has a package manager that installs the system basics and provides a number of libraries (mostly the ones needed for MinGW itself), this handful of precompiled libraries pales in comparison to the hundreds of packages provided by the typical package manager. In fact, the package manager for my Linux box has more MinGW-compiled libraries than the MinGW package manager has. This is as of this writing; by the time you read this, users like yourself may have contributed more packages to the MinGW repository.

Example 1-1 presents a quick sample program that does some amusing math (for me, at least; if the statistical jargon is Greek to you, that's OK). The C99-standard *error function*, erf(x), is closely related to the integral from zero to *x* of the Normal distribution with mean zero and standard deviation $\sqrt{2}$. Here, we use erf to verify an area popular among statisticians (the 95% confidence interval for a standard large-*n* hypothesis test). Let us name this file *erf.c*.

*Example 1-1. A one-liner from the standard library. (erf.c)*

```
#include <math.h>  //erf, sqrt
#include <stdio.h> //printf

int main(){
    printf("The integral of a Normal(0, 1) distribution "
           "between -1.96 and 1.96 is: %g\n", erf(1.96*sqrt(1/2.)));
}
```

The #include lines should be familiar to you. The compiler will paste *math.h* and *stdio.h* into the code file here, and thus paste in declarations for printf, erf, and sqrt. The declaration in *math.h* doesn't say anything about what erf does, only that it takes in a double and returns a double. That's enough information for the compiler to check the consistency of our usage and produce an object file with a note telling the computer: "once you get to this note, go find the erf function, and replace this note with erf's return value."

It is the job of the linker to reconcile that note by actually finding erf, which is in a library somewhere on your hard drive.

The math functions found in *math.h* are split off into their own library, and you will have to tell the linker about it by adding an -lm flag. Here, the -l is the flag indicating that a library needs to be linked in, and the library in this case has a single-letter name, m. You get printf for free, because there is an implicit -lc asking the linker to link the standard libc assumed at the end of the linking command. Later, we'll see GLib 2.0 linked in via -lglib-2.0, the GNU Scientific Library get linked via -lgsl, and so on.

So if the file were named *erf.c*, then the full command line using the gcc compiler, including several additional flags to be discussed shortly, would look like this:

```
gcc erf.c -o erf -lm -g -Wall -O3 -std=gnu11
```

So we've told the compiler to include math functions via an #include in the program, and told the linker to link to the math library via the -lm on the command line.

The -o flag gives the output name; otherwise, we'd get the default executable name of *a.out*.

## A Few of My Favorite Flags

You'll see that I use a few compiler flags every time, and I recommend you do, too.

- `-g` adds symbols for debugging. Without it, your debugger won't be able to give you variable or function names. They don't slow down the program, and we don't care if the program is a kilobyte larger, so there's little reason to not use this. It works for `gcc`, `clang`, and `icc` (Intel C Compiler).

- `-std=gnu11` is `clang`- and `gcc`-specific, and specifies that the compiler should allow code conforming to the C11 and POSIX standards (plus some GNU extensions). As of this writing, `clang` will default to using the C11 standard, and `gcc` the C89 standard. If your copy of `gcc`, `clang`, or `icc` predates C11, use `-std=gnu99` to get it to use C99. The POSIX standard specifies that `c99` be present on your system, so the compiler-agnostic version of the above line for compiling C99 code would be:

      c99 erf.c -o erf -lm -g -Wall -O3

  In the following makefiles, I get this effect by setting the variable `CC=c99`.

   Depending on the vintage of your Mac, `c99` may be a specially hacked version of `gcc`, which is probably not what you want. If you have a version of `c99` that halts on the `-Wall` flag, or it is missing entirely, make your own. Put a bash script named `c99` in the directory at the head of your path with the text:

      gcc --std=gnu99 $*

  or

      clang $*

  as you prefer. Make it executable via `chmod +x c99`.

- `-O3` indicates optimization level three, which tries every trick to build faster code. If, when you run the debugger, you find that too many variables have been optimized out for you to follow what's going on, then change this to `-O0`. This will be a common tweak in the `CFLAGS` variable, later. This works for `gcc`, `clang`, and `icc`.

- `-Wall` adds compiler warnings. This works for `gcc`, `clang`, and `icc`. For `icc`, you might prefer `-w1`, which displays the compiler's warnings, but not its remarks.

Use your compiler warnings, always. You may be fastidious and know the C standard inside out, but you aren't more fastidious or knowledgeable than your compiler. Old C textbooks filled pages admonishing you to watch out for the difference between = and ==, or to check that all variables are initialized before use. As a more modern textbook author, I have it easy, because I can summarize all those admonishments into one single tip: use your compiler warnings, always.

If your compiler advises a change, don't second-guess it or put off the fix. Do everything necessary to (1) understand why you got a warning and (2) fix your code so that it compiles with zero warnings and zero errors. Compiler messages are famously obtuse, so if you are having trouble with step (1), paste the warning message into your Internet search engine to see how many thousands of others were confounded by this warning before you. You may want to add -Werror to your compiler flags so your compiler will treat warnings as errors.

# Paths

I've got over 700,000 files on my hard drive, and one of them has the declarations for sqrt and erf, and another is the object file holding the compiled functions.[3] The compiler needs to know in which directories to look to find the correct header and object file, and the problem will only get more complicated when we use libraries that are not part of the C standard.

In a typical setup, there are at least three places where libraries may be installed:

- The operating system vendor may define a standard directory or two where libraries are installed by the vendor.

- There may be a directory for the local sysadmin to install packages that shouldn't be overwritten on the next OS upgrade from the vendor. For example, the sysadmin might have a specially hacked version of a library that should override the default version.

- Users typically don't have the rights to write to these locations, and so should be able to use libraries in their home directories.

The OS-standard location typically causes no problems, and the compiler should know to look in those places to find the standard C library, as well as anything installed alongside it. The POSIX standard refers to these directories as "the usual places."

---

3 You can try find / -type f | wc -l to get a rough file count on any POSIX-standard system.

But for the other stuff, you have to tell the compiler where to look. This is going to get byzantine: there is no standard way to find libraries in nonstandard locations, and it rates highly on the list of things that frustrate people about C. On the plus side, your compiler knows how to look in the usual locations, and library distributors tend to put things in the usual locations, so you might never need to specify a path manually. On another plus side, there are a few tools to help you with specifying paths. And on one last plus side, once you have located the nonstandard locations on your system, you can set them in a shell or makefile variable and never think about them again.

Let us say that you have a library named Libuseful installed on your computer, and you know that its various files were put in the */usr/local/* directory, which is the location officially intended for your sysadmin's local libraries. You already put #include <useful.h> in your code; now you have to put this on the command line:

```
gcc -I/usr/local/include use_useful.c -o use_useful -L/usr/local/lib -luseful
```

- -I adds the given path to the include search path, which the compiler searches for header files you #included in your code.

- -L adds to the library search path.

- Order matters. If you have a file named *specific.o* that depends on the Libbroad library, and Libbroad depends on Libgeneral, then you will need:

```
gcc specific.o -lbroad -lgeneral
```

Any other ordering, such as gcc -lbroad -lgeneral specific.o, will probably fail. You can think of the linker looking at the first item, specific.o, and writing down a list of unresolved function, structure, and variable names. Then it goes to the next item, -lbroad, and searches for the items on its still-missing list, all the while potentially adding new unresolved items, then checking -lgeneral for those items still on the missing list. If there are names still unlocated by the end of the list (including that implicit -lc at the end), then the linker halts and gives what is left of its missing-items list to the user.

OK, back to the location problem: where is the library that you want to link to? If it was installed via the same package manager that you used to install the rest of your operating system, then it is most likely in the usual places, and you don't have to worry about it.

You may have a sense of where your own local libraries tend to be, such as */usr/local* or */sw* or */opt*. You no doubt have on hand a means of searching the hard drive, such as a search tool on your desktop or the POSIX:

```
find /usr -name 'libuseful*'
```

to search */usr* for files with names beginning with *libuseful*. When you find Libuseful's shared object file is in */some/path/lib*, the headers are almost certainly in */some/path/include*.

Everybody else finds hunting the hard drive for libraries to be annoying, too, and pkg-config addresses this by maintaining a repository of the flags and locations that packages self-report as being necessary for compilation. Type **pkg-config** on your command line; if you get an error about specifying package names, then great, you have pkg-config and can use it to do the research for you. For example, on my PC, typing these two commands on the command line:

```
pkg-config --libs gsl libxml-2.0
pkg-config --cflags gsl libxml-2.0
```

gives me these two lines of output:

```
-lgsl -lgslcblas -lm -lxml2
-I/usr/include/libxml2
```

These are exactly the flags I need to compile using GSL and LibXML2. The -l flags reveal that GNU Scientific Library depends on a Basic Linear Algebra Subprograms (BLAS) library, and the GSL's BLAS library depends on the standard math library. It seems that all the libraries are in the usual places, because there are no -L flags, but the -I flag indicates the location for LibXML2's header files.

Back on the command line, when you surround a command by backticks, the shell replaces the command with its output. That is, when I type:

```
gcc `pkg-config --cflags --libs gsl libxml-2.0` -o specific specific.c
```

the compiler sees:

```
gcc -I/usr/include/libxml2 -lgsl -lgslcblas -lm -lxml2 -o specific specific.c
```

So pkg-config does a lot of the work for us, but it is not sufficiently standard that we can expect that everybody has it or that every library is registered with it. If you don't have pkg-config, then you'll have to do this sort of research yourself, by reading the manual for your library or searching your disk as we saw previously.

There are often environment variables for paths, such as CPATH or LIBRARY_PATH or C_INCLUDE_PATH. You would set them in your .bashrc or other such user-specific list of environment variables. They are hopelessly nonstandard—gcc on Linux and gcc on the Mac use different variables, and any other compiler may use others still. I find that it's easier to set these paths on a per-project basis in the makefile or its equivalent, using -I and -L flags. If you prefer these path variables, check the end of your compiler's manpage for the list of relevant variables for your situation.

Even with `pkg-config`, the need for something that will assemble all this for us is increasingly apparent. Each element is easy enough to understand, but it is a long, mechanical list of tedious parts.

## Runtime Linking

*Static libraries* are linked by the compiler by effectively copying the contents of the library into the final executable. So the program itself works as a more-or-less stand-alone system. *Shared libraries* are linked to your program at runtime, meaning that we have the same problem with finding the library that we had at compile time all over again at runtime. What is worse, *users* of your program may have this problem.

If the library is in one of the usual locations, life is good and the system will have no problem finding the library at runtime. If your library is in a nonstandard path, then you need to find a way to modify the runtime search path for libraries. Options:

- If you packaged your program with Autotools, Libtool knows how to add the right flags, and you don't have to worry about it.

- When compiling the program with `gcc`, `clang`, or `icc` based on a library in *libpath*, add:

    ```
    LDADD=-Llibpath -Wl,-Rlibpath
    ```

  to the subsequent makefile. The `-L` flag tells the compiler where to search for libraries to resolve symbols; the `-Wl` flag passes its flags through from `gcc/clang/icc` to the linker, and the linker embeds the given `-R` into the runtime search path for libraries to link to. Unfortunately, `pkg-config` often doesn't know about runtime paths, so you may need to enter these things manually.

- At runtime, the linker will use yet another path to find libraries not in the usual places and not annotated in an executable via `-Wl,R...`. This path can be set in your shell's startup script (`.bashrc`, `.zshrc`, or whatever is appropriate). To ensure that *libpath* is searched for shared libraries at runtime, use:

    ```
    export LD_LIBRARY_PATH=libpath:$LD_LIBRARY_PATH        #Linux, Cygwin
    export DYLD_LIBRARY_PATH=libpath:$DYLD_LIBRARY_PATH      #OS X
    ```

There are those who warn against overuse of the `LD_LIBRARY_PATH` (what if somebody puts a malicious impostor library in the path, thus replacing the real library without your knowledge?), but if all your libraries are in one place, it is not unreasonable to add one directory under your ostensible control to the path.

# Using Makefiles

The *makefile* provides a resolution to all this endless tweaking. It is basically an organized set of variables and sequences of one-line shell scripts. The POSIX-standard make program reads the makefile for instructions and variables, and then assembles the long and tedious command lines for us. After this segment, there will be little reason to call the compiler directly.

In "Makefiles vs. Shell Scripts" on page 77, I'll cover a few more details about the makefile; here, I'm going to show you the smallest practicable makefile that will compile a basic program that depends on a library. Here it is, all six lines of it:

```
P=program_name
OBJECTS=
CFLAGS = -g -Wall -O3
LDLIBS=
CC=c99

$(P): $(OBJECTS)
```

Usage:

- Once ever: Save this (with the name *makefile*) in the same directory as your *.c* files. If you are using GNU Make, you have the option of capitalizing the name to *Makefile* if you feel that doing so will help it to stand out from the other files. Set your program's name on the first line (use *progname*, not *progname.c*).

- Every time you need to recompile: Type make.

> **Your Turn:** Here's the world-famous *hello.c* program (Kernighan, 1978), in two lines:
>
> ```
> #include <stdio.h>
> int main(){ printf("Hello, world.\n"); }
> ```
>
> Save that and the preceding makefile to a directory, and try the previous steps to get the program compiled and running.

# Setting Variables

We'll get to the actual functioning of the makefile soon, but five out of six lines of this makefile are about setting variables (two of which are currently set to be blank), indicating that we should take a moment to consider environment variables in a little more detail.

Historically, there have been two main threads of shell grammar: one based primarily on the Bourne shell, and another based primarily on the C shell. The C shell has a slightly different syntax for variables, e.g., `set CFLAGS="-g -Wall -O3"` to set the value of `CFLAGS`. But the POSIX standard is written around the Bourne-type variable-setting syntax, so that is what I focus on through the rest of this book.

The shell and `make` use the `$` to indicate the value of a variable, but the shell uses `$var`, whereas `make` wants any variable names longer than one character in parens: `$(var)`. So, given the preceding makefile, `$(P): $(OBJECTS)` will be evaluated to mean

```
program_name:
```

There are several ways to tell `make` about a variable:

- Set the variable from the shell before calling `make`, and *export* the variable, meaning that when the shell spawns a child process, it has the variable in its list of environment variables. To set `CFLAGS` from a POSIX-standard command line:

  ```
  export CFLAGS='-g -Wall -O3'
  ```

  At home, I omit the first line in this makefile, P=*program_name*, and instead set it once per session via `export P=`*program_name*, which means I have to edit the makefile itself still less frequently.

- You can put these export commands in your shell's startup script, like `.bashrc` or `.zshrc`. This guarantees that every time you log in or start a new shell, the variable will be set and exported. If you are confident that your `CFLAGS` will be the same every time, you can set them here and never think about them again.

- You can export a variable for a single command by putting the assignment just before the command. The `env` command lists the environment variables it knows about, so when you run the following:

  ```
  PANTS=kakhi env | grep PANTS
  ```

  you should see the appropriate variable and its value. This is why the shell won't let you put spaces around the equals sign: the space is how it distinguishes between the assignment and the command.

  Using this form sets and exports the given variables for one line only. After you try this on the command line, try running `env | grep PANTS` again to verify that `PANTS` is no longer an exported variable.

  Feel free to specify as many variables as you'd like:

  ```
  PANTS=kakhi PLANTS="ficus fern" env | grep 'P.*NTS'
  ```

This form is a part of the shell specification's *simple command* description, meaning that the assignment needs to come before an actual command. This will matter when we get to noncommand shell constructs. Writing:

```
VAR=val if [ -e afile ] ; then ./program_using_VAR ; fi
```

will fail with an obscure syntax error. The correct form is:

```
if [ -e afile ] ; then VAR=val ./program_using_VAR ; fi
```

- As in the earlier makefile, you can set the variable at the head of the makefile, with the lines like CFLAGS=. In the makefile, you can have spaces around the equals sign without anything breaking.

- make will let you set variables on the command line, independent of the shell. Thus, these two lines are close to equivalent:

```
make CFLAGS="-g -Wall"    Set a makefile variable.
CFLAGS="-g -Wall" make    Set an environment variable visible to make and its children.
```

All of these means are equivalent, as far as your makefile is concerned, with the exception that child programs called by make will know new environment variables but won't know any makefile variables.

---

# Environment Variables in C

In your C code, get environment variables with getenv. Because getenv is so easy to use, it can be useful for quickly setting options from the command prompt.

Example 1-2 prints a message to the screen as often as the user desires. The message is set via the environment variable msg and the number of repetitions via reps. Notice how there are defaults of 10 and "Hello." in case getenv returns NULL (typically meaning that the environment variable is unset).

*Example 1-2. Environment variables provide a quick way to tweak details of a program (getenv.c)*

```c
#include <stdlib.h> //getenv, atoi
#include <stdio.h>  //printf

int main(){
    char *repstext = getenv("reps");
    int reps = repstext ? atoi(repstext) : 10;

    char *msg = getenv("msg");
    if (!msg) msg = "Hello.";

    for (int i=0; i< reps; i++)
        printf("%s\n", msg);
}
```

As previously, we can export a variable for just one line, which makes sending a variable to the program still more convenient. Usage:

```
reps=10 msg="Ha" ./getenv
msg="Ha" ./getenv
reps=20 msg=" " ./getenv
```

You might find this to be odd—the inputs to a program should come *after* the program name, darn it—but the oddness aside, you can see that it took little setup within the program itself, and we get to have named parameters on the command line almost for free.

When your program is a little further along, you can take the time to set up the POSIX-standard getopt or the GNU-standard argp_parse to process input arguments the usual way.

make also offers several built-in variables. Here are the (POSIX-standard) ones that you will need to read the following rules:

$@

> The full target filename. By *target*, I mean the file that needs to be built, such as a *.o* file being compiled from a *.c* file or a program made by linking *.o* files.

$*

> The target file with the suffix cut off. So if the target is *prog.o*, $* is *prog*, and $*.c would become *prog.c*.

$<

> The name of the file that caused this target to get triggered and made. If we are making *prog.o*, it is probably because *prog.c* has recently been modified, so $< is *prog.c*.

## The Rules

Now, let us focus on the procedures the makefile will execute, and then get to how the variables influence that.

Setting the variables aside, segments of the makefile have the form:

```
target: dependencies
        script
```

If the target gets called, via the command make *target*, then the dependencies are checked. If the target is a file, the dependencies are all files, and the target is newer than the dependencies, then the file is up-to-date and there's nothing to do. Otherwise, the processing of the target gets put on hold, the dependencies are run or generated, probably via another target, and when the dependency scripts are all finished, the target's script gets executed.

For example, before this was a book, it was a series of tips posted to a blog (*http://modelingwithdata.org*). Every blog post had an HTML and PDF version, all generated via LaTeX. I'm omitting a lot of details for the sake of a simple example (like the many options for latex2html), but here's the sort of makefile one could write for the process.

 If you are copying any of these makefile snippets from a version on your screen or on paper to a file named *makefile*, don't forget that the whitespace at the head of each line must be a tab, not spaces. Blame POSIX.

```
all: html doc publish

doc:
    pdflatex $(f).tex

html:
    latex -interaction batchmode $(f)
    latex2html $(f).tex

publish:
    scp $(f).pdf $(Blogserver)
```

I set f on the command line via a command like export f=tip-make. When I then type make on the command line, the first target, all, gets checked. That is, the command make by itself is equivalent to make *first_target*. That depends on html, doc, and publish, so those targets get called in sequence. If I know it's not yet ready to copy out to the world, then I can call make html doc and do only those steps.

In the simple makefile from earlier, we had only one target/dependency/script group. For example:

```
P=domath
OBJECTS=addition.o subtraction.o

$(P): $(OBJECTS)
```

This follows a sequence of dependencies and scripts similar to what my blogging makefile did, but the scripts are implicit. Here, P=domath is the program to be compiled, and it depends on the object files *addition.o* and *subtraction.o*. Because *addition.o* is not listed as a target, make uses an implicit rule, listed below, to compile from the *.c* to the *.o* file. Then it does the same for *subtraction.o* and *domath.o* (because GNU make implicitly assumes that domath depends on *domath.o* given the setup here). Once all the objects are built, we have no script to build the $(P) target, so GNU make fills in its default script for linking *.o* files into an executable.

POSIX-standard make has this recipe for compiling a *.o* object file from a *.c* source code file:

```
$(CC) $(CFLAGS) $(LDFLAGS) -o $@ $*.c
```

The $(CC) variable represents your C compiler; the POSIX standard specifies a default of CC=c99, but current editions of GNU make set CC=cc, which is typically a link to gcc. In the minimal makefile at the head of this segment, $(CC) is explicitly set to c99, $(CFLAGS) is set to the list of flags earlier, and $(LDFLAGS) is unset and therefore replaced with nothing. So if make determines that it needs to produce *your_pro gram.o*, then this is the command that will be run, given that makefile:

```
c99 -g -Wall -O3 -o your_program.o your_program.c
```

When GNU make decides that you have an executable program to build from object files, it uses this recipe:

```
$(CC) $(LDFLAGS) first.o second.o $(LDLIBS)
```

Recall that order matters in the linker, so we need two linker variables. In the previous example, we needed:

```
cc specific.o -lbroad -lgeneral
```

as the relevant part of the linking command. Comparing the correct compilation command to the recipe, we see that we need to set LDLIBS=-lbroad -lgeneral.

 If you'd like to see the full list of default rules and variables built in to your edition of make, try:

```
make -p > default_rules
```

So, that's the game: find the right variables and set them in the makefile. You still have to do the research as to what the correct flags are, but at least you can write them down in the makefile and never think about them again.

> **Your Turn:** Modify your makefile to compile *erf.c*.

If you use an IDE, or CMAKE, or any of the other alternatives to POSIX-standard make, you're going to be playing the same find-the-variables game. I'm going to continue discussing the preceding minimal makefile, and you should have no problem finding the corresponding variables in your IDE.

- The `CFLAGS` variable is an ingrained custom, but the variable that you'll need to set for the linker changes from system to system. Even `LDLIBS` isn't POSIX-standard, but it is what GNU make uses.

- The `CFLAGS` and `LDLIBS` variables are where we're going to hook all the compiler flags locating and identifying libraries. If you have `pkg-config`, put the back-ticked calls here. For example, the makefile on my system, where I use Apophenia and GLib for just about everything, looks like:

```
CFLAGS=`pkg-config --cflags apophenia glib-2.0` -g -Wall -std=gnu11 -O3
LDLIBS=`pkg-config --libs apophenia glib-2.0`
```

Or, specify the `-I`, `-L`, and `-l` flags manually, like:

```
CFLAGS=-I/home/b/root/include -g -Wall -O3
LDLIBS=-L/home/b/root/lib -lweirdlib
```

- After you add a library and its locations to the `LDLIBS` and `CFLAGS` lines and you know it works on your system, there is little reason to ever remove it. Do you really care that the final executable might be 10 kilobytes larger than if you customized a new makefile for every program? That means you can write one makefile summarizing where all the libraries are on your system and copy it from project to project without any rewriting.

- If your program requires a second (or more) C file, add *second.o*, *third.o*, and so on to the `OBJECTS` line (no commas, just spaces between names) in the makefile at the head of this section.

- If you have a program that is one *.c* file, you may not need a makefile at all. In a directory with no makefile and *erf.c* from earlier, try using your shell to:

```
export CFLAGS='-g -Wall -O3 -std=gnu11'
export LDLIBS='-lm'
make erf
```

and watch make use its knowledge of C compilation to do the rest.

---

## What Are the Linker Flags for Building a Shared Library?

To tell you the truth, I have no idea. It's different across operating systems, both by type and by year, and even on one system the rules are often hairy.

Instead, *Libtool*, one of the tools introduced in Chapter 3, knows every detail of every shared library generation procedure on every operating system. I recommend investing your time getting to know Autotools and thus solve the shared object compilation problem once and for all, rather than investing that time in learning the right compiler flags and linking procedure for every target system.

# Using Libraries from Source

So far, the story has been about compiling your own code using `make`. Compiling code provided by others is often a different story.

Let's try a sample package. The GNU Scientific Library includes a host of numeric computation routines.

The GSL is packaged via *Autotools*, a set of tools that will prepare a library for use on any machine, by testing for every known quirk and implementing the appropriate workaround. "Packaging Your Code with Autotools" on page 79 will go into detail about how you can package your own programs and libraries with Autotools. But for now, we can start off as users of the system and enjoy the ease of quickly installing useful libraries.

The GSL is often provided in precompiled form via package manager, but for the purposes of going through the steps of compilation, here's how to get the GSL as source code and set it up, assuming you have root privileges on your computer.

```
wget ftp://ftp.gnu.org/gnu/gsl/gsl-1.16.tar.gz  ❶
tar xvzf gsl-*gz                                ❷
cd gsl-1.16
./configure                                     ❸
make
sudo make install                               ❹
```

❶  Download the zipped archive. Ask your package manager to install `wget` if you don't have it, or type this URL into your browser.

❷  Unzip the archive: x=extract, v=verbose, z=unzip via `gzip`, f=filename.

❸  Determine the quirks of your machine. If the `configure` step gives you an error about a missing element, then use your package manager to obtain it and run `configure` again.

❹  Install to the right location—if you have permissions.

If you are trying this at home, then you probably have root privileges, and this will work fine. If you are at work and using a shared server, the odds are low that you have superuser rights, so you won't be able to provide the password needed to do the last step in the script as superuser. In that case, hold your breath until the next section.

Did it install? Example 1-3 provides a short program to try finding that 95% confidence interval using GSL functions; try it and see if you can get it linked and running:

*Example 1-3. Redoing Example 1-1 with the GSL (gsl_erf.c)*

```
#include <gsl/gsl_cdf.h>
#include <stdio.h>

int main(){
    double bottom_tail = gsl_cdf_gaussian_P(-1.96, 1);
    printf("Area between [-1.96, 1.96]: %g\n", 1-2*bottom_tail);
}
```

To use the library you just installed, you'll need to modify the makefile of your library-using program to specify the libraries and their locations.

Depending on whether you have `pkg-config` on hand, you can do one of:

```
LDLIBS=`pkg-config --libs gsl`
#or
LDLIBS=-lgsl -lgslcblas -lm
```

If it didn't install in a standard location and `pkg-config` is not available, you will need to add paths to the heads of these definitions, such as `CFLAGS=-I/usr/local/include` and `LDLIBS=-L/usr/local/lib -Wl,-R/usr/local/lib`.

# Using Libraries from Source (Even if Your Sysadmin Doesn't Want You To)

You may not have root access if you are using a shared computer at work, or at home if you have an especially controlling significant other. Then you have to go underground and make your own private root directory.

The first step is to simply create the directory:

```
mkdir ~/root
```

I already have a *~/tech* directory where I keep all my technical logistics, manuals, and code snippets, so I made a *~/tech/root* directory. The name doesn't matter, but I'll use *~/root* as the dummy directory here.

 Your shell replaces the tilde with the full path to your home directory, saving you a lot of typing. The POSIX standard only requires that the shell do this at the beginning of a word or just after a colon (which you'd need for a path-type variable), but most shells expand midword tildes as well. Other programs, like make, may or may not recognize the tilde as your home directory. In these cases, you can use the POSIX-mandated HOME environment variable, as in the examples to follow.

The second step is to add the right part of your new root system to all the relevant paths. For programs, that's the PATH in your *.bashrc* (or equivalent):

```
PATH=~/root/bin:$PATH
```

By putting the *bin* subdirectory of your new directory before the original PATH, it will be searched first, and your copy of any programs will be found first. Thus, you can substitute in your preferred version of any programs that are already in the standard shared directories of the system.

For libraries you will fold into your C programs, note the new paths to search in the preceding makefile:

```
LDLIBS=-L$(HOME)/root/lib   (plus the other flags, like -lgsl -lm ...)
CFLAGS=-I$(HOME)/root/include  (plus -g -Wall -O3 ...)
```

Now that you have a local root, you can use it for other systems as well, such as Java's CLASSPATH.

The last step is to install programs in your new root. If you have the source code and it uses Autotools, all you have to do is add --prefix=$HOME/root in the right place:

```
./configure --prefix=$HOME/root && make && make install
```

You didn't need sudo to do the install step, because everything is now in territory you control.

Because the programs and libraries are in your home directory and have no more permissions than you do, your sysadmin can't complain that they are an imposition on others. If your sysadmin complains anyway, then, as sad as it may be, it might be time to break up.

---

## The Manual

I suppose there was once a time when the manual was actually a printed document, but in the present day, it exists in the form of the man command. For example, use man strtok to read about the strtok function, typically including what header to include, the input arguments, and basic notes about its usage. The manual pages tend to keep it simple, sometimes lack examples, and assume the reader already has a basic idea of how the function works. If you need a more basic tutorial, your favorite Internet search engine can probably offer several (and in the case of strtok, see the section "A Pæan to strtok" on page 194). The GNU C library manual, also easy to find online, is very readable and written for beginners.

- If you can't recall the name of what you need to look up, every manual page has a one-line summary, and man -k *searchterm* will search those summaries. Many systems also have the apropos command, which is similar to man -k but adds

---

some features. For extra refinement, I often find myself piping the output of `apro pos` through `grep`.

- The manual is divided into sections. Section 1 is command-line commands, and section 3 is library functions. If your system has a command-line program named `printf`, then `man printf` will show its documentation, and `man 3 printf` will show the documentation for the C library's `printf` command.

- For more on the usage of the `man` command (such as the full list of sections), try `man man`.

- Your text editor or IDE may have a means of calling up manpages quickly. For example, vim users can put the cursor on a word and use *K* to open that word's manpage.

# Compiling C Programs via Here Document

At this point, you have seen the pattern of compilation a few times:

1. Set a variable expressing compiler flags.
2. Set a variable expressing linker flags, including a `-l` flag for every library that you use.
3. Use `make` or your IDE's recipes to convert the variables into full compile and link commands.

The remainder of this chapter will do all this one last time, using an absolutely minimal setup: just the shell. If you are a kinetic learner who picked up scripting languages by cutting and pasting snippets of code into the interpreter, you'll be able to do the same with pasting C code onto your command prompt.

## Include Header Files from the Command Line

`gcc` and `clang` have a convenient flag for including headers. For example:

```
gcc -include stdio.h
```

is equivalent to putting

```
#include <stdio.h>
```

at the head of your C file; likewise for `clang -include stdio.h`.

By adding that to our compiler invocation, we can finally write *hello.c* as the one line of code it should be:

```
int main(){ printf("Hello, world.\n"); }
```

which compiles fine via:

```
gcc -include stdio.h hello.c -o hi --std=gnu99 -Wall -g -O3
```

or shell commands like:

```
export CFLAGS='-g -Wall -include stdio.h'
export CC=c99
make hello
```

This tip about -include is compiler-specific and involves moving information from the code to the compilation instructions. If you think this is bad form, well, skip this tip.

## The Unified Header

Allow me to digress for a few paragraphs onto the subject of header files. To be useful, a header file must include the typedefs, macro definitions, and function declarations for types, macros, and functions used by the code file including the header. Also, it should not include typdefs, macro definitions, and function declarations that the code file will not use.

To truly conform to both of these conditions, you would need to write a separate header for every code file, with exactly the relevant parts for the current code file. Nobody actually does this.

There was once a time when compilers took several seconds or minutes to compile even relatively simple programs, so there was human-noticeable benefit to reducing the work the compiler has to do. My current copies of *stdio.h* and *stdlib.h* are each about 1,000 lines long (try wc -l /usr/include/stdlib.h) and *time.h* another 400, meaning that this seven-line program:

```
#include <time.h>
#include <stdio.h>
#include <stdlib.h>
int main(){
    srand(time(NULL));        // Initialize RNG seed.
    printf("%i\n", rand());   // Make one draw.
}
```

is actually a ~2,400-line program.

Your compiler doesn't think 2,400 lines is a big deal anymore, and this compiles in under a second. So the trend has been to save users time picking headers by including more elements in a single header.

You will see examples using GLib later, with an #include <glib.h> at the top. That header includes 74 subheaders, covering all the subsections of the GLib library. This is good user interface design by the GLib team, because those of us who don't want to spend time picking just the right subsections of the library can speed through the header paperwork in one line, and those who want detailed control can pick and choose exactly the headers they need. It would be nice if the C standard library had a quick-and-easy header like this; it wasn't the custom in the 1980s, but it's easy to make one.

---

**Your Turn:** Write yourself a single header, let us call it *allheads.h*, and throw in every header you've ever used, so it'll look something like:

```
#include <math.h>
#include <time.h>
#include <stdio.h>
#include <unistd.h>
#include <stdlib.h>
#include <gsl/gsl_rng.h>
```

I can't tell you exactly what it'll look like, because I don't know exactly what you use day to day.

Now that you have this aggregate header, you can just throw one:

```
#include <allheads.h>
```

on top of every file you write, and you're done with thinking about headers. Sure, it will expand to perhaps 10,000 lines of extra code, much of it not relevant to the program at hand. But you won't notice, and unused declarations don't change the final executable.

---

If you are writing a public header for other users, then by the rule that a header should not include unnecessary elements, your header probably should not have an `#include "allheads.h"` reading in all the definitions and declarations of the standard library—in fact, it is plausible that your public header may not have any elements from the standard library at all. This is generally true: your library may have a code segment that uses GLib's linked lists to operate, but that means you need to `#include <glib.h>` in that code file, not in the public library header.

Getting back to the idea of setting up a quick compilation on the command line, the unified header makes writing quick programs more quick. Once you have a unified header, even a line like `#include <allheads.h>` is extraneous if you are a gcc or clang user, because you can instead add `-include allheads.h` to your CFLAGS and never think about which out-of-project headers to include again.

## Here Documents

Here documents are a feature of POSIX-standard shells that you can use for C, Python, Perl, or whatever else, and they will make this book much more useful and fun. Also, if you want to have a multilingual script, here documents are an easy way to do it. Do some parsing in Perl, do the math in C, then have Gnuplot produce the pretty pictures, and have it all in one text file.

Here's a Python example. Normally, you'd tell Python to run a script via:

```
python your_script.py
```

Python lets you give the filename - to use stdin as the input file:

```
echo "print 'hi.'" | python -
```

You could, in theory, put some lengthy scripts on the command line via `echo`, but you'll quickly see that there are a lot of small, undesired parsings going on—you might need `\"hi\"` instead of `"hi"`, for example.

Thus, the *here document*, which does no parsing at all. Try this:

```
python - <<"XXXX"
lines=2
print "\nThis script is %i lines long.\n" %(lines,)
XXXX
```

- Here documents are a standard shell feature, so they should work on any POSIX system.

- The `"XXXX"` is any string you'd like; `"EOF"` is also popular, and `"-----"` looks good as long as you get the dash count to match at top and bottom. When the shell sees your chosen string alone on a line, it will stop sending the script to the program's stdin. That's all the parsing that happens.

- There's also a variant that begins with `<<-`. This variant removes all tabs at the head of every line, so you can put a here document in an indented section of a shell script without breaking the flow of indentation. Of course, this would be disastrous for a Python here document.

- As another variant, there's a difference between `<<"XXXX"` and `<<XXXX`. In the second version, the shell parses certain elements, which means you can have the shell insert the value of `$shell_variables` for you. The shell relies heavily on the `$` for its variables and other expansions; the `$` is one of the few characters on a standard keyboard that has no special meaning to C. It's as if the people who wrote Unix designed it from the ground up to make it easy to write shell scripts that produce C code....

## Compiling from stdin

OK, back to C: we can use here documents to compile C code pasted onto the command line via `gcc` or `clang`, or have a few lines of C in a multilingual script.

We're not going to use the makefile, so we need a single compilation command. To make life less painful, let us alias it. Paste this onto your command line, or add it to your *.bashrc, .zshrc,* or wherever applicable:

```
go_libs="-lm"
go_flags="-g -Wall -include allheads.h -O3"
alias go_c="c99 -xc - $go_libs $go_flags"
```

where *allheads.h* is the aggregate header you'd put together earlier. Using the -include flag means one less thing to think about when writing the C code, and I've found that bash's history gets wonky when there are #s in the C code.

On the compilation line, you'll recognize the - to mean that instead of reading from a named file, use stdin. The -xc identifies this as C code, because *gcc* stands for GNU Compiler Collection, not GNU C Compiler, and with no input filename ending in *.c* to tip it off, we have to be clear that this is not Java, Fortran, Objective C, Ada, or C++ (and likewise for clang, even though its name is meant to invoke *C language*).

Whatever you did to customize the LDLIBS and CFLAGS in your makefile, do here.

Now we're sailing, and can compile C code on the command line:

```
go_c << '---'
int main(){printf("Hello from the command line.\n");}
---
./a.out
```

We can use a here document to paste short C programs onto the command line, and write little test programs without hassle. Not only do you not need a makefile, you don't even need an input file.[4]

Don't expect this sort of thing to be your primary mode of working. But cutting and pasting code snippets onto the command line can be fun, and being able to have a single step in C within a longer shell script is pretty fabulous.

---

4 There is a POSIX custom that if the first line of *file* is #!*aninterpreter*, then when you run *file* from the shell, the shell will actually run *aninterpreter file*. This works well for interpreted languages like Perl or Python (especially given that they take # as a comment marker and so ignore the first line). Given the hints in this segment, you could write a script (let us call it c99sh) that would do the right thing with a C file that started with #!c99sh: fix the first line, send the rest of the file via a pipe to the compiler, then execute the resulting program. However, Rhys Ulerich already wrote such a c99sh for you, and has published the script to GitHub (*http://bit.ly/rhysu-c99sh*).

# CHAPTER 2

# Debug, Test, Document

*Crawling*
*Over your window*
*You think I'm confused,*
*I'm waiting ...*
*To complete my current ruse.*
—Wire, "I Am the Fly"

This chapter will cover tools for debugging, testing, and documenting your writing—the essentials to take your writing from a potentially useful set of scripts to something you and others can rely on.

Because C gives you the freedom to do idiotic things with memory, debugging means both the quotidian problem of checking logic (with GDB) and the more technical problem of checking for memory misallocations and leaks (with Valgrind). On the documentation side, this chapter covers one tool at the interface level (Doxygen) and another that helps you document and develop every step of the program (CWEB).

The chapter also gives a quick introduction to the *test harness*, which will allow you to quickly write lots of tests for your code, and offers some considerations about error reporting and handling input or user errors.

## Using a Debugger

The first tip about the debugger is simple and brief:

*Use a debugger, always.*

Some of you will find this to be not much of a tip, because who possibly wouldn't use a debugger? Here in the second edition of the book, I can tell you that one of the most common requests regarding the first edition was a more extensive introduction to the debugger, which was entirely new to many readers.

Some people worry that bugs typically come from broad errors of understanding, while the debugger only gives information at the low level of variable states and back-traces. Indeed, after you pinpoint a bug using the debugger, it is worth taking the time to consider what underlying problem and failure of understanding you have just discovered, and whether it replicates itself elsewhere in your code. Some death certificates include an aggressive inquiry into the cause of death: *Subject died as a result of* _____, *as a result of* _____, *as a result of* _____, *as a result of* _____, *as a result of* _____. After the debugger has helped you make such an inquiry and understand your code better, you can encapsulate your understanding in more unit tests.

About that *always*: there is virtually no cost to running a program under the debugger. Nor is the debugger just something to pull out when something breaks. Linus Torvalds explains: "I use gdb all the time ... as a disassembler on steroids that you can program." (*http://bit.ly/lt-debugger*) It's great being able to pause anywhere, increase the verbosity level with a quick `print verbose++`, force out of a `for (int i=0; i<10; i++)` loop via `print i=100` and `continue`, or test a function by throwing a series of test inputs at it. The fans of interactive languages are right that interacting with your code improves the development process all the way along; they just never got to the debugging chapter in the C textbook, and so never realized that all of those interactive habits apply to C as well.

Whatever your intent, you will need to have human-readable debugging information (i.e., names for variables and functions) compiled into the program for any debugger to be at all useful. To include debugging symbols, use the `-g` flag in the compiler switches (i.e., your `CFLAGS` variable). Reasons to not use the `-g` flag are rare indeed—it doesn't slow down your program, and adding a kilobyte to your executable is irrelevant for most situations. Debugging may also be easier after turning off optimization via the `-O0` (oh zero) compiler flag, because the optimizer may eliminate variables useful for debugging and shuffle the code in surprising ways.

I'm mostly covering GDB, because on most POSIX systems, it's the only game in town. (By the way, a C++ compiler engages in what is known as *mangling* of the code. In `gdb` it shows, and I've always found debugging C++ code from the `gdb` prompt to be painful. Because C code compiles without mangling, I find `gdb` to be much more usable for C, and having a GUI that unmangles the names is not necessary.) LLDB (companion to the LLVM/`clang`) is gaining popularity, and I will cover it as well. Apple has ceased shipping GDB as part of its Xcode suite, but you can install it via a package manager, such as Macports, Fink, or Homebrew. On a Mac, you may need to run debug sessions via sudo(!), like `sudo lldb stddev_bugged`.

You might be working from an IDE or other visual front end that runs your program under the debugger every time you click run. I'm going to show you commands from the command line, and you should have no trouble translating the basics here into mouse clicks on your screen. Depending on the frontend, you might be able to use the macros defined in *.gdbinit*.

When working with the command line directly, you will probably need to have a text editor in another window or terminal displaying your code. The simple debugger/editor combination provides many of the conveniences of an IDE, and may be all you need.

## The Stack of Frames

To start your program, you ask the system to execute a function called main. The computer generates a *frame* into which information about the function is placed, such as the inputs (which for main are customarily named argc and argv) and the variables that are created by the function.

Let us say that, in the course of its execution, main calls another function, get_agents. Then execution of main stops and a new frame is generated for get_agents, holding its various details and variables. Perhaps get_agents calls another function, agent_address, at which point we have a growing *stack* of frames. Eventually, agent_address will finish execution, at which point it pops off the stack and get_agents resumes.

If your question is just "Where am I?" the easy answer is the line number in the code, and sometimes this is all you need. But more often, your question is "How did I get here?" and the answer, the *backtrace* or *call stack*, is a listing of the stack of frames. Here's a sample backtrace:

```
#0  0x00413bbe in agent_address (agent_number=312) at addresses.c:100
#1  0x004148b6 in get_agents () at addresses.c:163
#2  0x00404f9b in main (argc=1, argv=0x7fffffffe278) at addresses.c:227
```

The top of the stack is frame 0, down to main, which is currently frame 2 (but that will change as the stack grows and shrinks). The hexadecimal after the frame number gives the locations to which execution will return when the called function returns; as an application programmer, I always took it as visual noise to ignore. After that, we have the function name, its inputs (which in the case of argv is again a hex address), and the line in the source code where execution is happening.

If you found that the house listed in agent_address is clearly wrong, then maybe the agent_number input is somehow wrong, in which case you have to jump to frame 1 and ask what the state of get_agents was that set up the strange state of agent_address. Much of the skill of interrogating a program is in jumping around in the stack and tracing causes and effects from one function's frame to the next.

# A Debugging Detective Story

This section will go through an imaginary Q&A session with GDB or LLDB. In the set of code samples for this book, you will find *stddev_bugged.c*, a rewrite of Example 7-4 with a bug inserted. The change is small enough that you can refer to that listing of *stddev.c* to get a view of the program. Like any good detective story, the clues needed to identify the culprit are all available to you. The line of questions will help eliminate suspects until only one suspect remains and the bug becomes obvious.

After compiling the program (CFLAGS="-g" make stddev_bugged should do it), we start the inquiry by starting the debugger:

```
gdb stddev_bugged
# or
lldb stddev_bugged
```

We are now at the debugger command prompt, ready to ask questions.

**Q: What does this program do?**

A: The run command runs the program. Here, the GDB and LLDB command is the same; where they differ I will use the GDB command in the example and put the LLDB command in square brackets. Like all GDB and LLDB commands, it can be abbreviated:

```
(gdb) r

mean: 5687.496667 var: 194085710
mean: 0.83 var: 4.1334
[Inferior 1 (process 22734) exited normally]
```

It looks like the program produces some means and variances. It makes it to the end of the program without segfaults or other failures, and returns zero, indicating normal execution.

**Q: Does the code in main verify what we got from the output?**

A: The easiest way to look at the code is to simply open the source code in a text editor. There are ways to keep a text editor side-by-side with the debugger even when logging in to a terminal-only remote machine; see "Try a Multiplexer" on page 74. But GDB and LLDB will also display lines of code via the list command:

```
(gdb) l main

28              }
29              return (meanvar){.mean = avg,
30                          .var = avg2 - pow(avg, 2)}; //E[x^2] - E^2[x]
31      }
32
33      int main(){
34          double d[] = { 34124.75, 34124.48,
```

```
35                    34124.90, 34125.31,
36                    34125.05, 34124.98, NAN};
37
```

We get 10 lines of code, centered at the requested point. Rerunning list with no arguments gives us the next 10 lines:

```
(gdb) l
38          meanvar mv = mean_and_var(d);
39          printf("mean: %.10g var: %.10g\n", mv.mean, mv.var*6/5.);
40
41          double d2[] = { 4.75, 4.48,
42                          4.90, 5.31,
43                          5.05, 4.98, NAN};
44
45          mv = mean_and_var(d2);
46          mv.var *= 6./5;
47          printf("mean: %.10g var: %.10g\n", mv.mean, mv.var);
```

We see the call to the function mean_and_var on line 38, which is sent the list d. But there's a problem: the numbers in d are all around 34,125, but the mean output by the program was about 5,687 (not to mention the runaway variance). Similarly, the second call to mean_and_var sent in a list of numbers around 5, but the second mean was 0.83.

The remainder of the session is really asking a single question: *what is the first point in the code where something went wrong?* But to answer that central question, we will need more details.

**Q: How can we see what is happening in mean_and_var?**

A: We want the program to pause at mean_and_var, so we set a breakpoint there:

```
(gdb) b mean_and_var
Breakpoint 1 at 0x400820: file stddev_bugged.c, line 16.
```

With the breakpoint set, rerunning the program stops at that point:

```
(gdb) r
Breakpoint 1, mean_and_var (data=data@entry=0x7fffffffe130) at stddev_bugged.c:16
16      meanvar mean_and_var(const double *data){
(gdb)
```

We are now sitting at line 16, the head of the function, ready to ask further details about what is going on here.

**Q: Is data what we think it is?**

A: We can look at data within this frame via print, which abbreviates to p:

```
(gdb) p *data
$2 = 34124.75
```

That was disappointing: we only got the first element. But GDB has a specialized @-syntax for printing a sequence of elements in an array. Asking for 10 elements [LLDB: mem read -t*double* -c*10* *data*]:

```
(gdb) p *data@10
$3 =    {34124.75,
  34124.480000000003,
  34124.900000000001,
  34125.309999999998,
  34125.050000000003,
  34124.980000000003,
  nan(0x8000000000000),
  7.7074240751234461e-322,
  4.9406564584124654e-324,
  2.0734299798669383e-317}
```

Note the star at the head of the expression; without it, we'd get a sequence of 10 hexadecimal addresses.

I asked for 10 elements because I couldn't be bothered to count how many elements are in the data set, but the first 7 of these 10 elements look correct: a series of numbers, followed by a NaN marker. After that, we see whatever noise is in uninitialized space after the array.

**Q: Does this match what got sent by main?**

A: We can get a backtrace via bt:

```
(gdb) bt
#0  mean_and_var (data=data@entry=0x7fffffffe130) at stddev_bugged.c:16
#1  0x0000000000400680 in main () at stddev_bugged.c:38
```

The stack of frames is two frames deep, including the current frame, and its caller, main. Let us see what the data looks like in frame 1. First, we switch to it:

```
(gdb) f 1
#1  0x0000000000400680 in main () at stddev_bugged.c:38
38              meanvar mv = mean_and_var(d);
```

The debugger is now in the main frame, on line 38. Line 38 is where we expected it to be, so the sequence of execution is OK (and wasn't shuffled by the optimizer). In this frame, the data array is named d:

```
(gdb) p *d@7
$5 =   {34124.75,
  34124.480000000003,
  34124.900000000001,
  34125.309999999998,
  34125.050000000003,
  34124.980000000003,
  nan(0x8000000000000)}
```

This looks like it matches the data in the mean_and_var frame, so it seems nothing strange happened with the data set.

We don't have to explicitly return to frame zero to continue stepping through the program, but we could do so either via f 0 or by movement in the stack relative to the current frame:

```
(gdb) down
```

Note that up and down refer to the numeric order. Given that the list produced by bt (in both GDB and LLDB) puts the numerically lowest frame at the physical top of the list, up goes down the backtrace list and down goes up the backtrace list.

**Q: Is this a problem with parallel threads?**

A: We can get the list of threads via info threads [LLDB: thread list]:

```
(gdb) info threads
  Id   Target Id         Frame
* 1    Thread 0x7ffff7fcb7c0 (LWP 28903) "stddev_bugged" mean_and_var
                   (data=data@entry=0x7fffffffe180) at stddev_bugged.c:16
```

In this case, there is only one active thread, so this can't be a multithreading problem. The * shows us which thread the debugger is in right now. If there were a thread two, we could jump to it via GDB's thread 2 or LLDB's thread select 2.

 If your programs aren't spawning lots of new threads, they will be after you read Chapter 12. GDB users, add this line to your .gdbi nit to turn off those annoying notices about every new thread:

```
set print thread-events off
```

**Q: What is mean_and_var doing?**

A: We can repeatedly step through the next line of the program:

```
(gdb) n
18                  avg2 = 0;
(gdb) n
16        meanvar mean_and_var(const double *data){
```

Hitting the Enter key with no input repeats the previous command, so we don't even have to type the n:

```
(gdb)
18                  avg2 = 0;
(gdb)
20          size_t count= 0;
(gdb)
16      meanvar mean_and_var(const double *data){
(gdb)
21          for(size_t i=0;  !isnan(data[i]); i++){
(gdb)
21          for(size_t i=0;  !isnan(data[i]); i++){
(gdb)
22              ratio = count/(count+1);
(gdb)
26          avg   += data[i]/(count +0.0);
```

The line numbers indicate that the program is jumping around. This is because in each step, the debugger is executing machine-level instructions which are not necessarily ordered to match the C code that generated them. Even with optimization set to level zero, this is normal. The jumping around can also affect variables, as their value may be unreliable until after the second or third time a line gets hit in the out-of-order sequence.

There are other options for stepping through, typically one of snuc; see the table below. But stepping through like this will take all day. We see that there is a for loop stepping through data, so let us set another breakpoint in the middle of the loop:

```
(gdb) b 25
Breakpoint 2 at 0x400875: file stddev_bugged.c, line 25.
```

Now we have two breakpoints, which we can see via a GDB info break command or LLDB's break list:

```
(gdb) info break
Num     Type           Disp Enb Address            What
1       breakpoint     keep y   0x0000000000400820 in mean_and_var
                                                    at stddev_bugged.c:16
        breakpoint already hit 1 time
2       breakpoint     keep y   0x0000000000400875 in mean_and_var
                                                    at stddev_bugged.c:25
```

We don't really need the breakpoint at the head of mean_and_var anymore, so we can disable it [LLDB: break dis 1]:

```
(gdb) dis 1
```

After this, the Enb column from the output of info break will be n for breakpoint 1. You can later reenable the breakpoint via GDB's enable 1 or LLDB's break enable

1 if need be. Or if you know you will never need it again, delete the breakpoint via GDB's del 1 or LLDB's break del 1.

**Q: What do the variables look like in the middle of the loop?**

A: We can start over entirely via r, or we can continue from where we are via c:

```
(gdb) c
Breakpoint 2, mean_and_var (data=data@entry=0x7fffffffe130) at stddev_bugged.c:25
25              avg2  *= ratio;
```

We are now stopped at line 25, and can see all local variables [LLDB: frame variable]:

```
(gdb) info local
i = 0
avg = 0
avg2 = 0
ratio = 0
count = 1
```

We can also check the input arguments via GDB's info args, though we have already looked at data directly. LLDB's frame variable includes both local variables and input arguments.

**Q: We know the output mean is wrong, so how does avg change at each run?**

A: We could type p avg every time the we stop at this breakpoint, but the display command automates this:

```
(gdb) disp avg
1: avg = 0
```

Now, when we continue, the debugger will continue through the loop, and at each stop we see the current value of avg:

```
(gdb) c
Breakpoint 2, mean_and_var (data=data@entry=0x7fffffffe130) at stddev_bugged.c:25
25              avg2  *= ratio;
1: avg = 0

(gdb)
Breakpoint 2, mean_and_var (data=data@entry=0x7fffffffe130) at stddev_bugged.c:25
25              avg2  *= ratio;
1: avg = 0
```

This is a bad sign: the code has lines like

```
avg *= ratio;
...
avg += data[i]/(count +0.0);
```

so avg should be changing at each iteration of the loop, but is stuck at zero. Having established that it is broken, we are done looking at avg (which is labeled as display #1), so we can turn off autoprinting via undisp 1.

**Q: How do the inputs to avg look?**

A: We verified that data looks good; how are ratio and count?

```
(gdb) disp ratio
2: ratio = 0

(gdb) disp count
3: count = 3
```

Continuing through the loop a few times, we see that count is incrementing the way a variable named "count" should, but ratio is not moving:

```
(gdb) c
Breakpoint 2, mean_and_var (data=data@entry=0x7fffffffe130) at stddev_bugged.c:25
25                  avg2   *= ratio;
3: count = 4
2: ratio = 0
```

**Q: Where did ratio get set?**

A: Inspecting the code, in the text editor or via l, we see that ratio is only set on line 22:

```
ratio = count/(count+1);
```

We already verified that count is incrementing as it should, but there must be something wrong on this line. At this point, the error may be obvious to you: if count is an integer, then count/(count+1) is integer-arithmetic division, which returns an integer (3/4==0), not the floating-point division we all learned in elementary school (3/4==0.75). The correct thing to do (see "Cast Less" on page 147) is to ensure that either the numerator or denominator is floating-point, which we can do by changing the integer constant 1 to the floating-point constant 1.0:

```
ratio = count/(count+1.0);
```

The debugger didn't remind us about this common error, but it helped us find the first point in the code where something went wrong, and it is certainly easier to find an error on one line than to find an error in a 50-line code block. Along the way, we got to check and verify all sorts of details about the code, and get a better understanding of the flow of the program and the stack of frames.

Table 2-1 provides a list of the more common debugger commands. Both GDB and LLDB have dozens more, but these are the 10% that you will likely use 90% of the time. Most of the variable names are taken from the *New York Times* headline downloader from "libxml and cURL" on page 337.

*Table 2-1. Common debugger commands*

| Group | Command | Meaning |
|---|---|---|
| Go | run | Run the program from the start. |
| | run *args* | Run the program from the start, with the given command-line arguments. |
| Stop | b *get_rss* | Pause your program at a certain function. |
| | b *nyt_feeds.c:105* | Pause just before a certain line of code. |
| | break *105* | Same as b *nyt_feeds.c:105* if you are already stopped in *nyt_feeds.c*. |
| | info break [GDB] | List breakpoints. |
| | break list [LLDB] | |
| | watch *curl* [GDB] | Break if the value of the given variable changes. |
| | watch set var *curl* [LLDB] | |
| | dis *3* / ena *3* / del *3* [GDB] | Disable/reenable/delete breakpoint *3*. If you have a lot of breakpoints set, disable by itself turns them all off, and then you can enable the one or two that you need at the moment; likewise for enable/delete. |
| | break dis *3* / break ena *3* / break del *3* [LLDB] | |
| Inspect variables | p *url* | Print the value of *url*. You may specify any expression, including function calls. |
| | p *\*an_array@10* [GDB] | Print the first 10 elements of *an_array*. The next 10 are p *\*(an_array+10)@10*. |
| | mem read -t*double* -c*10* an_array | Read a count of 10 items of type double from an_array. The next 10 are mem read -t*double* -c*10* an_array+10. |
| | info args / info vars [GDB] | Get the values of all arguments to the function or all local variables. |
| | frame var [LLDB] | Get the values of all arguments to the function and all local variables. |
| | disp *url* | Display the value of *url* every time the program stops. |

| Group | Command | Meaning |
| --- | --- | --- |
| | undisp 3 | Stop the display the of display item 3. GDB: with no number, turn them all off. |
| Threads | info thread [GDB] | List the active threads. |
| | thread list [LLDB] | |
| | thread 2 [GDB] | Switch focus to thread 2 |
| | thread select 2 [LLDB] | |
| Frames | bt | List the stack of frames. |
| | f 3 | Look at frame 3. |
| | up / down | Go numerically one up or down in the stack of frames. |
| Step | s | Step one line, even if that means entering another function. |
| | n | Next line, but do not enter subfunctions, and possibly back up to the head of a loop. |
| | u | Until the next line forward from the current line (so let an already-visited loop run through until forward progress). |
| | c | Continue until the next breakpoint or the end of the program. |
| | ret or ret 3 [GDB] | Return from the current function immediately with the given return value (if any). |
| | j 105 [GDB] | Jump to whatever line you please (within reason). |
| Look at code | l | list prints the 10 lines around the line you are currently on. |
| Repeat | Enter | Just hitting Enter will repeat the last command, which makes stepping easier, or after l, Enter will list the next 10 lines after those you just saw. |
| Compile | make [GDB] | Run make without exiting GDB. You can also specify a target, like make myprog. |
| Get help | help | Explore everything else the debugger offers. |

# GDB Variables

This segment covers some useful debugger features that will help you look at your data with as little cognitive effort as possible. All of the commands to follow go on the debugger command line; IDE debuggers based on GDB often provide a means of hooking in to these facilities as well.

Here's a sample program that does nothing, but that you can type in for the sake of having a variable to interrogate. Because it is such a do-nothing program, be sure to set the compiler's optimization flag to -O0, or else x will disappear entirely.

```
int main(){
    int x[20] = {};
    x[0] = 3;
}
```

The first tip will only be new to those of you who didn't read the GDB manual (Stallman, 2002), which is probably all of you. You can generate convenience variables, to save typing. For example, if you want to inspect an element deep within a hierarchy of structures, you can do something like:

```
(gdb) set $vd = my_model->dataset->vector->data
p *$vd@10

(lldb) p double *$vd = my_model->dataset->vector->data
mem read -tdouble -c10 $vd
```

That first line generated the convenience variable to substitute for the lengthy path. Following the lead of the shell, a dollar sign indicates a variable. Unlike the shell, GDB uses set and a dollar sign on the variable's first use, and LLDB uses clang's parser to evaluate expressions, so the LLDB declaration is a typical C declaration. The second line in both versions demonstrates a simple use. We don't save much typing here, but if you suspect a variable of guilty behavior, giving it a short name makes it easier to give it a thorough interrogation.

These aren't just names; they're real variables that you can modify. After breaking at line 3 or line 4 of the do-nothing program, try:

```
(gdb) set $ptr=&x[3]
p *$ptr = 8
p *($ptr++)    #print the pointee, and step forward one

(lldb) p int *$ptr = &x[3]
p *$ptr = 8
p *($ptr++)
```

The second line changes the value in the given location. Adding one to a pointer steps forward to the next item in the list (as per "All the Pointer Arithmetic You Need to Know" on page 138), so after the third line, $ptr is now pointing to x[4].

That last form is especially useful because hitting the Enter key without any input repeats the last command. Because the pointer stepped forward, you'll get a new next value every time you hit Enter, until you get the gist of the array. This is also useful should you find yourself dealing with a linked list. Pretend we have a function named `show_structure` that displays an element of the linked list and sets `$list` equal to the given element, and we have the head of the list at `list_head`. Then:

```
p $list=list_head
show_structure $list->next
```

and leaning on the Enter key will step through the list. Later, we'll make that imaginary function to display a data structure a reality.

But first, here's one more trick about these `$` variables. Let me cut and paste a few lines of interaction with a debugger in the other screen:

```
(gdb|lldb) p x+3
$17 = (int *) 0xbffff9a4
```

You probably don't even look at it anymore, but notice how the output to the print statement starts with `$17`. Indeed, every output is assigned a variable name, which we can use like any other:

```
(gdb|lldb) p *$17
$18 = 8
(gdb|lldb) p *$17+20
$19 = 28
```

To be even more brief, GDB uses a lone `$` as a shorthand variable assigned to the last output. So if you get a hex address when you thought you would get the value at that address, just put `p *$` on the next line to get the value. With this, the above steps could have been:

```
(gdb) p x+3
$20 = (int *) 0xbffff9a4
(gdb) p *$
$21 = 8
(gdb) p $+20
$22 = 28
```

## Print Your Structures

You can define simple macros, which are especially useful for displaying nontrivial data structures—which is most of the work one does in a debugger. Even a simple 2D array hurts your eyes when it's displayed as a long line of numbers. In a perfect world, every major structure you deal with will have a debugger command associated to quickly view that structure in the manner(s) most useful to you.

The facility is rather primitive, but you probably already wrote a C-side function that prints any complex structures you might have to deal with, so the macro can simply call that function with a few keystrokes.

You can't use any of your C preprocessor macros at the debugger prompt, because they were substituted out long before the debugger saw any of your code. So if you have a valuable macro in your code, you may have to reimplement it in the debugger as well.

Here is a GDB function you can try by putting a breakpoint about halfway through the parse function in "libxml and cURL" on page 337, at which point you'll have a doc structure representing an XML tree. Put these macros in your .gdbinit.

```
define pxml
    p xmlElemDump(stdout, $arg0, xmlDocGetRootElement($arg0))
end
document pxml
Print the tree of an already opened XML document (i.e., an xmlDocPtr) to the
screen. This will probably be several pages long.
E.g., given: xmlDocPtr doc = xmlParseFile(infile);
use: pxml doc
end
```

Notice how the documentation follows right after the function itself; view it via help pxml or help user-defined. The macro itself just saves some typing, but because the primary activity in the debugger is looking at data, those little things add up.

I'll discuss the LLDB versions of these macros below.

GLib has a linked-list structure, so we should have a linked-list viewer. Example 2-1 implements it via two user-visible macros (phead to view the head of the list, then pnext to step forward) and one macro the user should never have to call (plistdata, to remove redundancy between phead and pnext).

*Example 2-1. A set of macros to easily display a linked list in GDB—about the most elaborate debugging macro you'll ever need (gdb_showlist)*

```
define phead
    set $ptr = $arg1
    plistdata $arg0
end
document phead
Print the first element of a list. E.g., given the declaration
    Glist *datalist;
    g_list_add(datalist, "Hello");
view the list with something like
gdb> phead char datalist
gdb> pnext char
gdb> pnext char
This macro defines $ptr as the current pointed-to list struct,
```

and $pdata as the data in that list element.
end

```
define pnext
    set $ptr = $ptr->next
    plistdata $arg0
end
document pnext
You need to call phead first; that will set $ptr.
This macro will step forward in the list, then show the value at
that next element. Give the type of the list data as the only argument.

This macro defines $ptr as the current pointed-to list struct, and
$pdata as the data in that list element.
end

define plistdata
    if $ptr
        set $pdata = $ptr->data
    else
        set $pdata= 0
    end
    if $pdata
        p ($arg0*)$pdata
    else
        p "NULL"
    end
end
document plistdata
This is intended to be used by phead and pnext, q.v. It sets $pdata and prints its value.
end
```

Example 2-2 offers some simple code that uses the GList to store char*s. You can break around line 8 or 9 and call the previous macros.

*Example 2-2. Some sample code for trying debugging, or a lightning-quick intro to GLib linked lists (glist.c)*

```c
#include <stdio.h>
#include <glib.h>

GList *list;

int main(){
    list = g_list_append(list, "a");
    list = g_list_append(list, "b");
    list = g_list_append(list, "c");

    for ( ; list!= NULL; list=list->next)
        printf("%s\n", (char*)list->data);
}
```

You can define functions to run before or after every use of a given command. To give an example in GDB:

```
define hook-print
echo <----\n
end
```

```
define hookpost-print
echo ---->\n
end
```

will print cute brackets before and after anything you print. The most exciting hook is hook-stop. The display command will print the value of any expression every time the program stops, but if you want to make use of a macro or other GDB command at every stop, redefine hook-stop:

```
define hook-stop
pxml suspect_tree
end
```

When you are done with your suspect, redefine hook-stop to be nothing:

```
define hook-stop
end
```

LLDB users: see target stop-hook add.

---

**Your Turn:** GDB macros can also include a while that looks much like the ifs in Example 2-2 (start with a line like while $ptr and conclude with end). Use this to write a macro to print an entire list at once.

---

LLDB does things a little differently.

First, you may have noticed that LLDB commands are often verbose, because the authors expect you to write your own aliases for the commands you use more often. For example, you could write an alias for the commands to print double or int arrays via:

```
(lldb) command alias dp memory read -tdouble -c%1
command alias ip memory read -tint -c%1

# Usage:
dp 10 data
ip 10 idata
```

The aliasing mechanism is intended for abbreviating existing commands. There is no way to assign a help string to the aliased command, because LLDB recycles the help string associated with the full command. To write macros like the GDB macros above, LLDB uses regular expressions.

Here is the LLDB version to put in .lldbinit:

```
command regex pxml
            's/(.+)/p xmlElemDump(stdout, %1, xmlDocGetRootElement(%1))/'
            -h "Dump the contents of an XML tree."
```

A full discussion of regexes is beyond the scope of this book (and there are hundreds of regex tutorials online), but the contents of a set of parens between the first and second slash will be inserted into the %1 marker between the second and third slashes.

---

## Profiling

It doesn't matter how fast your program is: you will still want it faster. In most languages, the first piece of advice is to rewrite everything in C, but you're already writing in C. The next step is to find the functions that are taking up the most time and therefore would provide the most payoff to more optimization efforts.

First, add the -pg flag to gcc's or icc's CFLAGS (yes, this is compiler-specific; gcc will prep the program for gprof; Intel's compiler will prep the program for prof, and has a similar workflow to the gcc-specific details I give here). With this flag, your program will stop every few microseconds and note in which function it is currently working. The annotations get written in binary format to *gmon.out*.

Only the executable is profiled, not libraries that are linked to it. Therefore, if you need to profile a library as it runs a test program, you'll have to copy all of the library and program code into one place and recompile everything as one big executable.

After running your program, call gprof *your_program* > *profile* (or prof ...), then open *profile* in your text editor to view a human-readable listing of functions, their calls, and what percentage of the program's time was spent in each function. You might be surprised by where the bottlenecks turn out to be.

---

# Using Valgrind to Check for Errors

Most of our time spent debugging is spent finding the first point in the program where something looks wrong. Good code and a good system will find that point for you. That is, a good system fails fast.

C gets mixed scores on this. In some languages, a typo like conut=15 would generate a new variable that has nothing to do with the count you meant to set; with C, it fails at the compilation step. On the other hand, C will let you assign to the 10th element of a 9-element array and then trundle along for a long time before you find out that there's garbage in what you thought was element 10.

---

Those memory mismanagement issues are a hassle, and so there are tools to confront them. Within these, Valgrind is a big winner. It is ported to most POSIX systems (including OS X), where you can get a copy via your package manager. Windows users might want to try Dr. Memory (*http://bit.ly/dr-memory*).

Valgrind runs a virtual machine that keeps better tabs on memory than the real machine does, so it knows when you hit the 10th element in an array of 9 items.

Once you have a program compiled (with debugging symbols included via gcc's or clang's -g flag, of course), run:

```
valgrind your_program
```

If you have an error, Valgrind will give you two backtraces that look a lot like the backtraces your debugger gives you. The first is where the misuse was first detected, and the second is Valgrind's best guess as to what line the misuse clashed with, such as where a double-freed block was first freed, or where the closest malloced block was allocated. The errors are often subtle, but having the exact line to focus on goes a long way toward finding the bug. Valgrind is under active development—programmers like nothing better than writing programming tools—so I'm amused to watch how much more informative the reports have gotten over time and only expect better in the future.

To give you an example of a Valgrind backtrace, I inserted an error in the code of Example 9-1 by doubling line 14, free(cmd), thus causing the cmd pointer to be freed once on line 14 and again on line 15. Here's the backtrace I got:

```
Invalid free() / delete / delete[] / realloc()
   at 0x4A079AE: free (vg_replace_malloc.c:427)
   by 0x40084B: get_strings (sadstrings.c:15)
   by 0x40086B: main (sadstrings.c:19)
 Address 0x4c3b090 is 0 bytes inside a block of size 19 free'd
   at 0x4A079AE: free (vg_replace_malloc.c:427)
   by 0x40083F: get_strings (sadstrings.c:14)
   by 0x40086B: main (sadstrings.c:19)
```

The top frame in both backtraces is in the standard library code for freeing pointers, but we can be confident that the standard library is well debugged. Focusing on the part of the stack referring to code that I wrote, the backtrace points me to lines 14 and 15 of *sadstrings.c*, which are indeed the two calls to free(cmd) in my modified code.

Valgrind is very good at finding conditional jumps that depend on uninitialized values. You can use this to trace back exactly when a variable is or is not initialized by inserting lines like

```
if(suspect_var) printf(" ");
```

into your code and seeing if Valgrind complains about the variable at that point.

You can also start the debugger at the first error, by running:

```
valgrind --db-attach=yes your_program
```

With this sort of startup, you'll be asked if you want to run the debugger on every detected error, and then you can check the value of the implicated variables as usual. At this point, we're back to having a program that fails on the first line where a problem is detected.

Valgrind also does memory leaks:

```
valgrind --leak-check=full your_program
```

This is typically slower, so you might not want to run it every time. When it finishes, you'll have a backtrace for where every leaked pointer was allocated.

For some code bases, chasing leaks can be very time-consuming. A leak in a library function that could conceivably run a million times in the center of a user program's loop, or in a program that should have 100% runtime for months, will eventually cause potentially major problems for users. But it is easy to find programs broadly deemed to be reliable (on my machine, doxygen, git, TeX, vi, others) that Valgrind reports as definitely losing kilobytes. For such cases, we can adapt a certain cliché about trees falling in the woods: if a bug does not cause incorrect results or user-perceivable slowdowns, is it really a high-priority bug?

## Unit Testing

Of course you're writing tests for your code. You're writing *unit tests* for the smaller components and *integration tests* to make sure that the components get along amicably. You may even be the sort of person who writes the unit tests first and then builds the program to pass the tests.

Now you've got the problem of keeping all those tests organized, which is where a *test harness* comes in. A test harness is a system that sets up a small environment for every test, runs the test, and reports whether the result is as expected. Like the debugger, I expect that some of you are wondering who it is that doesn't use a test harness, and to others, it's something you never really considered.

There are abundant choices. It's easy to write a macro or two to call each test function and compare its return value to the expected result, and more than enough authors have let that simple basis turn into yet another implementation of a full test harness. From *How We Test Software at Microsoft*: "Microsoft's internal repository for shared tools includes more than 40 entries under *test harness*." For consistency with the rest of the book, I'll show you GLib's test harness, and because they are all so similar, and because I'm not going to go into so much detail that I'm effectively reading the GLib manual to you, what I cover here should carry over to other test harnesses as well.

A test harness has a few features that beat the typical homemade test macro:

- You need to test the failures. If a function is supposed to abort or exit with an error message, you need a facility to test that the program actually exited when you expected it to.

- Each test is kept separate, so you don't have to worry that test 3 affected the outcome of test 4. If you want to make sure the two procedures don't interact badly, run them in sequence as an integration test after running them separately.

- You probably need to build some data structures before you can run your tests. Setting up the scene for a test sometimes takes a good amount of work, so it would be nice to run several tests given the same setup.

Example 2-3 shows a few basic unit tests of the dictionary object from "Implementing a Dictionary" on page 251, implementing these three test harness features. It demonstrates how that last item largely dictates the flow of test harness use: a new struct type is defined at the beginning of the program, then there are functions for setting up and tearing down an instance of that struct type, and once we have all that in place it is easy to write several tests using the built environment.

The dictionary is a simple set of key/value pairs, so most of the testing consists of retrieving a value for a given key and making sure that it worked OK. Notice that a key of NULL is not acceptable, so we check that the program will halt if such a key gets sent in.

*Example 2-3. A test of the dictionary from "Implementing a Dictionary" on page 251 (dict_test.c)*

```
#include <glib.h>
#include "dict.h"

typedef struct {                                          ❶
    dictionary *dd;
} dfixture;

void dict_setup(dfixture *df, gconstpointer test_data){   ❷
    df->dd = dictionary_new();
    dictionary_add(df->dd, "key1", "val1");
    dictionary_add(df->dd, "key2", NULL);
}
```

```
void dict_teardown(dfixture *df, gconstpointer test_data){
    dictionary_free(df->dd);
}

void check_keys(dictionary const *d){                          ❸
    char *got_it = dictionary_find(d, "xx");
    g_assert(got_it == dictionary_not_found);
    got_it = dictionary_find(d, "key1");
    g_assert_cmpstr(got_it, ==, "val1");
    got_it = dictionary_find(d, "key2");
    g_assert_cmpstr(got_it, ==, NULL);
}

void test_new(dfixture *df, gconstpointer ignored){
    check_keys(df->dd);
}

void test_copy(dfixture *df, gconstpointer ignored){
    dictionary *cp = dictionary_copy(df->dd);
    check_keys(cp);
    dictionary_free(cp);
}

void test_failure(){                                           ❹
    if (g_test_trap_fork(0, G_TEST_TRAP_SILENCE_STDOUT |
    G_TEST_TRAP_SILENCE_STDERR)){
        dictionary *dd = dictionary_new();
        dictionary_add(dd, NULL, "blank");
    }
    g_test_trap_assert_failed();
    g_test_trap_assert_stderr("NULL is not a valid key.\n");
}

int main(int argc, char **argv){
    g_test_init(&argc, &argv, NULL);
    g_test_add ("/set1/new test", dfixture, NULL,          ❺
                        dict_setup, test_new, dict_teardown);
    g_test_add ("/set1/copy test", dfixture, NULL,
                        dict_setup, test_copy, dict_teardown);
    g_test_add_func ("/set2/fail test", test_failure);   ❻
    return g_test_run();
}
```

❶ The elements used in a set of tests is called a *fixture*. GLib requires that each fixture be a struct, so we create a throwaway struct to be passed from the setup to
   the test to the teardown.

❷ Here are the setup and teardown scripts that create the data structure to be used
   for a number of tests.

❸ Now that the setup and teardown functions are defined, the tests themselves are just a sequence of simple operations on the structures in the fixture and assertions that the operations went according to plan. The GLib test harness provides some extra assertion macros, like the string comparison macro, `g_assert_compstr`, used here.

❹ GLib tests for failure via the POSIX `fork` system call (which means that this won't run on Windows without a POSIX subsystem). The `fork` call generates a new program that runs the contents of the `if` statement, which should fail and call `abort`. This program watches for the forked version and checks that it failed and that the right message was written to `stderr`.

❺ Tests are organized into sets via path-like strings. The `NULL` argument could be a pointer to a data set to be used by the test, but not built/torn down by the system. Notice how both the new and copy tests use the same setup and teardown.

❻ If you don't have setup/teardown to do before/after the call, use this simpler form to run the test.

## Using a Program as a Library

The only difference between a function library and a program is that a program includes a `main` function that indicates where execution should start.

Now and then I have a file that does one thing that's not quite big enough to merit being set up as a standalone shared library. It still needs tests, and I can put them in the same file as everything else, via a preprocessor condition. In the following snippet, if `Test_operations` is defined (via the various methods discussed later), then the snippet is a program that runs the tests; if `Test_operations` is not defined (the usual case), then the snippet is compiled without `main` and so is a library to be used by other programs.

```
int operation_one(){
    ...
}

int operation_two(){
    ...
}

#ifdef Test_operations

    void optest(){
        ...
    }
```

```
    int main(int argc, char **argv){
        g_test_init(&argc, &argv, NULL);
        g_test_add_func ("/set/a test", test_failure);
    }

#endif
```

There are a few ways to define the `Test_operations` variable. In with the usual flags, probably in your makefile, add:

```
CFLAGS=-DTest_operations
```

The `-D` flag is the POSIX-standard compiler flag that is equivalent to putting `#define` *Test_operations* at the top of every *.c* file.

When you see Automake in Chapter 3, you'll see that it provides a `+=` operator, so given the usual flags in `AM_CFLAGS`, you could add the `-D` flag to the checks via:

```
check_CFLAGS  = $(AM_CFLAGS)
check_CFLAGS += -DTest_operations
```

The conditional inclusion of `main` can also come in handy in the other direction. For example, I often have an analysis to do based on some quirky data set. Before writing the final analysis, I first have to write a function to read in and clean the data, and then a few functions producing summary statistics that sanity-check the data and my progress. This will all be in *modelone.c*. Next week, I may have an idea for a new descriptive model, which will naturally make heavy use of the existing functions to clean data and display basic statistics. By conditionally including `main` in *modelone.c*, I can quickly turn the original program into a library. Here is a skeleton for *modelone.c*:

```
void read_data(){
    [database work here]
}

#ifndef MODELONE_LIB
int main(){
    read_data();
    ...
}
#endif
```

I use `#ifndef` rather than `#ifdef`, because the norm is to use *modelone.c* as a program, but this otherwise functions the same way as the conditional inclusion of `main` for testing purposes did.

# Coverage

What's your test coverage? Are there lines of code that you wrote that aren't touched by your tests? gcc has the companion gcov, which will count how many times each line of code was touched by a program. The procedure:

- Add -fprofile-arcs -ftest-coverage to your CFLAGS for gcc. You might want to set the -O0 flag, so that no lines of code are optimized out.

- When the program runs, each source file *yourcode.c* will produce one or two data files, *yourcode.gcda* and *yourcode.gcno*.

- Running gcov *yourcode*.gcda will write to stdout the percentage of runnable lines of code that your program hit (declarations, #include lines, and so on don't count) and will produce *yourcode.c.cov*.

- The first column of *yourcode.c.cov* will show how often each runnable line was hit by your tests, and will mark the lines not hit with a big fat #####. Those are the parts for which you should consider writing another test.

Example 2-4 shows a shell script that adds up all the steps. I use a here document to generate the makefile, so I could put all the steps in one script, and after compiling, running, and gcov-ing the program, I grep for the ##### markers. The -C3 flag to GNU grep requests three lines of context around matches. It isn't POSIX-standard, but then, neither are pkg-config or the test coverage flags.

*Example 2-4. A script to compile for coverage testing, run the tests, and check for lines of code not yet tested (gcov.sh)*

```
cat > makefile << '------'
P=dict_test
objects= keyval.o dict.o
CFLAGS = `pkg-config --cflags glib-2.0` -g -Wall -std=gnu99 \
         -O0 -fprofile-arcs -ftest-coverage
LDLIBS = `pkg-config --libs glib-2.0`
CC=gcc

$(P):$(objects)
------

make
./dict_test
for i in *gcda; do gcov $i; done;
grep -C3 '#####' *.c.gcov
```

# Error Checking

A complete programming textbook must include at least one lecture to the reader about how important it is to handle errors sent by functions you have called.

OK, consider yourself lectured. Now let's consider the side of how and when you will return errors from the functions you write. There are a lot of different types of errors in a lot of different contexts, so we have to break down the inquiry into several subcases:

- What is the user going to do with the error message?
- Is the receiver a human or another function?
- How can the error be communicated to the user?

I will leave the third question for later ("Return Multiple Items from a Function" on page 222), but the first two questions already give us a lot of cases to consider.

## What is the User's Involvement in the Error?

Thoughtless error-handling, wherein authors pepper their code with error-checks because you can't have too many, is not necessarily the right approach. You need to maintain lines of error-handling code like any other, and every user of your function has internalized endless lectures about how every possible error code needs to be handled, so if you throw error codes that have no reasonable resolution, the function user will be left feeling guilty and unsure. There is such a thing as too much information (TMI).

To approach the question of how an error will be used, consider the complementary question of how the user was involved in the error to begin with.

*Sometimes the user can't know if an input is valid before calling the function.*
The classic example of this is looking up a key in a key/value list and finding out that the key is not in the list. In this case, you could think of the function as a lookup function that throws errors if the key is missing from the list, or you could think of it as a dual-purpose function that either looks up keys or informs the caller whether the key is present or not.

Or to give an example from high-school algebra, the quadratic formula requires calculating sqrt(b*b - 4*a*c), and if the term in parens is negative, the square root is not a real number. It's awkward to expect the function user to calculate b*b - 4*a*c to establish feasibility, so it is reasonable to think of the quadratic formula function as either returning the roots of the quadratic equation or reporting whether the roots will be real or not.

In these examples of nontrivial input-checking, bad inputs aren't even an error, but are a routine and natural use of the function. If an error-handling function aborts or otherwise destructively halts on errors (as does the error-handler that follows), then it shouldn't be called in situations like these.

*Users passed in blatantly wrong input, such as a* NULL *pointer or other sort of malformed data.*

Your function has to check for these things, to prevent it from segfaulting or otherwise failing, but it is hard to imagine what the caller will do with the information. The documentation for *yourfn* told users that the pointer can't be NULL, so when they ignore it and call int* indata=NULL; *yourfn*(indata), and you return an error like Error: NULL pointer input, it's hard to imagine what the caller will do differently.

A function usually has several lines like if (input1==NULL) return -1; ... if (input20==NULL) return -1; at the head, and I find in the contexts where I work that reporting exactly which of the basic requirements enumerated in the documentation the caller missed is TMI.

*The error is entirely an error of internal processing.*

This includes "shouldn't happen" errors, wherein an internal calculation somehow got an impossible answer—what *Hair: The American Tribal Love Rock Musical* called a failure of the flesh, such as unresponsive hardware or a dropped network or database connection.

The flesh failures can typically be handled by the recipient (e.g., by wiggling the network cable). Or, if the user requests that a gigabyte of data be stored in memory and that gigabyte is not available, it makes sense to report an out-of-memory error. However, when allocation for a 20-character string fails, the machine is either overburdened and about to become unstable or it is on fire, and it's typically hard for a calling system to use that information to recover gracefully. Depending on the context in which you are working, *your computer is on fire-*type errors might be counterproductive and TMI.

Errors of internal processing (i.e., errors unrelated to external conditions and not directly tied to a somehow-invalid input value) cannot be handled by the caller. In this case, detailing to the user what went wrong is probably TMI. The caller needs to know that the output is unreliable, but enumerating lots of different error conditions just leaves the caller (duty-bound to handle all errors) with more work.

## The Context in Which the User is Working

As above, we often use a function to check on the validity of a set of inputs; such usage is not an error per se, and the function is most useful if it returns a meaningful value for these cases rather than calling an error handler. The rest of this section considers the bona fide errors.

- If the user of the program has access to a debugger and is in a context where using one is feasible, then the fastest way to fail is to call abort and cause the program to stop. Then the user has the local variables and backtrace right at the scene of the crime. The abort function has been C-standard since forever (you'll need to #include <stdlib.h>).
- If the user of the program is actually a Java program, or has no idea what a debugger is, then abort is an abomination, and the correct response is to return some sort of error code indicating a failure.

Both of these cases are very plausible, so it is sensible to have an if-else branch that lets the user select the correct mode of operation for the context.

It's been a long time since I've seen a nontrivial library that didn't implement its own error-handling macro. It's at just that level where the C standard doesn't provide one, but it's easy to implement with what C does offer, so everybody writes a new one.

The standard assert macro (hint: #include <assert.h>) will check a claim you make, and then stop if and only if your claim turns out to be false. Every implementation will be a little bit different, but the gist is:

```
#define assert(test) (test) ? 0 : abort();
```

By itself, assert is useful to test whether intermediate steps in your function are doing what they should be doing. I also like to use assert as documentation: it's a test for the computer to run, but when I see assert(matrix_a->size1 == matrix_b->size2), then I as a human reader am reminded that the dimensions of the two matrices will match in this manner. However, assert provides only the first kind of response (aborting), so assertions have to be wrapped.

Example 2-5 presents a macro that satisfies both conditions; I'll discuss it further in "Variadic Macros" on page 210. Note also that some users deal well with stderr, and some have no means to work with it.

*Example 2-5. A macro for dealing with errors: report or record them, and let the user decide whether to stop on errors or move on (stopif.h)*

```
#include <stdio.h>
#include <stdlib.h> //abort

/** Set this to \c 's' to stop the program on an error.
    Otherwise, functions return a value on failure.*/
char error_mode;

/** To where should I write errors? If this is \c NULL, write to \c stderr. */
```

```
FILE *error_log;

#define Stopif(assertion, error_action, ...) {                     \
        if (assertion){                                            \
            fprintf(error_log ? error_log : stderr, __VA_ARGS__); \
            fprintf(error_log ? error_log : stderr, "\n");        \
            if (error_mode=='s') abort();                          \
            else                {error_action;}                   \
        } }
```

Here are some imaginary sample uses:

```
Stopif(!inval, return -1, "inval must not be NULL");
Stopif(isnan(calced_val), goto nanval, "Calced_val was NaN. Cleaning
up, leaving.");
...
nanval:
    free(scratch_space);
    return NAN;
```

The most common means of dealing with an error is to simply return a value, so if you use the macro as is, expect to be typing return often. This can be a good thing, however. Authors often complain that sophisticated try-catch setups are effectively an updated version of the morass of gotos that we all consider to be harmful. For example, Google's internal coding style guide advises against using try-catch constructs, using exactly the morass-of-gotos rationale. This advises that it is worth reminding readers that the flow of the program will be redirected on error (and to where), and that we should keep our error-handling simple.

## How Should the Error Indication Be Returned?

I'll get to this question in greater detail in the chapter on struct handling (notably, "Return Multiple Items from a Function" on page 222), because if your function is above a certain level of complexity, returning a struct makes a lot of sense, and then adding an error-reporting variable to that struct is an easy and sensible solution. For example, given a function that returns a struct named out that includes a char* element named error:

```
Stopif(!inval, out.error="inval must not be NULL"; return out
            , "inval must not be NULL");
```

GLib has an error-handling system with its own type, the GError, that must be passed in (via pointer) as an argument to any given function. It provides several additional features above the macro listed in Example 2-5, including error domains and easier passing of errors from subfunctions to parent functions, at the cost of added complexity.

# Interweaving Documentation

You need documentation. You know this, and you know that you need to keep it current when the code changes. Yet, somehow, documentation is often the first thing to fall by the wayside. It is so very easy to say *it runs; I'll document it later.*

So you need to make writing the documentation as easy as physically possible. The immediate implication is that you have the documentation for the code in the same file as the code, as close as possible to the code being documented, and that implies that you're going to need a means of extracting the documentation from the code file.

Having the documentation right by the code also means you're more likely to read the documentation. It's a good habit to reread the documentation for a function before modifying it, both so that you have a better idea of what's going on, and so that you will be more likely to notice when your changes to the code will also require a change in the documentation.

I'll present two means of weaving documentation into the code: Doxygen and CWEB. Your package manager should be happy to install either of them.

## Doxygen

Doxygen is a simple system with simple goals. It works best for attaching a description to each function, struct, or other such block. This is the case of documenting an interface for users who will never care to look at the code itself. The description will be in a comment block right on top of the function, struct, or whatever, so it is easy to write the documentation comment first, then write the function to live up to the promises you just made.

The syntax for Doxygen is simple enough, and a few bullet points will have you well on your way to using it:

- If a comment block starts with two stars, `/** like so */`, then Doxygen will parse the comment. One-star comments, `/* like so */`, are ignored.

- If you want Doxygen to parse a file, you will need a `/** \file */` comment at the head of the file; see the example. If you forget this, Doxygen won't produce output for the file and won't give you much of a hint as to what went wrong.

- Put the comment right before the function, struct, et cetera.

- Your function descriptions can (and should) include `\param` segments describing the input parameters and a `\return` line listing the expected return value. Again, see the example.

- Use `\ref` for cross-references to other documented elements (including functions or pages).

- You can use an @ anywhere I used a backslash above: @file, @mainpage, et cetera. This is in emulation of JavaDoc, which seems to be emulating WEB. As a LaTeX user, I am more used to the backslash.

To run Doxygen, you will need a configuration file, and there are a lot of options to configure. Doxygen has a clever trick for handling this; run:

```
doxygen -g
```

and it will write a configuration file for you. You can then open it and edit as needed; it is of course very well documented. After that, run doxygen by itself to generate the outputs, including HTML, PDF, XML, or manual pages, as per your specification.

If you have Graphviz installed (ask your package manager for it), then Doxygen can generate *call graphs*: box-and-arrow diagrams showing which functions call and are called by which other functions. If somebody hands you an elaborate program and expects you to get to know it quickly, this can be a nice way to get a quick feel for the flow.

I documented "libxml and cURL" on page 337 using Doxygen; have a look and see how it reads to you as code, or run it through Doxygen and check out the HTML documentation it produces.

Every snippet throughout the book beginning with /** is also in Doxygen format.

### The narrative

Your documentation should contain at least two parts: the technical documentation describing the function-by-function details, and a narrative explaining to users what the package is about and how to get their bearings.

Start the narrative in a comment block with the header \mainpage. If you are producing HTML output, this will be the *index.html* of your website—the first page readers should see. From there, add as many pages as you'd like. Subsequent pages have a header of the form:

```
/** \page onewordtag The title of your page
*/
```

Back on the main page (or any other, including function documentation), add \ref *onewordtag* to produce a link to the page you wrote. You can tag and name the main page as well, if need be.

The narrative pages can be anywhere in your code: you could put them close to the code itself, or the narrative might make sense as a separate file consisting entirely of Doxygen comment blocks, maybe named *documentation.h*.

# Literate Code with CWEB

TeX, a document formatting system, is often held up as a paragon of a complicated system done very right. It is about 35 years old as of this writing, and (in this author's opinion) still produces the most attractive math of any typesetting system available. Many more recent systems don't even try to compete, and use TeX as a backend for typesetting. Its author, Donald Knuth, used to offer a bounty for bugs, but eventually dropped the bounty after it went unclaimed for many years.

Dr. Knuth explains the high quality of TeX by discussing how it was written: *literate programming*, in which every procedural chunk is preceded by a plain-English explanation of that chunk's purpose and functioning. The final product looks like a free-form description of code with some actual code interspersed here and there to formalize the description for the computer (in contrast to typical documented code, which is much more code than exposition). Knuth wrote TeX using WEB, a system that intersperses English expository text with PASCAL code. Here in the present day, the code will be in C, and now that TeX works to produce beautiful documentation, we might as well use it as the markup language for the expository side. Thus, CWEB.

As for the output, it's easy to find textbooks that use CWEB to organize and even present the content (e.g., Hanson, 1996). If somebody else is going to study your code (for some of you this might be a coworker or a review team), then CWEB might make a lot of sense.

I wrote "Example: An Agent-Based Model of Group Formation" on page 282 using CWEB; here's a rundown of what you need to know to compile it and follow its CWEB-specific features:

- It's customary to save CWEB files with a *.w* extension.
- Run `cweave` *groups.w* to produce a *.tex* file; then run `pdftex` *groups.tex* to produce a PDF.
- Run `ctangle` *groups.w* to produce a *.c* file. GNU `make` knows about this in its catalog of built-in rules, so `make groups` will run `ctangle` for you.

The tangle step removes comments, which means that CWEB and Doxygen are incompatible. Perhaps you could produce a header file with a header for each public function and struct for doxygenization, and use CWEB for your main code set.

Here is the CWEB manual reduced to seven bullet points:

- Every special code for CWEB has an @ followed by a single character. Be careful to write `@<titles@>` and not `@<incorrect titles>@`.
- Every segment has a comment, then code. It's OK to have a blank comment, but that comment-code rhythm has to be there, or else all sorts of errors turn up.

- Start a text section with an @ following by a space. Then expound, using TeX formatting.
- Start an unnamed chunk of code with @c.
- Start a named block of code with a title followed by an equals sign (because this is a definition): @<an operation@>=.
- That block will get inserted verbatim wherever you use the title. That is, each chunk name is effectively a macro that expands to the chunk of code you specified, but without all the extra rules of C preprocessor macros.
- Sections (like the sections in the example about group membership, setting up, plotting with Gnuplot, and so on) start with @* and have a title ending in a period.

That should be enough for you to get started writing your own stuff in CWEB. Have a look at "Example: An Agent-Based Model of Group Formation" on page 282 and see how it reads to you.

---

## Becoming a Better Typist

I selected many of the topics in this book based on my experience helping colleagues work out C code, and in the process learning the things that give them trouble. For some, setting up the environment was a real roadblock; many had trouble getting comfortable with pointers; and a surprisingly large number of people are just uncomfortable with the keyboard. It might not be what we think about when discussing programming, but people who are not confident at the keyboard are disinclined to use a language where symbol-heavy text like for (i=0; i<10; i++) is standard fare.

Here's the advice I give when issues with typing come up: get a light t-shirt and drape it over the keyboard. Stick your hands under the shirt, and start typing.

The intent is to prevent that sneaking glance that we all do to check where the keys are. It turns out that the keys aren't very mobile and are always exactly where you left them. But those micropauses to check on things are how we keep our confidence and facility with the keyboard at a certain safe speed.

If not being able to see is frustrating at first, persist through the initial awkwardness, and get to know those occasional keys that you never quite learned. When you are more confident with the keyboard, you'll have more brain power to dedicate to writing.

# Packaging Your Project

*Everything is building and it appears*
*That you're all architects and engineers.*

—Fugazi, "Ex-spectator"

If you've read this far, then you have met the tools that solve the core problems for dealing with C code, like debugging and documenting it. If you're eager to get going with C code itself, then feel free to skip ahead to Part II. This chapter and the next will cover some heavy-duty tools intended for collaboration and distribution to others: package-building tools and a revision-control system. Along the way, there will be many digressions about how you can use these tools to write better even when working solo.

I mentioned it in the introduction, but nobody reads introductions, and it bears repeating: the C community holds itself to a very high standard of interoperability. Yes, if you look around your office or coffee shop, everybody is using a homogeneous set of tools, but there is great diversity outside of any local area. Personally, I get emails reasonably often from people using my code on systems that I've never seen in person; I think this is amazing, and am always gratified that I strove for interoperability over the easier path of writing code that runs fine on my platform.

In the present day, Autotools, a system for autogenerating the perfect makefile for a given system, is central to how code is distributed. You've already met it in "Using Libraries from Source" on page 24, where you used it to quickly install the GNU Scientific Library. Even if you've never dealt with it directly, it is probably how the people who maintain your package-management system produced just the right build for your computer.

But you'll have trouble following what Autotools is doing unless you have a good idea of how a makefile works, so we need to cover those in a little more detail first. But to a first approximation, makefiles are organized sets of shell commands, so you'll need to get to know the various facilities the shell offers for automating your work. The path is long, but at the end you will be able to:

- Use the shell to automate work.
- Use makefiles to organize all those tasks you have the shell doing.
- Use Autotools to let users autogenerate makefiles on any system.

## The Shell

A POSIX-standard shell will have the following:

- Abundant macro facilities, in which your text is replaced with new text—i.e., an *expansion* syntax
- A Turing-complete programming language
- An interactive frontend—the command prompt—which might include lots of user-friendly features
- A system for recording and reusing everything you typed: history
- Lots of other things I won't mention here, such as job control and many built-in utilities

There is *a lot* of shell scripting syntax, so this section covers only a few pieces of low-hanging syntactic fruit for these categories. There are many shells to be had (and later, a sidebar will suggest trying a different one from the default), but unless otherwise noted, this section will stick to the POSIX standard.

I won't spend much time on the interactive features, but I have to mention one that isn't even POSIX-standard: tab completion. In bash, if you type part of a filename and hit the Tab key, the name will be autocompleted if there's only one option, and if not, hit Tab again to see a list of options. If you want to know how many commands you can type on the command line, hit Tab twice on a blank line and bash will give you the whole list. Other shells go much further than bash: after typing make, hit Tab in the Z shell and it will read your makefile for the possible targets. The Friendly Interactive shell (fish) will check the manual pages for the summary lines, so when you type man Tab it will give you a one-line summary of every command beginning with L, which could save you the trouble of actually pulling up any manpage at all.

There are two types of shell users: those who didn't know about this tab-completion thing, and those who use it *all the time on every single line*. If you were one of those people in that first group, you're going to love being in the second.

## Replacing Shell Commands with Their Outputs

A shell largely behaves like a macro language, wherein certain blobs of text get replaced with other blobs of text. These are called *expansions* in the shell world, and there are many types: this section touches on variable substitution, command substitution, a smattering of history substitution, and will give examples of tilde expansion and arithmetic substitution for quick desk calculator math. I leave you to read your shell's manual on alias expansion, brace expansion, parameter expansion, word splitting, pathname expansion, and glob expansion.

Variables are a simple expansion. If you set a variable like

```
onething="another thing"
```

on the command line, then when you later type:

```
echo $onething
```

then `another thing` will print to screen.

Your shell will require that there be no spaces on either side of the =, which will annoy you at some point.

When one program starts a new program (in POSIX C, when the `fork()` system call is used), a copy of all environment variables is sent to the child program. Of course, this is how your shell works: when you enter a command, the shell forks a new process and sends all the environment variables to the child.

Environment variables, however, are a subset of the shell variables. When you make an assignment like the previous one, you have set a variable for the shell to use; when you:

```
export onething="another thing"
```

then that variable is available for use in the shell, and its export attribute is set. Once the export attribute is set, you can still change the variable's value.

For our next expansion, how about the backtick, `` ` ``, which is not the more vertical-looking single tick '.

> The vertical tick (', not the backtick) indicates that you don't want expansions done. The sequence:
>
> ```
> onething="another thing"
> echo "$onething"
> echo '$onething'
> ```
>
> will print:
>
> ```
> another thing
> $onething
> ```

The backtick replaces the command you give with its output, doing so macro-style, where the command text is replaced in place with the output text.

Example 3-1 presents a script that counts lines of C code by how many lines have a ;, ), or } on them. Given that lines of source code is a lousy metric for most purposes anyway, this is as good a means as any, and has the bonus of being one line of shell code.

*Example 3-1. Counting lines using shell variables and POSIX utilities (linecount.sh)*

```
# Count lines with a ;, ), or }, and let that count be named Lines.
Lines=`grep '[;)}]' *.c | wc -l`

# Now count how many lines there are in a directory listing; name it Files.
Files=`ls *.c |wc -l`

echo files=$Files and lines=$Lines

# Arithmetic expansion is a double-paren.
# In bash, the remainder is truncated; more on this later.
echo lines/file = $(($Lines/$Files))

# Or, use those variables in a here script.
# By setting scale=3, answers are printed to 3 decimal places.
# (Or use bc -l (ell), which sets scale=20)
bc << ---
scale=3
$Lines/$Files
---
```

You can run the shell script via . `linecount.sh`. The dot is the POSIX-standard command to source a script. Your shell probably also lets you do this via the non-standard but much more comprehensible source `linecount.sh`.

> On the command line, the backtick is largely equivalent to $(). For example: echo `date` and echo $(date). However, make uses $() for its own purposes, so the backtick is easier to use in makefiles.

## Use the Shell's for Loops to Operate on a Set of Files

Let's get to some proper programming, with if statements and for loops.

But first, some caveats and annoyances about shell scripting:

- Scope is awkward—pretty much everything is global.

- It's effectively a macro language, so all those text interactions that they warned you about when you write a few lines of C preprocessor code (see "Cultivate Robust and Flourishing Macros" on page 163) are largely relevant for every line of your shell script.
- There isn't really a debugger that can execute the level-jumping basics from "Using a Debugger" on page 33, though modern shells will provide some facilities to trace errors or verbosely run scripts.
- You'll have to get used to the little tricks that will easily catch you, like how you can't have spaces around the = in onething=another, but you must have spaces around the [ and ] in if [ -e ff ] (because they're keywords that just happen to not have any letters in them).

Some people don't see these details as much of an issue, and ♥ the shell. Me, I write shell scripts to automate what I would type at the command line, and once things get complex enough that there are functions calling other functions, I take the time to switch to Perl, Python, awk, or whatever is appropriate.

Having a programming language that you can type directly onto the command line makes it easy to run the same command on several files. Let's back up every *.c* file the old fashioned way, by copying it to a new file with a name ending in *.bkup*:

```
for file in *.c;
do
 cp $file ${file}.bkup;
done
```

You see where the semicolon is: at the end of the list of files the loop will use, on the same line as the for statement. I'm pointing this out because when cramming this onto one line, as in:

```
for file in *.c; do cp $file ${file}.bkup; done
```

I always forget that the order is ; do and not do ;.

The for loop is useful for dealing with a sequence of *n* runs of a program. By way of a simple example, *benford.sh* searches C code for numbers beginning with a certain digit (i.e., the head of the line or a nondigit followed by the digit we are looking for), and writes each line that has the given number to a file, as shown in Example 3-2:

*Example 3-2. For each digit i, search for the (nondigit)i sequence in the text; count those lines (benford.sh)*

```
for i in 0 1 2 3 4 5 6 7 8 9; do grep -E '(^|[^0-9.])'$i *.c > lines_with_${i}; done
wc -l lines_with*          #A rough histogram of your digit usage.
```

Testing against Benford's law is left as an exercise for the reader.

The curly braces in ${i} are there to distinguish what is the variable name and what is subsequent text; you don't need it here, but you would if you wanted a filename like ${i}lines.

You probably have the seq command installed on your machine—it's BSD/GNU-standard but not POSIX-standard. Then we can use backticks to generate a sequence:

```
for i in `seq 0 9`; do grep -E '(^|[^0-9.])'$i *.c > lines_with_${i}; done
```

Using this form, running your program a thousand times is trivial:

```
for i in `seq 1 1000`; do ./run_program > ${i}.out; done
```

```
#or append all output to a single file:
for i in `seq 1 1000`; do
  echo output for run $i: >> run_outputs
  ./run_program >> run_outputs
done
```

## Test for Files

Now let's say that your program relies on a data set that has to be read in from a text file to a database. You only want to do the read-in once, or in pseudocode: if (database exists) then (do nothing), else (generate database from text).

On the command line, you would use test, a versatile command typically built into the shell. To try it, run a quick ls, get a filename you know is there, and use test to check that the file exists like this:

```
test -e a_file_i_know
echo $?
```

By itself, test outputs nothing, but because you're a C programmer, you know that every program has a main function that returns an integer, and we will use only that return value here. It's customary to read the return value as a problem number, so 0==no problem, and in this case 1==file does not exist (which is why, as will be discussed in "Don't Bother Explicitly Returning from main" on page 143, the default is that main returns zero). The shell doesn't print the return value to the screen, but stores it in a variable, $?, which you can print via echo.

The echo command itself has a return value, and $? will be set to that value after you run echo $?. If you want to use the value of $? for a specific command more than once, assign it to a variable, such as returnval=$?.

Example 3-3 uses test in an if statement to act only if a file does not exist. As in C, ! means *not*.

*Example 3-3. An if/then statement built around test—run it several times (.*
*iftest.sh; . iftest.sh; . iftest.sh) to watch the test file come in and out of existence*
*(iftest.sh)*

```
if test ! -e a_test_file; then
    echo test file had not existed
    touch a_test_file
else
    echo test file existed
    rm a_test_file
fi
```

Notice that, as with the `for` loop, the semicolon is in what I consider an awkward position, and we have the super-cute rule that we end `if` blocks with `fi`. By the way, `else if` is not valid syntax; use the `elif` keyword.

To make it easier for you to run this repeatedly, let's cram it onto one margin-busting line. The keywords [ and ] are equivalent to `test`, so when you see this form in other people's scripts and want to know what's going on, the answer is in `man test`.

```
if [ ! -e a_test_file ]; then echo test file had not existed; ↵
    touch a_test_file; else echo test file existed; rm a_test_file; fi
```

Because so many programs follow the custom that zero==OK and nonzero==problem, we can use `if` statements without `test` to express the clause *if the program ran OK, then....* For example, it's common enough to use `tar` to archive a directory into a single *.tgz* file, then delete the directory. It would be a disaster if the tar file somehow didn't get created but the directory contents were deleted anyway, so we should have some sort of test that the `tar` command completed successfully before deleting everything:

```
#generate a test file:
mkdir a_test_dir
echo testing ... testing > a_test_dir/tt

#Compress it, and remove only if the compression succeeded.
if tar cz a_test_dir > archived.tgz; then
    echo Compression went OK. Removing directory.
    rm -r a_test_dir
else
    echo Compression failed. Doing nothing.
fi
```

If you want to see this fail after running once, try `chmod 000 archived.tgz` to make the destination archive unwritable, then rerun.

Bear in mind that the above forms are about the return value of the program, be it `test` or some other program. Now and then you may want to use the actual output, which brings us back to the backtick. For example, `cat yourfile | wc -l` will produce a single number giving the line count of *yourfile* (assuming you have already established that it exists), so it is appropriate for embedding into a test:

```
if [ `cat yourfile | wc -l` -eq 0 ] ; then echo empty file.; fi
```

---

## Try a Multiplexer

I always have two terminals open when coding: one with the code in an editor, and one for compiling and running the program (probably in a debugger). Add another source file or two, and being able to deftly jump among terminals becomes essential.

There are two major terminal multiplexers to choose from, on either side of the great GNU-BSD rivalry: GNU Screen and tmux. Your package manager will probably install either or both of them.

Both work via a single command key. GNU Screen defaults to Ctrl-A. Tmux defaults to Ctrl-B, but the consensus seems to be that everybody remaps that to use Ctrl-A instead, by adding:

```
unbind C-b
set -g prefix C-a
bind a send-prefix
```

to *.tmux_conf* in their home directories. The manuals will list dozens of other things that you can add to your configuration files. When searching for tips and documentation, by the way, notice that *GNU Screen* is the name to type into your Internet search engine, because *Screen* by itself will get you nowhere.

Having set Ctrl-A as the command key, Ctrl-A Ctrl-A jumps between two windows, and you can read the manual for the Ctrl-A (other key) combinations that let you step forward or backward in the window list, or display the full list of windows so you can just pick from the list.

So both multiplexers solve the multiwindow problem. But they do so very much more:

- Ctrl-A-D will detach the session, meaning that your terminal no longer displays the various virtual terminals under the multiplexer's control. But they're still running in the background.
  - At the end of a long day with GNU Screen/Tmux, detach. Later, reattach from home or at work tomorrow using `screen -r` or `tmux attach`, and pick up exactly where you left off. The ability to keep going after a disconnect is also nice when working via a spotty connection to a server in Belize or Ukraine.
  - The multiplexer leaves the programs in its virtual terminals running after you've detached, which is useful for long processes that have to run overnight.
- There's a cut/paste feature.

---

> — Once in copy mode, you can mouselessly page through what's passed through the terminal lately, highlight a section, and copy it to the multiplexer's internal clipboard, then paste the copied text onto the command line.
>
> — While you're browsing for things to cut, you can scroll through the history and search for specific strings.
>
> These multiplexers really take that last step from the terminal being a place to work to being a fun place to work.

# fc

`fc` is a (POSIX-standard) command for turning your noodling on the shell into a repeatable script. Try:

```
fc -l    # The l is for list and is important.
```

You now have on the screen a numbered list of your last few commands. Your shell might let you type `history` to get the same effect.

The `-n` flag suppresses the line numbers, so you can write history items 100 through 200 to a file via:

```
fc -l -n 100 200 > a_script
```

then remove all the lines that were experiments that didn't work, and you've converted your futzing on the command line into a clean shell script.

If you omit the `-l` flag, then `fc` becomes a more immediate and volatile tool. It pulls up an editor (which means if you redirect with >, you're basically hung), doesn't display line numbers, and when you quit your editor, whatever is in that file gets executed immediately. This is great for a quick repetition of the last few lines, but can be disastrous if you're not careful. If you realize that you forgot the `-l` or are otherwise surprised to see yourself in the editor, delete everything on the screen to prevent unintended lines from getting executed.

But to end on a positive note, `fc` stands for *fix command*, and that is its simplest usage. With no options, it edits the prior line only, so it's nice for when you need to make elaborate corrections to a command.

## Try a New Shell

There are a lot of shells in the world beyond the shell your operating system vendor chose as the default. Here, I'll sample from the interesting things that the Z shell can do, to give you a hint of what switching from bash can get you.

Z shell's feature and variable lists go for dozens of pages, so there goes parsimony—but why bother being Spartan with interactive conveniences? (If you have Spartan æsthetics, then you still want to switch out of bash; try ash.) Set variables in ~/.zshrc (or just type them onto the command line to try them out); here is the one you'll need for the following examples:

```
setopt INTERACTIVE_COMMENTS
#now comments like this won't give an error
```

Expansion of globs, like replacing file.* with file.c file.o file.h is the responsibility of the shell. The most useful way in which Zsh extends this is that **/ tells the shell to recurse the directory tree when doing the expansion. A POSIX-standard shell reads ~ to be your home directory, so if you want every .c file anywhere in your purview, try ls ~/**/*.c.

Let's back up every last one of our .c files:

```
# This line may create a lot of files all over your home directory.
for ff in ~/**/*.c; do cp $ff ${ff}.bkup; done
```

Remember how bash only gives you arithmetic expansion on integers, so $((3/2)) is 1? Zsh and Ksh (and others) are C-like in giving you a real (more than integer) answer if you cast the numerator or denominator to float:

```
echo $((3/2.))        #works for zsh, syntax error for bash

#repeating the line-count example from earlier:
Files=`ls *.c |wc -l`
Lines=`grep '[)};]' *.c | wc -l`

echo lines/file = $(($Lines/($Files+0.0)))     #Add 0.0 to cast to float
```

Spaces in filenames can break things in bash, because spaces separate list elements. Zsh has an array syntax that doesn't depend on using spaces as an element delimiter.

```
# Generate two files, one of which has spaces in the name.
echo t1 > "test_file_1"
echo t2 > "test file 2"

# This fails in bash, is OK in Zsh.
for f in test* ; do cat $f; done
```

If you decide to switch shells, there are two ways to do it: you can use chsh to make the change official in the login system (/etc/passwd gets modified), or if that's somehow a problem, you can add exec -l /usr/bin/zsh (or whatever shell you like) as the last line of your .bashrc, so bash will replace itself with your preferred shell every time it starts.

If you want your makefile to use a nonstandard shell, add:

```
SHELL=command -v zsh
```

(or whatever shell you prefer) to your makefile. The POSIX-standard command -v prints the full path to a command, so you don't have to look it up yourself. SHELL is an odd variable in that it has to be in the makefile or set as an argument to make, because make ignores the environment variable named SHELL.

# Makefiles vs. Shell Scripts

You probably have a lot of little procedures associated with a project floating around (word count, spell check, run tests, write to revision control, push revision control out to a remote, back up), all of which could be automated by a shell script. But rather than producing a new one- or two-line script for every little task you have for your project, you can put them all into a makefile.

Makefiles were first covered in "Using Makefiles" on page 17, but now that we've covered the shell in more detail, we have more that we can put into a makefile. Here's one more example target from my daily life, which uses the if/then shell syntax and test. I use Git, but there are three Subversion repositories I have to deal with, and I never remember the procedures. As in Example 3-4, I now have a makefile to remember for me.

*Example 3-4. Folding an if/then and a test into a makefile (make_bit)*

```
push:
    @if [ "x$(MSG)" = 'x' ] ; then \          ❶
            echo "Usage: MSG='your message here.' make push"; fi
    @test "x$(MSG)" != 'x'                     ❷
    git commit -a -m "$(MSG)"
    git svn fetch
    git svn rebase
    git svn dcommit

pull:
    git svn fetch
    git svn rebase
```

❶  I need a message for each commit, so I do that via an environment variable set on the command line, via: MSG="This is a commit." make push. This line is an if-then statement that prints a reminder if I forget this.

❷  Test to ensure that "x$(MSG)" expands to something besides just "x", meaning that $(MSG) is not empty. Adding the x to both sides of the test adds protection for the case where $(MSG) is empty. If the test fails, make does not continue.

The commands executed in a makefile are in some ways just what you would type on the command line, and in some ways drastically different:

- *Every line runs independently, in a separate shell.* If you write this into your makefile:

```
clean:
        cd junkdir
        rm -f *          # Do not put this in a makefile.
```

then you will be a sad puppy. The two lines in the script are equivalent to C code like this:

```
system("cd junkdir");
system("rm -f *");
```

Or, because system("*cmd*") is equivalent to sh -c "*cmd*", our make script is also equivalent to:

```
sh -c "cd junkdir"
sh -c "rm -f *"
```

And for the shell geeks, (*cmd*) runs *cmd* in a subshell, so the make snippet is also equivalent to typing this at the shell prompt:

```
(cd junkdir)
(rm -f *)
```

In all cases, the second subshell knows nothing of what happened in the first subshell. make will first spawn a shell that changes into the directory you are emptying, then make is done with that subshell. Then it starts a new subshell from the directory you started in and calls rm -f *.

On the plus side, make will delete the erroneous makefile for you. If you want to express the thought in this form, do it like this:

```
cd junkdir && rm -f *
```

where the && runs commands in short-circuit sequence just like in C (i.e., if the first command fails, don't bother running the second). Or use a backslash to join two lines into one:

```
cd junkdir&& \
rm -f *
```

Though for a case like this, I wouldn't trust just a backslash. In real life, you're better off just using rm -f junkdir/* anyway.

- make replaces instances of $*x* (for one-letter or one-symbol variable names) or $(*xx*) (for multiletter variable names) with the appropriate values.
- If you want the shell, not make, to do the substitution, then drop the parens and double your $$s. For example, to use the shell's variable mangling to name backups from a makefile: for i in *.c; do cp $$i $${i%%.c}.bkup; done.

- Recall from "Using Makefiles" on page 17 that you can set an environment variable just before a command, e.g., CFLAGS=-O3 gcc test.c. That can come in handy now that each shell survives for a single line. Don't forget that the assignment has to come just before a command and not a shell keyword like if or while.

- An @ at the head of a line means run the command but don't echo anything to the screen as it happens.

- A - at the head of a line means that if the command returns a nonzero value, keep going anyway. Otherwise, the script halts on the first nonzero return.

For simpler projects and most of your day-to-day annoyances, a makefile using all those features from the shell will get you very far. You know the quirks of the computer you use every day, and the makefile will let you write them down in one place and stop thinking about them.

Will your makefile work for a colleague? If your program is a common set of .c files and any necessary libraries are installed, and the CFLAGS and LDLIBS in your makefile are right for your recipient's system, then perhaps it will all work fine, and at worst will require an email or two clarifying things. If you are generating a shared library, then forget about it—the procedure for generating a shared library is very different for Mac, Linux, Windows, Solaris, or different versions of each. When distributing to the public at large, everything needs to be as automated as possible, because it's hard to trade emails about setting flags with dozens or hundreds of people, and most people don't want to put that much effort into making a stranger's code work anyway. For all these reasons, we need to add another layer for publicly distributed packages.

# Packaging Your Code with Autotools

The Autotools are what make it possible for you to download a library or program, and run:

```
./configure
make
sudo make install
```

(and nothing else) to set it up. Please recognize what a miracle of modern science this is: the developer has no idea what sort of computer you have, where you keep your programs and libraries (/usr/bin? /sw? /cygdrive/c/bin?), and who knows what other quirks your machine demonstrates, and yet configure sorted everything out so that make could run seamlessly. And so Autotools is central to how code gets distributed in the modern day. If you want anybody who is not on a first-name basis with you to use your code (or if you want a Linux distro to include your program in their package manager), then having Autotools generate the build for you will significantly raise your odds.

It is easy to find packages that depend on some existing framework for installation, such as Scheme, Python ≥2.4 but <3.0, Red Hat Package Manager (RPM), and so on. The framework makes it easy for users to install the package—right after they install the framework. Especially for users without root privileges, such requirements can be a showstopper. The Autotools stand out in requiring only that the user have a computer with rudimentary POSIX compliance.

Using the Autotools can get complex, but the basics are simple. By the end of this, we will have written six lines of packaging text and run four commands, and will have a complete (albeit rudimentary) package ready for distribution.

The actual history of Autoconf, Automake, and Libtool is somewhat involved: these are distinct packages, each of which evolved independently of the others. But here's how I like to imagine it all happening.

**Meno:** I love make. It's so nice that I can write down all the little steps to building my project in one place.

**Socrates:** Yes, automation is great. Everything should be automated, all the time.

**Meno:** I have lots of targets in my makefile, so users can type make to produce the program, make install to install, make check to run tests, and so on. It's a lot of work to write all those makefile targets, but so smooth when it's all assembled.

**Socrates:** OK, I shall write a system—it will be called Automake—that will automatically generate makefiles with all the usual targets from a very short pre-makefile.

**Meno:** That's great. Producing shared libraries is especially annoying, because every system has a different procedure.

**Socrates:** It is annoying. Given the system information, I shall write a program for generating the scripts needed to produce shared libraries from source code, and then put those into automade makefiles.

**Meno:** Wow, so all I have to do is tell you my operating system, and whether my compiler is named cc or clang or gcc or whatever, and you'll drop in the right code for the system I'm on?

**Socrates:** That's error-prone. I will write a system called Autoconf that will be aware of every system out there and that will produce a report of everything Automake and your program needs to know about the system. Then Autoconf will run Automake, which will use the list of variables in my report to produce a makefile.

**Meno:** I am flabbergasted—you've automated the process of autogenerating makefiles. But it sounds like we've just changed the work I have to do from inspecting the various platforms to writing configuration files for Autoconf and makefile templates for Automake.

**Socrates:** You're right. I shall write a tool, Autoscan, that will scan the *Makefile.am* you wrote for Automake, and autogenerate Autoconf's *configure.ac* for you.

**Meno:** Now all you have to do is autogenerate *Makefile.am*.

**Socrates:** Yeah, whatever. RTFM and do it yourself.

Each step in the story adds a little more automation to the step that came before it: Automake uses a simple script to generate makefiles (which already go far in automating compilation over manual command-typing); Autoconf tests the environment and uses that information to run Automake; Autoscan checks your code for what you need to make Autoconf run. Libtool works in the background to assist Automake.

## An Autotools Demo

Example 3-5 presents a script that gets Autotools to take care of *Hello, World*. It is in the form of a shell script you can copy and paste onto your command line (as long as you make sure there are no spaces after the backslashes). Of course, it won't run until you ask your package manager to install the Autotools: Autoconf, Automake, and Libtool.

*Example 3-5. Packaging Hello, World. (auto.conf)*

```
if [ -e autodemo ]; then rm -r autodemo; fi
mkdir -p autodemo                            ❶
cd autodemo
cat > hello.c <<\
"-------------"
#include <stdio.h>

int main(){ printf("Hi.\n"); }
-------------

cat > Makefile.am <<\                         ❷
"-------------"
bin_PROGRAMS=hello
hello_SOURCES=hello.c
-------------

autoscan                                      ❸
sed -e 's/FULL-PACKAGE-NAME/hello/' \         ❹
    -e 's/VERSION/1/'   \
    -e 's|BUG-REPORT-ADDRESS|/dev/null|' \
    -e '10i\
AM_INIT_AUTOMAKE' \
        < configure.scan > configure.ac

touch NEWS README AUTHORS ChangeLog           ❺
```

```
autoreconf -iv                          ❻
./configure
make distcheck
```

❶ Create a directory and use a here document to write *hello.c* to it.

❷ We need to hand-write *Makefile.am*, which is two lines long. Even the `hello_SOURCES` line is optional, because Automake can guess that *hello* will be built from a source file named *hello.c*.

❸ `autoscan` produces *configure.scan*.

❹ Edit *configure.scan* to give the specs of your project (name, version, contact email), and add the line `AM_INIT_AUTOMAKE` to initialize Automake. (Yes, this is annoying, especially given that Autoscan used Automake's *Makefile.am* to gather info, so it is well aware that we want to use Automake.) You could do this by hand; I used `sed` to directly stream the customized version to *configure.ac*.

❺ These four files are required by the GNU coding standards, and so GNU Autotools won't proceed without them. I cheat by creating blank versions using the POSIX-standard `touch` command; yours should have actual content.

❻ Given *configure.ac*, run `autoreconf` to generate all the files to ship out (notably, *configure*). The `-i` flag will produce extra boilerplate files needed by the system.

How much do all these macros do? The *hello.c* program itself is a leisurely three lines and *Makefile.am* is two lines, for five lines of user-written text. Your results may differ a little, but when I run `wc -l *` in the post-script directory, I find 11,000 lines of text, including a 4,700-line `configure` script.

It's so bloated because it's so portable: your recipients probably don't have Autotools installed, and who knows what else they're missing, so this script depends only on rudimentary POSIX compliance.

I count 73 targets in the 600-line makefile.

- The default target, when you just type `make` on the command line, produces the executable.

- `sudo make install` would install this program if you so desire; run `sudo make uninstall` to clear it out.

- There is even the mind-blowing option to `make Makefile` (which actually comes in handy if you tweak *Makefile.am* and want to quickly regenerate the makefile).

---

- As the author of the package, you will be interested in `make distcheck`, which generates a tar file with everything a user would need to unpack and run the usual `./configure && make && sudo make install` (without the aid of the Autotools system that you have on your development box), and verifies that the distribution is OK, such as running any tests you may have specified.

Figure 3-1 summarizes the story as a flow diagram.

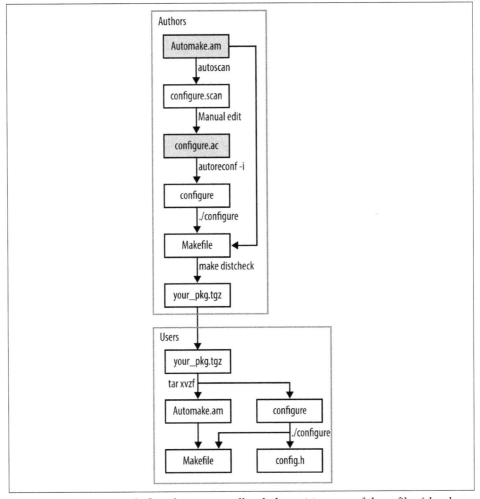

*Figure 3-1. An Autotools flowchart: you will only be writing two of these files (the shaded ones); everything else is autogenerated by the given command*

You will only be writing two of these files (the shaded ones); everything else is autogenerated by the given command. Let's start from the bottom portion: the user gets your package as a tarball, and untars it via `tar xvzf your_pkg.tgz`, which produces a directory with your code, *Makefile.am*, *configure*, and a host of other auxiliary files that aren't worth discussing here. The user types `./configure`, and that produces *configure.h* and the *Makefile*. Now everything is in place for the user to type `make`; `sudo make install`.

As an author, your goal is to produce that tarball, with a high-quality *configure* and *Makefile.am*, so the user can run his or her part without a hitch. Start by writing *Makefile.am* yourself. Run `autoscan` to get a preliminary *configure.scan*, which you will manually edit to *configure.ac*. (Not shown: the four files required by the GNU coding standards: *NEWS*, *README*, *AUTHORS*, and *ChangeLog*.) Then run `autore conf -iv` to generate the `configure` script (plus many other auxiliary files). Given the configure script, you can now run it to produce the makefile; given the makefile, you can run `make distcheck` to generate the tarball to ship out.

Notice that there is some overlap: you will be using the same *configure* and *Makefile* as the user does, though your purpose is to produce a package, and the user's purpose is to install the package. That means you have the facilities to install and test the code without fully packaging it, and users have the facility to repackage the code if somehow so inclined.

## Describing the Makefile with Makefile.am

A typical makefile is half about the structure of what parts of your project depend on what other parts, and half about the specific variables and procedures to execute. Your *Makefile.am* will focus on the structure of what needs to be compiled and what it depends on, and the specifics will be filled in by Autoconf and Automake's built-in knowledge of compilation on different platforms.

*Makefile.am* will consist of two types of entry, which I will refer to as *form variables* and *content variables*.

### Form variables

A file that has to be handled by the makefile may have any of a number of intents, each of which Automake annotates by a short string.

*bin*
    Install to wherever programs go on the system, e.g., */usr/bin* or */usr/local/bin*.

*include*
    Install to wherever headers go, e.g., */usr/local/include*.

*lib*
    Install to wherever libraries go, e.g., */usr/local/lib*.

*pkgbin*

If your project is named `project`, install to a subdirectory of the main program directory, e.g., */usr/local/bin/project/* (the same goes for `pkginclude` or `pkglib`).

*check*

Use for testing the program, when the user types `make check`.

*noinst*

Don't install; just keep the file around for use by another target.

Automake generates boilerplate `make` scripts, and it's got different boilerplate for:

| | |
|---|---|
| PROGRAMS | |
| HEADERS | |
| LIBRARIES | *static libraries* |
| LTLIBRARIES | *shared libraries generated via Libtool* |
| DIST | *items to be distributed with the package, such as data files that didn't go elsewhere* |

An intent plus a boilerplate format equals a form variable. For example:

| | |
|---|---|
| bin_PROGRAMS | *programs to build and install* |
| check_PROGRAMS | *programs to build for testing* |
| include_HEADERS | *headers to install in the system-wide include directory* |
| lib_LTLIBRARIES | *dynamic and shared libraries, via Libtool* |
| noinst_LIBRARIES | *static library (no Libtool), to keep on hand for later* |
| noinst_DIST | *distribute with the package, but that's all* |
| python_PYTHON | *Python code, to byte-compile and install where Python packages go* |

Now that you have the form down, you can use these to specify how each file gets handled. In the Hello, World example earlier, there was only one file that had to be dealt with:

```
bin_PROGRAMS = hello
```

To give another example, `noinst_DIST` is where I put data that is needed for the post-compilation tests but is not worth installing. Put as many items on each line as you'd like. For example:

```
pkginclude_HEADERS = firstpart.h secondpart.h
noinst_DIST = sample1.csv sample2.csv \
              sample3.csv sample4.csv
```

## Content variables

Items under `noinst_DIST` just get copied into the distribution package, and `HEADERS` just get copied to the destination directory and have their permissions set appropriately. So those are basically settled.

For the compilation steps such as ..._PROGRAMS and ..._LDLIBRARIES, Automake needs to know more details about how the compilation works. At the very least, it needs to know what source files are being compiled. Thus, for every item on the right side of an equals sign of a form variable about compilation, we need a variable specifying the sources. For example, with these two programs we need two SOURCES lines:

```
bin_PROGRAMS= weather wxpredict
weather_SOURCES= temp.c barometer.c
wxpredict_SOURCES=rng.c tarotdeck.c
```

This may be all you need for a basic package.

 Here we have another failure of the principle that things that do different things should look different: the content variables have the same lower_UPPER look as the form variables shown earlier, but they are formed from entirely different parts and serve entirely different purposes.

Recall from the discussion about plain old makefiles that there are certain default rules built into make, which use variables like CFLAGS to tweak the details of what gets done. Automake's form variables effectively define more default rules, and they each have their own set of associated variables.

For example, the rule for linking together object files to form an executable might look something like:

```
$(CC) $(LDFLAGS) temp.o barometer.o $(LDADD) -o weather
```

 GNU Make uses LDLIBS for the library variable at the second half of the link command, and GNU Automake uses LDADD for the second half of the link command.

It's not all that hard to use your favorite Internet search engine to find the documentation that explains how a given form variable blows up into a set of targets in the final makefile, but I've found that the fastest way to find out what Automake does is to just run it and look at the output makefile in a text editor.

You can set all of these variables on a per-program or per-library basis, such as weather_CFLAGS=-O1. Or, use AM_VARIABLE to set a variable for all compilations or linkings. Here are my favorite compiler flags, which you met in the section "Using Makefiles" on page 17:

```
AM_CFLAGS=-g -Wall -O3
```

I didn't include `-std=gnu99` to get `gcc` to use a less obsolete standard, because this is a compiler-specific flag. If I put `AC_PROG_CC_C99` in *configure.ac*, then Autoconf will set the `CC` variable to `gcc  -std=gnu99` for me. Autoscan isn't (yet) smart enough to put this into the *configure.scan* that it generates for you, so you will probably have to put it into *configure.ac* yourself. (As of this writing, there isn't yet an `AC_PROG_CC_C11` macro.)

Specific rules override `AM_`-based rules, so if you want to keep the general rules and add on an override for one flag, you would need a form like:

```
AM_CFLAGS=-g -Wall -O3
hello_CFLAGS = $(AM_CFLAGS) -O0
```

### Adding testing

I haven't yet presented to you the dictionary library (which is covered in "Extending Structures and Dictionaries" on page 249), but I have shown you the test harness for it, in "Unit Testing" on page 52. When Autotools pushes out the library, it makes sense to run the tests again. The agenda is now to build:

- A library, based on *dict.c* and *keyval.c*. It has headers, *dict.h* and *keyval.h*, which will need to ship out with the library.
- A testing program, which Automake needs to be aware is for testing, not for installation.
- The program, `dict_use`, that makes use of the library.

Example 3-6 expresses this agenda. The library gets built first, so that it can be used to generate the program and the test harness. The `TESTS` variable specifies which programs or scripts get run when the user types `make  check`.

*Example 3-6. An Automake file that handles testing (dict.automake)*

```
AM_CFLAGS=`pkg-config --cflags glib-2.0` -g -O3 -Wall    ❶

lib_LTLIBRARIES=libdict.la                               ❷
libdict_la_SOURCES=dict.c keyval.c                       ❸

include_HEADERS=keyval.h dict.h

bin_PROGRAMS=dict_use
dict_use_SOURCES=dict_use.c
dict_use_LDADD=libdict.la                                ❹

TESTS=$(check_PROGRAMS)                                   ❺
check_PROGRAMS=dict_test
dict_test_LDADD=libdict.la
```

❶ Here, I cheated, because other users might not have pkg-config installed. If we can't assume pkg-config, the best we can do is check for the library via Autoconf's AC_CHECK_HEADER and AC_CHECK_LIB, and if something is not found, ask the user to modify the CFLAGS or LDFLAGS environment variables to specify the right -I or -L flags. Because we haven't gotten to the discussion of *configure.ac*, I just use pkg-config.

❷ The first course of business is generating the shared library (via Libtool, and thus the *LT* in LTLIBRARIES).

❸ When writing a content variable from a filename, change anything that is not a letter, number, or @ sign into an underscore, as with libdict.la → libdict_la.

❹ Now that we've specified how to generate a shared library, we can use the shared library for assembling the program and tests.

❺ The TESTS variable specifies the tests that run when users type make check. Because these are often shell scripts that need no compilation, it is a distinct variable from check_PROGRAMS, which specifies programs intended for checking that have to be compiled. In our case, the two are identical, so we set one to the other.

### Adding makefile bits

If you've done the research and found that Automake can't handle some odd target, then you can write it into *Makefile.am* as you would to the usual makefile. Just write a target and its associated actions as in:

```
target: deps
    script
```

anywhere in your *Makefile.am*, and Automake will copy it into the final makefile verbatim. For example, the *Makefile.am* in "Python Host" on page 116 explicitly specifies how to compile a Python package, because Automake by itself doesn't know how (it just knows how to byte-compile standalone *.py* files).

Variables outside of Automake's formats also get added verbatim. This will especially be useful in conjunction with Autoconf, because if *Makefile.am* has variable assignments such as:

```
TEMP=@autotemp@
HUMIDITY=@autohum@
```

and your configure.ac has:

```
#configure is a plain shell script; these are plain shell variables
autotemp=40
autohum=.8
```

```
AC_SUBST(autotemp)
AC_SUBST(autohum)
```

then the final makefile will have text reading:

```
TEMP=40
HUMIDITY=.8
```

So you have an easy conduit from the shell script that Autoconf spits out to the final makefile.

## The configure Script

The *configure.ac* shell script produces two outputs: a makefile (with the help of Automake), and a header file named *config.h*.

If you've opened one of the sample *configure.ac* files produced so far, you might have noticed that it looks nothing at all like a shell script. This is because it makes heavy use of a set of macros (in the m4 macro language) that are predefined by Autoconf. Rest assured that every one of them will blow up into familiar-looking lines of shell script. That is, *configure.ac* isn't a recipe or specification to generate the configure shell script, it *is* configure, just compressed by some very impressive macros.

The m4 language doesn't have all that much syntax. Every macro is function-like, with parens after the macro name listing the comma-separated arguments (if any; else the parens are typically dropped). Where most languages write 'literal text', m4-via-Autoconf writes [literal text], and to prevent surprises where m4 parses your inputs a little too aggressively, wraps all of your macro inputs in those square brackets.

The first line that Autoscan generated is a good example:

```
AC_INIT([FULL-PACKAGE-NAME], [VERSION], [BUG-REPORT-ADDRESS])
```

We know that this is going to generate a few hundred lines of shell code, and somewhere in there, the given elements will be set. Change the values in square brackets to whatever is relevant. You can often omit elements, so something like:

```
AC_INIT([hello], [1.0])
```

is valid if you don't want to hear from your users. At the extreme, one might give zero arguments to a macro like AC_OUTPUT, in which case you don't need to bother with the parentheses.

The current custom in m4 documentation is to mark optional arguments with—I am not making this up—square brackets. So bear in mind that in m4 macros for Autoconf, square brackets mean literal not-for-expansion text, and in m4 macro documentation it means an optional argument.

Recall that the shell allows you to write if test ...; as if [ ... ];. Because *configure.ac* is just a compressed shell script, it can include shell code like this. But you will need to use the if test ...; form, because square brackets will be eaten by m4.

What macros do we need for a functional Autoconf file? In order of appearance:

- AC_INIT(...), already shown.
- AM_INIT_AUTOMAKE, to have Automake generate the makefile.
- LT_INIT sets up Libtool, which you need if and only if you are installing a shared library.
- AC_CONFIG_FILES([*Makefile subdir/Makefile*]), which tells Autoconf to go through those files listed and replace variables like @cc@ with their appropriate value. If you have several makefiles (typically in subdirectories), then list them here.
- AC_OUTPUT to ship out.

So we have the specification for a functional build package for any POSIX system anywhere in four or five lines, three of which Autoscan probably wrote for you.

But the real art that takes *configure.ac* from functional to intelligent is in predicting problems some users might have and finding the Autoconf macro that detects the problem (and, where possible, fixes it). You saw one example earlier: I recommended adding AC_PROG_CC_C99 to *configure.ac* to check for a C99 compiler. The POSIX standard requires that one be present via the command name c99, but just because POSIX says so doesn't mean that every system will have one, so it is exactly the sort of thing that a good configure script checks for.

Having libraries on hand is the star example of a prerequisite that has to be checked. Getting back to Autoconf's outputs for a moment, *config.h* is a standard C header consisting of a series of #define statements. For example, if Autoconf verified the presence of the GSL, you would find:

```
#define HAVE_LIBGSL 1
```

in *config.h*. You can then put #ifdefs into your C code to behave appropriately under appropriate circumstances.

Autoconf's check doesn't just find the library based on some naming scheme and hope that it actually works. It writes a do-nothing program using any one function somewhere in the library, then tries linking the program with the library. If the link step succeeds, then the linker was able to find and use the library as expected. So Autoscan can't autogenerate a check for the library, because it doesn't know what functions are to be found in it. The macro to check for a library is a one-liner, to which you provide the library name and a function that can be used for the check. For example:

```
AC_CHECK_LIB([glib-2.0],[g_free])
AC_CHECK_LIB([gsl],[gsl_blas_dgemm])
```

Add one line to *configure.ac* for every library you use that is not 100% guaranteed by the C standard, and those one-liners will blossom into the appropriate shell script snippets in `configure`.

You may recall how package managers always split libraries into the binary shared object package and the devel package with the headers. Users of your library might not remember (or even know) to install the header package, so check for it with, for example:

```
AC_CHECK_HEADER([gsl/gsl_matrix.h], , [AC_MSG_ERROR(
    [Couldn't find the GSL header files (I searched for \
    <gsl/gsl_matrix.h> on the include path). If you are \
    using a package manager, don't forget to install the \
    libgsl-devel package, as well as libgsl itself.])])
```

Notice the two commas: the arguments to the macro are header to check, action if found, and action if not found, and we are leaving the second blank.

What else could go wrong in a compilation? It's hard to become an authority on all the glitches of all the world's computers, given that we each have only a couple of machines at our disposal. Autoscan will give you some good suggestions, and you might find that running `autoreconf` also spits out some further warnings about elements to add to *configure.ac*. It gives good advice—follow its suggestions. But the best reference I have seen—a veritable litany of close readings of the POSIX standard, implementation failures, and practical advice—is the Autoconf manual itself. Some of it catalogs the glitches that Autoconf takes care of and are thus (thankfully) irrelevant nitpicking for the rest of us,[1] some of it is good advice for your code-writing, and some of the descriptions of system quirks are followed by the name of an Autoconf macro to include in your project's *configure.ac* should it be relevant to your situation.

---

1 For example, "Solaris 10 dtksh and the UnixWare 7.1.1 Posix shell … mishandle braced variable expansion that crosses a 1024- or 4096-byte buffer boundary within a here-document."

# VPATH builds

Say you have a source package in *~/pkgsrc;* the typical way to compile it is from that directory: `cd ~/pkgsrc; ./configure`. But you can compile it from anywhere:

```
mkdir tempbuild
cd tempbuild
~/pkgsrc/configure
```

This is referred to as a vpath build, and can be convenient when *pkgsrc* is a shared or read-only directory, or when building multiple variants of the same package.

To facilitate vpath builds, Autoconf defines a `srcdir` environment variable, which you can refer to

- in shell snippets in `configure.ac` as `$srcdir`
- in the automade makefile as `$(srcdir)`
- in files listed in the `AC_CONFIG_FILES` of `configure.ac`, via `@srcdir@`, which Autoconf will rewrite to the correct path.

It is worth testing that your project can be built in a different directory now and then. If a file is not found (I always have this problem with data files for tests), then you probably need to use one of the above forms to specify the location of the file.

### More Bits of Shell

Because *configure.ac* is a compressed version of the `configure` script the user will run, you can throw in any arbitrary shell code you'd like. Before you do, double-check that what you want to do isn't yet handled by any macros—is your situation really so unique that it never happened to any Autotools users before?

If you don't find it in the Autoconf package itself, you can check the GNU Autoconf macro archive (*http://bit.ly/autoconf-a*) for additional macros, which you can save to an *m4* subdirectory in your project directory, where Autoconf will be able to find and use them. See also (Calcote, 2010), an invaluable overview of the hairy details of Autotools.

A banner notifying users that they've made it through the configure process might be nice, and there's no need for a macro, because all you need is echo. Here's a sample banner:

```
echo \
"-----------------------------------------------------------

Thank you for installing ${PACKAGE_NAME} version ${PACKAGE_VERSION}.
```

```
Installation directory prefix: '${prefix}'.
Compilation command: '${CC} ${CFLAGS} ${CPPFLAGS}'

Now type 'make&& sudo make install' to generate the program
and install it to your system.

----------------------------------------------------------"
```

The banner uses several variables defined by Autoconf. There's documentation about what shell variables the system defines for you to use, but you can also find the defined variables by skimming `configure` itself.

There's one more extended example of Autotools at work, linking to a Python library in "Python Host" on page 116.

# CHAPTER 4

# Version Control

*Look at the world through your Polaroid glasses*
*Things'll look a whole lot better for the working classes.*

—Gang of Four, "I Found that Essence Rare"

This chapter is about revision control systems (RCSes), which maintain snapshots of the many different versions of a project as it develops, such as the stages in the development of a book, a tortured love letter, or a program.

Using an RCS has changed how I work. To explain it with a metaphor, think of writing as rock climbing. If you're not a rock climber yourself, you might picture a solid rock wall and the intimidating and life-threatening task of getting to the top. But in the modern day, the process is much more incremental. Attached to a rope, you climb a few meters, and then clip the rope to the wall using specialized equipment (cams, pins, carabiners, and so on). Now, if you fall, your rope will catch at the last carabiner, which is reasonably safe. While on the wall, your focus is not reaching the top, but the much more reachable problem of finding where you can clip your next carabiner.

Coming back to writing with an RCS, a day's work is no longer a featureless slog toward the summit, but a sequence of small steps. What one feature could I add? What one problem could I fix? Once a step is made and you are sure that your code base is in a safe and clean state, commit a revision, and if your next step turns out disastrously, you can fall back to the revision you just committed instead of starting from the beginning.

But structuring the writing process and allowing us to mark safe points is just the beginning:

- Our filesystem now has a time dimension. We can query the RCS's repository of file information to see what a file looked like last week and how it changed from then to now. Even without the other powers, I have found that this alone makes me a more confident writer.

- We can keep track of multiple versions of a project, such as my copy and my coauthor's copy. Even within my own work, I may want one version of a project (a *branch*) with an experimental feature, which should be kept segregated from the stable version that needs to be able to run without surprises.

- GitHub (*http://github.com*) has about 314,000 projects that self-report as being primarily in C as of this writing, and there are more C projects in other, smaller RCS repository hosts, such as the GNU's Savannah. Even if you aren't going to modify the code, cloning these repositories is a quick way to get the program or library onto your hard drive for your own use. When your own project is ready for public use (or before then), you can make the repository public as another means of distribution.

- Now that you and I both have versions of the same project, and both have equal ability to hack our versions of the code base, revision control gives us the power to merge together our multiple threads as easily as possible.

This chapter will cover Git, which is a *distributed revision control system*, meaning that any given copy of the project works as a standalone repository of the project and its history. There are others, with Mercurial and Bazaar the other front-runners in the category. There is largely a one-to-one mapping among the features of these systems, and what major differences had existed have merged over the years, so you should be able to pick the others up immediately after reading this chapter.

# Changes via diff

The most rudimentary means of revision control is via `diff` and `patch`, which are POSIX-standard and therefore most certainly on your system. You probably have two files on your drive somewhere that are reasonably similar; if not, grab any text file, change a few lines, and save the modified version with a new name. Try:

```
diff f1.c f2.c
```

and you will get a listing, a little more machine-readable than human-readable, that shows the lines that have changed between the two files. Piping output to a text file via `diff f1.c f2.c > diffs` and then opening *diffs* in your text editor may give you a colorized version that is easier to follow. You will see some lines giving the name of the file and location within the file, perhaps a few lines of context that did not change between the two files, and lines beginning with + and - showing the lines that got added and removed. Run `diff` with the `-u` flag to get a few lines of context around the additions and subtractions.

Given two directories holding two versions of your project, *v1* and *v2*, generate a single diff file in the unified diff format for the entire directories via the recursive (`-r`) option:

```
diff -ur v1 v2 > diff-v1v2
```

The `patch` command reads diff files and executes the changes listed there. If you and a friend both have *v1* of the project, you could send *diff-v1v2* to your friend, and she could run:

```
patch < diff-v1v2
```

to apply all of your changes to her copy of *v1*.

Or, if you have no friends, you can run `diff` from time to time on your own code and thus keep a record of the changes you have made over time. If you find that you have inserted a bug in your code, the diffs are the first place to look for hints about what you touched that you shouldn't have. If that isn't enough, and you already deleted *v1*, you could run the patch in reverse from the *v2* directory, `patch -R < diff-v1v2`, reverting version 2 back to version 1. If you were at version 4, you could even conceivably run a sequence of diffs to move further back in time:

```
cd v4
patch -R < diff-v3v4
patch -R < diff-v2v3
patch -R < diff-v1v2
```

I say *conceivably* because maintaining a sequence of diffs like this is tedious and error-prone. Thus, the revision control system, which will make and track the diffs for you.

# Git's Objects

Git is a C program like any other, and is based on a small set of objects. The key object is the commit object, which is akin to a unified diff file. Given a previous commit object and some changes from that baseline, a new commit object encapsulates the information. It gets some support from the *index*, which is a list of the changes registered since the last commit object, the primary use of which will be in generating the next commit object.

The commit objects link together to form a tree much like any other tree. Each commit object will have (at least) one parent commit object. Stepping up and down the tree is akin to using `patch` and `patch -R` to step among versions.

The repository itself is not formally a single object in the Git source code, but I think of it as an object, because the usual operations one would define, such as new, copy, and free, apply to the entire repository. Get a new repository in the directory you are working in via:

```
git init
```

OK, you now have a revision control system in place. You might not see it, because Git stores all its files in a directory named .git, where the dot means that all the usual utilities like ls will take it to be hidden. You can look for it via, e.g., ls -a or via a show hidden files option in your favorite file manager.

Alternatively, copy a repository via git clone. This is how you would get a project from Savannah or Github. To get the source code for Git using git:

```
git clone https://github.com/gitster/git.git
```

The reader may also be interested in cloning the repository with the examples for this book:

```
git clone https://github.com/b-k/21st-Century-Examples.git
```

If you want to test something on a repository in ~/myrepo and are worried that you might break something, go to a temp directory (say mkdir ~/tmp; cd ~/tmp), clone your repository with git clone ~/myrepo, and experiment away. Deleting the clone when done (rm -rf ~/tmp/myrepo) has no effect on the original.

Given that all the data about a repository is in the .git subdirectory of your project directory, the analog to freeing a repository is simple:

```
rm -rf .git
```

Having the whole repository so self-contained means that you can make spare copies to shunt between home and work, copy everything to a temp directory for a quick experiment, and so on, without much hassle.

We're almost ready to generate some commit objects, but because they summarize diffs since the starting point or a prior commit, we're going to have to have on hand some diffs to commit. The index (Git source: struct index_state) is a list of changes that are to be bundled into the next commit. It exists because we don't actually want every change in the project directory to be recorded. For example, gnomes.c and gnomes.h will beget gnomes.o and the executable gnomes. Your RCS should track gnomes.c and gnomes.h and let the others regenerate as needed. So the key operation with the index is adding elements to its list of changes. Use:

```
git add gnomes.c gnomes.h
```

to add these files to the index. Other typical changes to the list of files tracked also need to be recorded in the index:

```
git add newfile
git rm oldfile
git mv flie file
```

Changes you made to files that are already tracked by Git are not automatically added to the index, which might be a surprise to users of other RCSes (but see below). Add each individually via git add *changedfile*, or use:

```
git add -u
```

to add to the index changes to all the files Git already tracks.

At some point you have enough changes listed in the index that they should be recorded as a commit object in the repository. Generate a new commit object via:

```
git commit -a -m "here is an initial commit."
```

The -m flag attaches a message to the revision, which you'll read when you run git log later on. If you omit the message, then Git will start the text editor specified in the environment variable EDITOR so you can enter it (the default editor is typically vi; export that variable in your shell's startup script, e.g., .bashrc or .zshrc, if you want something different).

The -a flag tells Git that there are good odds that I forgot to run git add -u, so please run it just before committing. In practice, this means that you never have to run git add -u explicitly, as long as you always remember the -a flag in git commit -a.

 It is easy to find Git experts who are concerned with generating a coherent, clean narrative from their commits. Instead of commit messages like "added an index object, plus some bug fixes along the way," an expert Git author would create two commits, one with the message "added an index object" and one with "bug fixes." These authors have such control because nothing is added to the index by default, so they can add only enough to express one precise change in the code, write the index to a commit object, then add a new set of items to a clean index to generate the next commit object.

I found one blogger who took several pages to describe his commit routine: "For the most complicated cases, I will print out the diffs, read them over, and mark them up in six colors of highlighter…" However, until you become a Git expert, this will be much more control over the index than you really need or want. That is, not using -a with git commit is an advanced use that many people never bother with. In a perfect world, the -a would be the default, but it isn't, so don't forget it.

Calling `git commit -a` writes a new commit object to the repository based on all the changes the index was able to track, and clears the index. Having saved your work, you can now continue to add more. Further—and this is the real, major benefit of revision control so far—you can delete whatever you want, confident that it can be recovered if you need it back. Don't clutter up the code with large blocks of commented-out obsolete routines—delete!

 After you commit, you will almost certainly slap your forehead and realize something you forgot. Instead of performing another commit, you can run `git commit --amend -a` to redo your last commit.

---

## Diff/Snapshot Duality

Physicists sometimes prefer to think of light as a wave and sometimes as a particle; similarly, a commit object is sometimes best thought of as a complete snapshot of the project at a moment in time and sometimes as a diff from its parent. From either perspective, it includes a record of the author, the name of the object (as we'll see later), the message you attached via the `-m` flag, and (unless it is the initial commit) a pointer to the parent commit object(s).

Internally, is a commit a diff or a snapshot? It could be either or both. There was once a time when Git always stored a snapshot, unless you ran `git gc` (garbage collect) to compress the set of snapshots into a set of deltas (aka diffs). Users complained about having to remember to run `git gc`, so it now runs automatically after certain commands, meaning that Git is probably (but by no means always) storing diffs.

---

Having generated a commit object, your interactions with it will mostly consist of looking at its contents. You'll use `git diff` to see the diffs that are the core of the commit object and `git log` to see the metadata.

The key metadata is the name of the object, which is assigned via an unpleasant but sensible naming convention: the SHA1 hash, a 40-digit hexadecimal number that can be assigned to an object, in a manner that lets us assume that no two objects will have the same hash, and that the same object will have the same name in every copy of the repository. When you commit your files, you'll see the first few digits of the hash on the screen, and you can run `git log` to see the list of commit objects in the history of the current commit object, listed by their hash and the human-language message you wrote when you did the commit (and see `git help log` for the other available metadata). Fortunately, you need only as much of the hash as will uniquely identify your commit. So if you look at the log and decide that you want to check out revision number fe9c49cddac5150dc974de1f7248a1c5e3b33e89, you can do so with:

```
git checkout fe9c4
```

This does the sort of time-travel via diffs that `patch` almost provided, rewinding to the state of the project at commit `fe9c4`.

Because a given commit only has pointers to its parents, not its children, when you check `git log` after checking out an old commit, you will see the trace of objects that led up to this commit, but not later commits. The rarely used `git reflog` will show you the full list of commit objects the repository knows about, but the easier means of jumping back to the most current version of the project is via a *tag*, a human-friendly name that you won't have to look up in the log. Tags are maintained as separate objects in the repository and hold a pointer to a commit object being tagged. The most frequently used tag is `master`, which refers to the last commit object on the master branch (which, because we haven't covered branching yet, is probably the only branch you have). Thus, to return from back in time to the latest state, use:

```
git checkout master
```

Getting back to `git diff`, it shows what changes you have made since the last committed revision. The output is what would be written to the next commit object via `git commit -a`. As with the output from the plain `diff` program, `git diff > diffs` will write to a file that may be more legible in your colorized text editor.

Without arguments, `git diff` shows the diff between the index and what is in the project directory; if you haven't added anything to the index yet, this will be every change since the last commit. With one commit object name, `git diff` shows the sequence of changes between that commit and what is in the project directory. With two names, it shows the sequence of changes from one commit to the other:

```
git diff                Show the diffs between the working directory and the index.
git diff --staged       Show the diffs between the index and the previous commit.
git diff 234e2a         Show the diffs between the working directory and the given commit object.
git diff 234e2a 8b90ac  Show the changes from one commit object to another.
```

 There are a few naming conveniences to save you some hexadecimal. The name HEAD refers to the last checked-out commit. This is usually the tip of a branch; when it isn't, git error messages will refer to this as a "detached HEAD."

Append ~1 to a name to refer to the named commit's parent, ~2 to refer to its grandparent, and so on. Thus, all of the following are valid:

```
git diff HEAD~4        #Compare the working directory to four commits ago.
git checkout master~1  #Check out the predecessor to the head of the master branch.
git checkout master~   #Shorthand for the same.
git diff b0897~ b8097  #See what changed in commit b8097.
```

At this point, you know how to:

- Save frequent incremental revisions of your project.
- Get a log of your committed revisions.
- Find out what you changed or added recently.
- Check out earlier versions so that you can recover earlier work if needed.

Having a backup system organized enough that you can delete code with confidence and recover as needed will already make you a better writer.

## The Stash

Commit objects are the reference points from which most Git activity occurs. For example, Git prefers to apply patches relative to a commit, and you can jump to any commit, but if you jump away from a working directory that does not match a commit you have no way to jump back. When there are uncommitted changes in the current working directory, Git will warn you that you are not at a commit and will typically refuse to perform the operation you asked it to do. One way to go back to a commit would be to write down all the work you had done since the last commit, revert your project to the last commit, execute the operation, then redo the saved work after you are finished jumping or patching.

Thus we employ the *stash*, a special commit object mostly equivalent to what you would get from `git commit -a`, but with a few special features, such as retaining all the untracked junk in your working directory. Here is the typical procedure:

```
git stash
# Code is now as it was at last checkin.
git checkout fe9c4

# Look around here.

git checkout master      # Or whatever commit you had started with
# Code is now as it was at last checkin, so replay stashed diffs with:
git stash pop
```

Another sometimes-appropriate alternative for checking out given changes in your working directory is `git reset --hard`, which takes the working directory back to the state it was in when you last checked out. The command sounds severe because it is: you are about to throw away all work you have done since the last checkout.

# Trees and Their Branches

There is one tree in a repository, which got generated when the first author of a new repository ran `git init`. You are probably familiar with tree data structures, consisting of a set of nodes, where each node has links to some number of children and a link to a parent (and in exotic trees like Git's, possibly several parents).

Indeed, all commit objects but the initial one have a parent, and the object records the diffs between itself and the parent commit. The terminal node in the sequence, the tip of the branch, is tagged with a branch name. For our purposes, there is a one-to-one correspondence between branch tips and the series of diffs that led to that branch. The one-to-one correspondence means we can interchangeably refer to branches and the commit object at the tip of the branch. Thus, if the tip of the `master` branch is commit `234a3d`, then `git checkout master` and `git checkout 234a3d` are entirely equivalent (until a new commit gets written, and that takes on the `master` label). It also means that the list of commit objects on a branch can be rederived at any time by starting at the commit at the named tip and tracing back to the origin of the tree.

The typical custom is to keep the master branch fully functional at all times. When you want to add a new feature or try a new thread of inquiry, create a new branch for it. When the branch is fully functioning, you will be able to merge the new feature back into the master using the methods to follow.

There are two ways to create a new branch splitting off from the present state of your project:

```
git branch newleaf        # Create a new branch...
git checkout newleaf      # then check out the branch you just created.
      # Or execute both steps at once with the equivalent:
git checkout -b newleaf
```

Having created the new branch, switch between the tips of the two branches via `git checkout master` and `git checkout newleaf`.

What branch are you on right now? Find out with:

```
git branch
```

which will list all branches and put a * by the one that is currently active.

What would happen if you were to build a time machine, go back to before you were born, and kill your parents? If we learned anything from science fiction, it's that if we change history, the present doesn't change, but a new alternate history splinters off. So if you check out an old version, make changes, and check in a new commit object with your newly made changes, then you now have a new branch distinct from the master branch. You will find via `git branch` that when the past forks like this, you will be on `(no branch)`. Untagged branches tend to create problems, so if ever you

find that you are doing work on (no branch), then run git branch -m
*new_branch_name* to name the branch to which you've just splintered.

# Merging

So far, we have generated new commit objects by starting with a commit object as a
starting point and applying a list of diffs from the index. A branch is also a series of
diffs, so given an arbitrary commit object and a list of diffs from a branch, we should
be able to create a new commit object in which the branch's diffs are applied to the
existing commit object. This is a *merge*. To merge all the changes that occurred over
the course of *newleaf* back into master, switch to master and use git merge:

```
git checkout master
git merge newleaf
```

For example, you have used a branch off of master to develop a new feature, and it
finally passes all tests; then applying all the diffs from the development branch to mas
ter would create a new commit object with the new feature soundly in place.

Let us say that, while working on the new feature, you never checked out master and
so made no changes to it. Then applying the sequence of diffs from the other branch
would simply be a fast replay of all of the changes recorded in each commit object in
the branch, which Git calls a *fast-forward*.

But if you made any changes to master, then this is no longer a simple question of a
fast application of all of the diffs. For example, say that at the point where the branch
split off, *gnomes.c* had:

```
short int height_inches;
```

In master, you removed the derogatory type:

```
int height_inches;
```

The purpose of *newleaf* was to convert to metric:

```
short int height_cm;
```

At this point, Git is stymied. Knowing how to combine these lines requires knowing what you as a human intended. Git's solution is to modify your text file to include both versions, something like:

```
<<<<<<< HEAD
int height_inches;
=======
short int height_cm;
>>>>>>> 3c3c3c
```

The merge is put on hold, waiting for you to edit the file to express the change you would like to see. In this case, you would probably reduce the five-line chunk Git left in the text file to:

```
int height_cm;
```

Here is the procedure for committing merges in a non-fast-forward, meaning that there have been changes in both branches since they diverged:

1. Run git merge *other_branch*.

2. In all likelihood, get told that there are conflicts you have to resolve.

3. Check the list of unmerged files using git status.

4. Pick a file to manually check on. Open it in a text editor and find the merge-me marks if it is a content conflict. If it's a filename or file position conflict, move the file into place.

5. Run git add *your_now_fixed_file*.

6. Repeat steps 3–5 until all unmerged files are checked in.

7. Run git commit to finalize the merge.

Take comfort in all this manual work. Git is conservative in merging and won't automatically do anything that could, under some storyline, cause you to lose work.

When you are done with the merge, all of the relevant diffs that occurred in the side branch are represented in the final commit object of the merged-to branch, so the custom is to delete the side branch:

```
git branch -d other_branch
```

The *other_branch* tag is deleted, but the commit objects that led up to it are still in the repository for your reference.

## The Rebase

Say you have a main branch and split off a testing branch from it on Monday. Then on Tuesday through Thursday, you make extensive changes to both the main and testing branch. On Friday, when you try to merge the test branch back into the main, you have an overwhelming number of little conflicts to resolve.

Let's start the week over. You split the testing branch off from the main branch on Monday, meaning that the last commits on both branches share a common ancestor of Monday's commit on the main branch. On Tuesday, you have a new commit on the main branch; let it be commit `abcd123`. At the end of the day, you replay all the diffs that occurred on the main branch onto the testing branch:

```
git branch testing    # get on the testing branch
git rebase abcd123     # or equivalently: git rebase main
```

With the `rebase` command, all the changes made on the main branch since the common ancestor are replayed on the testing branch. You might need to manually merge things, but by only having one day's work to merge, we can hope that the task of merging is more manageable.

Now that all changes up to `abcd123` are present in both branches, it is as if the branches had actually split off from that commit, rather than Monday's commit. This is where the name of the procedure comes from: the testing branch has been rebased to split off from a new point on the main branch.

You also perform rebases at the end of Wednesday, Thursday, and Friday, and each of them is reasonably painless, as the testing branch kept up with the changes on the main branch throughout the week.

Rebases are often cast as an advanced use of Git, because other systems that aren't as capable with diff application don't have this technique. But in practice rebasing and merging are about on equal footing: both apply diffs from another branch to produce a commit, and the only question is whether you are tying together the ends of two branches (in which case, merge) or want both branches to continue their separate lives for a while longer (in which case, rebase). The typical usage is to rebase the diffs from the master into the side branch, and merge the diffs from the side branch into the master, so there is a symmetry between the two in practice. And as noted, letting diffs pile up on multiple branches can make the final merge a pain, so it is good form to rebase reasonably often.

# Remote Repositories

Everything to this point has been occurring within one tree. If you cloned a repository from elsewhere, then at the moment of cloning, you and the origin both have identical trees with identical commit objects. However, you and your colleagues will continue working, so you will all be adding new and different commit objects.

Your repository has a list of *remotes*, which are pointers to other repositories related to this one elsewhere in the world. If you got your repository via `git clone`, then the repository from which you cloned is named `origin` as far as the new repository is concerned. In the typical case, this is the only remote you will ever use.

When you first clone and run `git branch`, you'll see one lonely branch, regardless of how many branches the origin repository had. But run `git branch -a` to see all the branches that Git knows about, and you will see those in the remote as well as the local ones. If you cloned a repository from Github, et al, you can use this to check whether other authors had pushed other branches to the central repository.

Those copies of the branches in your local repository are as of the first time you pulled. Next week, to update those remote branches with the information from the origin repository, run `git fetch`.

Now that you have up-to-date copies of the remote branches in your repository, you could merge one with the local branch you are working on using the full name of the remote branch, for example, `git merge remotes/origin/master`.

Instead of the two-step `git fetch; git merge remotes/origin/master`, you can update the branch via

    git pull origin master

which fetches the remote changes and merges them into your current repository all at once.

The converse is `push`, which you'll use to update the remote repository with your last commit (not the state of your index or working directory). If you are working on a branch named `bbranch` and want to push to the remote with the same name, use:

    git push origin bbranch

There are good odds that when you push your changes, applying the diffs from your branch to the remote branch will not be a fast-forward (if it is, then your colleagues haven't been doing any work). Resolving a non-fast-forward merge typically requires human intervention, and there is probably not a human at the remote. Thus, Git will allow only fast-forward pushes. How can you guarantee that your push is a fast-forward?

1. Run `git pull origin` *bbranch* to get the changes made since your last pull.
2. Merge as seen earlier, wherein you as a human resolve those changes a computer cannot.
3. Run `git commit -a -m "dealt with merges"`.
4. Run `git push origin` *bbranch*, because now Git only has to apply a single diff, which can be done automatically.

To this point, I have assumed that you are on a local branch with the same name as the remote branch (probably `master` on both sides). If you are crossing names, give a colon-separated pair of *source:destination* branch names.

```
git fetch origin new_changes:master  #Merge remote new_changes into local master
git push origin my_fixes:version2    #Merge the local branch into a differently named remote.
git push origin :prune_me            #Delete a remote branch.
git fetch origin new_changes:        #Pull to no branch; create a commit named FETCH_HEAD.
```

None of these operations change your current branch, but some create a new branch that you can switch to via the usual `git checkout`.

---

## The Central Repository

Despite all the discussion of decentralization, the easiest setup for sharing is still to have a central repository that everybody clones, meaning that everybody has the same origin repository. This is how downloading from Github and Savannah typically works. When setting up a repository for this sort of thing, use `git init --bare`, which means that nobody can actually do work in that directory, and users will have to clone to do anything at all. There are also some permissions flags that come in handy, such as `--shared=group` to allow all members of a POSIX group to read and write to the repository.

You can't push to a branch in a nonbare remote repository that the repository owner has checked out; doing so will cause chaos. If this happens, ask your colleague to `git branch` to a different branch, then push while the target branch is in the background.

Or, your colleague can set up a public bare repository and a private working repository. You push to the public repository, and your colleague pulls the changes to his or her working repository when convenient.

---

The structure of a Git repository is not especially complex: there are commit objects representing the changes since the parent commit object, organized into a tree, with an index gathering together the changes to be made in the next commit. But with these elements, you can organize multiple versions of your work, confidently delete things, create experimental branches and merge them back to the main thread when they pass all their tests, and merge your colleagues' work with your own. From there, `git help` and your favorite Internet search engine will teach you many more tricks and ways to do these things more smoothly.

# CHAPTER 5

# Playing Nice with Others

The count of programming languages approaches infinity, and a huge chunk of them have a C interface. This short chapter offers some general notes about the process and demonstrates in detail the interface with one language, Python.

Every language has its own customs for packaging and distribution, which means that after you write the bridge code in C and the host language, you get to face the task of getting the packaging system to compile and link everything. This gives me a chance to present more advanced features of Autotools, such as conditionally processing a subdirectory and adding install hooks.

## Dynamic Loading

Before jumping into other languages, it is worth taking a moment to appreciate the C functions that make it all possible: `dlopen` and `dlsym`. These functions open a dynamic library and extract a symbol, such as a static object or a function, from that library.

The functions are part of the POSIX standard. Windows systems have a similar setup, but the functions are named `LoadLibrary` and `GetProcAddress`; for simplicity of exposition, I'll stick to the POSIX names.

The name "shared object file" is nicely descriptive: such a file includes a list of objects, including functions and statically defined structures, that are intended for use in other programs.

Using such a file is much like retrieving an item from a text file holding a list of items. For the text file, you would first call `fopen` to get a handle for the file, and then call an appropriate function to search the file and return a pointer to the found item. For a shared object file, the file-opening function is `dlopen`, and the function to search for the symbol you want is dlsym. The magic is in what you can do with the returned pointer. For the list of text items, you have a pointer to plain text and can do quotidian text-handling things with it. If you used dlsym to retrieve a pointer to a function, you can call the function, and if you retrieved a pointer to a struct, you can immediately use the struct as the already-initialized object that it is.

When your C program calls a function in a linked-to library, this is how the function is retrieved and used. A program with a plugin system is doing this to load functions written by different authors after the main program was shipped. A scripting language that wants to call C code will do so by calling the same dlopen and dlsym functions.

To show off what dlopen/dlsym can do, Example 5-1 is the beginnings of a C interpreter, that:

1. Asks the user to type in the code for a C function
2. Compiles the function to a shared object file
3. Loads the shared object file via dlopen
4. Gets the function via dlsym
5. Executes the function the user just typed in

Here is a sample run:

```
I am about to run a function. But first, you have to write it for me.
Enter the function body. Conclude with a '}' alone on a line.

>>double fn(double in){
>> return sqrt(in)*pow(in, 2);
>> }
f(1) = 1
f(2) = 5.65685
f(10) = 316.228
```

*Example 5-1. A program to request a function from the user, compile it on the spot, and run the function. (dynamic.c)*

```
#include <dlfcn.h>
#include <stdio.h>
#include <stdlib.h>
#include <readline/readline.h>

void get_a_function(){
    FILE *f = fopen("fn.c", "w");
    fprintf(f, "#include <math.h>\n"                    ❶
               "double fn(double in){\n");
```

```
        char *a_line = NULL;
        char *prompt = ">>double fn(double in){\n>> ";
        do {
            free(a_line);
            a_line = readline(prompt);                    ❷
            fprintf(f, "%s\n", a_line);
            prompt = ">> ";
        } while (strcmp(a_line, "}"));
        fclose(f);
}

void compile_and_run(){
    if (system("c99 -fPIC -shared fn.c -o fn.so")!=0){   ❸
        printf("Compilation error.");
        return;
    }

    void *handle = dlopen("fn.so", RTLD_LAZY);            ❹
    if (!handle) printf("Failed to load fn.so: %s\n", dlerror());

    typedef double (*fn_type)(double);                    ❺
    fn_type f = dlsym(handle, "fn");
    printf("f(1) = %g\n", f(1));
    printf("f(2) = %g\n", f(2));
    printf("f(10) = %g\n", f(10));
}

int main(){
    printf("I am about to run a function. But first, you have to write it for me.\n"
        "Enter the function body. Conclude with a '}' alone on a line.\n\n");
    get_a_function();
    compile_and_run();
}
```

❶ This function writes the user's input to a function, including the math library
   header (so pow, sin, et al. are available) and the correct function declaration.

❷ Here is most of the interface to the Readline library. You give it a prompt to
   show the user, it furnishes facilities for the user to comfortably provide input
   based on your prompt, and it returns a string with the user's input.

❸ Now that the user's function is in a complete .c file, compile using a typical call to
   the C compiler. You may have to modify this line for your compiler's preferred
   flags.

❹ Open the shared object file for reading objects. Lazy binding indicates that function names are resolved only as needed.

❺ The dlsym function will return a void *, so you need to specify the type information for the function.

This is the most system-specific example in the book. I use the GNU Readline library, which is installed by default on some systems, because it reduces the problem of getting user input to a single line of code. I use the system command to call the compiler, but compiler flags are notoriously nonstandard, so the flags may need to be changed to work on your system.

## The Limits of Dynamic Loading

Wouldn't it be great to clean up this program, add the right #ifdefs to use LoadLibrary when running from Windows (though GLib already did this for us—see gmodules in the GLib documentation), and build this into a full read-evaluate-print loop for C?

Unfortunately, that is not possible using dlopen and dlsym. For example, if I wanted to pull a single line of executable code out of the object file, what would I tell dlsym to retrieve? Local variables are out, because the dlsym function can only pull static variables declared as file-global in the source or functions from a shared object library. So this half-baked example is already revealing limitations of dlopen and dlsym.

Even if our only view of the C language is functions and global variables, there is still a broad range of possibilities. The functions can create new objects as desired, and the global variables could be structs holding a list of functions, or even just strings giving function names that the calling program can retrieve via dlsym.

Of course, the calling system needs to know what symbols to retrieve and how to use them. In the example above, I dictated that the function have a prototype of double fn(double). For a plug-in system, the author of the calling system could write down a precise set of instructions about what symbols need to be present and how they will be used. For a scripting language loading arbitrary code, the author of the shared object file would need to write script code that correctly calls objects.

# The Process

This section goes over some of the considerations that go into writing code that is easily callable by a host system that relies on dlopen/dlsym:

- On the C side, writing functions to be easy to call from other languages.
- Writing the wrapper function that calls the C function in the host language.
- Handling C-side data structures. Can they be passed back and forth?

- Linking to the C library. That is, once everything is compiled, we have to make sure that at runtime, the system knows where to find the library.

## Writing to Be Read by Nonnatives

The limitations of dlopen/dlsym have some immediate implications for how callable C code should be written.

- Macros are read by the preprocessor, so that the final shared library has no trace of them. In Chapter 10, I discuss all sorts of ways for you to use macros to make using functions more pleasant from within C, so that you don't even need to rely on a scripting language for a friendlier interface. But when you do need to link to the library from outside of C, you won't have those macros on hand, and your wrapper function will have to replicate whatever the function-calling macro does.

- You will need to tell the host language how to use each object retrieved via dlsym, such as providing the function header in a manner the host language can understand. That means that every single visible object requires additional, redundant work on the host side, which means limiting the number of interface functions will be essential. Some C libraries (like libXML in "libxml and cURL" on page 337) have a set of functions for full control, and "easy" wrapper functions to do typical workflows with one call; if your library has dozens of functions, consider writing a few such easy interface functions. It's better to have a host package that provides only the core functionality of the C-side library than to have a host package that is unmaintainable and eventually breaks.

- Objects are great for this situation. The short version of Chapter 11, which discusses this in detail, is that one file defines a struct and several functions that interface with the struct, including *struct*_new, *struct*_copy, *struct*_free, *struct*_print, and so on. A well-designed object will have a small number of interface functions, or will at least have a minimal subset for use by the host language. As discussed in the next section, having a central structure holding the data will also make things easier.

## The Wrapper Function

For every C function you expect that users will call, you will also need a wrapper function on the host side. This function serves a number of purposes:

*Customer service*
Users of the host language who don't know C don't want to have to think about the C-calling system. They expect the help system to say something about your functions, and the help system is probably directly tied to functions and objects

in the host language. If users are used to functions being elements of objects, and you didn't set them up as such on the C side, then you can set up the object as per custom on the host side.

*Translation in and out*
> The host language's representation of integers, strings, and floating-point numbers may be int, char*, and double, but in most cases, you'll need some sort of translation between host and C data types. In fact, you'll need the translation twice: once from host to C, then after you call your C function, once from C to host. See the example for Python that follows.

Users will expect to interact with a host-side function, so it's hard to avoid having a host function for every C-side function, but suddenly you've doubled the number of functions you have to maintain. There will be redundancy, as defaults you specify for inputs on the C side will typically have to be respecified on the host side, and argument lists sent by the host will typically have to be checked every time you modify them on the C side. There's no point fighting it: you're going to have redundancy and will have to remember to check the host-side code every time you change the C side interfaces. So it goes.

## Smuggling Data Structures Across the Border

Forget about a non-C language for now; let's consider two C files, struct.c and user.c, where a data structure is generated as a local variable with internal linkage in the first and needs to be used by the second.

The easiest way to reference the data across files is a simple pointer: struct.c allocates the pointer, user.c receives it, and all is well. The definition of the structure might be public, in which case the user file can look at the data pointed to by the pointer and make changes as desired. Because the procedures in the user are modifying the pointed-to data, there's no mismatch between what struct.c and user.c are seeing.

Conversely, if struct.c sent a copy of the data, then once the user made any modification, we'd have a mismatch between data held internally by the two files. If we expect the received data to be used and immediately thrown away, or treated as read-only, or that struct.c will never care to look at the data again, then there's no problem handing ownership over to the user.

So for data structures that struct.c expects to operate on again, we should send a pointer; for throwaway results, we can send the data itself.

What if the structure of the data structure isn't public? It seems that the function in user.c would receive a pointer, and then wouldn't be able to do anything with it. But it can do one thing: it can send the pointer back to struct.c. When you think about it, this is a common form. You might have a linked-list object, allocated via a list allocation function (though GLib doesn't have one), then use `g_list_append` to add elements, then use `g_list_foreach` to apply an operation to all list elements, and so on, simply passing the pointer to the list from one function to the next.

When bridging between C and another language that doesn't understand how to read a C struct, this is referred to as an *opaque pointer* or an *external pointer*. Because typedefs are not objects in the shared object file that can be retrieved by `dlsym`, all structs in your C code will indeed be opaque to the calling language.[1] As in the case between two `.c` files, there's no ambiguity about who owns the data, and with enough interface functions, we can still get a lot of work done. A good percentage of host languages have an explicit mechanism for passing an opaque pointer.

If the host language doesn't support opaque pointers, then return the pointer anyway. An address is an integer, and writing it down as such doesn't produce any ambiguity (Example 5-2).

*Example 5-2. We can treat a pointer address as a plain integer. There's little if any reason to do this in plain C, but it may be necessary for talking to a host language (intptr.c)*

```
#include <stdio.h>
#include <stdint.h> //intptr_t

int main(){
    char *astring = "I am somwhere in memory.";
    intptr_t location = (intptr_t)astring;   ❶
    printf("%s\n", (char*)location);          ❷
}
```

❶ The `intptr_t` type is guaranteed to have a range large enough to store a pointer address [C99 §7.18.1.4(1) & C11 §7.20.1.4(1)].

❷ Of course, casting a pointer to an integer loses all type information, so we have to explicitly respecify the type of the pointer. This is error-prone, which is why this technique is only useful in the context of dealing with systems that don't understand pointers.

What can go wrong? If the range of the integer type in your host language is too small, then this will fail depending on where in memory your data lives, in which case

---

1 Now and then one finds languages, such as Julia or Cython, whose authors went the extra mile past the `dlopen`/`dlsym` mechanism and developed methods for describing C structs on the host side, making the contents of formerly opaque pointers easily visible on the host side. The people who do this are my personal heroes.

you might do better to write the pointer to a string, then when you get the string back, parse it back via `strtoll` (string to `long long int`). There's always a way.

Also, we are assuming that the pointer is not moved or freed between when it first gets handed over to the host and when the host asks for it again. For example, if there is a call to `realloc` on the C side, the new opaque pointer will have to get handed to the host.

## Linking

As you have seen, dynamically linking to your shared object file is a problem solved by `dlopen`/`dlsym` and their Windows equivalents.

But there's often one more level to linking: what if your C code requires a library on the system and thus needs runtime linking (as per "Runtime Linking" on page 16)? The easy answer in the C world is to use Autotools to search the library path for the library you need and set the right compilation flags. If your host language's build system supports Autotools, then you will have no problem linking to other libraries on the system. If you can rely on `pkg-config`, then that might also do what you need. If Autotools and `pkg-config` are both out, then I wish you the best of luck in working out how to robustly get the host's installation system to correctly link your library. There seem to be a lot of authors of scripting languages who still think that linking one C library to another is an eccentric special case that needs to be handled manually every time.

# Python Host

The remainder of this chapter presents an example via Python, which goes through the preceding considerations for the ideal gas function that will be presented in Example 10-12; for now, take the function as given as we focus on packaging it. Python has extensive online documentation to show you how the details work, but Example 5-3 suffices to show you some of the abstract steps at work: registering the function, converting the host-format inputs to common C formats, and converting the common C outputs to the host format. Then we'll get to linking.

The ideal gas library only provides one function: to calculate the pressure of an ideal gas given a temperature input, so the final package will be only slightly more interesting than one that prints "Hello, World" to the screen. Nonetheless, we'll be able to start up Python and run:

```
from pvnrt import *
pressure_from_temp(100)
```

The first line loads all elements from the `pvnrt` package into the current Python namespace. The next line calls the `pressure_from_temp` Python command, which will load the C function (`ideal_pressure`) that does all the work.

The story starts with Example 5-3, which provides C code using the Python API to wrap the C function and register it as part of the Python package to be set up subsequently.

*Example 5-3. The wrapper for the ideal gas function (py/ideal.py.c)*

```
#include <Python.h>
#include "../ideal.h"

static PyObject *ideal_py(PyObject *self, PyObject *args){
    double intemp;
    if (!PyArg_ParseTuple(args, "d", &intemp)) return NULL;      ❶
    double out = ideal_pressure(.temp=intemp);
    return Py_BuildValue("d", out);                              ❷
}

static PyMethodDef method_list[] = {                             ❸
    {"pressure_from_temp",  ideal_py, METH_VARARGS,
     "Get the pressure from the temperature of one mole of gunk"},
    { }
};

PyMODINIT_FUNC initpvnrt(void) {
    Py_InitModule("pvnrt", method_list);
}
```

❶ Python sends a single object listing all of the function arguments, akin to `argv`. This line reads them into a list of C variables, as specified by the format specifiers (akin to `scanf`). If we were parsing a double, a string, and an integer, it would look like: `PyArg_ParseTuple(args, "dsi", &indbl, &instr, &inint)`.

❷ The output also takes in a list of types and C values, returning a single bundle for Python's use.

❸ The rest of this file is registration. We have to build a { }-terminated list of the methods in the function (including Python name, C function, calling convention, one-line documentation), then write a function named init*pkgname* to read in the list.

The example shows how Python handles the input- and output-translating lines without much fuss (on the C side, though some other systems do it on the host side). The file concludes with a registration section, which is also not all that bad.

Now for the problem of compilation, which can require some real problem solving.

## Compiling and Linking

As you saw in "Packaging Your Code with Autotools" on page 79, setting up Auto-tools to generate the library requires a two-line *Makefile.am* and a slight modification of the boilerplate in the *configure.ac* file produced by Autoscan. On top of that, Python has its own build system, Distutils, so we need to set that up, then modify the Autotools files to make Distutils run automatically.

## The Conditional Subdirectory for Automake

I decided to put all the Python-related files into a subdirectory of the main project folder. If Autoconf detects the right Python development tools, then I'll ask it to go into that subdirectory and get to work; if the development tools aren't found, then it can ignore the subdirectory.

Example 5-4 shows a *configure.ac* file that checks for Python and its development headers, and compiles the *py* subdirectory if and only if the right components are found. The first several lines are as before, taken from what `autoscan` gave me, plus the usual additions from before. The next lines check for Python, which I cut and pasted from the Automake documentation. They will generate a PYTHON variable with the path to Python; for *configure.ac*, two variables by the name of HAVE_PYTHON_TRUE and HAVE_PYTHON_FALSE; and for the makefile, a variable named HAVE_PYTHON.

If Python or its headers are missing, then the PYTHON variable is set to the impracticable path of a single :, which we can check for later. If the requisite tools are present, then we use a simple shell if-then-fi block to ask Autoconf to configure the *py* subdirectory as well as the current directory.

*Example 5-4. A configure.ac file for the Python building task (py/configure.ac)*

```
AC_PREREQ([2.68])
AC_INIT([pvnrt], [1], [/dev/null])
AC_CONFIG_SRCDIR([ideal.c])
AC_CONFIG_HEADERS([config.h])

AM_INIT_AUTOMAKE
AC_PROG_CC_C99
LT_INIT

AM_PATH_PYTHON(,, [:])                              ❶
AM_CONDITIONAL([HAVE_PYTHON], [test "$PYTHON" != :])

if test "$PYTHON" != : ; then                       ❷
AC_CONFIG_SUBDIRS([py])
fi
```

```
AC_CONFIG_FILES([Makefile py/Makefile py/setup.py])          ❸
AC_OUTPUT
```

❶  These lines check for Python, setting a `PYTHON` variable to : if it is not found, then add a `HAVE_PYTHON` variable appropriately.

❷  If the `PYTHON` variable is set, then Autoconf will continue into the *py* subdirectory; else it will ignore this subdirectory.

❸  There's a *Makefile.am* in the *py* subdirectory that needs to be turned into a makefile. The *setup.py.in* that Autoconf will use to generate *setup.py* is listed below.

> You'll see a lot of new little bits of Autotools syntax in this chapter, such as the `AM_PATH_PYTHON` snippet from earlier, and Automake's `all-local` and `install-exec-hook` targets later. The nature of Autotools is that it is a basic system (which I hope I communicated in Chapter 3) with a hook for every conceivable contingency or exception. There's no point memorizing them, and for the most part, they can't be derived from basic principles. The nature of working with Autotools, then, is that when odd contingencies come up, we can expect to search the manuals or the Internet at large for the right recipe.

We also have to tell Automake about the subdirectory, which is also just another if-then block, as in Example 5-5.

*Example 5-5. A Makefile.am file for the root directory of a project with a Python subdirectory (py/Makefile.am)*

```
pyexec_LIBRARIES=libpvnrt.a
libpvnrt_a_SOURCES=ideal.c

SUBDIRS=.

if HAVE_PYTHON          ❶
SUBDIRS += py
endif
```

❶  Autoconf produced this `HAVE_PYTHON` variable, and here is where we use it. If it exists, Automake will add *py* to its list of directories to handle; or else it will only deal with the current directory.

The first two lines specify that a library named `libpvnrt` is to be installed with Python executables based on source code in *ideal.c*. After that, I specify the first subdirectory to handle, which is . (the current directory). The static library has to be built before the Python wrapper for the library, and we guarantee that it is handled first by putting . at the head of the SUBDIRS list. Then, if HAVE_PYTHON checks out OK, we can use Automake's += operator to add the *py* directory to the list.

At this point, we have a setup that handles the *py* directory if and only if the Python development tools are in place. Now, let us descend into the *py* directory itself and look at how to get Distutils and Autotools to talk to each other.

## Distutils Backed with Autotools

By now, you are probably used to the procedure for compiling programs and libraries:

- Specify the files involved (e.g., via *your_program*_SOURCES in *Makefile.am*, or go straight to the objects list in the sample makefile used throughout this book).
- Specify the flags for the compiler (universally via a variable named CFLAGS).
- Specify the flags and additional libraries for the linker (e.g., LDLIBS for GNU Make or LDADD for GNU Autotools).

Those are the three steps, and although there are many ways to screw them up, the contract is clear enough. To this point in the book, I've shown you how to communicate the three parts via a simple makefile, via Autotools, and even via shell aliases. Now we have to communicate them to Distutils. Example 5-6 provides a *setup.py.in* file, which Autoconf will use to produce a *setup.py* file to control the production of a Python package.

*Example 5-6. The template for a setup.py file to control the production of a Python package (py/setup.py.in)*

```
from distutils.core import setup, Extension

py_modules= ['pvnrt']

Emodule = Extension('pvnrt',
        libraries=['pvnrt'],              ❶
        library_dirs=['@srcdir@/..'],     ❷
        sources = ['ideal.py.c'])         ❸

setup (name = 'pvnrt',                    ❹
        version = '1.0',
        description = 'pressure * volume = n * R * Temperature',
        ext_modules = [Emodule])
```

❶ The sources and the linker flags. The libraries line indicates that there will be a -lpvnrt sent to the linker.

❷ This line indicates that a `-L` clause will be added to the linker's flags to indicate that it should search for libraries at the given absolute path. We can have Autoconf fill in the absolute path to the source directory, as per "VPATH builds" on page 92.

❸ List the sources here, as you would in Automake.

❹ Here we provide the metadata about the package for use by Python and Distutils.

The specification of the production process for Python's Distutils is given in *setup.py*, as per Example 5-6, which has some typical boilerplate about a package: its name, its version, a one-line description, and so on. This is where we will communicate the three elements listed:

- The C source files that represent the wrapper for the host language (as opposed to the library handled by Autotools itself) are listed in `sources`.
- Python recognizes the `CFLAGS` environment variable. Makefile variables are not exported to programs called by make, so the *Makefile.am* for the *py* directory, in Example 5-7, sets a shell variable named `CFLAGS` to Autoconf's `@CFLAGS@` just before calling `python setup.py build`.
- Python's Distutils require that you segregate the libraries from the library paths. Because they don't change very often, you can probably manually write the list of libraries, as in the example (don't forget to include the static library generated by the main Autotools build). The directories, however, differ from machine to machine, and are why we had Autotools generate `LDADD` for us. So it goes.

I chose to write a setup package where the user will call Autotools, and then Autotools calls Distutils. So the next step is to get Autotools to know that it has to call Distutils.

In fact, that is Automake's only responsibility in the *py* directory, so the *Makefile.am* for that directory deals only with that problem. As in Example 5-7, we need one step to compile the package and one to install, each of which will be associated with one makefile target. For setup, that target is `all-local`, which will be called when users run `make`; for installation, the target is `install-exec-hook`, which will be called when users run `make install`.

*Example 5-7. Setting up Automake to drive Python's Distutils (py/Makefile.py.am)*

```
all-local: pvnrt

pvnrt:
        CFLAGS='@CFLAGS@' python setup.py build
```

```
install-exec-hook:
        python setup.py install
```

At this point in the story, Automake has everything it needs in the main directory to generate the library, Distutils has all the information it needs in the *py* directory, and Automake knows to run Distutils at the right time. From here, the user can type the usual `./configure && make && sudo make install` sequence and build both the C library and its Python wrapper.

# PART II

# The Language

This is the part where we reconsider everything about the C language.

There are two parts to the process: working out what bits of the language not to use, and then finding out about the new things. Some of the new things are syntactic features, such as being able to initialize a list of struct elements by name; some of the new things are functions that have been written for us and are now common, such as the functions that will allow us to write to strings without quite as much pain.

I assume basic knowledge of C. Readers new to the language may want to read Appendix A first.

The chapters cover the material as follows:

Chapter 6 provides a guide for those perplexed (or perhaps made a bit uneasy) by pointers.

Chapter 7 is where we start building by tearing down. We'll go over a survey of concepts covered by the typical textbooks that I believe should be downplayed or considered deprecated.

Chapter 8 goes in the other direction, offering more in-depth discussion of concepts I found were mentioned only in passing or were missing entirely from typical textbooks.

In Chapter 9, we pay special attention to strings and work out how to handle them without memory allocation or character-counting madness. `malloc` will be lonely, because you'll never call it.

Chapter 10 presents newer syntax, which will let us write function calls in ISO-standard C with inputs such as lists of arbitrary length; e.g., `sum(1, 2.2, [...] 39, 40)` or named, optional elements like `new_person(.name="Joe", .age=32, .sex='M')`. Like rock and roll, these syntactic features saved my life. If I hadn't known about them, I would have abandoned C a long time ago.

Chapter 11 is a deconstruction of the concept of object-oriented programming. It is a many-headed hydra, and translating all of it to C would be a Herculean task of limited benefit, but there are some aspects of the paradigm that are easily implemented when needed.

It may sound too good to be true, but with one line of code, you can double or quadruple the speed of your program (or even better). The secret is in parallel threads, and Chapter 12 covers covers three systems for turning your single-threaded program into a multithreaded program.

Having covered the idea of how one would structure a library, let's use a few in Chapter 13 to do advanced math, talk to an Internet server via whatever protocol it speaks, run a database, and otherwise kick some ass.

# CHAPTER 6

# Your Pal the Pointer

*He's the one*
*Who likes all our pretty songs*
*And he likes to sing along*
*And he likes to shoot his gun*
*But he don't know what it means.*
—Nirvana, "In Bloom"

Like a song about music, or a movie about Hollywood, a pointer is data describing other data. It's certainly easy to get overwhelmed: all at once, you have to deal with getting lost in references to references, aliases, memory management, and `malloc`. But our outrageous fortune breaks down into separate components. For example, we can use pointers as aliases without bothering with `malloc`, which doesn't have to appear nearly as often as the textbooks from the '90s told us it did. On the one hand, C's syntax can be confusing with its use of stars; on the other hand, C's syntax provides us with tools for dealing with especially complicated setups like pointers to functions.

The topics in this chapter address common errors and common points of confusion. If you've been writing in C for a long time, these points will seem like second nature to you, and you might want to skip or quickly skim this chapter. It is intended for all those people (and their numbers are legion) who feel a little uneasy when working with pointers.

## Automatic, Static, and Manual Memory

C provides three basic models of memory management, which is two more than most languages and two more than you really want to care about. And as a bonus for you, the reader, I'll even throw in two more memory models later on (thread-local in "Thread Local" on page 300 and mmaped in "Using mmap for Gigantic Data Sets" on page 329).

*Automatic*

You declare a variable on first use, and it is removed when it goes out of scope. Without the `static` keyword, any variable inside a function is automatic. Your typical programming language has only automatic-type data.

*Static*

Static variables exist in the same place throughout the life of the program. Array sizes are fixed at startup, but values can change (so it's not entirely static). Data is initialized before `main` starts, and thus any initializations have to be done with constants that require no calculations. Variables declared outside of functions (in file scope) and inside functions with the `static` keyword are static. If you forget to initialize a static variable, it is initialized to all zeros (or `NULL`).

*Manual*

The manual type involves `malloc` and `free`, and is where most of your segfaults happen.[1] This memory model is why Jesus weeps when he has to code in C. Also, this is the only type of memory where arrays can be resized after declaration.

Table 6-1 shows the differences in the three places you could put data. I discuss most of these points at length over the next few chapters.

*Table 6-1. Three types of memory; three bundles of features*

| | Static | Auto | Manual |
|---|---|---|---|
| Set to zero on startup | ◊ | | |
| Scope-limited | ◊ | ◊ | |
| Can set values on init | ◊ | ◊ | |
| Can set nonconstant values on init | | ◊ | |
| `sizeof` measures array size | ◊ | ◊ | |
| Persists across function calls | ◊ | | ◊ |
| Can be global | ◊ | | ◊ |

---

1 C99 and C11 §6.2.4 refer to `malloc`ed memory as *allocated memory*, but I chose to use a term that better distinguishes this type of storage from storage allocated on the stack.

|  | Static | Auto | Manual |
| --- | --- | --- | --- |
| Array size can be set at runtime |  | ◊ | ◊ |
| Can be resized |  |  | ◊ |
| Jesus weeps |  |  | ◊ |

Some of these are features that we are looking for in a variable, such as resizing or convenient initialization. Some of these things, such as whether you get to set values on initialization, are technical consequences of the memory system. So if you want a different feature, such as being able to resize at runtime, suddenly you have to care about `malloc` and the pointer heap. If we could bomb it all out and start over, we wouldn't tie together three sets of features with three sets of technical annoyances. But here we are.

## The Stack and the Heap

Any one function has a space in memory, a *frame*, holding information about the function, such as where to return to when finished and spaces for all of the automatically allocated variables.

When a function (such as `main`) calls another function, action in the first function's frame halts, and a frame for the new function is added to the *stack* of frames. When a function completes, its frame is popped off the stack, and all variables in that frame disappear in the process.

Unfortunately, the stack has arbitrary size limits that are much smaller than general memory, in the ballpark of maybe 2 or 3 megabytes (via Linux defaults as of this writing). That's about enough to hold all of Shakespeare's tragedies, so don't worry about allocating an array of 10,000 integers. But it's easy to find data sets much larger, and the current limits on the stack will require that we allocate space for them elsewhere, using `malloc`.

Memory allocated via `malloc` is not on the stack, but is elsewhere in the system, in a space called the *heap*. The heap may or may not be size-restricted; on a typical PC, it is not unreasonable to assume that the size of the heap is roughly the size of all available memory.

Here are some words that do not appear in the C11 standard:

Transistor  C++

CPU  Frame

| Joy | Heap |
|-----|------|
| Love | Stack |

Details of environment and implementation are typically left out of the standard, and the stack of frames is such an implementation detail. However, there has always been broad consensus in this form of implementation. The description of automatically allocated variables given by the C standard thus closely matches the functioning of variables allocated and destroyed in a stack of frames, and the description of what it calls allocated storage closely matches the behavior of memory taken from the heap.

All of this is about where you put your data in memory. This is distinct from the variables themselves, which can make for another level of fun:

1. If you declared your struct, char, int, double, or other variable either outside of a function or inside a function with the static keyword, then it's static; otherwise, it's automatic.

2. If you declared a pointer, the pointer itself has a memory type, probably auto or static as per rule 1. But the pointer could be pointing to any of the three types of data: static pointer to malloced data, automatic pointer to static data—all the combinations are possible.

Rule 2 means that you can't identify the memory model by the typography. On the one hand, it's nice that we don't have to deal with one notation for auto arrays and a different notation for manual arrays; on the other hand, you still have to be aware of which you have, so you don't get tripped up resizing an automatic array or not freeing a manual array.

The distinction between pointer-to-manual and pointer-to-automatic clarifies one of the famous points of confusion among C beginners: what is the difference between int an_array[] and int *a_pointer?

When a program runs across this declaration in your code:

```
int an_array[32];
```

the program will:

- set aside a space on the stack big enough for 32 integers,
- declare that an_array is a pointer, and
- bind that pointer to point to the newly allocated space.

The space set aside is automatically allocated, meaning that you cannot resize the space or retain the space after it is automatically destroyed at the end of scope. As an additional restriction, you can not reassign an_array to point elsewhere. Because the variable an_array can not be divorced from the 32-integer space allocated for it, K&R and the C standard say that an_array *is* the array.

Despite the restrictions, an_array is a pointer to a place in memory, and the usual rules of dereferencing a pointer (discussed in more detail below) apply to it.

When a program runs across this declaration in your code:

```
int *a_pointer;
```

the program will only do one of the above steps:

- declare that a_pointer is a pointer

This pointer is not bound to any specific location in memory, and so is free to be assigned to point to anywhere. Valid uses include:

```
//manually allocating a new block; pointing a_pointer to it:
a_pointer = malloc(32*sizeof(int));

//pointing the pointer to an_array, as declared above.
a_pointer = an_array;
```

So the distinction between writing int an_array[] and int *a_pointer in a declaration has a real effect. But in other cases, such as in a typedef declaration (such as for a new struct) or a function call, there is less distinction to be made. For example, given a function declared via

```
int f(int *a_pointer, int an_array[]);
```

a_pointer and an_array behave identically. No memory is being allocated, so the pointer-to-manual versus pointer-to-automatic distinction is moot. A C function receives a copy of the input arguments, not the originals, and a copy of a pointer-to-automatic doesn't have the binding restrictions that the original array has. So as an argument to a function, there is no distinction at all, and C99 §6.7.5.3(7) and C11 §6.7.6.3(7) state that "A declaration of a parameter as 'array of type' shall be adjusted to 'qualified pointer to type'" (the qualifiers, const, restrict, volatile, or _Atomic, are retained in the conversion from array-of-*type* to pointer-to-*type*). The example above had no array size, but this *pointer decay* occurs even for a form like int g(int an_array[32]).

I have grown the habit of always using the *a_pointer form in-function headers and typedefs, because it is one less thing to think about and preserves the rule of reading complex declarations from right to left (see "Noun-Adjective Form" on page 180).

> **Your Turn:** Check back on some code you have and go through the typology: which data is static memory, auto, manual; which variables are auto pointers to manual memory, auto pointers to static values, et cetera. If you don't have anything immediately on hand, try this exercise with Example 6-6.

# Persistent State Variables

This chapter is mostly about the interaction of automatic memory, manual memory, and pointers, which leaves static variables somewhat out of the narrative. But it's worth pausing to consider the good work static variables can do for us.

Static variables can have local scope. That is, you can have variables that exist only in one function, but when the function exits, the variable retains its value. This is great for having an internal counter or a reusable scratch space. Because a static variable never moves, a pointer to a static variable will remain valid after a function exits.

Example 6-1 presents a traditional textbook example: the Fibonacci sequence. We declare the first two elements to be 0 and 1, and each element after those is the sum of the two prior elements.

*Example 6-1. The Fibonacci sequence generated by a state machine (fibo.c)*

```
#include <stdio.h>

long long int fibonacci(){
    static long long int first = 0;
    static long long int second = 1;
    long long int out = first+second;
    first=second;
    second=out;
    return out;
}

int main(){
    for (int i=0; i< 50; i++)
        printf("%lli\n", fibonacci());
}
```

Check out how insignificant main is. The fibonacci function is a little machine that runs itself; main just has to bump the function and it spits out another value. That is, the function is a simple *state machine*, and static variables are the key tool for implementing state machines via C.

How can we use these static state machines in a world where every function has to be thread-safe? The ISO C committee saw us coming, and C11 includes a _Thread_local memory type. Just put that into your declarations:

```
static _Thread_local int counter;
```

and you've got a distinct counter for each thread. I discuss this in greater detail in "Thread Local" on page 300.

---

### Declaring Static Variables

Static variables, even those inside of a function, are initialized when the program starts, before main, so you can't initialize them with a nonconstant value.

```
//this fails: can't call gsl_vector_alloc() before main() starts
static gsl_vector *scratch = gsl_vector_alloc(20);
```

This is an annoyance, but easily solved with a macro to start at zero and allocate on first use:

```
#define Staticdef(type, var, initialization) \
    static type var = 0; \
    if (!(var)) var = (initialization);
```

```
//usage:
Staticdef(gsl_vector*, scratch, gsl_vector_alloc(20));
```

This works as long as we don't ever expect initialization to be zero (or in pointer-speak, NULL). If it is, it'll get reinitialized on the next go-round. Maybe that's OK anyway.

---

## Pointers Without malloc

When I tell my computer *set A to B*, I could mean one of two things:

- Copy the value of B into A. When I increment A with A++, then B doesn't change.
- Let A be an alias for B. Then A++ also increments B.

Every time your code says *set A to B*, you need to know whether you are making a copy or an alias. This is in no way C-specific.

For C, you are always making a copy, but if you are copying the address of the data you care about, a copy of the pointer is a new alias for the data. That's a fine implementation of aliasing.

Other languages have different customs: LISP family languages lean heavily on aliasing and have set commands to copy; Python scalars are effectively copied[2] but aliases lists (unless you use copy or deepcopy). Again, knowing which to expect will clear up a whole lot of bugs all at once.

The GNU Scientific Library includes vector and matrix objects, which both have a data element, which is itself an array of doubles. Let us say that we have some vector/matrix pairs, via a typedef, and an array of these pairs:

```
typedef struct {
    gsl_vector* vector;
    gsl_matrix* matrix;
} datapair;

datapair your_data[100];
```

Say we have been dealing with this structure for a while, and are frequently dealing with the first element of the first matrix:

```
your_data[0].matrix->data[0]
```

If you are familiar with how the blocks fit together, this is easy to follow, but is it ever annoying to type. Let's alias it:

```
double *elmt1 = your_data[0].matrix->data;
```

Among the two types of assignment shown, the equals sign here is the aliasing type: only a pointer gets copied, and if we change *elmt1, then the data point buried in your_data gets modified as well.

Aliasing is a malloc-free experience, and demonstrates that we can get mileage out of pointers without fretting about memory management.

To give another example where malloc sometimes needlessly turns up, you may have a function that takes in a pointer as input:

```
void increment(int *i){
    (*i)++;
}
```

Users of the function who too closely associate pointers with malloc might think that this means that they have to allocate memory to pass in to the function:

```
int *i = malloc(sizeof(int)); //so much effort, wasted
*i = 12;
increment(i);
...
free(i);
```

---

2 Initially, a=b would alias a to b, but changes to either would cause the alias to be replaced by a separate copy. The behavior is thus effectively a lazy copy or copy-on-write.

Rather, the easiest use is to let automatic memory allocation do the work:

```
int i=12;
increment(&i);
```

> **Your Turn:** I gave you that advice earlier that every time you have a line that says *set A to B*, you need to know whether you are asking for an alias or a copy. Grab some code you have on hand (in whatever language) and go through line by line and ask yourself which is which. Were there cases where you could sensibly replace a copy with an alias?

## Structures Get Copied, Arrays Get Aliased

As in Example 6-2, copying the contents of a structure is a one-line operation.

*Example 6-2. No, you don't need to copy the elements of a struct element by element (copystructs.c)*

```
#include <assert.h>

typedef struct{
    int a, b;
    double c, d;
    int *efg;
} demo_s;

int main(){
    demo_s d1 = {.b=1, .c=2, .d=3, .efg=(int[]){4,5,6}};
    demo_s d2 = d1;

    d1.b=14;                    ❶
    d1.c=41;
    d1.efg[0]=7;

    assert(d2.a==0);            ❷
    assert(d2.b==1);
    assert(d2.c==2);
    assert(d2.d==3);
    assert(d2.efg[0]==7);
}
```

❶  Let's change *d1* and see if *d2* changed.

❷  These assertions will all pass.

As before, you should always know whether your assignment is a copy of the data or a new alias, so which is it here? We changed d1.b d1.b, and d1.c and d2 didn't change, so this is a copy. But a copy of a pointer still points to the original data, so when we change d1.efg[0], the change also affects the copy of a pointer d2.efg. This advises that if you need a *deep copy* where pointer contents are copied, you will need a struct copying function, and if you don't have any pointers to trace through, then a copy function is overkill and an equals sign will do.

For arrays, the equals sign will copy an alias, not the data itself. In Example 6-3, let's try the same test of making a copy, changing the original, and checking the copy's value.

*Example 6-3. Structs get copied, but setting one array to the other creates an alias (copystructs2.c)*

```
#include <assert.h>

int main(){
    int abc[] = {0, 1, 2};
    int *copy = abc;

    copy[0] = 3;
    assert(abc[0]==3);  ❶
}
```

❶ Passes: the original changed when the copy did.

Example 6-4 is a slow buildup to a train wreck. It is mostly two functions that automatically allocate two blocks: the first allocates a struct and the second allocates a short array. Being automatic memory, we know that at the end of each function, the respective blobs of memory will be freed.

A function that ends in return x will return the value of x to the calling function [C99 and C11 §6.8.6.4(3)]. Seems simple enough, but that value has to be copied out to the calling function, whose frame is about to be destroyed. As previously, for a struct, a number, or even a pointer, the calling function will get a copy of the returned value; for an array, the calling function will get a *pointer* to the array, not a copy of the data in the array.

That last one is a nasty trap, because the pointer returned may be pointing to an automatically allocated array of data, which is destroyed on function exit. A pointer to a block of memory that has already been automatically freed is worse than useless.

*Example 6-4. You can return a struct from a function, but not an array (automem.c)*

```
#include <stdio.h>

typedef struct powers {
    double base, square, cube;
```

```
} powers;

powers get_power(double in){
    powers out = {.base   = in,                                    ❶
                  .square = in*in,
                  .cube   = in*in*in};
    return out;                                                    ❷
}

int *get_even(int count){
    int out[count];
    for (int i=0; i< count; i++)
        out[i] = 2*i;
    return out;    //bad.                                          ❸
}

int main(){
    powers threes = get_power(3);
    int *evens = get_even(3);
    printf("threes: %g\t%g\t%g\n", threes.base, threes.square, threes.cube);
    printf("evens: %i\t%i\t%i\n", evens[0], evens[1], evens[2]);  ❹
}
```

❶ The initialization is via designated initializers. If you've never met them, hold tight for a few chapters.

❷ This is valid. On exit, a copy of the local, automatically allocated out is made, then the local copy is destroyed.

❸ This is invalid. Here, arrays really are treated like pointers, so on exit, a copy of the pointer to out gets made. But once the autoallocated memory is destroyed, the pointer is now pointing to bad data. If your compiler is on the ball, it will warn you of this.

❹ Back in the function that called get_even, evens is a valid pointer-to-int, but it is pointing to already freed data. This may segfault, print garbage, or get lucky and print the correct values (this time).

If you need a copy of an array, you can still do it on one line, but we're back to memory-twiddling syntax, as in Example 6-5.

*Example 6-5. Copying an array requires memmove—it's antediluvian, but it works (memmove.c)*

```
#include <assert.h>
#include <string.h> //memmove

int main(){
```

```
    int abc[] = {0, 1, 2};
    int *copy1, copy2[3];

    copy1 = abc;
    memmove(copy2, abc, sizeof(int)*3);

    abc[0] = 3;
    assert(copy1[0]==3);
    assert(copy2[0]==0);
}
```

## malloc and Memory-Twiddling

Now for the memory part, in which we deal with addresses in memory directly. These will often be allocated manually via malloc.

The easiest way to avoid bugs related to malloc is not to use malloc. Historically (in the 1980s and 1990s), we needed malloc for all sorts of string manipulations; Chapter 9 gives full coverage of strings without explicitly calling malloc once. We needed malloc to deal with arrays for which length had to be set at runtime, which is pretty common; as per "Set Array Size at Runtime" on page 146, that is also largely obsolete.

Here is my roughly comprehensive list of reasons left for using malloc:

1. Resizing an already extant array requires realloc, which only makes sense on blocks of memory initially allocated via malloc.

2. As explained earlier, you can't return an array from a function.

3. Some objects should persist long after their initialization function. Though, Chapter 11 will present several examples that wrap the memory management for such objects into new/copy/free functions so that they don't sully our procedures.

4. Automatic memory is allocated on the stack of function frames, which may be restricted to a few megabytes (or less). Therefore, large chunks of data (i.e., anything measured in megabytes) should be allocated on the heap, not the stack. Again, you probably have a function to store your data in an object of some sort, so this will in practice be a call to an *object*_new function rather than to malloc itself.

5. Now and then, you will find function forms that require that a pointer be returned. For example, in "Pthreads" on page 310, the template requires that we write a function that returns a void *. We dodge that bullet by just returning NULL, but now and then, we hit a form where we're stuck. Note also that "Return Multiple Items from a Function" on page 222 discusses returning structs from a

function, so we can send back relatively complex return values without memory allocation, obviating another common use of allocations within a function.

I wrote this list to show you that it's not all that long—and item 5 is a rarity, and item 4 is often a special case of item 3, because giant data sets tend to get put into object-like data structures. Production code tends to have few uses of `malloc`, typically wrapped in new/copy/free functions so the main code doesn't have to deal further with memory management.

## The Fault Is in Our Stars

OK, so we're clear that pointers and memory allocation are separate concepts, but dealing with pointers themselves can still be a problem, because, well, all those stars are just confusing.

The ostensible rationale for the pointer declaration syntax is that the use and the declaration look alike. What they mean by this is that when you declare:

```
int *i;
```

`*i` is an integer, so it's only natural that we'd declare that `*i` is an integer via `int *i`.

So that's all well and good, and if it helps you, great. I'm not sure that I could invent a less ambiguous way of doing it.

Here's a common design rule, espoused throughout The Design of Everyday Things, for example: *things that have drastically different functions should not look similar* (Norman, 2002). That book gives the example of airplane controls, where two identical-looking levers often do entirely different things. In a crisis situation, that's an invitation for human error.

Here, C syntax crashes and burns, because `*i` in a declaration and `*i` outside of a declaration do very different things. For example:

```
int *i = malloc(sizeof(int)); //right
*i = 23;                       //right
int *i = 23;                   //wrong
```

I've thrown the rule that declaration looks like usage out of my brain. Here's the rule I use, which has served me well: when used for a declaration, a star indicates a pointer; when not used as a declaration, a star indicates the value of the pointer.

Here is a valid snippet:

```
int i = 13;
int *j = &i;
int *k = j;
*j = 12;
```

Using the rule given, you can see that on the second line, the initialization is correct, because *j is a declaration, and so a pointer. On the third line, *k is also the declaration of a pointer, so it makes sense to assign to it j, also a pointer. On the last line, *j is not in a declaration, so it indicates a plain integer, and so we can assign 12 to it (and i will change as a result).

So there's your first tip: bear in mind that when you see *i on a declaration line, it is a pointer to something; when you see *i on a nondeclaration line, it is the pointed-to value.

After some pointer arithmetic, I'll come back with another tip for dealing with weird pointer declaration syntax.

## All the Pointer Arithmetic You Need to Know

An element of an array can be expressed as being at some offset from the base of the array. You could declare a pointer double *p; then that's your base, and you can use the offsets from that base as an array: at the base itself, you will find the contents of the first element, p[0]; go one step from the base and you have the contents of the second, p[1]; et cetera. So if you give me a pointer and the distance from one element to the next, I've got an array.

You could just write the base plus offset directly and literally, via a form like (p+1). As your textbooks will tell you, p[1] is exactly equivalent to *(p+1), which explains why the first element in an array is p[0] == *(p+0). K & R spend about six pages on this stuff [2nd ed., sections 5.4 and 5.5].

The theory implies a few rules for notating arrays and their elements in practice:

- Declare arrays either via the explicit pointer form, double *p or the static/automatic form, double p[100].

- In either case, the *n*th array item is p[n]. Don't forget that the first item is zero, not one; it can be referred to with the special form p[0] == *p.

- If you need the address of the *n*th element (not its actual value), use the ampersand: &p[n]. Of course, the zeroth pointer is just &p[0] == p.

Example 6-6 shows some of these rules in use.

*Example 6-6. Some simple pointer arithmetic (arithmetic.c)*

```
#include <stdio.h>

int main(){
    int evens[5] = {0, 2, 4, 6, 8};
    printf("The first even number is, of course, %i\n", *evens);    ❶
```

```
    int *positive_evens = &evens[1];                          ❷
    printf("The first positive even number is %i\n", positive_evens[0]);   ❸
}
```

❶  Writing evens[0] using the special form *evens

❷  The address of element 1, assigned to a new pointer

❸  The usual way of referring to the first element of an array

I'll throw in one nice trick, based on the pointer arithmetic rule that p+1 is the address of the next point in an array (that is, &p[1]). With this rule, you don't need an index for for loops that step through an array. Example 6-7 uses a spare pointer that starts at the head of a list, and then steps through the array with p++ until it hits the NULL marker at the end. The next pointer declaration tip will make this much more legible.

*Example 6-7. We can use the fact that p++ means "step to the next pointer" to streamline for loops (pointer_arithmetic1.c)*

```
#include <stdio.h>

int main(){
    char *list[] = {"first", "second", "third", NULL};
    for (char **p=list; *p != NULL; p++){
        printf("%s\n", p[0]);
    }
}
```

> **Your Turn:** How would you implement this if you didn't know about p++?

Base-plus-offset thinking doesn't give us much payoff in terms of cute syntactic tricks, but it does explain a lot about how C works. In fact, consider the struct. Given:

```
    typedef struct{
        int a, b;
        double c, d;
    } abcd_s;

    abcd_s list[3];
```

As a mental model, you can think of list as our base, and list[0].b is just far enough past that to refer to b. That is, given that the location of list is the integer (size_t)&list, b might be located at (size_t)&list + sizeof(int); and so list[2].d would be at the position (size_t)&list + 6*sizeof(int) +

`5*sizeof(double)`. Under this thinking, a struct is much like an array, except the elements have names instead of numbers and are of different types and sizes.

It's not quite correct, because of *alignment*: the system may decide that the data needs to be in chunks of a certain size, so fields may have extra space at the end so that the next field begins at the right point, and the struct may have padding at its end so that a list of structs is appropriately aligned [C99 and C11 §6.7.2.1(15) and (17)]. The header *stddef.h* defines the `offsetof` macro, which makes the base-plus-offset thinking accurate again: `list[2].d` really is at `(size_t)&list + 2*sizeof(abcd_s) + offsetof(abcd_s, d)`.

By the way, there can't be padding at the beginning of a struct, so `list[2].a` is at `(size_t)&list+ 2*sizeof(abcd_s)`.

Here is a silly function to recursively count the number of elements in a list until we hit a zero-valued element. Let us say (and this is a bad idea) that we'd like to be able to use this function for any type of list where a zero value makes sense, so it will take in a `void` pointer.

```
int f(void *in){
    if (*(char*)in==0) return 1;
    else return 1 + f(&(in[1]));   //This won't work.
}
```

The base-plus-offset rule explains why this won't work. To refer to `a_list[1]`, the compiler needs to know the exact length of `a_list[0]`, so it knows how far to offset from the base. But without a type attached, it can't calculate that size.

## Multidimensional Arrays

One way to do a multidimensional array is via an array of arrays of arrays, like `int an_array[2][3][7]`. This is a subtly different type from `int another_array[2][3][6]`, and using it in practice creates more headaches than it solves, especially when writing functions that are expected to operate on both of these types. Textbook examples usually stick to arrays of universally fixed size (we can expect that there will always be 12 months) or never pass an array of arrays to a function.

I say, forget it. It's too much of a pain to write around the subtly different types. Everybody has a different view of the world of code, but I rarely see this form outside of textbooks, and see a base-plus-stride-offset form much more frequently.

The more workable way to implement an $N_1$-by-$N_2$-by-$N_3$ multidimensional array of `double`s:

- Define a struct with a single data pointer (herein `data`) and a list of *strides*.

- Define an alloc routine that sets up the pointer via `data=malloc(sizeof(double)*N1*N2*N3)` and records the strides, S1=N1, S2=N2, S3=N3. You will also need a free routine to free the allocated memory.

- Define get/set routines: `get(x, y, z)` would retrieve `data[x + S1*y + S1*S2*z]`, and `set` would put a value in that same position. With these get/set functions, the first block of $S_1$ data points in `data` is of the form $(x, 0, 0)$. The next block of data points, from $S_1+0$ to $S_1+S_1$, is of the form $(x, 1, 0)$. Repeating this row-by-row pattern covers every value of the form $(x, y, 0)$, and requires $S_1 * S_2$ slots. The next slot will be position $(0, 0, 1)$, and so on until all $S_1 * S_2 * S_3$ cells are accounted for.

We can check whether the inputs to the get/set routines are outside the bounds of the array, because we recorded the strides. We don't need S3 to find any positions in the data grid, but it is worth recording in the struct to check bounds.

The GNU Scientific Library has a fine implementation of this for two-dimensional arrays. Their implementation is slightly different, including a stride for the first dimension and an offset marker. It is trivial to get subsets like column/row vectors or submatrices simply by changing the starting point and strides. For arrays of three or more dimensions, your favorite Internet search engine will provide several options using a base-plus-stride-offset system like the one described here.

## Typedef as a teaching tool

Any time you find yourself putting together a complex type, which frequently means a pointer-to-pointer-to-pointer sort of situation, ask yourself whether a typedef could clarify things.

For example, this popular definition:

```
typedef char* string;
```

reduces the visual clutter around arrays of strings and clarifies their intent. In the preceding pointer-arithmetic p++ example, did the declarations communicate to you that `char *list[]` is a list of strings, and that `*p` is a string? Example 6-8 shows a rewrite of the `for` loop of Example 6-7, replacing `char *` with `string`.

*Example 6-8. Adding a typedef makes awkward code a little more legible (pointer_arithmetic2.c)*

```
#include <stdio.h>
typedef char* string;

int main(){
    string list[] = {"first", "second", "third", NULL};
    for (string *p=list; *p != NULL; p++){
```

```
        printf("%s\n", *p);
    }
}
```

The declaration line for `list` is now as easy as C gets and clearly indicates that it is a list of strings, and the snippet `string *p` should indicate to you that p is a pointer-to-string, so *p is a string.

In the end, you'll still have to remember that a string is a pointer-to-`char`; for example, `NULL` is a valid value.

One could even take this further, such as declaring a 2D array of strings using the typedef above plus `typedef stringlist string*`. Sometimes this helps; sometimes it's just more notation to memorize.

Typedefs save the day when dealing with pointers to functions. If you have a function with a header like:

```
double a_fn(int, int); //a declaration
```

then just add a star (and parens to resolve precedence) to describe a pointer to this type of function:

```
double (*a_fn_type)(int, int);    //a type: pointer-to-function
```

Then put `typedef` in front of that to define a type:

```
typedef double (*a_fn_type)(int, int); //a typedef for a pointer to function
```

Now you can use it as a type like any other, such as to declare a function that takes another function as input:

```
double apply_a_fn(a_fn_type f, int first_in, int second_in){
    return f(first_in, second_in);
}
```

Being able to define specific pointer-to-function types takes writing functions that take other functions as inputs from being a daunting test of star placement to being kind of trivial.

In the end, dealing with pointers can be much simpler than the textbooks make it out to be, because it really is just a location or an alias—it's not about the different types of memory management at all. Complex constructs like pointers-to-pointers-to-strings are always confusing, because our hunter-gatherer ancestors never had a need to evolve skills to handle them. With the typedef, C at least gives us a tool to deal with them.

# CHAPTER 7

# Inessential C Syntax that Textbooks Spend a Lot of Time Covering

> *I believe it is good*
> *Let's destroy it.*
> —Porno for Pyros, "Porno for Pyros"

C may be a relatively simple language, but the C standard is about 700 pages, so unless you want to devote your life to studying it, it is important to know which parts can be ignored.

We can start with digraphs and trigraphs. If your keyboard is missing the { and } keys, you can use `<%` and `%>` as a replacement (like `int main() <% … %>`). This was relevant in the 1990s, when keyboards around the world followed diverse customs, but today it is hard to find a keyboard anywhere that is missing curly braces. The trigraph equivalents from C99 and C11 §5.2.1.1(1), `??<` and `??>`, are so useless that the authors of `gcc` and `clang` didn't bother to implement code to parse them.

Obscure corners of the language like trigraphs are easy to ignore, because nobody mentions them. But other parts of the language got heavy mention in textbooks from decades past, to address requirements in C89 or deal with limitations of computing hardware of the 1900s. With fewer restrictions, we can streamline our code. If you get joy from deleting code and eliminating redundancies, this chapter is for you.

## Don't Bother Explicitly Returning from main

As a warm-up, let's shave a line off every program you write.

Your program must have a `main` function, and it has to be of return type `int`, so you must absolutely have the following in your program:

```
int main(){ ... }
```

You would think that you therefore have to have a `return` statement that indicates what integer gets returned by `main`. However, the C standard states that "... reaching the `}` that terminates the main function returns a value of 0" [C99 and C11 §5.1.2.2(3)]. That is, if you don't write `return 0;` as the last line of your `main` function, then it will be assumed.

Recall that, after running your program, you can use `echo $?` to see its return value; you can use this to verify that programs that reach the end of `main` do indeed always return zero.

Earlier, I showed you this version of *hello.c*, and you can now see how I got away with a `main` containing only one #include plus one line of code:[1]

```
#include <stdio.h>
int main(){ printf("Hello, world.\n"); }
```

> **Your Turn:** Go through your programs and delete the `return 0` line from the end of `main`; see if it makes any difference.

## Let Declarations Flow

Think back to the last time you read a play. At the beginning of the text, there was the *Dramatis Personæ*, listing the characters. A list of character names probably didn't have much meaning to you before you started reading, so if you're like me you skipped that page and went straight to the start of the play. When you are in the thick of the plot and you forget who Benvolio is, it's nice to be able to flip back to the head of the play and get a one-line description (he is Romeo's friend and Montague's nephew), but that's because you're reading on paper. If the text were on a screen, you could search for Benvolio's first appearance.

In short, the *Dramatis Personæ* is not very useful to readers. It would be better to introduce characters when they first appear.

I see code like this pretty often:

---

1 By the way, there is one other way that this snippet shaves four keystrokes from the old requirements. In what even K& R 2nd ed. called "old style" declarations, having nothing inside the parens, like `int main()`, indicated no information about parameters, not definite information that there are zero parameters. Under the old rules, we would need `int main(void)` to be clear that `main` is taking no arguments. But since 1999, "An empty list in a function declarator that is part of a definition of that function specifies that the function has no parameters" [C99 §6.7.5.3(14) and C11 §6.7.6.3(14)].

```
#include <stdio.h>

int main(){
    char *head;
    int i;
    double ratio, denom;

    denom=7;
    head = "There is a cycle to things divided by seven.";
    printf("%s\n", head);
    for (i=1; i<= 6; i++){
        ratio = i/denom;
        printf("%g\n", ratio);
    }
}
```

It has three or four lines of introductory material (I'll let you decide how to count the whitespace), followed by the routine.

This is a throwback to ANSI C89, which required all declarations to be at the head of the block, due to technical limitations of early compilers. We still have to declare our variables, but we can minimize the burden on the author and reader by doing so at the first use:

```
#include <stdio.h>

int main(){
    double denom = 7;
    char *head = "There is a cycle to things divided by seven.";
    printf("%s\n", head);
    for (int i=1; i<= 6; i++){
        double ratio = i/denom;
        printf("%g\n", ratio);
    }
}
```

Here, the declarations happen as needed, so the onus of declaration reduces to sticking a type name before the first use. If you have color syntax highlighting, then the declarations are still easy to spot (and if you don't have a text editor that supports color, you are seriously missing out—and there are dozens to hundreds to choose from!).

When reading unfamiliar code, my first instinct when I see a variable is to go back and see where it was declared. If the declaration is at the first use or the line immediately before the first use, I'm saved from a few seconds of skimming back. Also, by the rule that you should keep the scope of a variable as small as possible, we're pushing the active variable count on earlier lines that much lower, which might start to matter for a longer function. And, as a final benefit, the decaration-in-loop form will prove to be easier to parallelize with OpenMP, in Chapter 12.

In this example, the declarations are at the beginning of their respective blocks, followed by nondeclaration lines. This is just how the example turned out, but you can freely intermix declarations and nondeclarations.

I left the declaration of denom at the head of the function, but we could move that into the loop as well, because it is only used inside the loop. We can trust that the compiler will know enough not to waste time and energy deallocating and reallocating the variable on every iteration of the loop [although this is what it theoretically does—see C99 and C11 §6.8(3)]. As for the index, it's a disposable convenience for the loop, so it's natural to reduce its scope to exactly the scope of the loop.

---

## Will This New Syntax Slow Down My Program?

No.

The compiler's first step is to parse your code into a language-independent internal representation. This is how the gcc (GNU Compiler Collection) can produce compatible object files for C, C++, ADA, and FORTRAN—by the end of the parsing step, they all look the same. Therefore, the grammatical conveniences provided by C99 to make your text more human-readable are typically abstracted away well before the executable is produced.

Along the same lines, the target device that will run your program will see nothing but postcompilation machine instructions, so it will be indifferent as to whether the original code conformed to C89, C99, or C11.

---

## Set Array Size at Runtime

Dovetailing with putting declarations wherever you want, you can allocate arrays to have a length determined at runtime, based on calculations before the declarations.

Again, this wasn't always true: a quarter-century ago, you either had to know the size of the array at compile time or use malloc.

To take a real-world example I happened upon once, let's say that you'd like to create a set of threads, but the number of threads is set by the user on the command line. The author did this by getting the size of the array from the user via atoi(argv[1]) (i.e., convert the first command-line argument to an integer), and then, having established that number at runtime, allocating an array of the right length.

```
pthread_t *threads;
int thread_count;
thread_count = atoi(argv[1]);
threads = malloc(thread_count * sizeof(pthread_t));
...
```

```
    free(threads);
```

But we can write this with less fuss:

```
    int thread_count = atoi(argv[1]);
    pthread_t threads[thread_count];
    ...
```

There are fewer places for anything to go wrong, and it reads like declaring an array, not initializing memory registers. We had to `free` the manually allocated array, but we can just drop the automatically allocated array on the floor, and it'll get cleaned up when the program leaves the given scope.[2]

# Cast Less

In the 1970s and 1980s, `malloc` returned a `char*` pointer and had to be cast (unless you were allocating a string), with a form like:

```
    //don't bother with this sort of redundancy:
    double* list = (double*) malloc(list_length * sizeof(double));
```

You don't have to do this anymore, because `malloc` now gives you a `void` pointer, which the compiler will comfortably autocast to any pointer type. The easiest way to do the cast is to declare a new variable with the right type. For example, functions that have to take in a `void` pointer will typically begin with a form like:

```
    int use_parameters(void *params_in){
        param_struct *params = params_in;    //Effectively casting pointer-to-NULL
        ...                                   //to a pointer-to-param_struct.
    }
```

More generally, if it's valid to assign an item of one type to an item of another type, then C will do it for you without your having to tell it to with an explicit cast. If it's not valid for the given type, then you'll have to write a function to do the conversion

---

2 The C99 standard required conforming compilers to accept variable-length arrays (VLAs). The C11 standard took a step back and made it optional. Personally, I found this move to be out of character for the standards committee, which is normally meticulous about making sure that all existing code (even trigraphs!) will continue to compile into the future.

Because VLAs are an optional part of the standard, we have to ask whether they are reliable. Compiler authors gain market share by writing compilers that work for as much existing code as possible, so it is not surprising that every major compiler that makes a serious effort to comply to the C11 standard does allow VLAs. Even if you are writing for an Arduino microcontroller (which is not a traditional stack-and-heap system), you will be using AVR-gcc, a variant of gcc that still handles VLAs. I consider code using VLAs to be reliable across a diverse range of platforms, and expect it to continue to be reliable in the future.

Readers who wish to prepare for a standards-compliant compiler that opts out of supporting VLAs can use a feature test macro to check whether VLAs can be used; see "Test Macros" on page 172.

anyway. This isn't true of C++, which depends more on types and therefore requires casts to be explicit.

There remain two reasons to use C's type-casting syntax to cast a variable from one type to another.

First, when dividing two numbers, an integer divided by an integer will always return an integer, so the following statements will both be true:

```
4/2 == 2
3/2 == 1
```

That second is the source of lots of errors. It's easy to fix: if i is an integer, then i + 0.0 is a floating-point number that matches the integer. Don't forget parentheses as needed, but that solves your problem. If you have a constant, 2 is an integer and 2.0 or even just 2. is floating point. Thus, all of these variants work:

```
int two=2;
3/(two+0.0) == 1.5
3/(2+0.0) == 1.5
3/2.0 == 1.5
3/2. == 1.5
```

You can also use the casting form:

```
3/(double)two == 1.5
3/(double)2 == 1.5
```

I'm partial to the add-zero form, for æsthetic reasons; you're welcome to prefer the cast-to-double form. But make a habit of one or the other every time you reach for that / key, because this is the source of many, many errors (and not just in C; lots of other languages also like to insist that int / int → int—not that that makes it OK).

Second, array indices have to be integers. It's the law [C99 and C11 §6.5.2.1(1)], and compilers will thus complain if you send a floating-point index. So, you may have to cast to an integer, even if you know that in your situation you will always have an integer-valued expression.

```
4/(double)2 == 2.0        //This is floating-point, not an int.
mylist[4/(double)2]       //So, an error: floating-point index

mylist[(int)(4/(double)2)] //Works. Take care with the parens.

int index=4/(double)2     //This form also works, and is more legible.
mylist[index]
```

You can see that even for the few legitimate reasons to cast, you have options to avoid the casting syntax: adding 0.0 and declaring an integer variable for your array indices.

Nor is this just a question of reducing clutter. Your compiler checks types for you and throws warnings or errors accordingly, but an explicit cast is a way of saying to the compiler, *leave me alone; I know what I'm doing.* For example, consider this short program, which tries to set `list[7]=12`, but twice commits the classic error of using a pointer instead of the pointed-to value:

```
int main(){
    double x = 7;
    double *xp = &x;
    int list[100];

    int val2 = xp;          //Clang warns about using a pointer as an int.
    list[val2] = 12;

    list[(int)xp] = 12;     //Clang gives no warning.
}
```

# Enums and Strings

Enums are a good idea that went bad.

The benefit is clear enough: integers are not at all mnemonic, and so wherever you are about to put a short list of integers in your code, you are better off naming them. Here's the even worse means of how we could do it without the `enum` keyword:

```
#define NORTH 0
#define SOUTH 1
#define EAST 2
#define WEST 3
```

With `enum`, we can shrink that down to one line of source code, and our debugger is more likely to know what `EAST` means. Here's the improvement over the sequence of `#defines`:

```
enum directions {NORTH, SOUTH, EAST, WEST};
```

But we now have five new symbols in our namespaces: `directions`, `NORTH`, `SOUTH`, `EAST`, and `WEST`.

For an enum to be useful, it typically has to be global (i.e., declared in a header file intended to be included in many places all over a project). For example, you'll often find enums typedefed in the public header file for a library. To minimize the chance of name clashes, library authors use names like `G_CONVERT_ERROR_NOT_ABSO LUTE_PATH` or the relatively brief `CblasConjTrans`.

At that point, an innocuous and sensible idea has fallen apart. I don't want to type these messes, and I use them so infrequently that I have to look them up every time (especially because many are infrequently used error values or input flags, so there's typically a long gap between each use). Also, all-caps reads like yelling.

My own habit is to use single characters, wherein I would mark transposition with 't' and a path error with 'p'. I think this is enough to be mnemonic—in fact, I'm far more likely to remember how to spell 'p' than how to spell that all-caps mess—and it requires no new entries in the namespace.

I think usability considerations trump efficiency issues at this level, but even so, bear in mind that an enumeration is typically an integer, and char is C-speak for a single byte. So when comparing enums, you will likely need to compare the states of 16 bits or more, whereas with a char, you need compare only 8. So even if the speed argument were relevant, it would advocate against enums.

We sometimes need to combine flags. When opening a file using the open system call, you might need to send O_RDWR|O_CREAT, which is the bitwise combination of the two enums. You probably don't use open directly all that often; you are probably making more use of fopen, which is more user friendly. Instead of using an enum, it uses a one- or two-letter string, like "r" or "r+", to indicate whether something is readable, writable, both, et cetera.

In the context, you know "r" stands for *read*, and if you don't have the convention memorized, you can confidently expect that you will after a few more uses of fopen, whereas I still have to check whether I need CblasTrans or CBLASTrans or Cblas Transpose every time.

On the plus side of enums, you have a small, fixed set of symbols, so if you mistype one, the compiler stops and forces you to fix your typo. With strings, you won't know you had a typo until runtime. Conversely, strings are not a small, fixed set of symbols, so you can more easily extend the set of enums. For example, I once ran into an error handler that offers itself for use by other systems—as long as the errors the new system generates match the handful of errors in the original system's enum. If the errors were short strings, extension by others would be trivial.

There are reasons for using enums: sometimes you have an array that makes no sense as a struct but that nonetheless requires named elements, and when doing kernel-level work, giving names to bit patterns is essential. But in cases where enums are used to indicate a short list of options or a short list of error codes, a single character or a short string can serve the purpose without cluttering up the namespace or users' memory.

# Labels, gotos, switches, and breaks

In the olden days, assembly code didn't have the modern luxuries of while and for loops. Instead, there were only conditions, labels, and jumps. Where we would write while (a[i] < 100) i++;, our ancestors might have written:

```
label 1
if a[i] >= 100
    go to label 2
increment i
go to label 1
label 2
```

If it took you a minute to follow what was going on in this block, imagine reading this in a real-world situation, where the loop would be interspersed, nested, or half-nested with other jumps. I can attest from my own sad and painful experience that following the flow of such code is basically impossible, which is why `goto` is considered harmful in the present day (Dijkstra, 1968).

You can see how welcome C's `while` keyword would have been to somebody stuck writing in assembly code all day. However, there is a subset of C that is still built around labels and jumps, including the syntax for labels, `goto`, `switch`, `case`, `default`, `break`, and `continue`. I personally think of this as the portion of C that is transitional from how authors of assembly code wrote to the more modern style. This segment will present these forms as such, and suggest when they are still useful. However, this entire subset of the language is technically optional, in the sense that you can write equivalent code using the rest of the language.

## goto Considered

A line of C code can be labeled by providing a name with a colon after it. You can then jump to that line via `goto`. Example 7-1 is a simple function that presents the basic idea, with a line labeled `outro`. It finds the sum of all the elements in two arrays, provided they are all not NaN (Not a Number; see "Marking Exceptional Numeric Values with NaNs" on page 160). If one of the elements is NaN, this is an error and we need to exit the function. But however we choose to exit, we will free both vectors as cleanup. We could place the cleanup code in the listing three times (once if `vector` has a NaN, once if `vector2` has one, and once on OK exit), but it's cleaner to have one exit segment and jump to it as needed.

*Example 7-1. Using goto for a clean getaway in case of errors*

```c
/* Sum to the first NaN in the vector.
   Sets error to zero on a clean summation, 1 if a NaN is hit.*/
double sum_to_first_nan(double* vector, int vector_size,
                        double* vector2, int vector2_size, int *error){
    double sum=0;
    *error=1;
    for (int i=0; i< vector_size; i++){
        if (isnan(vector[i])) goto outro;
        sum += vector[i];
    }
```

```
    for (int i=0; i< vector2_size; i++){
        if (isnan(vector2[i])) goto outro;
        sum += vector2[i];
    }
    *error=0;

    outro:
    printf("The sum until the first NaN (if any) was %g\n", sum);
    free(vector);
    free(vector2);
    return sum;
}
```

The goto will only work within one function. If you need to jump from one function to an entirely different one, have a look at longjmp in your C standard library documentation.

A single jump by itself tends to be relatively easy to follow, and can clarify if used appropriately and in moderation. Even Linus Torvalds, the lead author of the Linux kernel, recommends the goto for limited uses like cutting out of a function when there's an error or processing is otherwise finished early, as in the example. Also, when you get to working with OpenMP in Chapter 12, you'll find that it doesn't allow a return in the middle of a parallelized block. So to stop execution, you will need either a lot of if statements, or a goto jumping to the end of the block.

So, to revise the common wisdom on goto, it is generally harmful but is a common present-day idiom for cleaning up in case of different kinds of errors, and it is often cleaner than the alternatives.

---

# A Keyword for the Morbid

The goto is useful for executing a few cleanup operations on the way out of a single function when something goes wrong. On a global scale, you have the choice of three go-to-the-exit functions: exit, quick_exit, and _Exit, and you can use the the at_exit and at_quick_exit functions to register the cleanup operations. (C11 §7.22.4).

At an early point in your program, you can call at_exit(fn), to register fn to be called by exit before closing streams and shutting down. For example, if you have a database handle open, or need to close a network connection, or want your XML document to close all its open elements, you can put a function here to do so. It has to have the form void fn(void), so any information for the function has to be delivered via global variables. After the registered functions are called (in last-in first-out order), open streams and files are closed and the program terminates.

---

You can register an entirely separate set of functions via at_quick_exit. These functions (and not the ones registered via at_exit) are called should your program call quick_exit. This form of exit does not close streams or flush buffers.

Finally, the _Exit function leaves as quickly as possible: no registered functions are called, and no buffers flushed.

Example 7-2 presents a simple example that prints different things depending on which nonreturning function you uncomment.

*Example 7-2. Abandon hope, all ye who enter a function marked with the _Noreturn function specifier. (noreturn.c)*

```
#include <stdio.h>
#include <unistd.h> //sleep
#include <stdlib.h> //exit, _Exit, et al.

void wail(){
    fprintf(stderr, "OOOOooooooo.\n");
}

void on_death(){
    for (int i=0; i<4; i++)
        fprintf(stderr, "I'm dead.\n");
}

_Noreturn void the_count(){    ❶
    for (int i=5; i --> 0;){
        printf("%i\n", i); sleep(1);
    }
    //quick_exit(1);            ❷
    //_Exit(1);
    exit(1);
}

int main(){
    at_quick_exit(wail);
    atexit(wail);
    atexit(on_death);
    the_count();
}
```

❶ The _Noreturn keyword is advice to the compiler that there is no need to prepare return information for the function.

❷ Uncomment these to see what gets called by the other exit functions.

# switch

Here is a snippet of code for the textbook norm for using the POSIX-standard `getopt` function to parse command-line arguments:

```
char c;
while ((c = getopt(...))){
    switch(c){
        case 'v':
            verbose++;
            break;
        case 'w':
            weighting_function();
            break;
        case 'f':
            fun_function();
            break;
    }
}
```

So when `c == 'v'`, the verbosity level is increased, when `c == 'w'`, the weighting function is called, et cetera.

Note well the abundance of `break` statements (which cut to the end of the `switch` statement, not the `while` loop, which continues looping). The `switch` function just jumps to the appropriate label (recall that the colon indicates a label), and then the program flow continues along, as it would given any other jump to a label. Thus, if there were no `break` after `verbose++`, then the program would merrily continue on to execute `weighting_function`, and so on. This is called *fall-through*. There are reasons for when fall-through is actually desirable, but to me, it always seemed to be a lemonade-out-of-lemons artifact of how `switch-case` is a smoothed-over syntax for using labels, `goto`, and `break`. Peter van der Linden surveyed a large code base and found that fall-through was appropriate for only 3% of cases.

If the risk of inserting a subtle bug by forgetting a `break` or `default` seems great to you, there is a simple solution: don't use `switch`.

The alternative to the `switch` is a simple series of `if`s and `else`s:

```
char c;
while ((c = getopt(...))){
    if (c == 'v')      verbose++;
    else if (c == 'w') weighting_function();
    else if (c == 'f') fun_function();
}
```

It's redundant because of the repeated reference to `c`, but it's shorter because we don't need a `break` every three lines. Because it isn't a thin wrapper around raw labels and jumps, it's harder to get wrong.

# Deprecate Float

Floating-point math is challenging in surprising places. It's easy to write down a reasonable algorithm that introduces 0.01% error on every step, which over 1,000 iterations turns the results into complete slop. You can easily find volumes filled with advice about how to avoid such surprises. Much of it is still valid today, but much of it is easy to handle quickly: use double instead of float, and for intermediate values in calculations, it doesn't hurt to use long double.

For example, *Writing Scientific Software* advises users to avoid what the authors call the single-pass method of calculating variances (Oliveira, 2006; p 24). They give an example that is *ill-conditioned*. As you may know, a floating-point number is so named because the decimal floats to the right position in an otherwise scale-independent number. For exposition, let's pretend the computer works in decimal; then this sort of system can store 23,000,000 exactly as easily as it could store .23 or .00023—just let the decimal point float. But 23,000,000.00023 is a challenge, because there are only so many digits available for expressing the prefloat value, as shown in Example 7-3.

*Example 7-3. A float can't store this many significant digits (floatfail.c)*

```
#include <stdio.h>

int main(){
    printf("%f\n", (float)333334126.98);
    printf("%f\n", (float)333334125.31);
}
```

The output from Example 7-3 on my netbook, with a 32-bit float:

```
333334112.000000
333334112.000000
```

There went our precision. This is why computing books from times past worried so much about writing algorithms to minimize the sort of drift one could have with only seven reliable decimal digits.

That's for a 32-bit float, which is the minimum standard anymore. I even had to explicitly cast to float, because the system will otherwise store these numbers with a 64-bit value.

64 bits is enough to reliably store 15 significant digits: 100,000,000,000,001 is not a problem. (Try it! Hint: printf(%.20g, *val*) prints *val* to 20 significant decimal digits).

Example 7-4 presents the code to run Oliveira and Stewart's example, including a single-pass calculation of mean and variance. Once again, this code is only useful as a demonstration, because the GSL already implements means and variance calculators. It does the example twice: once with the ill-conditioned version, which gave our authors from 2006 terrible results, and once after subtracting 34,120 from every number, which thus gives us something that even a plain float can handle with full precision. We can be confident that the results using the not-ill-conditioned numbers are accurate.

*Example 7-4. Ill-conditioned data: not such a big deal anymore (stddev.c)*

```
#include <math.h>
#include <stdio.h> //size_t

typedef struct meanvar {double mean, var;} meanvar;

meanvar mean_and_var(const double *data){
    long double avg = 0,                                ❶
        avg2 = 0;
    long double ratio;
    size_t cnt= 0;
    for(size_t i=0;   !isnan(data[i]); i++){
        ratio = cnt/(cnt+1.0);
        cnt   ++;
        avg   *= ratio;
        avg2  *= ratio;
        avg   += data[i]/(cnt +0.0);
        avg2  += pow(data[i], 2)/(cnt +0.0);
    }
    return (meanvar){.mean = avg,                       ❷
                    .var = avg2 - pow(avg, 2)}; //E[x^2] - E^2[x]
}

int main(){
    double d[] = { 34124.75, 34124.48,
                   34124.90, 34125.31,
                   34125.05, 34124.98, NAN};

    meanvar mv = mean_and_var(d);
    printf("mean: %.10g var: %.10g\n", mv.mean, mv.var*6/5.);

    double d2[] = { 4.75, 4.48,
                    4.90, 5.31,
                    5.05, 4.98, NAN};

    mv = mean_and_var(d2);
    mv.var *= 6./5;                                     ❸
    printf("mean: %.10g var: %.10g\n", mv.mean, mv.var);  ❹
}
```

❶ As a rule of thumb, using a higher level of precision for intermediate variables can avoid incremental roundoff problems. That is, if our output is double, then avg, avg2, and `ratio` should be `long double`. Do the results from the example change if we just use `doubles`? (Hint: no.)

❷ The function returns a struct generated via designated initializers. If this form is unfamiliar to you, you'll meet it soon.

❸ The function above calculated the population variance; scale to produce the sample variance.

❹ I used `%g` as the format specifier in the `printfs`; that's the *general* form, which accepts both floats and doubles.

Here are the results:

```
mean: 34124.91167 var: 0.07901676614
mean: 4.911666667 var: 0.07901666667
```

The means are off by 34,120, because we set up the calculations that way, but they are otherwise precisely identical (the .66666 would continue off the page if we let it), and the ill-conditioned variance is off by 0.000125%. The ill-conditioning had no appreciable effect.

That, dear reader, is technological progress. All we had to do was throw twice as much space at the problem, and suddenly all sorts of considerations are basically irrelevant. *You can still construct realistic cases where numeric drift can create problems*, but it's much harder to do so. Even if there is a perceptible speed difference between a program written with all `doubles` and one written with all `floats`, it's worth extra microseconds to be able to ignore so many caveats.

Should we use `long ints` everywhere integers are used? The case isn't quite as open and shut. A `double` representation of π is more precise than a `float` representation of π, even though we're in the ballpark of 3; both `int` and `long int` representations of numbers up to a few billion are precisely identical. The only issue is overflow. There was once a time when the limit was scandalously short, like around 32,000. It's good to be living in the present, where the range of integers on a typical system might go up to about ±2.1 billion. But if you think there's even a remote possibility that you have a variable that might multiply its way up to the billions (that's just 200 × 200 × 100 × 500, for example), then you certainly need to use a `long int` or even a `long long int`, or else your answer won't just be imprecise—it'll be entirely wrong, as most implementations wrap around from +2.1 billion to -2.1 billion. Have a look at your copy of *limits.h* (typically in the usual locations like */include* or */usr/include/*) for details; on my netbook, for example, *limits.h* says that `int` and `long int` are identical.

If you are doing some exceptionally serious counting, then #include <stdint.h> and use the intmax_t type, which is guaranteed to have a range at least up to $2^{63}-1 = 9{,}223{,}372{,}036{,}854{,}775{,}807$ [C99 §7.18.1 and C11 §7.20.1].

If you do switch, remember that you'll need to modify all your printfs to use %li as the format specifier for long int and %ji for intmax_t.

## Comparing Unsigned Integers

Example 7-5 shows a simple program that compares an int to a size_t, which is an unsigned integer sometimes used for representing array offsets (formally, it is the type returned by sizeof):

*Example 7-5. Comparing unsigned and signed integers (uint.c)*

```
#include <stdio.h>

int main(){
    int neg = -2;
    size_t zero = 0;
    if (neg < zero) printf("Yes, -2 is less than 0.\n");
    else            printf("No, -2 is not less than 0.\n");
}
```

You can run this and verify that it gets the wrong answer. This snippet demonstrates that in most comparisons between signed and an unsigned integers, C will force the signed type to unsigned (C99 & C11 §6.3.1.8(1)), which is the opposite of what we as humans expect. I will admit to having been caught by this a few times, and it is hard to spot the bug because the comparison looks so natural.

C gives you a multitude of ways to represent a number, from unsigned short int up to long double. Having so many types was necessary back when even mainframe memory was measured in kilobytes. But in the present day, this section and the last advise against using the full range. Micromanaging types, using float for efficiency and breaking out double for special occasions, or using unsigned int because you are confident the variable will never store a negative number, opens the way to bugs caused by subtle numeric imprecision and C's not-quite-intuitive arithmetic conversions.

## Safely Parse Strings to Numbers

There are several functions available to parse the numeric value of a string of text. The most popular are atoi and atof (ASCII-to-int and ASCII-to-float). Their use is very simple, such as:

```
char twelve[] = "12";
int x = atoi(twelve);

char million[] = "1e6";
double m = atof(million);
```

But there is no error-checking: if `twelve` is "XII", then `atoi(twelve)` evaluates to zero and the program continues.

The safer alternative is using `strtol` and `strtod`. They have actually been around since C89 but often take a back seat because they do not appear in K&R, 1st ed., and take a little more work to use. Most of the authors I have surveyed (including myself in a prior book!) do not mention them or relegate them to an appendix.

The `strtod` function takes a second argument, a pointer-to-pointer-to-char, which will point to the first character that the parser could not interpret as part of a number. This can be used to continue parsing the rest of the text, or to check for errors if you expect that the string should consist only of a number. If that variable is declared as `char *end`, then at the end of reading a string that could be read in its entirety as a number, end points to the '\0' at the end of the string, so we can test for failure with a condition like `if (*end) printf("read failure.")`.

Example 7-6 gives a sample usage, in the form of a simple program to square a number given on the command line.

*Example 7-6. Using strtod to read in a number (strtod.c)*

```
#include "stopif.h"
#include <stdlib.h> //strtod
#include <math.h>    //pow

int main(int argc, char **argv){
    Stopif (argc < 2, return 1, "Give me a number on the command line to square.");
    char *end;
    double in = strtod(argv[1], &end);
    Stopif(*end, return 2, "I couldn't parse '%s' to a number. "
                "I had trouble with '%s'.", argv[1], end);
    printf("The square of %s is %g\n", argv[1], pow(in, 2));
}
```

Since C99, there have also been `strtof` and `strtold` to convert to float and long double. The integer versions, `strtol` or `strtoll`, to convert to a `long int` or a `long long int`, take three arguments: the string to convert, the pointer-to-end, and a base.

The traditional base is base 10, but you can set this to 2 to read binary numbers, 8 to read octal, 16 to read hexadecimal, and so on up to base 36.

---

# Marking Exceptional Numeric Values with NaNs

*Gonna make it through, gonna make it through. Divide by zero like a wrecking crew.*
—*The Offspring, "Dividing by Zero"*

The IEEE floating-point standard gives precise rules for how floating-point numbers are represented, including special forms for infinity, negative infinity, and Not-a-Number—NaN, which indicates a math error like 0/0 or log(-1). IEEE 754/IEC 60559 (as the standard is called, because the sort of people who deal with these things are fine with their standards having a number as a name) is distinct from the C or POSIX standards, but it is supported almost everywhere. If you are working on a Cray or some special-purpose embedded devices, you'll have to ignore the details of this section (but even AVR libc for Arduino and other microcontrollers defines NAN and INFINITY).

As in Example 10-1, NaN can be useful as a marker to indicate the end of a list, provided we are confident that the main part of the list will have all not-NaN values.

The other thing everybody needs to know about NaN is that testing for equality *always* fails—after setting x=NAN, even x==x will evaluate to false. Use isnan($x$) to test whether $x$ is NaN.

Those of you elbow deep in numeric data may be interested in other ways we can use NaNs as markers.

The IEEE standard has a *lot* of forms for NaN: the sign bit can be 0 or 1, then the exponent is all 1s, and the rest is nonzero, so you have a bunch of bits like this: S11111111MMMMMMMMMMMMMMMMMMMMMMM, where S is the sign and M the unspecified mantissa.

A zero mantissa indicates ±infinity, depending on the sign bit, but we can otherwise specify those Ms to be anything we want. Once we have a way to control those free bits, we can add all kinds of distinct semaphores into a cell of a numeric array.

The graceful way to generate a specific NAN is via the function nan(*tagp*) that returns a NAN "with content indicated through *tagp*." [C99 and C11 §7.12.11.2] The input should be a string representing a floating-point number—the nan function is a wrapper for strtod—which will be written to the mantissa of the NaN.

---

The program in Example 7-7 generates and uses an NA (not available) marker, which is useful in contexts where we need to distinguish between data that is missing and math errors.

*Example 7-7. Make an NA marker to annotate your floating-point data (na.c)*

```c
#include <stdio.h>
#include <math.h> //NAN, isnan, nan

double ref;

double set_na(){
    if (!ref) ref=nan("21");
    return ref;
}

int is_na(double in){                    ❶
    if (!ref) return 0;   //set_na was never called==>no NAs yet.

    char *cc = (char *)(&in);
    char *cr = (char *)(&ref);
    for (int i=0; i< sizeof(double); i++)
        if (cc[i] != cr[i]) return 0;
    return 1;
}

int main(){
    double x = set_na();
    double y = x;
    printf("Is x=set_na() NA? %i\n", is_na(x));
    printf("Is x=set_na() NAN? %i\n", isnan(x));
    printf("Is y=x NA? %i\n", is_na(y));
    printf("Is 0/0 NA? %i\n", is_na(0/0.));
    printf("Is 8 NA? %i\n", is_na(8));
}
```

❶ The is_na function checks whether the bit pattern of the number we're testing matches the special bit pattern that set_na made up. It does this by treating both inputs as character strings and doing character-by-character comparison.

I produced a single semaphore to store in a numeric data point, using 21 as the haphazardly chosen key. We can insert as many other distinct markers as desired directly into our data set using a minor modification of the preceding code to mark all sorts of different exceptions.

In fact, some widely used systems (such as WebKit) go much further than just a semaphore and actually insert an entire pointer into the mantissa of their NaNs. This method, *NaN boxing*, is left as an exercise for the reader.

# CHAPTER 8

# Important C Syntax that Textbooks Often Do Not Cover

The last chapter covered some topics that traditional C textbooks stressed but which may not be relevant in a current computing environment. This chapter covers some points that I have found many textbooks do not cover or only mention in passing. Like the last chapter, this chapter covers a lot of little topics, but it breaks down into three main segments:

- The preprocessor often gets short mention, I think because many people think of it as auxiliary or not real C. But it's there for a reason: there are things that macros can do that the rest of the C language can't. Not all standards-compliant compilers offer the same facilities, and the preprocessor is also how we determine and respond to the characteristics of the environment.

- In my survey of C textbooks, I found a book or two that do not even mention the `static` and `extern` keywords. So this chapter takes some time to discuss *linkage*, and break down the confusing uses of the `static` keyword.

- The `const` keyword fits this chapter because it is too useful to not use, but it has oddities in its specification in the standard and in its implementation in common compilers.

## Cultivate Robust and Flourishing Macros

Some situations have common trap doors that users must know to avoid, but if you can provide a macro that always dodges the trap, you have a safer user interface. Chapter 10 will present several options for making the user interface to your library friendlier and less error-inviting, and will rely heavily on macros to do it.

I read a lot of people who say that macros are themselves invitations for errors and should be avoided, but those people don't advise that you shouldn't use NULL, isalpha, isfinite, assert, type-generic math like log, sin, cos, or pow, or any of the dozens of other facilities defined by the GNU-standard library via macros. Those are well-written, robust macros that do what they should every time.

Macros perform text substitutions (referred to as *expansions* under the presumption that the substituted text will be longer), and text substitutions require a different mind-set from the usual functions, because the input text can interact with the text in the macro and other text in the source code. Macros are best used in cases where we want those interactions, and when we don't we need to take care to prevent them.

Before getting to the rules for making macros robust, of which there are three, let me distinguish between two types of macro. One type expands to an expression, meaning that it makes sense to evaluate these macros, print their values, or in the case of numeric results, use them in the middle of an equation. The other type is a block of instructions, that might appear after an if statement or in a while loop. That said, here are some rules:

- Parens! It's easy for expectations to be broken when a macro pastes text into place. Here's an easy example:

  ```
  #define double(x) 2*x                    Needs more parens.
  ```

  Now, the user tries double(1+1)*8, and the macro expands it to 2*1+1*8, equals 10, not 32. Parens make it work:

  ```
  #define double(x) (2*(x))
  ```

  Now (2*(1+1))*8 is what it should be. The general rule is to put all inputs in parens unless you have a specific reason not to. If you have an expression-type macro, put the macro expansion itself in parens.

- Avoid double usage. This textbook example is a little risky:

  ```
  #define max(a, b)    ((a) > (b) ? (a) : (b))
  ```

  If the user tries int x=1, y=2; int m=max(x, y++), the expectation is that m will be 2 (the preincrement value of y), and then y will bump up to 3. But the macro expands to:

  ```
  m = ((x) > (y++) ? (x) : (y++))
  ```

  which will evaluate y++ twice, causing a double increment where the user expected only a single, and m=3 where the user expected m=2.

  If you have a block-type macro, then you can declare a variable to take on the value of the input at the head of the block, and then use your copy of the input for the rest of the macro.

---

This rule is not adhered to as religiously as the parens rule—the max macro often appears in the wild—so bear in mind as a macro user that side effects inside calls to unknown macros should be kept to a minimum.

- Curly braces for blocks. Here's a simple block macro:

```
#define doubleincrement(a, b) \      Needs curly braces.
    (a)++;                    \
    (b)++;
```

We can make it do the wrong thing by putting it after an `if` statement:

```
int x=1, y=0;
if (x>y)
    doubleincrement(x, y);
```

Adding some indentation to make the error obvious, this expands to:

```
int x=1, y=0;
if (x>y)
    (x)++;
(y)++;
```

Another potential pitfall: what if your macro declares a variable `total`, but the user defined a `total` already? Variables declared in the block can conflict with variables declared outside the block. Example 8-1 has the simple solution to both problems: put curly braces around your macro.

Putting the whole macro in curly braces allows us to have an intermediate variable named `total` that lives only inside the scope of the curly braces around the macro, and it therefore in no way interferes with the `total` declared in `main`.

*Example 8-1. We can control the scope of variables with curly braces, just as with typical nonmacro code (curly.c)*

```
#include <stdio.h>

#define sum(max, out) {           \
    int total=0;                  \
    for (int i=0; i<= max; i++)   \
        total += i;               \
    out = total;                  \
}

int main(){
    int out;
    int total = 5;
    sum(5, out);
    printf("out= %i original total=%i\n", out, total);
}
```

But there is one small glitch remaining. Getting back to the simple `doubleincre`
`ment` macro, this code:

```
#define doubleincrement(a, b) { \
    (a)++;                      \
    (b)++;                      \
}

if (a>b) doubleincrement(a, b);
else      return 0;
```

expands to this:

```
if (a>b) {
    (a)++;
    (b)++;
};
else      return 0;
```

The extra semicolon just before the `else` confuses the compiler. Users will get a
compiler error, which means that they cannot ship erroneous code, but the solution of removing the semicolon or wrapping the statement in a seemingly extraneous set of curly braces will not be apparent and makes for a not-transparent
UI. To tell you the truth, there's not much you can do about this. The common
solution to this is to wrap the macro still further in a run-once `do-while` loop:

```
#define doubleincrement(a, b) do { \
    (a)++;                          \
    (b)++;                          \
} while(0)

if (a>b) doubleincrement(a, b);
else      return 0;
```

In this case, the problem is solved, and we have a macro that users won't know is
a macro. But what if we have a macro which has a `break` either built in or somehow provided by the user? Here is another assertion macro, and a usage which
won't work:

```
#define AnAssert(expression, action) do { \
    if (!(expression)) action;             \
} while(0)

double an_array[100];
double total=0;
...
for (int i=0; i< 100; i++){
    AnAssert(!(isnan(an_array[i])), break);
    total += an_array[i];
}
```

The user is unaware that the break statement provided is embedded in an internal-to-macro do-while loop, and thus may compile and run incorrect code. In cases where a do-while wrapper would break the expected behavior of break, it is probably easier to leave off the do-while wrapper and warn users about the quirk regarding semicolons before an else.[1]

Using gcc -E curly.c, we see that the preprocessor expands the sum macro as shown next, and following the curly braces shows us that there's no chance that the total in the macro's scope will interfere with the total in the main scope. So the code would print total as 5:

```
int main(){
    int out;
    int total = 5;
    { int total=0; for (int i=0; i<= 5; i++) total += i; out = total; };
    printf("out= %i total=%i\n", out, total);
}
```

 Limiting a macro's scope with curly braces doesn't protect us from all name clashes. In the previous example, what would happen if we were to write int out, i=5; sum(i, out);?

If you have a macro that is behaving badly, use the -E flag for gcc, Clang, or icc to only run the preprocessor, printing the expanded version of everything to stdout. Because that includes the expansion of #include <stdio.h> and other voluminous boilerplate, I usually redirect the results to a file or to a pager, with a form like gcc -E *mycode.c* |less, and then search the results for the macro expansion I'm trying to debug.

That's about it for macro caveats. The basic principle of keeping macros simple still makes sense, and you'll find that macros in production code tend to be one-liners that prep the inputs in some way and then call a standard function to do the real work. The debugger and non-C systems that can't parse macro definitions themselves don't have access to your macro, so whatever you write should still have a way of being usable without the macros. "Linkage with static and extern" on page 176 will have one suggestion for reducing the hassle when writing down simple functions.

---

1 There is also the option of wrapping the block in if (1){ … } else (void)0, which again absorbs a semicolon. This technically works, but triggers warnings when the macro is itself embedded in an if-else statement when using the -Wall compiler flag, and so is also not transparent to users.

# The Preprocessor

The token reserved for the preprocessor is the octothorp, #, and the preprocessor makes three entirely different uses of it: to mark directives, to stringize an input, and to concatenate tokens.

You know that a preprocessor directive like #define begins with a # at the head of the line.

As an aside, whitespace before the # is ignored [K&R 2nd ed. §A12, p. 228], which has some typographical utility. For example, you can put throwaway macros in the middle of a function, just before they get used, and indent them to flow with the function. According to the old school, putting the macro right where it gets used is against the "correct" organization of a program (which puts all macros at the head of the file), but having it right there makes it easy to refer to and makes the throwaway nature of the macro evident. In "OpenMP" on page 294, we'll annotate for loops with #pragmas, and putting the # flush with the left margin would produce an unreadable mess.

The next use of the # is in a macro: it turns a macro argument into a string. Example 8-2 shows a program demonstrating a point about the use of sizeof (see the sidebar), though the main focus is on the use of the preprocessor macro.

*Example 8-2. In which text is both printed and evaluated (sizesof.c)*

```c
#include <stdio.h>

#define Peval(cmd) printf(#cmd ": %g\n", cmd);

int main(){
    double *plist = (double[]){1, 2, 3};          ❶
    double list[] = {1, 2, 3};
    Peval(sizeof(plist)/(sizeof(double)+0.0));
    Peval(sizeof(list)/(sizeof(double)+0.0));
}
```

❶ This is a compound literal. If you're unfamiliar with them, I'll introduce them to you later. When considering how sizeof treats plist, bear in mind that plist is a pointer to an array, not the array itself.

When you try it, you'll see that the input to the macro is printed as plain text, and then its value is printed, because #cmd is equivalent to "cmd" as a string. So Peval(list[0]) would expand to:

```c
printf("list[0]" ": %g\n", list[0]);
```

Does that look malformed to you, with the two strings `"list[0]"` `": %g\n"` next to each other? The next preprocessor feature is that if two literal strings are adjacent, the preprocessor merges them into one: `"list[0]: %g\n"`. And this isn't just in macros:

```
printf("You can use the preprocessor's string "
       "concatenation to break long strings of text "
       "in your program. I think this is easier than "
       "using backslashes, but be careful with spacing.");
```

---

## The Limits of sizeof

Did you try the sample code? It is based on a common trick in which you can get the size of an automatic or static array by dividing its total size by the size of one element (see c-faq (*http://bit.ly/q-623*); K&R 1st ed. p. 126, 2nd ed. p 135; example 2 in C99 & C11 §6.5.3.4), e.g.:

```
//This is not reliable:
#define arraysize(list) sizeof(list)/sizeof(list[0])
```

The `sizeof` operator (it's a C keyword, not a plain function) refers to the automatically allocated variable (which might be an array or a pointer), not to the data a pointer might be pointing to. For an automatic array like `double list[100]`, the compiler had to allocate a hundred `doubles`, and will have to make sure that much space (probably 800 bytes) is not trampled by the next variable to go on the stack. For manually allocated memory (`double *plist; plist = malloc(sizeof(double *100));`), the pointer on the stack is maybe 8 bytes long (certainly not 100), and `sizeof` will return the length of that pointer, not the length of what it is pointing to.

Some cats, when you point to a toy, will go and inspect the toy; some cats will sniff your finger.

---

Conversely, you might want to join together two things that are not strings. Here, use two octothorps, which I herein dub the hexadecathorp: `##`. If the value of `name` is `LL`, then when you see `name ## _list`, read it as `LL_list`, which is a valid and usable variable name.

*Gee*, you comment, *I sure wish every array had an auxiliary variable that gave its length.* OK, Example 8-3 writes a macro that declares a local variable ending in `_len` for each list you tell it to care about. It'll even make sure every list has a terminating marker, so you don't even need the length.

That is, this macro is total overkill, and I don't recommend it for immediate use, but it does demonstrate how you can generate lots of little temp variables that follow a naming pattern that you choose.

*Example 8-3. Creating auxiliary variables using the preprocessor (preprocess.c)*

```c
#include <stdio.h>
#include <math.h> //NAN

#define Setup_list(name, ...)                                      \
    double *name ## _list = (double []){__VA_ARGS__, NAN};     \  ❶
    int name ## _len = 0;                                          \
    for (name ## _len =0;                                          \
            !isnan(name ## _list[name ## _len]);                   \
            ) name ## _len ++;


int main(){
    Setup_list(items, 1, 2, 4, 8);                                    ❷
    double sum=0;
    for (double *ptr= items_list; !isnan(*ptr); ptr++)                ❸
        sum += *ptr;
    printf("total for items list: %g\n", sum);

    #define Length(in) in ## _len                                     ❹

    sum=0;
    Setup_list(next_set, -1, 2.2, 4.8, 0.1);
    for (int i=0; i < Length(next_set); i++)                          ❺
        sum += next_set_list[i];
    printf("total for next set list: %g\n", sum);
}
```

❶ The lefthand side demonstrates the use of ## to produce a variable name follow-ing the given template. The right-hand side foreshadows Chapter 10, which dem-onstrates uses of variadic macros.

❷ Generates items_len and items_list.

❸ Here is a loop using the NaN marker.

❹ Some systems let you query an array for its own length using a form like this.

❺ Here is a loop using the next_set_len length variable.

As a stylistic aside, there has historically been a custom to indicate that a function is actually a macro by putting it in all caps, as a warning to be careful to watch for the surprises associated with text substitution. I think this looks like yelling, and prefer to mark macros by capitalizing the first letter. Others don't bother with the capitaliza-tion thing at all.

## Macro Arguments Are Optional

Here's a sensible assertion-type macro that returns if an assertion fails:

```
#define Testclaim(assertion, returnval) if (!(assertion))         \
        {fprintf(stderr, #assertion " failed to be true. \
        Returning " #returnval "\n"); return returnval;}
```

Sample usage:

```
int do_things(){
    int x, y;
    ...
    Testclaim(x==y, -1);
    ...
    return 0;
}
```

But what if you have a function that has no return value? In this case, you can leave the second argument blank:

```
void do_other_things(){
    int x, y;
    ...
    Testclaim(x==y, );
    ...
    return;
}
```

Then the last line of the macro expands to `return ;`, which is valid and appropriate for a function that returns `void`.[2]

If so inclined, you could even use this to implement default values:

```
#define Blankcheck(a) {int aval = (#a[0]=='\0') ? 2 : (a+0);  \
        printf("I understand your input to be %i.\n", aval); \
        }
```

```
//Usage:

Blankcheck(0); //will set aval to zero.
Blankcheck( ); //will set aval to two.
```

---

2 On the validity of blank macro arguments, see C99 and C11 §6.10.3(4), which explicitly allow "arguments consisting of no preprocessing tokens."

# Test Macros

The set of things that can run a C program is very diverse—from Linux PCs to Arduino microcontrollers to GE refrigerators. Your C code finds out the capabilities of the compiler and target platform via test macros, which may be defined by the compiler, -D... flags in the compilation command, or #included files listing local capabilities, like *unistd.h* on POSIX systems or *windows.h* (and the headers it calls in) on Windows.

Once you have a handle on what macros can be tested for, you can use the preprocessor to handle diverse environments.

gcc and clang will give you a list of defined macros via the -E -dM flags (-E: run only the preprocessor; -dM: dump macro values). On the box I'm writing on,

```
echo "" | clang -dM -E -xc -
```

produces 157 macros.

It would be impossible to write down a complete list of feature macros, including those defined for the hardware, the brand of standard C library, and the compiler, but Table 8-1 lists some of the more common and stable macros and their meaning. I chose macros that are relevant to this book or are broad checks for system type. The ones that begin with __STDC_... are defined by the C standard.

*Table 8-1. Some commonly defined feature macros*

| Macro | Meaning |
|-------|---------|
| _POSIX_C_SOURCE | Conforms with IEEE 1003.1, aka ISO/IEC 9945. Usually set to a revision date. |
| _WINDOWS | A Windows box, with the *windows.h* header and everything defined therein. |
| __MACOSX__ | A Mac running OS X. |
| __STDC_HOSTED__ | The program is being compiled for a computer with an operating system that will call main. |
| __STDC_IEC_559__ | Conforms to IEEE 754, the floating-point standard that eventually became ISO/IEC/IEEE 60559. Notably, the processor can represent NaN, INFINITY, and -INFINITY. |
| __STDC_VERSION__ | The version of the standard the compiler implements: many use 199409L for C89 (as fixed in a 1995 revision), 199901L for C99, 201112L for C11 as of this writing. |
| __STDC_NO_ATOMICS__ | Set to 1 if the implementation does not support _Atomic variables and does not provide *stdatomic.h* |
| __STDC_NO_COMPLEX__ | Set to 1 if the implementation does not support complex types. |

| Macro | Meaning |
|---|---|
| __STDC_NO_VLA__ | Set to 1 if the implementation does not support variable-length arrays. |
| __STDC_NO_THREADS__ | Set to 1 if the implementation does not support the C-standard *threads.h* and the elements defined therein. You may be able to use POSIX threads, OpenMP, fork, and other alternatives. |

One of Autoconf's key strengths is generating macros to describe capabilities. Let us say that you are using Autoconf, that your *config.ac* file includes a line with this macro:

```
AC_CHECK_FUNCS([strcasecmp asprintf])
```

and that the system where ./configure was run has (POSIX-standard) strcasecmp but is missing (GNU/BSD-standard) asprintf. Then Autoconf will produce a header named *config.h* including these two lines:

```
#define HAVE_STRCASECMP 1
/* #undef HAVE_ASPRINTF */
```

You can then accommodate all options using the #ifdef (if defined) or #ifndef (if not defined) preprocessor directives, like:

```
#include "config.h"

#ifndef HAVE_ASPRINTF
[paste the source code for asprintf (Example 9-3) here.]
#endif
```

There are times when there is nothing to be done about a missing feature but to stop, in which case you can use the #error preprocessor directive:

```
#ifndef HAVE_ASPRINTF
    #error "HAVE_ASPRINTF undefined. I simply refuse to " \
           "compile on a system without asprintf."
#endif
```

Since C11, there is also the _Static_assert keyword. A static assertion takes two arguments: the static expression to be tested, and a message to be sent to the person compiling the program. A C11-compliant *assert.h* header defines the less typographically awkward static_assert to expand to the _Static_assert keyword [C11 §7.2(3)]. Sample usage:

```
#include <limits.h> //INT_MAX
#include <assert.h>

_Static_assert(INT_MAX < 33000L, "Your compiler uses very short integers.");

#ifndef HAVE_ASPRINTF
static_assert(0, "HAVE_ASPRINTF undefined. I still refuse to "
```

```
                      "compile on a system without asprintf.");
      #endif
```

The Ls at the end of 33000L and some of the year-month values above indicate that the given numbers should be read as a long int, in case you are on a compiler where integers this large overflow on a regular int.

This may be a more convenient form than the #if/#error/#endif form, but because it was introduced in a standard published in December 2011, it is itself a portability issue. For example, the designers of Visual Studio implement a _STATIC_ASSERT macro which only takes one argument (the assertion), and do not recognize the standard _Static_assert.[3]

Also, the #ifdef/#error/#endif setup and _Static_assert are largely equivalent: The C standard indicates that both check *constant-expressions* and print a *string-literal*, though one should do so in the preprocessing phase and one during compilation. [C99 §6.10.1(2) and C11 §6.10.1(3); C11 §6.7.10] So as of this writing, it is probably safest to stick to using the preprocessor to stop on missing capabilities.

## Header Guards

What if you were to paste the same typedef for the same struct into a file? For instance, you could put

```
typedef struct {
    int a;
    double b;
} ab_s;

typedef struct {
    int a;
    double b;
} ab_s;
```

into a file named *header.h*.

A human can easily verify that these structs are the same, but the compiler is required to read any new struct declaration in a file as a new type [C99 §6.7.2.1(7) and C11 §6.7.2.1(8)]. So the above code won't compile, as ab_s is redeclared to be two separate (albeit equal) types.[4]

---

3 See the Microsoft Developer Network (*http://bit.ly/static-a*).

4 If the types are the same, then the duplicate typedefs are not a problem, as per C11 §6.7(3): "A typedef name may be redefined to denote the same type as it currently does, provided that type is not a variably modified type."

We can achieve the error of double-declaring by listing the typedef only once, but then including the header twice, like

```
#include "header.h"
#include "header.h"
```

Because include files frequently include other include files, this error can crop up in subtle ways involving longer chains of headers within headers. The C-standard solution to ensure that this cannot happen is generally referred to as an *include guard*, in which we define a variable specific to the file, and then wrap the rest of the file in an #ifndef:

```
#ifndef Already_included_head_h
#define Already_included_head_h 1

[paste all of header.h here]

#endif
```

The first time through, the variable is not defined and the file is parsed; the second time through the variable is defined and so the rest of the file is skipped.

This form has been in use since forever (see K & R 2nd ed., §4.11.3), but it is slightly easier to use the once pragma. At the head of the file to be included only once, add

```
#pragma once
```

and the compiler will understand that the file is not to be double-included. Pragmas are compiler-specific, with only a few defined in the C standard. However, every major compiler, including gcc, clang, Intel, C89-mode Visual Studio, and several others, all understand #pragma once.

## Comment Out Code with the Preprocessor

A block surrounded by #if 0 and #endif is ignored, so you can use this form to comment out a block of code. Unlike comments via /* ... */, this style of commenting can be nested:

```
#if 0
    ...
    #if 0
        /* code that was already ignored */
    #endif
    ...
#endif
```

But if the nesting is not correct, like

```
#if 0
    ...
    #ifdef This_line_has_no_matching_endif
```

```
     · · ·
  #endif
```
you will get an error as the preprocessor matches the #endif with the wrong #if.

## Linkage with static and extern

In this section, we write code that will tell the compiler what kind of advice it should give to the linker. The compiler works one *.c* file at a time, (typically) producing one *.o* file at at a time, then the linker joins those *.o* files together to produce one library or executable.

What happens if there are two declarations in two separate files for the variable x? It could be that the author of one file just didn't know that the author of the other file had chosen x, so the two xes should be stored in two separate spaces. Or perhaps the authors were well aware that they are referring to the same variable, and the linker should take all references of x to be pointing to the same spot in memory.

*External linkage* means that symbols that match across files should be treated as the same thing by the linker. The extern keyword will be useful to indicate external linkage (see later).[5]

*Internal linkage* indicates that a file's instance of a variable x or a function f() is its own and matches only other instances of x or f() in the same scope (which for things declared outside of any functions would be file scope). Use the static keyword to indicate internal linkage.

It's funny that external linkage has the extern keyword, but instead of something sensible like intern for internal linkage, there's static. In "Automatic, Static, and Manual Memory" on page 125, I discussed the three types of memory model: static, automatic, and manual. Using the word static for both linkage and memory model is joining together two concepts that may at one time have overlapped for technical reasons, but are now distinct.

- For file scope variables, static affects only the linkage:
  - The default linkage is external, so use the static keyword to change this to internal linkage.
  - Any variable in file scope will be allocated using the static memory model, regardless of whether you used static *int x,* extern *int x,* or just plain *int x.*

---

5 This is from C99 and C11 §6.2.3, which is actually about resolving symbols across different scopes, not just files. But trying crazy linkage tricks across different scopes within one file is generally not done.

---

- For block scope variables, `static` affects only the memory model:

  — The default linkage is internal, so the `static` keyword doesn't affect linkage. You could change the linkage by declaring the variable to be `extern`, but this is rarely done.

  — The default memory model is automatic, so the `static` keyword changes the memory model to static.

- For functions, `static` affects only the linkage:

  — Functions are only defined in file scope (though `gcc` offers nested functions as an extension). As with file-scope variables, the default linkage is external, but use the `static` keyword for internal linkage.

  — There's no confusion with memory models, because functions are always static, like file-scope variables.

The norm for declaring a function to be shared across *.c* files is to put the header in a *.h* file to be reincluded all over your project, and put the function itself in one *.c* file (where it will have the default external linkage). This is a good norm, and is worth sticking to, but it is reasonably common for authors to want to put one- or two-line utility functions (like `max` and `min`) in a *.h* file to be included everywhere. You can do this by preceding the declaration of your function with the `static` keyword, for example:

```
//In common_fns.h:
static long double max(long double a, long double b){
    (a > b) ? a : b;
}
```

When you `#include "common_fns.h"` in each of a dozen files, the compiler will produce a new instance of the `max` function in each of them. But because you've given the function internal linkage, none of the files has made public the function name `max`, so all dozen separate instances of the function can live independently with no conflicts. Such redeclaration might add a few bytes to your executable and a few milliseconds to your compilation time, but that's irrelevant in typical environments.

## Externally Linked Variables in Header Files

The `extern` keyword is a simpler issue than `static`, because it is only about linkage, not memory models. The typical setup for a variable with external linkage:

- In a header to be included anywhere the variable will be used, declare your variable with the `extern` keyword. E.g., `extern int x`.

- In exactly one .c file, declare the variable as usual, with an optional initializer. E.g., `int x=3`. As with all static-memory variables, if you leave off the initial value (just `int x`), the variable is initialized to zero or NULL.

That's all you have to do to use variables with external linkage.

You may be tempted to put the `extern` declaration not in a header, but just as a loose declaration in your code. In *file1.c*, you have declared `int x`, and you realize that you need access to x in *file2.c*, so you throw a quick `extern int x` at the top of the file. This will work—today. Next month, when you change *file1.c* to declare `double x`, the compiler's type checking will still find *file2.c* to be entirely internally consistent. The linker blithely points the routine in *file2.c* to the location where the `double` named x is stored, and the routine blithely misreads the data there as an `int`. You can avoid this disaster by leaving all `extern` declarations in a header to `#include` in both *file1.c* and *file2.c*. If any types change anywhere, the compiler will then be able to catch the inconsistency.

Under the hood, the system is doing a lot of work to make it easy for you to declare one variable several times while allocating memory for it only once. Formally, a declaration marked as `extern` is a declaration (a statement of type information so the compiler can do consistency checking), and not a definition (instructions to allocate and initialize space in memory). But a declaration without the `extern` keyword is a *tentative definition*: if the compiler gets to the end of the unit (defined below) and doesn't see a definition, then the tentative definitions get turned into a single definition, with the usual initialization to zero or NULL. The standard defines *unit* in that sentence as a single file, after `#include`s are all pasted in [a translation unit; see C99 and C11 §6.9.2(2)].

Compilers like `gcc` and `clang` typically read *unit* to mean the entire program, meaning that a program with several non-extern declarations and no definitions rolls all these tentative definitions up into a single definition. Even with the `--pedantic` flag, `gcc` doesn't care whether you use the `extern` keyword or leave it off entirely. In practice, that means that the `extern` keyword is largely optional: your compiler will read a dozen declarations like `int x=3` as a single definition of a single variable with external linkage. This is technically nonstandard, but K&R (2nd ed, p 227) describe this behavior as "usual in UNIX systems and recognized as a common extension by the [ANSI '89] Standard." (Harbison, 1991) §4.8 documents four distinct interpretations of the rules for `extern`s.

This means that if you want two variables with the same name in two files to be distinct, but you forget the `static` keyword, a compiler may link those variables together as a single variable with external linkage; subtle bugs can easily ensue. So be careful to use `static` for all file-scope variables intended to have internal linkage.

---

# The const Keyword

The const keyword is fundamentally useful, but the rules around const have several surprises and inconsistencies. This segment will point them out so they won't be surprises anymore, which should make it easier for you to use const wherever good style advises that you do.

Early in your life, you learned that *copies* of input data are passed to functions, but you can still have functions that change input data by sending in a *copy of a pointer* to the data. When you see that an input is plain, not-pointer data, then you know that the caller's original version of the variable won't change. When you see a pointer input, it's unclear. Lists and strings are naturally pointers, so the pointer input could be data to be modified, or it could just be a string.

The const keyword is a literary device for you, the author, to make your code more readable. It is a *type qualifier* indicating that the data pointed to by the input pointer will not change over the course of the function. It is useful information to know when data shouldn't change, so do use this keyword where possible.

The first caveat: the compiler does not lock down the data being pointed to against all modification. Data that is marked as const under one name can be modified using a different name. In Example 8-4, a and b point to the same data, but because a is not const in the header for set_elmt, it can change an element of the b array. See Figure 8-1.

*Example 8-4. Data that is marked as const under one name can be modified using a different name (constchange.c)*

```
void set_elmt(int *a, int const *b){
    a[0] = 3;
}

int main(){
    int a[10] = {};      ❶
    int const *b = a;
    set_elmt(a, b);
}                        ❷
```

❶ Initialize the array to all zeros.

❷ This is a do-nothing program intended only to compile and run without errors. If you want to verify that b[0] did change, you can run this in your debugger, break at the last line, and print the value of b.

So const is a literary device, not a lock on the data.

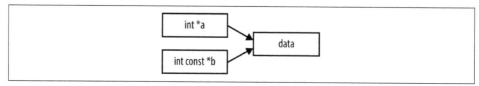

*Figure 8-1. We can modify the data via a, even though b is const; this is valid*

## Noun-Adjective Form

The trick to reading declarations is to read from right to left. Thus:

`int const`
  A constant integer

`int const *`
  A (variable) pointer to a constant integer

`int * const`
  A constant pointer to a (variable) integer

`int * const *`
  A pointer to a constant pointer to an integer

`int const * *`
  A pointer to a pointer to a constant integer

`int const * const *`
  A pointer to a constant pointer to a constant integer

You can see that the `const` always refers to the text to its left, just as the `*` does.

You can switch a type name and `const`, and so write either `int const` or `const int` (though you can't do this switch with `const` and `*`). I prefer the `int const` form because it provides consistency with the more complex constructions and the right-to-left rule. There's a custom to use the `const int` form, perhaps because it reads more easily in English or because that's how it's always been done. Either works.

---

### What About restrict and inline?

I wrote some sample code both using the `restrict` and `inline` keywords and not using them, so that I could demonstrate to you the speed difference that these keywords make.

I had high hopes, and in years past, I found real gains from using `restrict` in numeric routines. But when I wrote up the tests here in the present day, the difference in speed with and without the keywords was minuscule.

---

As per my recommendations throughout the book, I set CFLAGS=-g -Wall -O3 when compiling, and that means gcc threw every optimization trick it knew at my sample programs, and those optimizations knew when to treat pointers as restrict and when to inline functions without my explicitly instructing the compiler.

## Tension

In practice, you will find that const sometimes creates tension that needs to be resolved: when you have a pointer that is marked const but want to send it as an input to a function that does not have a const marker in the right place. Maybe the function author thought that the keyword was too much trouble, or believed the chatter about how shorter code is always better code, or just forgot.

Before proceeding, you'll have to ask yourself if there is any way that the pointer could change in the const-less function being called. There might be an edge case where something gets changed, or some other odd reason. This is stuff worth knowing anyway.

If you've established that the function does not break the promise of const-ness that you made with your pointer, then it is entirely appropriate to cheat and cast your const pointer to a non-const for the sake of quieting the compiler.

```
//No const in the header this time...
void set_elmt(int *a, int *b){
    a[0] = 3;
}

int main(){
    int a[10];
    int const *b = a;
    set_elmt(a, (int*)b);      //...so add a type-cast to the call.
}
```

The rule seems reasonable to me. You can override the compiler's const-checking, as long as you are explicit about it and indicate that you know what you are doing.

If you are worried that the function you are calling won't fulfill your promise of const-ness, then you can take one step further and make a full copy of the data, not just an alias. Because you don't want any changes in the variable anyway, you can throw out the copy afterward.

## Depth

Let us say that we have a struct type—name it counter_s—and we have a function that takes in such a struct, of the form f(counter_s const *in). Can the function modify the elements of the structure?

Let's try it: Example 8-5 generates a struct with two pointers, and in `ratio`, that struct becomes `const`, yet when we send one of the pointers held by the structure to the `const`-less subfunction, the compiler doesn't complain.

*Example 8-5. The elements of a const struct are not const (conststruct.c)*

```
#include <assert.h>
#include <stdlib.h>   //assert

typedef struct {
    int *counter1, *counter2;
} counter_s;

void check_counter(int *ctr){ assert(*ctr !=0); }

double ratio(counter_s const *in){          ❶
    check_counter(in->counter2);            ❷
    return *in->counter1/(*in->counter2+0.0);
}

int main(){
    counter_s cc = {.counter1=malloc(sizeof(int)),   ❸
                    .counter2=malloc(sizeof(int))};
    *cc.counter1 = *cc.counter2 = 1;
    ratio(&cc);
}
```

❶ The incoming struct is marked as `const`.

❷ We send an element of the `const` struct to a function that takes not-`const` inputs. The compiler does not complain.

❸ This is declaration via designated initializers—coming soon.

In the definition of your struct, you can specify that an element be `const`, though this is typically more trouble than it is worth. If you really need to protect only the lowest level in your hierarchy of types, your best bet is to put a note in the documentation.

## The char const ** Issue

Example 8-6 is a simple program to check whether the user gave Iggy Pop's name on the command line. Sample usage from the shell (recalling that $? is the return value of the just-run program):

```
iggy_pop_detector Iggy Pop; echo $?       #prints 1
iggy_pop_detector Chaim Weitz; echo $?     #prints 0
```

*Example 8-6. Ambiguity in the standard causes all sorts of problems for the pointer-to-pointer-to-const (iggy_pop_detector.c)*

```
#include <stdbool.h>
#include <strings.h> //strcasecmp (from POSIX)

bool check_name(char const **in){  ❶
    return   (!strcasecmp(in[0], "Iggy") && !strcasecmp(in[1], "Pop"))
           ||(!strcasecmp(in[0], "James") && !strcasecmp(in[1], "Osterberg")));
}

int main(int argc, char **argv){
    if (argc < 2) return 0;
    return check_name(&argv[1]);
}
```

❶ If you haven't seen Booleans before, I'll introduce you to them in a sidebar later.

The check_name function takes in a pointer to constant string, because there is no need to modify the input strings. But when you compile it, you'll find that you get a warningclang says: "passing char ** to parameter of type const char ** discards qualifiers in nested pointer types." In a sequence of pointers, all the compilers I could find will convert to const what you could call the top-level pointer (casting to char * const *), but complain when asked to const-ify what that pointer is pointing to (char const **, aka const char **).

Again, you'll need to make an explicit cast—replace check_name(&argv[1]) with:

```
check_name((char const**)&argv[1]);
```

Why doesn't this entirely sensible cast happen automatically? We need some creative setup before a problem arises, and the story is inconsistent with the rules to this point. So the explanation is a slog; I will understand if you skip it.

The code in Example 8-7 creates the three links in the diagram: the direct link from constptr -> fixed, and the two steps in the indirect link from constptr -> var and var -> fixed. In the code, you can see that two of the assignments are made explicitly: constptr -> var and constptr -> -> fixed. But because *constptr == var, that second link implicitly creates the var -> fixed link. When we assign *var=30, that assigns fixed = 30.

*Example 8-7. We can modify the data via an alternate name, even though it is const via one name—this is deemed to be illegal. The relationships among the variables are displayed in Figure 8-2. (constfusion.c)*

```
#include <stdio.h>

int main(){
    int *var;
```

```
    int const **constptr = &var; // the line that sets up the failure
    int const fixed = 20;
    *constptr = &fixed;          // 100% valid
    *var = 30;
    printf("x=%i y=%i\n", fixed, *var);
}
```

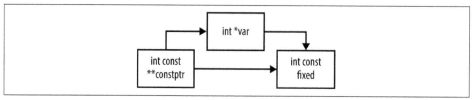

*Figure 8-2. The links among the variables in Example 8-7*

We would never allow int *var to point directly at int const fixed. We only managed it via a sleight-of-pointer where var winds up implicitly pointing to fixed without explicitly stating it.

> **Your Turn:** Is it possible to cause a failure of const like this one, but where the disallowed type cast happens over the course of a function call, as per the Iggy Pop detector?

As earlier, data that is marked as const under one name can be modified using a different name. So, really, it's little surprise that we were able to modify the const data using an alternative name.[6]

I enumerate this list of problems with const so that you can surmount them. As literature goes, it isn't all that problematic, and the recommendation that you add const to your function declarations as often as appropriate still stands—don't just grumble about how the people who came before you didn't provide the right headers. After all, some day others will use your code, and you don't want them grumbling about how they can't use the const keyword because your functions don't have the right headers.

---

6 The code here is a rewrite of the example in C99 and C11 §6.5.16.1(6), where the line analogous to constptr=&var is marked as a constraint violation. Whether it is a constraint violation seems to depend on how one reads "both operands [on either side of an =] are pointers to qualified or unqualified versions of compatible types" in the "constraints" section of C99 and C11 §6.5.16.1. I'm not the only one who thinks it's ambiguous: compilers are supposed to throw an error and refuse to compile the program on constraint violations, but gcc and clang mark this form with a warning and continue.

## True and False

C originally had no Boolean (true/false) type, instead using the convention that if something is zero or NULL, then it is false, and if it is anything else it is true. Thus, if(`ptr`!=NULL) and if(`ptr`) are equivalent.

C99 introduced the _Bool type, which is technically unnecessary, because you can always use an integer to represent a true/false value. But to a human reading the code, the Boolean type clarifies that the variable can only take on true/false values, and so gives some indication of its intent.

The string _Bool was chosen by the standards committee because it is in the space of strings reserved for additions to the language, but it is certainly awkward. The *stdbool.h* header defines three macros to improve readability: bool expands to _Bool, so you don't have to use the unappealing underscore in your declarations; true expands to 1; false expands to 0.

Just as the bool type is more for the human reader, the true and false macros can clarify the intent of an assignment: if I forgot that outcome was declared as bool, out come=true adds a reminder of intent that outcome=1 does not.

However, there is really no reason to compare any expression to true or false: we all know to read if (x) to mean *if x is true, then...*, without the ==true explicitly written on the page. Further, given int x=2, if (x) does what everybody expects and if (x==true) doesn't.

# CHAPTER 9

# Easier Text Handling

*I believe that in the end the word will break cement.*
—Pussy Riot, paraphrasing Aleksandr Solzhenitsyn in a
statement on August 8, 2012

A string of letters is an array of indeterminate length, and automatically allocated arrays (allocated on the stack) can't be resized, and that in a nutshell is the problem with text in C. Fortunately, many others before us have already faced this problem and produced at least partial solutions. A handful of C-standard and POSIX-standard functions are sufficient to handle many of our string-building needs.

Also, C was designed in the 1970s, before the invention of non-English languages. Again, with the right functions (and the right understanding of how language is encoded), C's original focus on English is not a real problem.

## Making String Handling Less Painful with asprintf

The `asprintf` function allocates the amount of string space you will need, and then fills the string. That means you never really have to worry about string-allocating again.

`asprintf` is not part of the C standard, but it's available on systems with the GNU or BSD standard library, which covers a big range of users. Further, the GNU Libiberty library provides a version of `asprintf` that you can either cut and paste into your own code base or call from the library with a `-liberty` flag for the linker. Libiberty ships with some systems with no native `asprintf`, like MSYS for Windows. And if cutting and pasting from `libiberty` is not an option, I'll present a quick reimplementation using the standard `vsnprintf` function.

The old way made people homicidal (or suicidal, depending on temperament), because they first had to get the length of the string they were about to fill, allocate space, and then actually write to the space. Don't forget the extra slot for the null terminator!

Example 9-1 demonstrates the painful way of setting up a string, for the purpose of using C's `system` command to run an external utility. The thematically appropriate utility, `strings`, searches a binary for printable plain text. The `get_strings` function will receive `argv[0]`, the name of the program itself, so the program searches itself for strings. This is perhaps amusing, which is all we can ask of demo code.

*Example 9-1. The tedious way of setting up strings (sadstrings.c)*

```
#include <stdio.h>
#include <string.h> //strlen
#include <stdlib.h> //malloc, free, system

void get_strings(char const *in){
    char *cmd;
    int len = strlen("strings ") + strlen(in) + 1;   ❶
    cmd = malloc(len);                                ❷
    snprintf(cmd, len, "strings %s", in);
    if (system(cmd)) fprintf(stderr, "something went wrong running %s.\n", cmd);
    free(cmd);
}

int main(int argc, char **argv){
    get_strings(argv[0]);
}
```

❶  Premeasuring lengths is such a waste of time.

❷  The C standard says `sizeof(char)==1`, so we at least don't need `malloc( len*sizeof(char))`.

Example 9-2 uses `asprintf`, so `malloc` gets called for you, which means that you also don't need the step where you measure the length of the string.

*Example 9-2. This version cuts only two lines from Example 9-1, but they're the most misery-inducing lines (getstrings.c)*

```
#define _GNU_SOURCE //cause stdio.h to include asprintf
#include <stdio.h>
#include <stdlib.h> //free

void get_strings(char const *in){
    char *cmd;
    asprintf(&cmd, "strings %s", in);
```

```
    if (system(cmd)) fprintf(stderr, "something went wrong running %s.\n", cmd);
    free(cmd);
}

int main(int argc, char **argv){
    get_strings(argv[0]);
}
```

The actual call to asprintf looks a lot like the call to sprintf, except you need to send the location of the string, not the string itself, because new space will be mal loced and the location written into the char ** you input.

Say that, for whatever reason, the GNU asprintf isn't available for your use. Counting the length that a printf statement and its arguments will eventually expand to is error-prone, so how can we get the computer to do it for us? The answer has been staring at us all along, in C99 §7.19.6.12(3) and C11 §7.21.6.12(3): "The vsnprintf function returns the number of characters that would have been written had $n$ been sufficiently large, not counting the terminating null character, or a negative value if an encoding error occurred." The snprintf function also returns a would-have-been value.

So if we do a test run with vsnprintf on a 1-byte string, we can get a return value with the length that the string should be. Then we can allocate the string to that length and run vsnprintf for real. We're running the function twice, so it may take twice as long to work, but it's worth it for the safety and convenience.

Example 9-3 presents an implementation of asprintf via this procedure of running vsnprintf twice. I wrapped it in a HAVE_ASPRINTF check to be Autoconf-friendly; see below.

*Example 9-3. An alternative implementation of asprintf (asprintf.c)*

```
#ifndef HAVE_ASPRINTF
#define HAVE_ASPRINTF
#include <stdio.h>  //vsnprintf
#include <stdlib.h> //malloc
#include <stdarg.h> //va_start et al

/* The declaration, to put into a .h file. The __attribute___ tells the compiler
to check printf-style type-compliance. It's not C-standard, but a lot of compilers
support it; just remove it if yours doesn't. */

int asprintf(char **str, char* fmt, ...) __attribute__ ((format (printf,2,3)));


int asprintf(char **str, char* fmt, ...){
    va_list argp;
    va_start(argp, fmt);
```

```
    char one_char[1];
    int len = vsnprintf(one_char, 1, fmt, argp);
    if (len < 1){
        fprintf(stderr, "An encoding error occurred. Setting the input pointer to NULL.\n");
        *str = NULL;
        return len;
    }
    va_end(argp);

    *str = malloc(len+1);
    if (!str) {
        fprintf(stderr, "Couldn't allocate %i bytes.\n", len+1);
        return -1;
    }
    va_start(argp, fmt);
    vsnprintf(*str, len+1, fmt, argp);
    va_end(argp);
    return len;
}
#endif

#ifdef Test_asprintf
int main(){
    char *s;
    asprintf(&s, "hello, %s.", "–Reader–");
    printf("%s\n", s);

    asprintf(&s, "%c", '\0');
    printf("blank string: [%s]\n", s);

    int i = 0;
    asprintf(&s, "%i", i++);
    printf("Zero: %s\n", s);
}
#endif
```

## Security

If you have a string of predetermined length, str, and write data of unknown length
to it using sprintf, then you might find that data gets written to whatever is adjacent
to str—a classic security breach. Thus, sprintf is effectively deprecated in favor of
snprintf, which limits the amount of data written.

Using asprintf effectively prevents this problem, because as much memory as is
needed will get written. It's not perfect: eventually, whatever mangled and improper
input string will hit a \0 somewhere, but the amount of data could conceivably
exceed the amount of free memory, or the additional data written to str might be
sensitive information like a password.

If memory is exceeded, then `asprintf` will return -1, so in a situation involving user inputs, the careful author would use something like the `Stopif` macro (which I introduce in "Variadic Macros" on page 210) with a form like:

```
Stopif(asprintf(&str, "%s", user_input)==-1, return -1, "asprintf failed.")
```

But if you got as far as sending an unchecked string to `asprintf`, you've already lost. Check that strings from untrusted inputs are of a sane length beforehand. The function might also fail on a string of reasonable length because the computer is out of memory or is being eaten by gremlins.

C11 (Appendix K) also offers all the usual formatted printing functions with an `_s` attached: `printf_s`, `snprintf_s`, `fprintf_s`, and so on. They are intended to be more secure than the no-`_s` versions. Input strings may not be `NULL`, and if an attempt is made to write more than `RINT_MAX` bytes to a string, (where `RINT_MAX` is intended to be half the maximum capacity of a `size_t`) the function fails with a "runtime constraint violation." However, support for these functions in the standard C libraries is still spotty.

## Constant Strings

Here is a program that sets up two strings and prints them to the screen:

```
#include <stdio.h>

int main(){
    char *s1 = "Thread";

    char *s2;
    asprintf(&s2, "Floss");

    printf("%s\n", s1);
    printf("%s\n", s2);
}
```

Both forms will leave a single word in the given string. However, the C compiler treats them in a very different manner, which can trip up the unaware.

Did you try the earlier sample code that showed what strings are embedded into the program binary? In the example here, `Thread` would be such an embedded string, and `s1` could thus point to a location in the executable program itself. How efficient —you don't need to spend runtime having the system count characters or waste memory repeating information already in the binary. I suppose in the 1970s, this mattered.

Both the baked-in `s1` and the allocated-on-demand `s2` behave identically for reading purposes, but you can't modify or free `s1`. Here are some lines you could add to the example, and their effects:

```
s2[0]='f'; //Switch Floss to lowercase.
s1[0]='t'; //Segfault.

free(s2); //Clean up.
free(s1); //Segfault.
```

Your system may point directly to the string embedded in the executable, or it may copy the string to a read-only data segment; in fact, C99 §6.4.5(6) and C11 §6.4.5(7) say the method of storing constant strings is unspecified, and what happens if they are modified is undefined. Because that undefined behavior could be and often is a segfault, that means we should take s1's contents as read-only.

The difference between constant and variable strings is subtle and error-prone, and it makes hardcoded strings useful only in limited contexts. I can't think of a scripting language where you would need to care about this distinction.

But here is one simple solution: strdup, which is POSIX-standard, and is short for *string duplicate*. It works like this:

```
char *s3 = strdup("Thread");
```

The string Thread is still hardcoded into the program, but s3 is a copy of that constant blob, and so can be freely modified as you wish. With liberal use of strdup, you can treat all strings equally, without worrying about which are constant and which are pointers.

If you are unable to use the POSIX standard and are worried that you don't have a copy of strdup on your machine, it's easy enough to write a version for yourself. For example, we can once again use asprintf:

```
#ifndef HAVE_STRDUP
char *strdup(char const* in){
    if (!in) return NULL;
    char *out;
    asprintf(&out, "%s", in);
    return out;
}
#endif
```

And where does that HAVE_STRDUP macro come from? If you are using Autotools, then putting this line:

```
AC_CHECK_FUNCS([asprintf strdup])
```

into *configure.ac* would produce a segment in the configure script that generates a *configure.h* with HAVE_STRDUP and HAVE_ASPRINTF defined or not defined as appropriate.

# Extending Strings with asprintf

Here is an example of the basic form for appending another bit of text to a string using `asprintf`:

```
asprintf(&q, "%s and another clause %s", q, addme);
```

I use this for generating database queries. I would put together a chain, such as this contrived example:

```
int col_number=3, person_number=27;
char *q =strdup("select ");
asprintf(&q, "%scol%i \n", q, col_number);
asprintf(&q, "%sfrom tab \n", q);
asprintf(&q, "%swhere person_id = %i", q, person_number);
```

And in the end I have:

```
select col3
from tab
where person_id = 27
```

This is a rather nice way of putting together a long and painful string, which becomes essential as the subclauses get convoluted.

But it's a memory leak, because the blob at the original address of q isn't released when q is given a new location by `asprintf`. For one-off string generation, it's not even worth caring about—you can drop a few million query-length strings on the floor before anything noticeable happens.

If you are in a situation where you might produce an unknown number of strings of unknown length, then you will need a form like that in Example 9-4.

*Example 9-4. A macro to cleanly extend strings (sasprintf.c)*

```
#include <stdio.h>
#include <stdlib.h> //free

//Safer asprintf macro
#define Sasprintf(write_to,  ...) {                \
    char *tmp_string_for_extend = (write_to); \
    asprintf(&(write_to), __VA_ARGS__);        \
    free(tmp_string_for_extend);               \
}

//sample usage:
int main(){
    int i=3;
    char *q = NULL;
    Sasprintf(q, "select * from tab");
    Sasprintf(q, "%s where col%i is not null", q, i);
```

```
    printf("%s\n", q);
}
```

The `Sasprintf` macro, plus occasional use of `strdup`, may be enough for all of your string-handling needs. Except for one glitch and the occasional `free`, you don't have to think about memory issues at all.

The glitch is that if you forget to initialize q to `NULL` or via `strdup`, then the first use of the `Sasprintf` macro will be freeing whatever junk happened to be in the uninitialized location q—a segfault.

For example, the following fails—wrap that declaration in `strdup` to make it work:

```
char *q = "select * from";   //fails—needs strdup().
Sasprintf(q, "%s %s where col%i is not null", q, tablename, i);
```

In extensive usage, this sort of string concatenation can theoretically cause slow-downs, as the first part of the string gets rewritten over and over. In this case, you can use C as a prototyping language for C: if and only if the technique here proves to be too slow, take the time to replace it with more traditional `snprintf`s.

## A Pæan to strtok

*Tokenizing* is the simplest and most common parsing problem, in which we split a string into parts at delimiters. This definition covers all sorts of tasks:

- Splitting words at whitespace delimiters such as one of `" \t\n\r"`
- Given a path such as `"/usr/include:/usr/local/include:."`, cutting it at the colons into the individual directories
- Splitting a string into lines using a simple newline delimiter, `"\n"`
- You might have a configuration file with lines of the form `value = key`, in which case your delimiter is `"="`
- Comma-delimited values in a datafile are of course cut at the comma

Two levels of splitting will get you still further, such as reading a full configuration file by first splitting at newlines, then splitting each line at the =.

If your needs are more complex than splitting at single-character delimiters, you may need regular expressions. See "Parsing Regular Expressions" on page 324 for a discussion of the POSIX-standard regular expression parsers and how they can pull subsections of strings for you.

Tokenizing comes up often enough that there's a standard C library function to do it, strtok (string tokenize), which is one of those neat little functions that does its job quietly and well.

The basic working of strtok is to step through the string you input until it hits the first delimiter, then overwrite the delimiter with a '\0'. Now the first part of the input string is a valid string representing the first token, and strtok returns a pointer to the head of that substring for your use. The function holds the original string's information internally, so when you call strtok again, it can search for the end of the next token, nullify that end, and return the head of that token as a valid string.

The head of each substring is a pointer to a spot within an already-allocated string, so the tokenizing does a minimum of data writing (just those \0s) and no copying. The immediate implication is that the string you input is mangled, and because substrings are pointers to the original string, you can't free the input string until you are done using the substrings (or, you can use strdup to copy out the substrings as they come out).

The strtok function holds the rest of the string you first input in a single static internal pointer, meaning that it is limited to tokenizing one string (with one set of delimiters) at a time, and it can't be used while threading. Therefore, consider strtok to be deprecated.

Instead, use strtok_r or strtok_s, which are threading-friendly versions of strtok. The POSIX standard provides strtok_r, and the C11 standard provides strtok_s. The use of either is a little awkward, because the first call is different from the subsequent calls.

- The first time you call the function, send in the string to be parsed as the first argument.
- On subsequent calls, send in NULL as the first argument.
- The last argument is the scratch string. You don't have to initialize it on first use; on subsequent uses it will hold the string as parsed so far.

Here's a line counter for you (actually, a counter of nonblank lines; see warning later on). Tokenizing is often a one-liner in scripting languages, but this is about as brief as it gets with strtok_r. Notice the *if* ? *then* : *else* to send in the original string only on the first use.

```
#include <string.h> //strtok_r

int count_lines(char *instring){
    int counter = 0;
    char *scratch, *txt, *delimiter = "\n";
    while ((txt = strtok_r(!counter ? instring : NULL, delimiter, &scratch)))
```

```
        counter++;
    return counter;
}
```

The Unicode section will give a full example, as will the Cetology example of "Count References" on page 277.

The C11-standard `strtok_s` works just like `strtok_r`, but has an extra argument (the second) which gives the length of the input string, and is updated to shrink to the length of the remaining string on each call. If the input string is not `\0`-delimited, this extra element would be useful. We could redo the earlier example with:

```
#include <string.h> //strtok_s

//first use
size_t len = strlen(instring);
txt = strtok_s(instring, &len, delimiter, &scratch);

//subsequent use:
txt = strtok_s(NULL, &len, delimiter, &scratch);
```

 Two or more delimiters in a row are treated as a single delimiter, meaning that blank tokens are simply ignored. For example, if your delimiter is "`:`" and you are asking `strtok_r` or `strtok_s` to break down `/bin:/usr/bin::/opt/bin`, then you will get the three directories in sequence—the `::` is treated like a `:`. This is also why the preceding line counter is actually a nonblank line counter, as the double newline in a string like `one \n\n three \n four` (indicating that line two is blank) would be treated by `strtok` and its variants as a single newline.

Ignoring double delimiters is often what you want (as in the path example), but sometimes it isn't, in which case you'll need to think about how to detect double delimiters. If the string to be split was written by you, then be sure to generate the string with a marker for intentionally blank tokens. Writing a function to precheck strings for doubled delimiters is not too difficult (or try the BSD/GNU-standard `strsep`). For inputs from users, you can add stern warnings about not allowing delimiters to double up, and warn them of what to expect, like how the line-counter here ignores blank lines.

Example 9-6 presents a small library of string utilities that might be useful to you, including some of the macros from earlier in this book.

There are two key functions: `string_from_file` reads a complete file into a string. This saves us all the hassle of trying to read and process smaller chunks of a file. If you routinely deal with text files larger than a few gigabytes, you won't be able to rely on this, but for situations in which text files never make it past a few megabytes, there's no point screwing around with incrementally reading a text file one chunk at a time. I'll use this function for several examples over the course of the book.

The second key function is ok_array_new, which tokenizes a string and writes the output to a struct, an ok_array.

Example 9-5 is the header.

*Example 9-5. A header for a small set of string utilities (string_utilities.h)*

```
#include <string.h>
#define _GNU_SOURCE //asks stdio.h to include asprintf
#include <stdio.h>

//Safe asprintf macro
#define Sasprintf(write_to,  ...) {              \        ❶
    char *tmp_string_for_extend = write_to;  \
    asprintf(&(write_to), __VA_ARGS__);       \
    free(tmp_string_for_extend);              \
}

char *string_from_file(char const *filename);

typedef struct ok_array {
    char **elements;
    char *base_string;
    int length;
} ok_array;                                          ❷

ok_array *ok_array_new(char *instring, char const *delimiters);  ❸

void ok_array_free(ok_array *ok_in);
```

❶  This is the Sasprintf macro from earlier, reprinted for your convenience.

❷  This is an array of tokens, which you get when you call ok_array_new to tokenize a string.

❸  This is the wrapper to strtok_r that will produce the ok_array.

Example 9-6 does the work of having GLib read a file into a string and using strtok_r to turn a single string into an array of strings. You'll see some examples of usage in Example 9-7, Example 12-2, and Example 12-3.

*Example 9-6. Some useful string utilities (string_utilities.c)*

```
#include <glib.h>
#include <string.h>
```

```
#include "string_utilities.h"
#include <stdio.h>
#include <assert.h>
#include <stdlib.h> //abort

char *string_from_file(char const *filename){
    char *out;
    GError *e = NULL;
    GIOChannel *f = g_io_channel_new_file(filename, "r", &e);          ❶
    if (!f) {
        fprintf(stderr, "failed to open file '%s'.\n", filename);
        return NULL;
    }
    if (g_io_channel_read_to_end(f, &out, NULL, &e) != G_IO_STATUS_NORMAL){
        fprintf(stderr, "found file '%s' but couldn't read it.\n", filename);
        return NULL;
    }
    return out;
}

ok_array *ok_array_new(char *instring, char const *delimiters){          ❷
    ok_array *out= malloc(sizeof(ok_array));
    *out = (ok_array){.base_string=instring};
    char *scratch = NULL;
    char *txt = strtok_r(instring, delimiters, &scratch);
    if (!txt) return NULL;
    while (txt) {
        out->elements = realloc(out->elements, sizeof(char*)*++(out->length));
        out->elements[out->length-1] = txt;
        txt = strtok_r(NULL, delimiters, &scratch);
    }
    return out;
}

/* Frees the original string, because strtok_r mangled it, so it
   isn't useful for any other purpose. */
void ok_array_free(ok_array *ok_in){
    if (ok_in == NULL) return;
    free(ok_in->base_string);
    free(ok_in->elements);
    free(ok_in);
}

#ifdef test_ok_array
int main (){                                                             ❸
    char *delimiters = " `~!@#$%^&*()_-+={[]}|\\;:\",<>./?\n";
    ok_array *o = ok_array_new(strdup("Hello, reader. This is text."), delimiters);
    assert(o->length==5);
    assert(!strcmp(o->elements[1], "reader"));
    assert(!strcmp(o->elements[4], "text"));
    ok_array_free(o);
    printf("OK.\n");
```

```
}
#endif
```

❶ Although it doesn't work in all situations, I've grown enamored of just reading an entire text file into memory at once, which is a fine example of eliminating programmer annoyances by throwing hardware at the problem. If we expect files to be too big for memory, we could use mmap (q.v.) to the same effect.

❷ This is the wrapper to strtok_r. If you've read to this point, you are familiar with the while loop that is all but obligatory in its use, and the function here records the results from it into an ok_array struct.

❸ If test_ok_array is not set, then this is a library for use elsewhere. If it is set (CFLAGS=-Dtest_ok_array), then it is a program that tests that ok_array_new works, by splitting the sample string at nonalphanumeric characters.

# Unicode

Back when all the computing action was in the United States, ASCII (American Standard Code for Information Interchange) defined a numeric code for all of the usual letters and symbols printed on a standard US QWERTY keyboard, which I will refer to as the naïve English character set. A C char is 8 bits (binary digits) = 1 byte = 256 possible values. ASCII defined 128 characters, so it fit into a single char with even a bit to spare. That is, the eighth bit of every ASCII character will be zero, which will turn out to be serendipitously useful later.

Unicode follows the same basic premise, assigning a hexadecimal numeric value, typically between 0000 and FFFF, to every glyph used for human communication.[1] By custom, these *code points* are written in the form U+0000. The work is much more ambitious and challenging, because it requires cataloging all the usual Western letters, tens of thousands of Chinese and Japanese characters, all the requisite glyphs for Ugaritic, Deseret, and so on, throughout the world and throughout human history.

The next question is how it is to be encoded, and at this point, things start to fall apart. The primary question is how many bytes to set as the unit of analysis. UTF-32 (UTF stands for UCS Transformation Format; UCS stands for Universal Character

---

[1] The range from 0000 to FFFF is the *basic multilingual plane* (BMP), and includes most but not all of the characters used in modern languages. Later code points (conceivably from 10000 to 10FFFF) are in the *supplementary planes*, including mathematical symbols (like the symbol for the real numbers, $\mathbb{R}$) and a unified set of CJK ideographs. If you are one of the ten million Chinese Miao, or one of the hundreds of thousands of Indian Sora Sompeng or Chakma speakers, your language is here. Yes, the great majority of text can be expressed with the BMP, but rest assured that if you assume that all text is in the Unicode range below FFFF, then you will be wrong on a regular basis.

Set) specifies 32 bits = 4 bytes as the basic unit, which means that every character can be encoded in a single unit, at the cost of a voluminous amount of empty padding, given that naïve English can be written with only 7 bits. UTF-16 uses 2 bytes as the basic unit, which handles most characters comfortably with a single unit but requires that some characters be written down using two. UTF-8 uses 1 byte as its unit, meaning still more code points written down via multiunit amalgams.

I like to think about the UTF encodings as a sort of trivial encryption. For every code point, there is a single byte sequence in UTF-8, a single byte sequence in UTF-16, and a single byte sequence in UTF-32, none of which are necessarily related. Barring an exception discussed below, there is no reason to expect that the code point and any of the encrypted values are numerically the same, or even related in an obvious way, but I know that a properly programmed decoder can easily and unambiguously translate among the UTF encodings and the correct Unicode code point.

What do the machines of the world choose? On the Web, there is a clear winner: as of this writing over 83% of websites use UTF-8.[2] Also, Mac and Linux boxes default to using UTF-8 for everything, so you have good odds that an unmarked text file on a Mac or Linux box is in UTF-8.

About 8% of the world's websites still aren't using Unicode at all, but are using a relatively archaic format, ISO/IEC 8859 (which has code pages, with names like Latin-1). And Windows, the free-thinking flipping-off-the-POSIX-man operating system, uses UTF-16.

Displaying Unicode is up to your host operating system, and it already has a lot of work to do. For example, when printing the naïve English set, each character gets one spot on the line of text, but the Hebrew ב = b, for instance, can be written as a combination of ב (U+05D1) and ‎ (U+05BC). Vowels are added to the consonant to further build the character: בַּ = ba (U+05D1 and U+05BC and U+05B8). And how many bytes it takes to express these three code points in UTF-8 (in this case, six) is another unrelated layer. Now, when we talk about string length, we could mean number of code points, width on the screen, or the number of bytes required to express the string.

So, as the author of a program that needs to communicate with humans who speak all kinds of languages, what are your responsibilities? You need to:

- Work out what encoding the host system is using, so that you aren't fooled into using the wrong encoding to read inputs and can send back outputs that the host can correctly decode
- Successfully store text somewhere, unmangled

---

2 See Web Technology Surveys (*http://bit.ly/w3techs-en*).

- Recognize that one character is not a fixed number of bytes, so any base-plus-offset code you write (given a Unicode string us, things like us++) may give you fragments of a code point
- Have on hand utilities to do any sort of comprehension of text: toupper and tolower work only for naïve English, so we will need replacements

Meeting these responsibilities will require picking the right internal encoding to prevent mangling, and having on hand a good library to help us when we need to decode.

## The Encoding for C Code

The choice of internal coding is especially easy. UTF-8 was designed for you, the C programmer.

- The UTF-8 unit is 8 bits: a char.[3] It is entirely valid to write a UTF-8 string to a char * string, as with naïve English text.
- The first 128 Unicode code points exactly match ASCII. For example, *A* is 41 (hexadecimal) in ASCII and is Unicode code point U+0041. Therefore, if your Unicode text happens to consist entirely of naïve English, then you can use the usual ASCII-oriented utilities on them, or UTF-8 utilities. If the eighth bit of a char is 0, then the char represents an ASCII character; if it is 1, then that char is one chunk of a multibyte character. Thus, no part of a UTF-8 non-ASCII Unicode character will ever match an ASCII character.
- U+0000 is a valid code point, which we C authors like to write as '\0'. Because \0 is the ASCII zero as well, this rule is a special case of the last one. This is important because a UTF-8 string with one \0 at the end is exactly what we need for a valid C char * string. Recall how the unit for UTF-16 and UTF-32 is several bytes long, and for naïve English, there will be padding for most of the unit; that means that the first 8 bits have very good odds of being entirely zero, which means that dumping UTF-16 or UTF-32 text to a char * variable is likely to give you a string littered with null bytes.

So we C coders have been well taken care of: UTF-8 encoded text can be stored and copied with the char * string type we have been using all along. Now that one character may be several bytes long, be careful not to change the order of any of the bytes and to never split a multibyte character. If you aren't doing these things, you're as OK

---

3 There may once have been ASCII-oriented machines where compilers used 7-bit chars, but C99 and C11 §5.2.4.2.1(1) define CHAR_BIT to be 8 or more; see also §6.2.6.1(4), which defines a byte as CHAR_BIT bits.

as you would be if the string were naïve English. Therefore, here is a partial list of standard library functions that are UTF-8 safe:

- `strdup` and `strndup`
- `strcat` and `strncat`
- `strcpy` and `strncpy`
- The POSIX `basename` and `dirname`
- `strcmp` and `strncmp`, but only if you use them as zero/nonzero functions to determine whether two strings are equal. If you want to meaningfully sort, you will need a collation function; see the next section.
- `strstr`
- `printf` and family, including `sprintf`, where `%s` is still the marker to use for a string
- `strtok_r`, `strtok_s` and `strsep`, provided that you are splitting at an ASCII character like one of " `\t\n\r:|;,`"
- `strlen` and `strnlen`, but recognize that you will get the number of bytes, which is not the number of Unicode code points or width on the screen. For these you'll need a new library function, as discussed in the next section.

These are pure byte-slinging functions, but most of what we want to do with text requires decoding it, which brings us to the libraries.

## Unicode Libraries

Our first order of business is to convert from whatever the rest of the world dumped on us to UTF-8 so that we can use the data internally. That is, you'll need gatekeeper functions that encode incoming strings to UTF-8, and decode outgoing strings from UTF-8 to whatever the recipient wants on the other end, leaving you safe to do all internal work in one sensible encoding.

This is how Libxml (which we'll meet in "libxml and cURL" on page 337) works: a well-formed XML document states its encoding at the header (and the library has a set of rules for guessing if the encoding declaration is missing), so Libxml knows what translation to do. Libxml parses the document into an internal format, and then you can query and edit that internal format. Barring errors, you are guaranteed that the internal format will be UTF-8, because Libxml doesn't want to deal with alternate encodings either.

If you have to do your own translations at the door, then you have the POSIX-standard `iconv` function. This is going to be an unbelievably complicated function, given that there are so many encodings to deal with. The GNU provides a portable libiconv in case your computer doesn't have the function on hand.

 The POSIX standard also specifies that there be a command-line iconv program, a shell-friendly wrapper to the C function.

GLib provides a few wrappers to iconv, and the ones you're going to care about are g_locale_to_utf8 and g_locale_from_utf8. And while you're in the GLib manual, you'll see a long section on Unicode manipulation tools. You'll see that there are two types: those that act on UTF-8 and those that act on UTF-32 (which GLib stores via a gunichar).

Recall that 8 bits is not nearly enough to express all characters in one unit, so a single character is between one and six units long. Thus, UTF-8 counts as a *multibyte encoding*, and therefore, the problems you'll have are getting the true length of the string (using a character-count or screen-width definition of *length*), getting the next full character, getting a substring, or getting a comparison for sorting purposes (a.k.a. *collating*).

UTF-32 has enough padding to express any character with the same number of blocks, and so it is called a *wide character*. You'll often see reference to multibyte-to-wide conversions; this is the sort of thing they're talking about.

Once you have a single character in UTF-32 (GLib's gunichar), you'll have no problem doing character-content things with it, like getting its type (alpha, numeric, ...), converting it to upper- or lowercase, et cetera.

If you read the C standard, you no doubt noticed that it includes a wide character type, and all sorts of functions to go with it. The wchar_t is from C89, and therefore predates the publication of the first Unicode standard. I'm not sure what it's useful for anymore. The width of a wchar_t isn't fixed by the standard, so it could mean 32-bit or 16-bit (or anything else). Compilers on Windows machines like to set it at 16-bit, to accommodate Microsoft's preference for UTF-16, but UTF-16 is still a multibyte encoding, so we need yet another type to guarantee a true fixed-width encoding. C11 fixes this by providing a char16_t and char32_t, but we don't have much code written around those types yet.

## The Sample Code

Example 9-7 presents a program to take in a file and break it into "words," by which I mean use strtok_r to break it at spaces and newlines, which are pretty universal. For each word, I use GLib to convert the first character from multibyte UTF-8 to wide character UTF-32, and then comment on whether that first character is a letter, a number, or a CJK-type wide symbol (where CJK stands for Chinese/Japanese/Korean, which are often printed with more space per character).

The `string_from_file` function reads the whole input file to a string, then `local string_to_utf8` converts it from the locale of your machine to UTF-8. The notable thing about my use of `strtok_r` is that there is nothing notable. If I'm splitting at spaces and newlines, then I can guarantee you that I'm not splitting a multibyte character in half.

I output to HTML, because then I can specify UTF-8 and not worry about the encoding on the output side. If you have a UTF-16 host, open the output file in your browser.

Because this program uses GLib and `string_utilities`, my makefile looks like:

```
CFLAGS==`pkg-config --cflags glib-2.0` -g -Wall -O3
LDADD=`pkg-config --libs glib-2.0`
CC=c99
objects=string_utilities.o

unicode: $(objects)
```

For another example of Unicode character dealings, see Example 10-21, which enumerates every character in every UTF-8-valid file in a directory.

*Example 9-7. Take in a text file and print some useful information about its characters (unicode.c)*

```
#include <glib.h>
#include <locale.h> //setlocale
#include "string_utilities.h"
#include "stopif.h"

//Frees instring for you—we can't use it for anything else.
char *localstring_to_utf8(char *instring){ ❶
    GError *e=NULL;
    setlocale(LC_ALL, ""); //get the OS's locale.
    char *out = g_locale_to_utf8(instring, -1, NULL, NULL, &e);
    free(instring); //done with the original
    Stopif(!g_utf8_validate(out, -1, NULL), free(out); return NULL,
            "Trouble: I couldn't convert your file to a valid UTF-8 string.");
    return out;
}

int main(int argc, char **argv){
    Stopif(argc==1, return 1, "Please give a filename as an argument. "
                    "I will print useful info about it to uout.html.");

    char *ucs = localstring_to_utf8(string_from_file(argv[1]));
    Stopif(!ucs, return 1, "Exiting.");
```

```
    FILE *out = fopen("uout.html", "w");
    Stopif(!out, return 1, "Couldn't open uout.html for writing.");
    fprintf(out, "<head><meta http-equiv=\"Content-Type\" "
                "content=\"text/html; charset=UTF-8\" />\n");
    fprintf(out, "This document has %li characters.<br>",
                g_utf8_strlen(ucs, -1)); ❷
    fprintf(out, "Its Unicode encoding required %zu bytes.<br>", strlen(ucs));
    fprintf(out, "Here it is, with each space-delimited element on a line "
                "(with commentary on the first character):<br>");

    ok_array *spaced = ok_array_new(ucs, " \n"); ❸
    for (int i=0; i< spaced->length; i++, (spaced->elements)++){
        fprintf(out, "%s", *spaced->elements);
        gunichar c = g_utf8_get_char(*spaced->elements); ❹
        if (g_unichar_isalpha(c)) fprintf(out, " (a letter)");
        if (g_unichar_isdigit(c)) fprintf(out, " (a digit)");
        if (g_unichar_iswide(c)) fprintf(out, " (wide, CJK)");
        fprintf(out, "<br>");
    }
    fclose(out);
    printf("Info printed to uout.html. Have a look at it in your browser.\n");
}
```

❶ This is the incoming gateway, which converts from whatever it is that your box likes to use to UTF-8. There's no outgoing gateway because I write to an HTML file, and browsers know how to deal with UTF-8. An outgoing gateway would look a lot like this function, but use g_locale_from_utf8.

❷ strlen is one of those functions that assumes one character equals 1 byte, and so we need a replacement for it.

❸ Use the ok_array_new function from earlier in the chapter to split at spaces and newlines.

❹ Here are some per-character operations, which will only work after you convert from the multibyte UTF-8 to a fixed-width (wide-character) encoding.

## Gettext

Your program probably writes a lot of messages to readers, such as error messages and prompts for user input. Truly user-friendly software has translations of these bits of text in as many human languages as possible. GNU Gettext provides a framework for organizing the translations. The Gettext manual is pretty readable, so I refer you there for details, but here is a rough overview of the procedure to give you a sense of the system:

- Replace every instance of "*Human message*" in your code with `_(`"*Human message*"`)`. The underscore is a macro that will eventually expand to a function call that selects the right string given the user's runtime locale.

- Run `xgettext` to produce an index of strings that need translating, in the form of a portable object template (*.pot*) file.

- Send the *.pot* file to your colleagues around the globe who speak diverse languages, so they can send you *.po* files providing translations of the strings for their language.

- Add `AM_GNU_GETTEXT` to your *configure.ac* (along with any optional macros to specify where to find the *.po* files and other such details).

# CHAPTER 10

# Better Structures

*Twenty-nine different attributes and only seven that you like.*
—The Strokes, "You Only Live Once"

This chapter is about functions that take structured inputs, and improving the user interface to our libraries.

It starts by covering three bits of syntax introduced to C in the ISO C99 standard: compound literals, variable-length macros, and designated initializers. The chapter is to a great extent an exploration of all the things that combinations of these elements can do for us.

With just compound literals, we can more easily send lists to a function. Then, a variable-length macro lets us hide the compound literal syntax from the user, leaving us with a function that can take a list of arbitrary length: f(1, 2) or f(1, 2, 3, 4) would be equally valid.

We could use similar forms to implement the foreach keyword as seen in many other languages, or vectorize a one-input function so that it operates on several inputs.

Designated initializers make working with structs much easier, to the point that I've almost entirely stopped using the old method. Instead of illegible and error-prone junk like person_struct p = {"Joe", 22, 75, 20}, we can write self-documenting declarations such as person_struct p = {.name="Joe", .age=22, .weight_kg=75, .education_years=20}.

Now that initializing a struct doesn't hurt, returning a struct from a function is also painless and can go far to clarify our function interfaces.

Sending structs to functions also becomes a more viable option. By wrapping everything in another variable-length macro, we can now write functions that take a variable number of named arguments, and even assign default values to those the function user doesn't specify. A loan calculator example will provide a function where both amortization(.amount=200000, .rate=4.5, .years=30) and amortiza tion(.rate=4.5, .amount=200000) are valid uses. Because the second call does not give a loan term, the function uses its default of a 30-year mortgage.

The remainder of the chapter gives some examples of situations where input and output structs can be used to make life easier, including when dealing with function interfaces based on void pointers, and when saddled with legacy code with a horrendous interface that needs to be wrapped into something usable.

# Compound Literals

You can send a literal value into a function easily enough: given the declaration dou ble a_value, C has no problem understanding f(a_value).

But if you want to send a list of elements—a compound literal value like {20.38, a_value, 9.8}—then there's a syntactic caveat: you have to put a typecast before the compound literal, or else the parser will get confused. The list now looks like (dou ble[]) {20.38, a_value, 9.8}, and the call looks like this:

```
f((double[]) {20.38, a_value, 9.8});
```

Compound literals are automatically allocated, meaning that you need neither mal loc nor free to use them. At the end of the scope in which the compound literal appears, it just disappears.

Example 10-1 begins with a rather typical function, sum, that takes in an array of dou ble, and sums its elements up to the first NaN (Not-a-Number, see "Marking Exceptional Numeric Values with NaNs" on page 160). If the input array has no NaNs, the results will be a disaster; we'll impose some safety below. The example's main has two ways to call it: the traditional via a temp variable and the compound literal.

*Example 10-1. We can bypass the temp variable by using a compound literal (sum_to_nan.c)*

```
#include <math.h> //NAN
#include <stdio.h>

double sum(double in[]){                                          ❶
    double out=0;
    for (int i=0; !isnan(in[i]); i++) out += in[i];
    return out;
}

int main(){
    double list[] = {1.1, 2.2, 3.3, NAN};                         ❷
```

```
    printf("sum: %g\n", sum(list));

    printf("sum: %g\n", sum((double[]){1.1, 2.2, 3.3, NAN}));   ❸
}
```

❶ This unremarkable function will add the elements of the input array, until it reaches the first NaN marker.

❷ This is a typical use of a function that takes in an array, where we declare the list via a throwaway variable on one line, and then send it to the function on the next.

❸ Here, we do away with the intermediate variable and use a compound literal to create an array and send it directly to the function.

There's the simplest use of compound literals; the rest of this chapter will make use of them to all sorts of benefits. Meanwhile, does the code on your hard drive use any quick throwaway lists whose use could be streamlined by a compound literal?

This form is setting up an auto-allocated array, not a pointer to an array, so you'll be using the (double[]) type, not (double*).

## Initialization via Compound Literals

Let me delve into a hairsplitting distinction, which might give you a more solid idea of what compound literals are doing.

You are probably used to declaring arrays via a form like:

```
    double list[] = {1.1, 2.2, 3.3, NAN};
```

Here we have allocated a named array, list. If you called sizeof(list), you would get back whatever 4 * sizeof(double) is on your machine. That is, list *is* the array (as discussed in "Automatic, Static, and Manual Memory" on page 125).

You could also perform the declaration via a compound literal, which you can identify by the (double[]) header:

```
    double *list = (double[]){1.1, 2.2, 3.3, NAN};
```

Here, the system first generated an anonymous list, put it into the function's memory frame, and then it declared a pointer, list, pointing to the anonymous list. So list is an *alias*, and sizeof(list) will equal sizeof(double*). Example 8-2 demonstrates this.

# Variadic Macros

I broadly consider variable-length functions in C to be broken (more in "Flexible Function Inputs" on page 225). But variable-length macro arguments are easy. The keyword is __VA_ARGS__, and it expands to whatever set of elements were given.

In Example 10-2, I revisit Example 2-5, a customized variant of printf that prints a message if an assertion fails.

*Example 10-2. A macro for dealing with errors, reprinted from Example 2-5 (stopif.h)*

```
#include <stdio.h>
#include <stdlib.h> //abort

/** Set this to \c 's' to stop the program on an error.
    Otherwise, functions return a value on failure.*/
char error_mode;

/** To where should I write errors? If this is \c NULL, write to \c stderr. */
FILE *error_log;

#define Stopif(assertion, error_action, ...) {              \
        if (assertion){                                     \
            fprintf(error_log ? error_log : stderr, __VA_ARGS__); \
            fprintf(error_log ? error_log : stderr, "\n");  \
            if (error_mode=='s') abort();                   \
            else            {error_action;}                 \
        } }

    //sample usage:
    Stopif(x<0 || x>1, return -1, "x has value %g, "
                    "but it should be between zero and one.", x);
```

Whatever the user puts down in place of the ellipsis (...) gets plugged in at the __VA_ARGS__ mark.

As a demonstration of just how much variable-length macros can do for us, Example 10-3 rewrites the syntax of for loops. Everything after the second argument —regardless of how many commas are scattered about—will be read as the ... argument and pasted in to the __VA_ARGS__ marker.

*Example 10-3. The ... of the macro covers the entire body of the for loop (varad.c)*

```
#include <stdio.h>

#define forloop(i, loopmax, ...) for(int i=0; i< loopmax; i++) \
                    {__VA_ARGS__}

int main(){
```

```
    int sum=0;
    forloop(i, 10,
            sum += i;
            printf("sum to %i: %i\n", i, sum);
    )
}
```

I wouldn't actually use Example 10-3 in real-world code, but chunks of code that are largely repetitive but for a minor difference across repetitions happen often enough, and it sometimes makes sense to use variable-length macros to eliminate the redundancy.

# Safely Terminated Lists

Compound literals and variadic macros are the cutest couple, because we can now use macros to build lists and structures. We'll get to the structure building shortly; let's start with lists.

A few pages ago, you saw the function that took in a list and summed until the first NaN. When using this function, you don't need to know the length of the input array, but you do need to make sure that there's a NaN marker at the end; if there isn't, you're in for a segfault. We could guarantee that there is a NaN marker at the end of the list by calling sum using a variadic macro, as in Example 10-4.

*Example 10-4. Using a variadic macro to produce a compound literal (safe_sum.c)*

```
#include <math.h> //NAN
#include <stdio.h>

double sum_array(double in[]){                              ❶
    double out=0;
    for (int i=0; !isnan(in[i]); i++) out += in[i];
    return out;
}

#define sum(...) sum_array((double[]){__VA_ARGS__, NAN})    ❷

int main(){
    double two_and_two = sum(2, 2);                          ❸
    printf("2+2 = %g\n", two_and_two);
    printf("(2+2)*3 = %g\n", sum(two_and_two, two_and_two, two_and_two));
    printf("sum(asst) = %g\n", sum(3.1415, two_and_two, 3, 8, 98.4));
}
```

❶ The name is changed, but this is otherwise the sum-an-array function from before.

❷ This line is where the action is: the variadic macro dumps its inputs into a compound literal. So the macro takes in a loose list of doubles but sends to the function a single list, which is guaranteed to end in NAN.

❸ Now, main can send to sum loose lists of numbers of any length, and it can let the macro worry about appending the terminal NAN.

Now that's a stylish function. It takes in as many inputs as you have, and you don't have to pack them into an array beforehand, because the macro uses a compound literal to do it for you.

In fact, the macro version only works with loose numbers, not with anything you've already set up as an array. If you already have an array—and if you can guarantee the NAN at the end—then call sum_array directly.

## Multiple Lists

Now what if you want to send *two* lists of arbitrary length? For example, say that you've decided that your program should emit errors in two ways: print a more human-friendly message to screen and print a machine-readable error code to a log (I'll use stderr here). It would be nice to have one function that takes in printf-style arguments to both output functions, but then how would the compiler know when one set of arguments ends and the next begins?

We can group arguments the way we always do: using parens. With a call to my_macro of the form my_macro(f(a, b), c), the first macro argument is all of f(a, b)—the comma inside the parens is not read as a macro argument divider, because that would break up the parens and produce nonsense [C99 and C11 §6.10.3(11)].

And thus, here is a workable example to print two error messages at once:

```
#define fileprintf(...) fprintf(stderr, __VA_ARGS__)
#define doubleprintf(human, machine) do {printf human; fileprintf machine;} while(0)

//usage:
if (x < 0) doubleprintf(("x is negative (%g)\n", x), ("NEGVAL: x=%g\n", x));
```

The macro will expand to:

```
do {printf ("x is negative (%g)\n", x); fileprintf ("NEGVAL: x=%g\n", x);}
while(0);
```

I added the fileprintf macro to provide consistency across the two statements. Without it, you would need the human printf arguments in parens and the log printf arguments not in parens:

```
#define doubleprintf(human, ...) do {printf human;\
                             fprintf (stderr, __VA_ARGS__);} while(0)

//and so:
if (x < 0) doubleprintf(("x is negative (%g)\n", x), "NEGVAL: x=%g\n", x);
```

This is valid syntax, but I don't like this from the user interface perspective, because symmetric things should look symmetric.

What if users forget the parens entirely? It won't compile: there isn't much that you can put after printf besides an open paren that won't give you a cryptic error message. On the one hand, you get a cryptic error message; on the other, there's no way to accidentally forget the parens and ship wrong code into production.

To give another example, Example 10-5 will print a product table: given two lists $R$ and $C$, each cell $(i, j)$ will hold the product $R_i$ $C_j$. The core of the example is the matrix_cross macro and its relatively user-friendly interface.

*Example 10-5. Sending two variable-length lists to one function (times_table.c)*

```
#include <math.h> //NAN
#include <stdio.h>

#define make_a_list(...) (double[]){__VA_ARGS__, NAN}

#define matrix_cross(list1, list2) matrix_cross_base(make_a_list list1, \
    make_a_list list2)

void matrix_cross_base(double *list1, double *list2){
    int count1 = 0, count2 = 0;
    while (!isnan(list1[count1])) count1++;
    while (!isnan(list2[count2])) count2++;

    for (int i=0; i<count1; i++){
        for (int j=0; j<count2; j++)
            printf("%g\t", list1[i]*list2[j]);
        printf("\n");
    }
    printf("\n\n");
}

int main(){
    matrix_cross((1, 2, 4, 8), (5, 11.11, 15));

    matrix_cross((17, 19, 23), (1, 2, 3, 5, 7, 11, 13));

    matrix_cross((1, 2, 3, 5, 7, 11, 13), (1));   //a column vector
}
```

# Foreach

Earlier, you saw that you can use a compound literal anywhere you would put an array or structure. For example, here is an array of strings declared via a compound literal:

```
char **strings = (char*[]){"Yarn", "twine"};
```

Now let's put that in a for loop. The first element of the loop declares the array of strings, so we can use the preceding line. Then, we step through until we get to the NULL marker at the end. For additional comprehensibility, I'll typedef a string type:

```
#include <stdio.h>

typedef char* string;

int main(){
    string str = "thread";
    for (string *list = (string[]){"yarn", str, "rope", NULL}; *list; list++)
        printf("%s\n", *list);
}
```

It's still noisy, so let's hide all the syntactic noise in a macro. Then main is as clean as can be:

```
#include <stdio.h>
//I'll do it without the typedef this time.

#define Foreach_string(iterator, ...)\
    for (char **iterator = (char*[]){__VA_ARGS__, NULL}; *iterator; iterator++)

int main(){
    char *str = "thread";
    Foreach_string(i, "yarn", str, "rope"){
        printf("%s\n", *i);
    }
}
```

# Vectorize a Function

The free function takes exactly one argument, so we often have a long cleanup at the end of a function of the form:

```
free(ptr1);
free(ptr2);
free(ptr3);
free(ptr4);
```

How annoying! No self-respecting LISPer would ever allow such redundancy to stand, but would write a vectorized free function that would allow:

```
free_all(ptr1, ptr2, ptr3, ptr4);
```

If you've read the chapter to this point, then the following sentence will make complete sense to you: we can write a variadic macro that generates an array (ended by a stopper) via compound literal, then runs a for loop that applies the function to each element of the array. Example 10-6 adds it all up.

*Example 10-6. The machinery to vectorize any function that takes in any type of pointer (vectorize.c)*

```
#include <stdio.h>
#include <stdlib.h> //malloc, free

#define Fn_apply(type, fn, ...) {                                   \  ❶
    void *stopper_for_apply = (int[]){0};                           \  ❷
    type **list_for_apply = (type*[]){__VA_ARGS__, stopper_for_apply}; \
    for (int i=0; list_for_apply[i] != stopper_for_apply; i++)      \
        fn(list_for_apply[i]);                                      \
}

#define Free_all(...) Fn_apply(void, free, __VA_ARGS__);

int main(){
    double *x= malloc(10);
    double *y= malloc(100);
    double *z= malloc(1000);

    Free_all(x, y, z);
}
```

❶ For added safety, the macro takes in a type name. I put it before the function name, because the type-then-name ordering is reminiscent of a function declaration.

❷ We need a stopper that we can guarantee won't match any in-use pointers, including any NULL pointers, so we use the compound literal form to allocate an array holding a single integer and point to that. Notice how the stopping condition of the for loop looks at the pointers themselves, not what they are pointing to.

Now that the machinery is in place, we can wrap this vectorizing macro around anything that takes in a pointer. For the GSL, you could define:

```
#define Gsl_vector_free_all(...) \
        Fn_apply(gsl_vector, gsl_vector_free, __VA_ARGS__);
#define Gsl_matrix_free_all(...) \
        Fn_apply(gsl_matrix, gsl_matrix_free, __VA_ARGS__);
```

We still get compile-time type-checking (unless we set the pointer type to void), which ensures that the macro inputs are a list of pointers of the same type. To take in a set of heterogeneous elements, we need one more feature—designated initializers.

# Designated Initializers

I'm going to define this term by example. Here is a short program that prints a 3-by-3 grid to the screen, with a star in one spot. You get to specify whether you want the star to be in the upper right, left center, or wherever by setting up a direction_s structure.

The focus of Example 10-7 is in main, where we declare three of these structures using designated initializers—i.e., we designate the name of each structure element in the initializer.

*Example 10-7. Using designated initializers to specify a structure (boxes.c)*

```
#include <stdio.h>

typedef struct {
    char *name;
    int left, right, up, down;
} direction_s;

void this_row(direction_s d); //these functions are below
void draw_box(direction_s d);

int main(){
    direction_s D = {.name="left", .left=1};              ❶
    draw_box(D);

    D = (direction_s) {"upper right", .up=1, .right=1};   ❷
    draw_box(D);

    draw_box((direction_s){});                            ❸
}

void this_row(direction_s d){                             ❹
    printf( d.left    ? "*..\n"
            : d.right ? "..*\n"
            : ".*.\n");
}

void draw_box(direction_s d){
    printf("%s:\n", (d.name ? d.name : "a box"));
    d.up                ? this_row(d) : printf("...\n");
    (!d.up && !d.down)  ? this_row(d) : printf("...\n");
    d.down              ? this_row(d) : printf("...\n");
```

```
    printf("\n");
}
```

❶ This is our first designated initializer. Because .right, .up, and .down are not specified, they are initialized to zero.

❷ It seems natural that the name goes first, so we can use it as the first initializer, with no label, without ambiguity.

❸ This is the extreme case, where everything is initialized to zero.

❹ Everything after this line is about printing the box to the screen, so there's nothing novel after this point.

The old school method of filling structs was to memorize the order of struct elements and initialize all of them without any labels, so the upper right declaration without a label would be:

```
    direction_s upright = {NULL, 0, 1, 1, 0};
```

This is illegible and makes people hate C. Outside of the rare situation where the order is truly natural and obvious, please consider the unlabeled form to be deprecated.

- Did you notice that in the setup of the upper right struct, I had designated elements out of order relative to the order in the structure declaration? Life is too short to remember the order of arbitrarily ordered sets—let the compiler sort 'em out.
- The elements not declared are initialized to zero. No elements are left undefined. [C99 § 6.7.8(21) and C11 § 6.7.9(21)]
- You can mix designated and not-designated initializers. In Example 10-7, it seemed natural enough that the name comes first (and that a string like "upper right" isn't an integer), so when the name isn't explicitly tagged as such, the declaration is still legible. The rule is that the compiler picks up where it left off:

```
    typedef struct{
        int one;
        double two, three, four;
    } n_s;

    n_s justone = {10, .three=8};     //10 with no label gets dropped into
                                       //the first slot: .one=10
    n_s threefour = {.two=8, 3, 4};   //By the pick up where you left off rule, 3 gets put in
                                       //the next slot after .two: .three=3 and .four=4
```

- I had introduced compound literals in terms of arrays, but being that structs are more or less arrays with named and oddly sized elements, you can use them for structs, too, as I did in the upper right and center structs in the sample code. As before, you need to add a cast-like (typename) before the curly braces. The first example in main is a direct declaration and so doesn't need a compound initializer syntax, while later assignments set up an anonymous struct via compound literal and then copy that anonymous struct to D or send it to a subfunction.

---

**Your Turn:** Rewrite every struct declaration in all of your code to use designated initializers. I mean this. The old school way, without markers for which initializer went where, was terrible. Notice also that you can rewrite junk like

```
direction_s D;
D.left = 1;
D.right = 0;
D.up = 1;
D.down = 0;
```

with

```
direction_s D = {.left=1, .up=1};
```

---

# Initialize Arrays and Structs with Zeros

If you declare a variable inside a function, then C won't zero it out automatically (which is perhaps odd for things called automatic variables). I'm guessing that the rationale here is a speed savings: when setting up the frame for a function, zeroing out bits is extra time spent, which could potentially add up if you call the function a million times and it's 1985.

But here in the present, leaving a variable undefined is asking for trouble.

For simple numeric data, set it to zero on the line where you declare the variable. For pointers, including strings, set it to NULL. That's easy enough, as long as you remember (and a good compiler will warn you if you risk using a variable before it is initialized).

For structs and arrays of constant size, I just showed you that if you use designated initializers but leave some elements blank, those blank elements get set to zero. You can therefore set the whole structure to zero by assigning a complete blank. Here's a do-nothing program to demonstrate the idea:

```
typedef struct {
    int la, de, da;
} ladeda_s;

int main(){
    ladeda_s emptystruct = {};
    int ll[20] = {};
}
```

Isn't that easy and sweet?

Now for the sad part: let us say that you have a variable-length array (i.e., one whose length is set by a runtime variable). The only way to zero it out is via `memset`:

```
int main(){
    int length=20;
    int ll[length];
    memset(ll, 0, 20*sizeof(int));
}
```

So it goes.[1]

---

**Your Turn:** Write yourself a macro to declare a variable-length array and set all of its elements to zero. You'll need inputs listing the type, name, and size.

---

For arrays that are sparse but not entirely empty, you can use designated initializers:

```
//By the pick up where you left off rule, equivalent to {0, 0, 1.1, 0, 0, 2.2, 3.3}:
double list1[7] = {[2]=1.1, [5]=2.2, 3.3}
```

# Typedefs Save the Day

Designated initializers give new life to structs, and the rest of this chapter is largely a reconsideration of what structs can do for us now that they don't hurt so much to use.

But first, you've got to declare the format of your structs. Here's a sample of the format I use:

```
typedef struct newstruct_s {
    int a, b;
    double c, d;
} newstruct_s;
```

---

1 You can blame ISO C standard §6.7.8(3) for this, because it insists that variable length arrays can't be initialized. I say the compiler should be able to work it out.

This declares a new type (newstruct_s) that happens to be a structure of the given form (struct newstruct_s). You'll here and there find authors who come up with two different names for the struct tag and the typedef, such as typedef struct _nst { ... } newstruct_s;. This is unnecessary: struct tags have a separate namespace from other identifiers [K&R 2nd ed. §A8.3 (p. 213); C99 and C11 §6.2.3(1)], so there is never ambiguity to the compiler. I find that repeating the name doesn't produce any ambiguity for us humans either, and saves the trouble of inventing another naming convention.

The POSIX standard reserves names ending in _t for future types that might one day be added to the standard. Formally, the C standard only reserves int...._t and uint...._t, but each new standard slips in all sorts of new types ending in _t via optional headers. A lot of people don't spend a second worrying about potential name clashes their code will face when C22 comes out, and use the _t ending freely. In this book, I end struct names with _s.

You can declare a structure of this type in two ways:

```
newstruct_s ns1;
struct newstruct_s ns2;
```

There are only a few reasons for why you would need the struct newstruct_s name instead of just newstruct_s:

- If you've got a struct that includes one of its own kind as an element (such as how the next pointer of a linked-list structure is to another linked-list structure). For example:

    ```
    typedef struct newstruct_s {
        int a, b;
        double c, d;
        struct newstruct_s *next;
    } newstruct_s;
    ```

- The standard for C11 anonymous structs goes out of its way to require that you use the struct newstruct_s form. This will come up in "C, with fewer seams" on page 255.

- Some people just kinda like using the struct newstruct_s format, which brings us to a note on style.

# A Style Note

I was surprised to see that there are people in the world who think that typedefs are obfuscatory. For example, from the Linux-kernel style file: "When you see a `vps_t a;` in the source, what does it mean? In contrast, if it says `struct virtual_container *a;` you can actually tell what `a` is." The natural response to this is that having a longer name—and even one ending in *container*—clarifies the code, not the word `struct` hanging at the beginning.

But this typedef aversion had to come from somewhere. Further research turned up several sources that advise using typedefs to define units. For example:

```
typedef double inches;
typedef double meters;

inches length1;
meters length2;
```

Now you have to look up what `inches` really is every time it is used (`unsigned int`? `double`?), and it doesn't even afford any error protection. A hundred lines down, when you assign:

```
length1 = length2;
```

you have already forgotten about the clever type declaration, and the typical C compiler won't flag this as an error. If you need to take care of units, attach them to the variable name, so the error will be evident:

```
double length1_inches, length2_meters;
```

*//100 lines later:*

```
length1_inches = length2_meters;  //this line is self-evidently wrong.
```

It makes sense to use typedefs that are global, and their internals should be known by the user as sparingly as those of any other global elements, because looking up their declaration is as much a distraction as looking up the declaration of a variable, so they can impose cognitive load at the same time that they impose structure.

That said, it's hard to find a production library that doesn't rely heavily on typdefed global structures, like the GSL's `gsl_vectors` and `gsl_matrixes`; or GLib's hashes, trees, and plethora of other objects. Even the source code for Git, written by Linus Torvalds to be the revision control system for the Linux kernel, has a few carefully placed typedefed structures.

Also, the scope of a typedef is the same as the scope of any other declaration. That means that you can typedef things inside a single file and not worry about them cluttering up the namespace outside that file, and you might even find reason to have typedefs inside a single function. You might have noticed that most of the typedefs so far are local, meaning that the reader can look up the definition by scanning back a few lines, and when they are global (i.e., in a header to be included everywhere), they are somehow hidden in a wrapper, meaning that the reader never has to look up the definition at all. So we can write structs that do not impose cognitive load.

# Return Multiple Items from a Function

A mathematical function doesn't have to map to one dimension. For example, a function that maps to a 2D point *(x, y)* is nothing at all spectacular.

Python (among other languages) lets you return multiple return values using lists, like this:

```
#Given the standard paper size name, return its width, height
def width_length(papertype):
    if (papertype=="A4"):
        return [210, 297]
    if (papertype=="Letter"):
        return [216, 279]
    if (papertype=="Legal"):
        return [216, 356]

[a, b] = width_length("A4");
print("width= %i, height=%i" %(a, b))
```

In C, you can always return a struct, and thus as many subelements as desired. This is why I was praising the joys of having throwaway structs earlier: generating a function-specific struct is not a big deal.

Let's face it: C is still going to be more verbose than languages that have a special syntax for returning lists. But as demonstrated in Example 10-8, it is not impossible to clearly express that the function is returning a value in $\mathbb{R}^2$.

*Example 10-8. If you need to return multiple values from a function, return a struct (papersize.c)*

```
#include <stdio.h>
#include <strings.h> //strcasecmp (from POSIX)
#include <math.h>    //NaN

typedef struct {
    double width, height;
} size_s;

size_s width_height(char *papertype){
  return
    !strcasecmp(papertype, "A4")     ? (size_s) {.width=210, .height=297}
  : !strcasecmp(papertype, "Letter") ? (size_s) {.width=216, .height=279}
  : !strcasecmp(papertype, "Legal")  ? (size_s) {.width=216, .height=356}
                                     : (size_s) {.width=NAN, .height=NAN};
```

```
}
int main(){
    size_s a4size = width_height("a4");
    printf("width= %g, height=%g\n", a4size.width, a4size.height);
}
```

 The code sample uses the *condition? iftrue : else* form, which is a single expression, and so can appear after the return. Notice how a sequence of these cascades neatly into a sequence of cases (including that last catchall else clause at the end). I like to format this sort of thing into a nice little table; you can find people who call this terrible style.

The alternative is to use pointers, which is common and not considered bad form, but it certainly obfuscates what is input and what is output, and makes the version with the extra typedef look stylistically great:

```
//Return height and width via pointer:
void width_height(char *papertype, double *width, double *height);
```

```
//or return width directly and height via pointer:
double width_height(char *papertype, double *height);
```

## Reporting Errors

Pete Goodliffe discusses the various means of returning an error code from a function and is somewhat pessimistic about the options.

- In some cases, the value returned can have a specific semaphore value, like -1 for integers or NaN for floating-point numbers (but cases where the full range of the variable is valid are common enough).

- You can set a global error flag, but in 2006, Goodliffe was unable to recommend using the C11 _Thread_local keyword to allow multiple threads to allow the flag to work properly when running in parallel. Although a global-to-the-program error flag is typically unworkable, a small suite of functions that work closely together could conceivably be written with a _Thread_local file-scope variable.

- The third option is to "return a compound data type (or tuple) containing both the return value and an error code. This is rather clumsy in the popular C-like languages and is seldom seen in them."

To this point in the chapter, you have seen that there are many benefits to returning a struct, and modern C provides lots of facilities (typedefs, designated initalizers) that eliminate most of the clumsiness.

Any time you are writing a new struct, consider adding an error or status element. Whenever your new struct is returned from a function, you'll then have a built-in means of communicating whether it is valid for use.

Example 10-9 turns a physics 101 equation into an error-checked function to answer the question: given that an ideal object of a given mass has been in freefall to Earth for a given number of seconds, what is its kinetic energy?

I tricked it up with a lot of macros, because I find that authors tend to be more comfortable writing error-handling macros in C than for most other problems, perhaps because nobody wants error-checking to overwhelm the central flow of the story.

*Example 10-9. If your function returns a value and an error, you can use a struct to do so (errortuple.c)*

```
#include <stdio.h>
#include <math.h> //NaN, pow

#define make_err_s(intype, shortname) \        ❶
    typedef struct {                  \
        intype value;                 \
        char const *error;            \        ❷
    } shortname##_err_s;

make_err_s(double, double)
make_err_s(int, int)
make_err_s(char *, string)

double_err_s free_fall_energy(double time, double mass){
    double_err_s out = {};  //initialize to all zeros.
    out.error = time < 0      ? "negative time"        ❸
              : mass < 0      ? "negative mass"
              : isnan(time) ? "NaN time"
              : isnan(mass) ? "NaN mass"
                            : NULL;
    if (out.error) return out;                         ❹

    double velocity = 9.8*time;
    out.value = mass*pow(velocity, 2)/2.;
    return out;
}

#define Check_err(checkme, return_val) \             ❺
    if (checkme.error) {fprintf(stderr, "error: %s\n", checkme.error); return return_val;}

int main(){
    double notime=0, fraction=0;
    double_err_s energy = free_fall_energy(1, 1);     ❻
```

```
    Check_err(energy, 1);
    printf("Energy after one second: %g Joules\n", energy.value);

    energy = free_fall_energy(2, 1);
    Check_err(energy, 1);
    printf("Energy after two seconds: %g Joules\n", energy.value);

    energy = free_fall_energy(notime/fraction, 1);
    Check_err(energy, 1);
    printf("Energy after 0/0 seconds: %g Joules\n", energy.value);
}
```

❶ If you like the idea of returning a value/error tuple, then you'll want one for every type. So I thought I'd really trick this up by writing a macro to make it easy to produce one tuple type for every base type. See the usage a few lines down, to generate double_err_s, int_err_s, and string_err_s. If you think this is one layer too many, then you don't have to use it.

❷ Why not let errors be a string instead of an integer? The error messages will typically be constant strings, so there is no messing about with memory management, and nobody needs to look up the translations for obscure enums. See "Enums and Strings" on page 149 for discussion.

❸ Another table of return values. This sort of thing is common in the input-checking preliminaries to a function. Notice that the out.error element points to one of the literal strings listed. Because no strings get copied, nothing has to be allocated or freed. To clarify this further, I made error a pointer to char const.

❹ Or, use the Stopif macro from "Error Checking" on page 58: Stopif(out.error, return out, out.error).

❺ Macros to check for errors on return are a common C idiom. Because the error is a string, the macro can print it to stderr (or perhaps an error log) directly.

❻ Usage is as expected. Authors often lament how easy it is for users to traipse past the error codes returned from their functions, and in that respect, putting the output value in a tuple is a good reminder that the output includes an error code that the user of the function should take into account.

# Flexible Function Inputs

A *variadic function* is one that takes a variable number of inputs. The most famous example is printf, where both printf("Hi.") and printf("%f %f %i\n", first, second, third) are valid, even though the first example has one input and the second has four.

Simply put, C's variadic functions provide exactly enough power to implement `printf`, and nothing more. You must have an initial fixed argument, and it's more or less expected that that first argument provides a catalog to the types of the subsequent elements, or at least a count. In the preceding example, the first argument (`"%f %f %i \n"`) indicates that the next two items are expected to be floating-point, and the last an integer.

There is no type safety: if you pass an `int` like 1 when you thought you were passing a `float` like 1.0, results are undefined. If the function expects to have three elements passed in but you sent only two, you're likely to get a segfault. Because of issues like this, CERT, a software security group, considers variadic functions to be a security risk (severity: high; likelihood: probable).[2]

Earlier, you met one way to provide some safety to variable-length function inputs of homogeneous type: by writing a wrapper macro that appends a stopper to the end of a list, we can guarantee that the base function will not receive a never-ending list. The compound literal will also check the input types and fail to compile if you send in an input of the wrong type.

This section covers two more ways to implement variadic functions with some type-checking safety. The last method will let you name your arguments, which can also help to reduce your error rate. I concur with CERT in considering free-form variadic functions too risky and use only the forms here for variadic functions in my own code.

The first safe format in this segment free-rides on the compiler's checking for `printf`, extending the already-familiar form. The second format in this segment uses a variadic macro to prep the inputs to use the designated initializer syntax in function headers.

## Declare Your Function as printf-Style

First, let's go the traditional route, and use C89's variadic function facilities. I mention this because you might be in a situation where macros somehow can't be used. Such situations are typically social, not technical—there are few if any cases where a variadic function can't be replaced by a variadic macro using one of the techniques discussed in this chapter.

---

2 See the CERT website (*http://bit.ly/SAJTl7*).

To make the C89 variadic function safe, we'll need an addition from gcc, but widely adopted by other compilers: the `__attribute__`, which allows for compiler-specific features.[3]

```
#include "config.h"
#ifndef HAVE__ATTRIBUTE__
#define __attribute__(...)
#endif
```

It goes on the declaration line of a variable, struct, or function (so if your function isn't declared before use, you'll need to do so).

gcc and clang will let you set an attribute to declare a function to be in the style of printf, meaning that the compiler will type-check and warn you should you have an int or a double* in a slot reserved for a double.

Say that we want a version of system that will allow printf-style inputs. In Example 10-10, the system_w_printf function takes in printf-style inputs, writes them to a string, and sends them to the standard system command. The function uses vasprintf, the va_list-friendly analog to asprintf. Both of these are BSD/GNU-standard. If you need to stick to C99, replace them with the snprintf analog vsnprintf (and so, #include <stdarg.h>).

The main function is a simple sample usage: it takes the first input from the command line and runs ls on it.

*Example 10-10. The olden way of processing variable-length inputs (olden_varargs.c)*

```
#define _GNU_SOURCE //cause stdio.h to include vasprintf
#include <stdio.h>  //printf, vasprintf
#include <stdarg.h> //va_start, va_end
#include <stdlib.h> //system, free
#include <assert.h>

int system_w_printf(char const *fmt, ...) __attribute__ ((format (printf,1,2)));   ❶

int system_w_printf(char const *fmt, ...){
    char *cmd;
    va_list argp;
    va_start(argp, fmt);
    vasprintf(&cmd, fmt, argp);
    va_end(argp);
```

---

3 If you are worried that users will have a compiler that does not support __attribute__, Autotools can allay your concerns. Get the AX_C___ATTRIBUTE__ macro from the Autoconf archive and paste it into a file named *aclocal.m4* in your project directory, add the call AX_C___ATTRIBUTE__ to *configure.ac*, then have the C preprocessor define __attribute__ to be blank should Autoconf find the user's compiler doesn't support it, via

```
    int out= system(cmd);
    free(cmd);
    return out;
}

int main(int argc, char **argv){
    assert(argc == 2);                                          ❷
    return system_w_printf("ls %s", argv[1]);
}
```

❶  Mark this as a `printf`-like function where input one is the format specifier, and
    the list of additional parameters starts at input two.

❷  I confess: I'm being lazy here. Use the raw `assert` macro only to check inter-
    mediate values under the author's control, not inputs sent in by the user. See
    "Error Checking" on page 58 for a macro appropriate for input testing.

The one advantage this has over the variadic macro is that it is awkward to get a
return value from a macro. However, the macro version in Example 10-11 is shorter
and easier, and if your compiler type-checks the inputs to `printf`-family functions,
then it'll do so here (without any `gcc`/`clang`-specific attributes).

*Example 10-11. The macro version has fewer moving parts (macro_varargs.c)*

```
#define _GNU_SOURCE //cause stdio.h to include vasprintf
#include <stdio.h>  //printf, vasprintf
#include <stdlib.h> //system
#include <assert.h>

#define System_w_printf(outval, ...) {              \
    char *string_for_systemf;                       \
    asprintf(&string_for_systemf, __VA_ARGS__); \
    outval = system(string_for_systemf);            \
    free(string_for_systemf);                       \
}

int main(int argc, char **argv){
    assert(argc == 2);
    int out;
    System_w_printf(out, "ls %s", argv[1]);
    return out;
}
```

# Optional and Named Arguments

I've already shown how you can send a list of identical arguments to a function more
cleanly via compound literal plus a variable-length macro, in "Safely Terminated
Lists" on page 211.

---

A struct is in many ways just like an array, but holding not-identical types, so it seems like we could apply the same routine: write a wrapper macro to clean and pack all the elements into a struct, then send the completed struct to the function. Example 10-12 makes it happen.

It puts together a function that takes in a variable number of named arguments. There are three parts to defining the function: the throwaway struct, which the user will never use by name (but that still has to clutter up the global space if the function is going to be global); the macro that inserts its arguments into a struct, which then gets passed to the base function; and the base function.

*Example 10-12. A function that takes in a variable number of named arguments—the arguments not set by the user have default values (ideal.c)*

```c
#include <stdio.h>

typedef struct {                                                    ❶
    double pressure, moles, temp;
} ideal_struct;

/** Find the volume (in cubic meters) via the ideal gas law: V =nRT/P
Inputs:
pressure in atmospheres (default 1)
moles of material (default 1)
temperature in Kelvins (default freezing = 273.15)
  */
#define ideal_pressure(...) ideal_pressure_base((ideal_struct){.pressure=1,   \   ❷
                                .moles=1, .temp=273.15, __VA_ARGS__})

double ideal_pressure_base(ideal_struct in){                        ❸
    return 8.314 * in.moles*in.temp/in.pressure;
}

int main(){
    printf("volume given defaults: %g\n", ideal_pressure() );
    printf("volume given boiling temp: %g\n", ideal_pressure(.temp=373.15) );   ❹
    printf("volume given two moles: %g\n", ideal_pressure(.moles=2) );
    printf("volume given two boiling moles: %g\n",
                        ideal_pressure(.moles=2, .temp=373.15) );
}
```

❶  First, we need to declare a struct holding the inputs to the function.

❷  The input to the macro will be plugged into the definition of an anonymous struct, wherein the arguments the user puts in the parens will be used as designated initializers.

❸  The function itself takes in an `ideal_struct`, rather than the usual free list of inputs.

❹  The user inputs a list of designated initializers; the ones not listed get given a default value; and then `ideal_pressure_base` will have an input structure with everything it needs.

Here's how the function call (don't tell the user, but it's actually a macro) on the last line will expand:

```
ideal_pressure_base((ideal_struct){.pressure=1, .moles=1, .temp=273.15,
                                     .moles=2, .temp=373.15})
```

The rule is that if an item is initialized multiple times, then the last initialization takes precedence [C99 § 6.7.8(19) and C11 § 6.7.9(19)]. So `.pressure` is left at its default of one, while the other two inputs are set to the user-specified value.

 `clang` flags the repeated initialization of `moles` and `temp` with a warning when using `-Wall`, because the compiler authors expect that the double-initialization is more likely to be an error than a deliberate choice of default values. Turn off this warning by adding `-Wno-initializer-overrides` to your compiler flags. gcc flags this as an error only if you ask for `-Wextra` warnings; use `-Wextra -Woverride-init` if you make use of this option.

---

**Your Turn:** In this case, the throwaway struct might not be so throwaway, because it might make sense to run the formula in multiple directions:

- pressure = 8.314 moles * temp/volume
- moles = pressure *volume /(8.314 temp)
- temp = pressure *volume /(8.314 moles)

Rewrite the struct to also have a volume element, and use the same struct to write the functions for these additional equations.

Then, use these functions to produce a unifying function that takes in a struct with three of `pressure`, `moles`, `temp`, and `volume` (the fourth can be NAN, or you can add a `what_to_solve` element to the struct) and applies the right function to solve for the fourth.

---

Now that arguments are optional, you can add a new argument six months from now without breaking every program that used your function in the meantime. You are free to start with a simple working function and build up additional features as

---

needed. However, we should learn a lesson from the languages that had this power from day one: it is easy to get carried away and build functions with literally dozens of inputs, each handling only an odd case or two.

## Polishing a Dull Function

To this point, the examples have focused on demonstrating simple constructs without too much getting in the way, but short examples can't cover the techniques involved in integrating everything together to form a useful and robust program that solves real-world problems. So the examples from here on in are going to get longer and include more realistic considerations.

Example 10-13 is a dull and unpleasant function. For an amortized loan, the monthly payments are fixed, but the percentage of the loan that is going toward interest is much larger at the outset (when more of the loan is still owed), and diminishes to zero toward the end of the loan. The math is tedious (especially when we add the option to make extra principal payments every month or to sell off the loan early), and you would be forgiven for skipping the guts of the function. Our concern here is with the interface, which takes in 10 inputs in basically arbitrary order. Using this function to do any sort of financial inquiry would be painful and error-prone.

That is, `amortize` looks a lot like many of the legacy functions floating around the C world. It is punk rock only in the sense that it has complete disdain for its audience. So in the style of glossy magazines everywhere, this segment will spruce up this function with a good wrapper. If this were legacy code, we wouldn't be able to change the function's interface (other programs might depend on it), so on top of the procedure that the ideal gas example used to generate named, optional inputs, we will need to add a prep function to bridge between the macro output and the fixed legacy-function inputs.

*Example 10-13. A difficult-to-use function with too many inputs and no error-checking (amortize.c)*

```
#include <math.h> //pow.
#include <stdio.h>
#include "amortize.h"

double amortize(double amt, double rate, double inflation, int months,
                int selloff_month, double extra_payoff, int verbose,
                double *interest_pv, double *duration, double *monthly_payment){
    double total_interest = 0;
    *interest_pv = 0;
    double mrate = rate/1200;

    //The monthly rate is fixed, but the proportion going to interest changes.
    *monthly_payment = amt * mrate/(1-pow(1+mrate, -months)) + extra_payoff;
    if (verbose) printf("Your total monthly payment: %g\n\n", *monthly_payment);
```

```
        int end_month = (selloff_month && selloff_month < months )
                            ? selloff_month
                            : months;
        if (verbose) printf("yr/mon\t Princ.\t\tInt.\t| PV Princ.\t PV Int.\t Ratio\n");
        int m;
        for (m=0; m < end_month && amt > 0; m++){
            double interest_payment = amt*mrate;
            double principal_payment = *monthly_payment - interest_payment;
            if (amt <= 0)
                principal_payment =
                interest_payment  = 0;
            amt -= principal_payment;
            double deflator = pow(1+ inflation/100, -m/12.);
            *interest_pv   += interest_payment * deflator;
            total_interest += interest_payment;
            if (verbose) printf("%i/%i\t%7.2f\t\t%7.2f\t| %7.2f\t %7.2f\t%7.2f\n",
                    m/12, m-12*(m/12)+1, principal_payment, interest_payment,
                    principal_payment*deflator, interest_payment*deflator,
                    principal_payment/(principal_payment+interest_payment)*100);
        }
        *duration = m/12.;
        return total_interest;
}
```

Example 10-14 and Example 10-15 set up a user-friendly interface to the function. Most of the header file is Doxygen-style documentation, because with so many inputs it would be insane not to document them all, and because we now have to tell the user what the defaults will be, should the user omit an input.

*Example 10-14. The header file, which is mostly documentation, plus a macro and a header for a prep function (amortize.h)*

```
double amortize(double amt, double rate, double inflation, int months,
            int selloff_month, double extra_payoff, int verbose,
            double *interest_pv, double *duration, double *monthly_payment);

typedef struct {
    double amount, years, rate, selloff_year, extra_payoff, inflation;   ❶
    int months, selloff_month;
    _Bool show_table;
    double interest, interest_pv, monthly_payment, years_to_payoff;
    char *error;
} amortization_s;


/** Calculate the inflation-adjusted amount of interest you would pay   ❷
    over the life of an amortized loan, such as a mortgage.

\li \c amount  The dollar value of the loan. No default--if unspecified,
               print an error and return zeros.
\li \c months  The number of months in the loan. Default: zero, but see years.
```

```
\li \c years   If you do not specify months, you can specify the number of
               years. E.g., 10.5=ten years, six months.
               Default: 30 (a typical U.S. mortgage).
\li \c rate   The interest rate of the loan, expressed in annual
               percentage rate (APR). Default: 4.5 (i.e., 4.5%), which
               is typical for the current (US 2012) housing market.
\li \c inflation   The inflation rate as an annual percent, for calculating
               the present value of money. Default: 0, meaning no
               present-value adjustment. A rate of about 3 has been typical
               for the last few decades in the US.
\li \c selloff_month   At this month, the loan is paid off (e.g., you resell
               the house). Default: zero (meaning no selloff).
\li \c selloff_year   If selloff_month==0 and this is positive, the year of
               selloff. Default: zero (meaning no selloff).
\li \c extra_payoff   Additional monthly principal payment. Default: zero.
\li \c show_table   If nonzero, display a table of payments. If zero, display
               nothing (just return the total interest). Default: 1

All inputs but \c extra_payoff and \c inflation must be nonnegative.

\return   an \c amortization_s structure, with all of the above values set as
          per your input, plus:

\li \c interest   Total cash paid in interest.
\li \c interest_pv   Total interest paid, with present-value adjustment for inflation.
\li \c monthly_payment   The fixed monthly payment (for a mortgage, taxes and
                         interest get added to this)
\li \c years_to_payoff   Normally the duration or selloff date, but if you make early
                         payments, the loan is paid off sooner.
\li \c error             If <tt>error != NULL</tt>, something went wrong and the results
                         are invalid.

*/
#define amortization(...) amortize_prep((amortization_s){.show_table=1, \
                                        __VA_ARGS__})  ❸

amortization_s amortize_prep(amortization_s in);
```

❶ The structure used by the macro to transfer data to the prep function. It has to be part of the same scope as the macro and prep function themselves. Some elements are input elements that are not in the amortize function but can make the user's life easier; some elements are output elements to be filled.

❷ The documentation, in Doxygen format. It's a good thing when the documentation takes up most of the interface file. Notice how each input has a default listed.

❸ This macro stuffs the user's inputs—perhaps something like amortization (.amount=2e6, .rate=3.0)—into a designated initializer for an amortization_s. We have to set the default to show_table here, because without it, there's no way to distinguish between a user who explicitly sets `.show_table=0` and a user who omits `.show_table` entirely. So if we want a default that isn't zero for a variable where the user could sensibly send in zero, we have to use this form.

The three ingredients to the named-argument setup are still apparent: a typedef for a struct, a macro that takes in named elements and fills the struct, and a function that takes in a single struct as input. However, the function being called is a prep function, wedged in between the macro and the base function, the declaration of which is here in the header. Its guts are in Example 10-15.

*Example 10-15. The nonpublic part of the interface (amort_interface.c)*

```
#include "stopif.h"
#include <stdio.h>
#include "amortize.h"

amortization_s amortize_prep(amortization_s in){                    ❶
    Stopif(!in.amount || in.amount < 0 || in.rate < 0              ❷
            || in.months < 0 || in.years < 0 || in.selloff_month < 0
            || in.selloff_year < 0,
            return (amortization_s){.error="Invalid input"},
            "Invalid input. Returning zeros.");

    int months = in.months;
    if (!months){
        if (in.years) months = in.years * 12;
        else          months = 12 * 30; //home loan
    }

    int selloff_month = in.selloff_month;
    if (!selloff_month && in.selloff_year)
        selloff_month = in.selloff_year * 12;

    amortization_s out = in;
    out.rate = in.rate ? in.rate : 4.5;                             ❸
    out.interest = amortize(in.amount, out.rate, in.inflation,
            months, selloff_month, in.extra_payoff, in.show_table,
            &(out.interest_pv), &(out.years_to_payoff), &(out.monthly_payment));
    return out;
}
```

❶  This is the prep function that `amortize` should have had: it sets nontrivial, intelligent defaults, and checks for an input errors. Now it's OK that `amortize` goes straight to business, because all the introductory work happened here.

❷  See "Error Checking" on page 58 for discussion of the `Stopif` macro. As per the discussion there, the check on this line is more to prevent segfaults and check sanity than to allow users to do automated testing of error conditions.

❸ Because it's a simple constant, we could also have set the rate in the `amortiza tion` macro, along with the default for `show_table`. You've got options.

The immediate purpose of the prep function is to take in a single struct and call the `amortize` function with the struct's elements, because we can't change the interface to `amortize` directly. But now that we have a function dedicated to preparing function inputs, we can really do error-checking and default-setting right. For example, we can now give users the option of specifying time periods in months or years, and can use this prep function to throw errors if the inputs are out of bounds or insensible.

Defaults are especially important for a function like this one, by the way, because most of us don't know (and have little interest in finding out) what a reasonable inflation rate is. If a computer can offer the user subject-matter knowledge that he or she might not have, and can do so with an unobtrusive default that can be overridden with no effort, then rare will be the user who is ungrateful.

The `amortize` function returns several different values. As per "Return Multiple Items from a Function" on page 222, putting them all in a single struct is a nice alternative to how `amortize` returns one value and then puts the rest into pointers sent as input. Also, the form using designated initializers via variadic macros requires another structure intermediating; why not combine the two structures? The result is an output structure that retains all of the input specifications.

After all that interface work, we now have a well-documented, easy-to-use, error-checked function, and the program in Example 10-16 can run lots of what-if scenarios with no hassle. It uses *amortize.c* and *amort_interface.c* from earlier, and the former file uses `pow` from the math library, so your makefile will look like:

```
P=amort_use
objects=amort_interface.o amortize.o
CFLAGS=-g -Wall -O3 #the usual
LDLIBS=-lm
CC=c99

$(P):$(objects)
```

*Example 10-16. At this point, we can use the amortization macro/function to write readable what-if scenarios (amort_use.c)*

```
#include <stdio.h>
#include "amortize.h"

int main(){
    printf("A typical loan:\n");
    amortization_s nopayments = amortization(.amount=200000, .inflation=3);
    printf("You flushed real $%g down the toilet, or $%g in present value.\n",
            nopayments.interest, nopayments.interest_pv);
```

```
amortization_s a_hundred = amortization(.amount=200000, .inflation=3,
                                         .show_table=0, .extra_payoff=100);
printf("Paying an extra $100/month, you lose only $%g (PV), "
       "and the loan is paid off in %g years.\n",
       a_hundred.interest_pv, a_hundred.years_to_payoff);

printf("If you sell off in ten years, you pay $%g in interest (PV).\n",
       amortization(.amount=200000, .inflation=3,
                    .show_table=0, .selloff_year=10).interest_pv);  ❶
}
```

❶ The `amortization` function returns a struct, and in the first two uses, the struct was given a name, and the named struct's elements were used. But if you don't need the intermediate named variable, don't bother. This line pulls the one element of the struct that we need from the function. If the function returned a piece of `malloced` memory you couldn't do this, because you'd need a name to send to the memory-freeing function, but notice how this entire chapter is about passing structs, not pointers-to-structs.

There are a lot of lines of code wrapping the original function, but the boilerplate struct and macros to set up named arguments are only a few of them. The rest is documentation and intelligent input-handling that is well worth adding. As a whole, we've taken a function with an almost unusable interface and made it as user-friendly as an amortization calculator can be.

# The Void Pointer and the Structures It Points To

This segment is about the implementation of generic procedures and generic structures. One example in this segment will apply some function to every file in a directory hierarchy, letting the user print the filenames to screen, search for a string, or whatever else comes to mind. Another example will use GLib's hash structure to record a count of every character encountered in a file, which means associating a Unicode character key with an integer value. Of course, GLib provides a hash structure that can take any type of key and any type of value, so the Unicode character counter is an application of the general container.

All this versatility is thanks to the void pointer, which can point to anything. The hash function and directory processing routine are wholly indifferent to what is being pointed to and simply pass the values through as needed. Type safety becomes our responsibility, but structs will help us retain type safety and will make it easier to write and work with generic procedures.

# Functions with Generic Inputs

A *callback function* is a function that is passed to another function for the other function's use. In this example to to recurse through a directory and do something to every file found there, the callback is the function handed to the directory-traversal procedure for it to apply to each file.

The problem is depicted in Figure 10-1. With a direct function call, the compiler knows the type of your data, it knows the type the function requires, and if they don't match the compiler will tell you. But a generic procedure should not dictate the format for the function or the data the function uses. "Pthreads" on page 310 makes use of pthread_create, which (omitting the irrelevant parts) might be declared with a form like:

```
typedef void *(*void_ptr_to_void_ptr)(void *in);
int pthread_create(..., void *ptr, void_ptr_to_void_ptr fn);
```

If we make a call like pthread_create(..., *indata*, *myfunc*), then the type information for *indata* has been lost, as it was cast to a void pointer. We can expect that somewhere in pthread_create, a call of the form *myfunc(indata)* will occur. If *indata* is a double*, and *myfunc* takes a char*, then this is a disaster the compiler can't prevent.

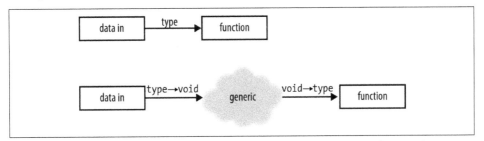

*Figure 10-1. Calling a function directly versus having a generic procedure perform the call*

Example 10-17 is the header file for an implementation of the function that applies functions to every directory and file within a given directory. It includes Doxygen documentation of what the process_dir function is expected to do. As it should be, the documentation is roughly as long as the code will be.

*Example 10-17. A header file for a generic directory-recursing function (process_dir.h)*

```
struct filestruct;
typedef void (*level_fn)(struct filestruct path);

typedef struct filestruct{
    char *name, *fullname;
```

```
        level_fn directory_action, file_action;
        int depth, error;
        void *data;
    } filestruct;                                                            ❶

    /** I get the contents of the given directory, run \c file_action on each
        file, and for each directory run \c dir_action and recurse into the directory.
        Note that this makes the traversal depth first.

        Your functions will take in a \c filestruct, qv. Note that there is an \c error
        element, which you can set to one to indicate an error.

        Inputs are designated initializers, and may include:

        \li \c .name The current file or directory name
        \li \c .fullname The path of the current file or directory
        \li \c .directory_action A function that takes in a \c filestruct.
                I will call it with an appropriately-set \c filestruct
                for every directory (just before the files in the directory
                are processed).
        \li \c .file_action Like the \c directory_action, but the function
                I will call for every non-directory file.
        \li \c .data A void pointer to be passed in to your functions.

        \return 0=OK, otherwise the count of directories that failed + errors thrown
                by your scripts.

        Sample usage:
    \code
        void dirp(filestruct in){ printf("Directory: <%s>\n", in.name); }
        void filep(filestruct in){ printf("File: %s\n", in.name); }

        //list files, but not directories, in current dir:
        process_dir(.file_action=filep);

        //show everything in my home directory:
        process_dir(.name="/home/b", .file_action=filep, .directory_action=dirp);
    \endcode
    */
    #define process_dir(...) process_dir_r((filestruct){__VA_ARGS__})         ❷

    int process_dir_r(filestruct level);                                     ❸
```

❶  Here they are again: the three parts of a function that takes in named arguments.
    Even setting that aside, this struct will be essential to retaining type safety when
    passing void pointers.

❷  The macro that stuffs designated initializers from the user into a compound lit-
    eral struct.

❸ The function that takes in the struct built by the `process_dir` macro. Users won't call it directly.

Comparing this with Figure 10-1, this header already indicates a partial solution to the type-safety problem: defining a definite type, the `filestruct`, and requiring the callback take in a struct of that type. There's still a void pointer buried at the end of the struct. I could have left the void pointer outside of the struct, as in:

```
typedef void (*level_fn)(struct filestruct path, void *indata);
```

But as long as we're defining an ad hoc struct as a helper to the `process_dir` function, we might as well throw the void pointer in there. Further, now that we have a struct associated with the `process_dir` function, we can use it to implement the form where a macro turns designated initializers into a function input, as per "Optional and Named Arguments" on page 228. Structs make everything easier.

Example 10-18 presents a use of `process_dir`—the portions before and after the cloud of Figure 10-1. These callback functions are simple, printing some spacing and the file/directory name. There isn't even any type unsafety yet, because the input to the callback was defined to be a certain type of struct.

Here's sample output, for a directory that has two files and a subdirectory named *cfiles*, holding another three files:

```
Tree for sample_dir:
├ cfiles
└──┐
   │ c.c
   │ a.c
   │ b.c
│ a_file
│ another_file
```

*Example 10-18. A program to display a tree of the current directory structure (show_tree.c)*

```c
#include <stdio.h>
#include "process_dir.h"

void print_dir(filestruct in){
    for (int i=0; i< in.depth-1; i++) printf("    ");
    printf("├ %s\n", in.name);
    for (int i=0; i< in.depth-1; i++) printf("    ");
    printf("└──┐\n");
}

void print_file(filestruct in){
    for (int i=0; i< in.depth; i++) printf("    ");
    printf("│ %s\n", in.name);
}
```

```
}

int main(int argc, char **argv){
    char *start = (argc>1) ? argv[1] : ".";
    printf("Tree for %s:\n", start ? start: "the current directory");
    process_dir(.name=start, .file_action=print_file, .directory_action=print_dir);
}
```

As you can see, main hands the `print_dir` and `print_file` functions to pro
cess_dir, and trusts that `process_dir` will call them at the right time with the appropriate inputs.

The `process_dir` function itself is in Example 10-19. Most of the work of the function is absorbed in generating an up-to-date struct describing the file or directory
currently being handled. The given directory is opened, via `opendir`. Then, each call
to `readdir` will pull another entry from the directory, which will describe one file,
directory, link, or whatever else in the given directory. The input `filestruct` is updated with the current entry's information. Depending on whether the directory entry
describes a directory or a file, the appropriate callback is called with the newly prepared `filestruct`. If it's a directory, then the function is recursively called using the
current directory's information.

*Example 10-19. Recurse through a directory, and apply file_action to every file found
and directory_action to every directory found (process_dir.c)*

```
#include "process_dir.h"
#include <dirent.h> //struct dirent
#include <stdlib.h> //free

int process_dir_r(filestruct level){
    if (!level.fullname){
        if (level.name) level.fullname=level.name;
        else            level.fullname=".";
    }
    int errct=0;

    DIR *current=opendir(level.fullname);                                    ❶
    if (!current) return 1;
    struct dirent *entry;
    while((entry=readdir(current))) {
        if (entry->d_name[0]=='.') continue;
        filestruct next_level = level;                                       ❷
        next_level.name = entry->d_name;
        asprintf(&next_level.fullname, "%s/%s", level.fullname, entry->d_name);

        if (entry->d_type==DT_DIR){
            next_level.depth ++;
            if (level.directory_action) level.directory_action(next_level); ❸
            errct+= process_dir_r(next_level);
```

```
    }
    else if (entry->d_type==DT_REG && level.file_action){
        level.file_action(next_level);                              ❹
        errct+= next_level.error;
    }
    free(next_level.fullname);                                      ❺
    }
    closedir(current);
    return errct;
}
```

❶ The opendir, readdir, and closedir functions are POSIX-standard.

❷ For each entry in the directory, make a new copy of the input filestruct, then update it as appropriate.

❸ Given the up-to-date filestruct, call the per-directory function. Recurse into subdirectory.

❹ Given the up-to-date filestruct, call the per-file function.

❺ The filestructs that get made for each step are not pointers and are not mal loced, so they require no memory-management code. However, asprintf does implicitly allocate fullname, so that has to be freed to keep things clean.

The setup successfully implemented the appropriate encapsulation: the printing functions didn't care about POSIX directory handling, and *process_dir.c* knew nothing of what the input functions did. And the function-specific struct made the flow relatively seamless.

## Generic Structures

Linked lists, hashes, trees, and other such data structures are applicable in all sorts of situations, so it makes sense that they would be provided with hooks for void pointers, and then you as a user would check types on the way in and on the way out.

This segment will present a typical textbook example: a character-frequency hash. A hash is a container that holds key/value pairs, with the intent of allowing users to quickly look up values using a key.

Before getting to the part where we process files in a directory, we need to customize the generic GLib hash to the form that the program will use, with a Unicode key and a value holding a single integer. Once this component (which is already a good example of dealing with callbacks) is in place, it will be easy to implement the callbacks for the file traversal part of the program.

As you will see, the equal_chars and printone functions are intended as callbacks for use by functions associated with the hash, so the hash will send to these callbacks two void pointers. Thus, the first lines of these functions declare variables of the correct type, effectively casting the void pointer input to a type.

Example 10-20 presents the header, showing what is for public use out of Example 10-21.

*Example 10-20. The header for unictr.c (unictr.h)*

```
#include <glib.h>

void hash_a_character(gunichar uc, GHashTable *hash);
void printone(void *key_in, void *val_in, void *xx);
GHashTable *new_unicode_counting_hash();
```

*Example 10-21. Functions built around a hash with a Unicode character as key and a purpose-built counter value (unictr.c)*

```
#include "string_utilities.h"
#include "process_dir.h"
#include "unictr.h"
#include <glib.h>
#include <stdlib.h> //calloc, malloc

typedef struct {                                              ❶
    int count;
} count_s;

void hash_a_character(gunichar uc, GHashTable *hash){
    count_s *ct = g_hash_table_lookup(hash, &uc);
    if (!ct){
        ct = calloc(1, sizeof(count_s));
        gunichar *newchar = malloc(sizeof(gunichar));
        *newchar = uc;
        g_hash_table_insert(hash, newchar, ct);
    }
    ct->count++;
}

void printone(void *key_in, void *val_in, void *ignored){      ❷
    gunichar const *key= key_in;                               ❸
    count_s const *val= val_in;
    char utf8[7];                                              ❹
    utf8[g_unichar_to_utf8(*key, utf8)]='\0';
    printf("%s\t%i\n", utf8, val->count);
}

static gboolean equal_chars(void const * a_in, void const * b_in){  ❺
    const gunichar *a= a_in;                                        ❻
```

```
    const gunichar *b= b_in;
    return (*a==*b);
}

GHashTable *new_unicode_counting_hash(){
    return g_hash_table_new(g_str_hash, equal_chars);
}
```

❶ Yes, this is a struct holding a single integer. One day, it might save your life.

❷ This is going to be a callback for `g_hash_table_foreach`, so it will take in void pointers for the key, value, and an optional void pointer that this function doesn't use.

❸ If a function takes in a void pointer, the first line needs to set up a variable with the correct type, thus casting the void pointer to something usable. Do not put this off to later lines—do it right at the top, where you can verify that you got the type cast correct.

❹ Six `chars` is enough to express any UTF-8 encoding of a Unicode character. Add another byte for the terminating `'\0'`, and 7 bytes is enough to express any one-character string.

❺ Because a hash's keys and values can be any type, GLib asks that you provide the comparison function to determine whether two keys are equal. Later, `new_unicode_counting_hash` will send this function to the hash creation function.

❻ Did I mention that the first line of a function that takes in a void pointer needs to assign the void pointer to a variable of the correct type? Once you do this, you're back to type safety.

Now that we have a set of functions in support of a hash for Unicode characters, Example 10-22 uses them, along with `process_dir` from before, to count all the characters in the UTF-8-readable files in a directory.

It uses the same `process_dir` function defined earlier, so the generic procedure and its
use should now be familiar to you. The callback to process a single file, `hash_a_file`, takes in a `filestruct`, but buried within that `filestruct` is a void pointer. The functions here use that void pointer to point to a GLib hash structure. Thus, the first line of `hash_a_file` casts the void pointer to the structure it points to, thus returning us to type safety.

Each component can be debugged in isolation, just knowing what will get input and when. But you can follow the hash from component to component and verify that it gets sent to `process_dir` via the `.data` element of the input `filestruct`, then `hash_a_file` casts `.data` to a `GHashTable` again, then it gets sent to `hash_a_charac ter`, which will modify it or add to it as you saw earlier. Then, `g_hash_table_fore ach` uses the `printone` callback to print each element in the hash.

*Example 10-22. A character frequency counter; usage: charct your_dir |sort -k 2 -n (charct.c)*

```
#define _GNU_SOURCE            //get stdio.h to define asprintf
#include "string_utilities.h"  //string_from_file
#include "process_dir.h"
#include "unictr.h"
#include <glib.h>
#include <stdlib.h>            //free

void hash_a_file(filestruct path){
    GHashTable *hash = path.data;                            ❶
    char *sf = string_from_file(path.fullname);
    if (!sf) return;
    char *sf_copy = sf;
    if (g_utf8_validate(sf, -1, NULL)){
        for (gunichar uc; (uc = g_utf8_get_char(sf))!='\0'; ❷
                sf = g_utf8_next_char(sf))
                    hash_a_character(uc, hash);
    }
    free(sf_copy);
}

int main(int argc, char **argv){
    GHashTable *hash;
    hash = new_unicode_counting_hash();
    char *start=NULL;
    if (argc>1) asprintf(&start, "%s", argv[1]);
    printf("Hashing %s\n", start ? start: "the current directory");
    process_dir(.name=start, .file_action=hash_a_file, .data=hash);
    g_hash_table_foreach(hash, printone, NULL);
}
```

❶ Recall that the `filestruct` includes a void pointer, data. So the first line of the function will of course declare a variable with the correct type for the input void pointer.

❷ UTF-8 characters are variable-length, so you need a special function to get the current character or step to the next character in a string.

I am a klutz who makes every possible error, yet I have rarely (if ever!) put the wrong type of struct in a list, tree, et cetera. Here are my own rules for ensuring type safety:

- If I have a linked list based on void pointers named `active_groups` and another named `persons`, it is obvious to me as a human being that a line like `g_list_append(active_groups, next_person)` is matching the wrong type of struct to the wrong list, without the compiler having to throw up a flag. So the first secret to my success is that I use names that make it very clear when I'm doing something dumb.

- Put the two sides of Figure 10-1 as close together as possible in your code, so when you change one, you can easily change the other.

- I may have mentioned this before, but the first line of a function that takes in a void pointer should declare a variable with the correct type, effectively casting to the correct type, as in `printone` and `equal_chars`. Having it right at the front raises the odds that you do the cast right, and once the cast is done, the type-safety problem is resolved.

- Associating a purpose-built structure with a given use of a generic procedure or structure makes a whole lot of sense.

  — Without a purpose-built struct, when you change the input type, you'll have to remember to hunt down every cast from a void pointer to the old type and change it to a cast to the new type, and the compiler won't help you with this. If you are sending a purpose-built struct holding the data, all you have to do is change the struct definition.

  — Along similar lines, when you realize that you need to pass one more piece of information to the callback function—and the odds are good that you will— then all you have to do is add the element to the struct's definition.

  — It might seem like passing a single number doesn't merit a whole new structure, but this is actually the riskiest case. Say that we have a generic procedure that takes in a callback and a void pointer to be sent to the callback, and call it like so:

```
void callback (void *voidin){
    double *input = voidin;
    ...
}

int i=23;
generic_procedure(callback, &i);
```

Did you notice that this innocuous code is a type disaster? Whatever the bit pattern of an `int` representing 23 might be, rest assured that when it is read as a `double` by `callback`, it won't be anywhere near 23. Declaring a new struct seems like a lot of bureaucracy, but it prevents an easy and natural error:

```
typedef struct {
    int level;
} one_lonely_integer;
```

— I find that there is some cognitive ease in knowing that there is a single type defined for all dealings in some segment of the code. When I cast to a type clearly purpose-built for the current situation, then I know I'm right; there are no lingering doubts that I should double-check that `char *` is the correct type instead of `char **` or `wchar_t *` or whatever else.

This chapter has covered the many ways that sending structs in and out of a function can be easy: with a good macro, the input struct can be filled with defaults and provide named function inputs; the output structure can be built on the fly using a compound literal; if the function has to copy the structure around (as in the recursion), then all you need is an equals sign; returning a blank structure is a trivial case of using designated initializers with nothing set. And associating a purpose-built struct with a function solves many of the problems with using generic procedures or containers, so applying a generic to a given situation is the perfect time to pull out all the struct-related tricks. Having a struct even gave you a place to put error codes, so you don't have to shoehorn them into the arguments to the function. That's a lot of payoff for the investment of writing up a quick type definition.

# CHAPTER 11

# Object-Oriented Programming in C

> *We favor the simple expression of the complex thought.*
>
> *...*
>
> *We are for flat forms*
>
> *Because they destroy illusion and reveal truth.*
>
> —Le Tigre, "Slideshow at Free University"

Here is the common format for the typical library, in C or in any other language:

- A small set of data structures that represent key aspects of the field the library addresses
- A set of functions (often referred to as *interface functions*) that manipulate those data structures

An XML library, for example, would have a structure representing an XML document and perhaps views of the document, plus lots of functions for going between the data structure and the XML file on disk, querying the structure for elements, et cetera. A database library would have a structure representing the state of communications with the database, and perhaps structures representing tables, plus lots of functions for talking to the database and dissecting the data it sends.

This is an eminently sensible way to organize a program or a library. It is the means by which an author can represent concepts with nouns and verbs that are appropriate to the problem at hand.

I won't waste time (and invite flame wars) by giving a precise definition of object-oriented programming (OOP), but the preceding description of an object-oriented library should give you a feel for what we are going after: a few central data structures, each with a set of functions that act on those central data structures.

For every expert who insists that a feature is essential for OOP, you will find another who sees it as a distraction from the core of OOP.[1] Nonetheless, here are a few extensions to the basic struct-plus-functions object that are very common:

- Inheritance, in which a struct is extended to add new elements to it
- Virtual functions, which have a default behavior for any object in the class, but which can have specific behaviors for different instances of the object (or its descendants on the inheritance tree)
- Fine control over scope, like dividing struct elements into private and public
- Operator overloading, wherein the same operation changes meaning depending on the type it operates on
- Reference counting, allowing objects to be freed if and only if all related resources are no longer in use

Segments in this chapter will consider how these things can be implemented in C. None of them are especially difficult: reference counting basically requires maintaining a counter; function (but not operator) overloading uses the _Generic keyword which is designed for this purpose; and virtual functions can be implemented via a dispatch function optionally backed by a key/value table of alternate functions.

This brings us to an interesting question: if these extensions to the basic struct-plus-functions object are so easy to do and only require a few lines of code, why don't authors writing in C use them all the time?

The Sapir-Whorf hypothesis, linking language and cognition, has been stated in many different ways; the statement I prefer is that some languages force us to think about some things that other languages do not force us to consider. Many languages force us to think about gender, because it is often awkward to compose sentences about a person that avoid gender markers like *he*, *she*, *his*, or *her*. C requires that you think about memory allocation more than other languages do (which may give rise to the stereotypes from non-C users who see C code as nothing but memory-twiddling). Languages that implement extensive scope operators force us to think precisely about when and to what objects a variable is visible—even if the language technically allows you to compile code with all your object's members declared as public, somebody will call you lazy and remind you of the norms around the language that force you to think about fine-grained scope.

---

1 "I once attended a Java user group meeting where James Gosling (Java's inventor) was the featured speaker. During the memorable Q&A session, someone asked him: 'If you could do Java over again, what would you change?' 'I'd leave out classes,' he replied."
— Allen Holub, *Why extends is evil* (*http://bit.ly/W7r7ao*)

Working in C thus puts us in a good position that we would not be in if we used an officially OOP language like C++ or Java: we can implement a number of extensions to the basic struct-plus-functions object via simple forms, but we are never forced to, and we can leave them out when they would add more moving parts with little benefit.

# Extending Structures and Dictionaries

Early in this segment, I'll present an example of the workhorse form for organizing libraries: a struct plus a set of functions that operate on that struct. But, as per the name, this segment is about how to make extensions: how can we add new elements to the struct, and how can we add new functions that work correctly on both already-extant structs and on new ones?

In 1936, in response to a formal mathematical question (The *Entscheidungsproblem*), Alonso Church developed a *lambda calculus*, a formal means of describing functions and variables. In 1937, in response to the same question, Alan Turing described a formal language in the form of a machine with a tape holding data and a head that can be shifted along the tape to read and write to the tape. Later, Church's lambda calculus and Turing's machine were shown to be equivalent—any calculation you could express in one, you could express in the other. It's been the same divide ever since, and Church's and Turing's constructions continue to be the root of how we structure our data.

The lambda calculus relies heavily on named lists; in lambda-inspired pseudocode, we might express a person's information as:

```
(person (
    (name "Sinead")
    (age 28)
    (height 173)
))
```

With Turing's machine, we would have a block of the tape set aside for the structure. The first few blocks would be a name, the next few would hold the age, and so on. Almost a century later, Turing's tape is still a not-bad description of computer memory: recall from "All the Pointer Arithmetic You Need to Know" on page 138 that this base-plus-offset form is exactly how C treats structures. We would write

```
typedef struct {
    char * name;
    double age, height;
} person;

person sinead = {.name="Sinead", .age=28, .height=173};
```

and sinead would point to a block of memory, and sinead.height would point to the tape immediately after name and age (and after any padding for alignment purposes).

Here are some differences between the list approach and the block-of-memory approach:

- Telling the computer to go to a certain offset from a certain address is still among the fastest operations a machine can execute. Your C compiler even does the translation from labels to offsets during compile time. Conversely, finding something in the list requires a lookup: given the label "age", which element in the list corresponds and where is its data in memory? Every system has techniques to make this as fast a lookup as possible, but a lookup will always be more work than a simple base-plus-offset.

- Adding a new element to a list is a much easier process than adding to a struct, which is basically fixed at compile time.

- A C compiler can tell you at compile time that hieght is a typo, because it can look in the struct's definition and see that there is no such element. Because a list is extensible, we won't know that there is no hieght element until the program runs and checks on the list.

Those last two items demonstrate a direct tension: we want extensibility, wherein we can add elements to a structure; we want registration, wherein things that are not in the structure are flagged as errors. That's a balance that has to be struck, and everybody implements controlled extension of an existing list differently.

C++, Java, and their siblings have a syntax for producing a new type that is an instance of the type to be extended but that inherits the old type's elements. You still get base-plus-offset speed and compile-time checking, but at the price of voluminous paperwork; where C has struct and its absurdly simple scoping rules (see "Scope" on page 269), Java has implements, extends, final, instanceof, class, this, interface, private, public, and protected.

Perl, Python, and many LISP-inspired languages are based on named lists, so that is a natural means of implementing a structure. Extend the list by just adding elements to it. Pros: fully extensible by just adding a new named item. Cons: as previously, we don't get registration, and although you can improve the name search via various tricks, you're a long way from the speed of a single base-plus-offset step. Many languages in this family have a class definition system, so that you can register a certain set of list items and thus check whether future uses conform to the definition, which, when done right, provides a nice compromise between checking and ease of extension.

Getting back to plain old C, its structs are the fastest way to access a structure's elements, and we get compile-time checking at the price of runtime extensibility. If you want a flexible list that can grow as the runtime need arises, you will need a list structure, such as the GLib's hashes, or the sample dictionary described later.

## Implementing a Dictionary

A dictionary is an easy structure to generate, given what we have in struct-based C. Doing so is a fine chance to try building some objects and demonstrate the struct-plus-functions form that is the basis of this chapter. Please note, however, that fleshing this out and making it bulletproof has already been done by other authors; see the GLib's keyed data tables or GHashTable, for example. The point here is simply that having compound structs plus simple arrays equals a short hop to a dictionary object.

We're going to start with a simple key/value pair. Its mechanism will be in *keyval.c*. The header in Example 11-1 lists the structure and its interface functions.

*Example 11-1. The header, or the public-facing portion of the key/value class (keyval.h)*

```
typedef struct keyval{
    char *key;
    void *value;
} keyval;

keyval *keyval_new(char *key, void *value);
keyval *keyval_copy(keyval const *in);
void keyval_free(keyval *in);
int keyval_matches(keyval const *in, char const *key);
```

Those of you with experience in traditional object-oriented programming languages will find this to be very familiar. The first instinct when establishing a new object is to write down new/copy/free functions, and that is what the example does. After that, there are typically a few structure-specific functions, such as the keyval_matches function to check whether the key in a keyval pair matches the input string.

Having new/copy/free functions mean that your memory management worries are brief: in the new and copy functions, allocate the memory with malloc; in the free function, remove the structure with free; having set up these functions, code that uses the object will never explicitly use malloc or free on them, but will trust that keyval_new, keyval_copy, and keyval_free will do all the memory management correctly.

Example 11-2 implements these new/copy/free functions for a key-value pair.

*Example 11-2. The typical boilerplate for a key/value object: a structure plus new/copy/ free functions (keyval.c)*

```c
#include <stdlib.h> //malloc
#include <strings.h> //strcasecmp (from POSIX)
#include "keyval.h"

keyval *keyval_new(char *key, void *value){
    keyval *out = malloc(sizeof(keyval));
    *out = (keyval){.key = key, .value=value};      ❶
    return out;
}

/** Copy a key/value pair. The new pair has pointers to
  the values in the old pair, not copies of their data.   */
keyval *keyval_copy(keyval const *in){
    keyval *out = malloc(sizeof(keyval));
    *out = *in;                                     ❷
    return out;
}

void keyval_free(keyval *in){ free(in); }

int keyval_matches(keyval const *in, char const *key){
    return !strcasecmp(in->key, key);
}
```

❶  Designated initializers make filling a struct easy.

❷  Remember, you can copy the contents of structs with an equals sign. If we wanted to copy the contents of pointers in the struct (rather than copy the pointers themselves), we would need more lines of code after this one.

Now that we have an object representing a single key/value pair, we can move on to establishing a dictionary as a list of these. Example 11-3 provides the header.

*Example 11-3. The public parts of the dictionary structure (dict.h)*

```c
#include "keyval.h"

extern void *dictionary_not_found;      ❶

typedef struct dictionary{
    keyval **pairs;
    int length;
} dictionary;

dictionary *dictionary_new (void);
dictionary *dictionary_copy(dictionary *in);
void dictionary_free(dictionary *in);
```

```
void dictionary_add(dictionary *in, char *key, void *value);
void *dictionary_find(dictionary const *in, char const *key);
```

❶   This will be the marker for when a key is not found in the dictionary. It has to be
     public.

As you can see, you get the same new/copy/free functions, plus a few other
dictionary-specific functions, and a marker to be described later. Example 11-4 provides the private implementation.

*Example 11-4. The implementation of the dictionary object (dict.c)*

```
#include <stdio.h>
#include <stdlib.h>
#include "dict.h"

void *dictionary_not_found;

dictionary *dictionary_new (void){
    static int dnf;                                                    ❶
    if (!dictionary_not_found) dictionary_not_found = &dnf;
    dictionary *out= malloc(sizeof(dictionary));
    *out= (dictionary){ };
    return out;
}

static void dictionary_add_keyval(dictionary *in, keyval *kv){         ❷
    in->length++;
    in->pairs = realloc(in->pairs, in->length*sizeof(keyval*));
    in->pairs[in->length-1] = kv;
}

void dictionary_add(dictionary *in, char *key, void *value){
    if (!key){fprintf(stderr, "NULL is not a valid key.\n"); abort();}  ❸
    dictionary_add_keyval(in, keyval_new(key, value));
}

void *dictionary_find(dictionary const *in, char const *key){
    for (int i=0; i< in->length; i++)
        if (keyval_matches(in->pairs[i], key))
            return in->pairs[i]->value;
    return dictionary_not_found;
}

dictionary *dictionary_copy(dictionary *in){
    dictionary *out = dictionary_new();
    for (int i=0; i< in->length; i++)
        dictionary_add_keyval(out, keyval_copy(in->pairs[i]));
    return out;
}
```

```
void dictionary_free(dictionary *in){
    for (int i=0; i< in->length; i++)
        keyval_free(in->pairs[i]);
    free(in);
}
```

❶ It is reasonable to have a NULL value in the key/value table, so we need a unique marker to indicate a missing value. I don't know where dnf will be stored in memory, but its address will certainly be unique.

❷ Recall that a function marked as static can not be used outside the file, so this is one more reminder that the function is private to the implementation.

❸ A confession: using abort like this is bad form; better would be to use a macro like the one in *stopif.h*. I did it this way to demonstrate a feature of the test harness.

Now that we have a dictionary, Example 11-5 can use it without thinking about memory management, which the new/copy/free/add functions take care of, and without making reference to key/value pairs, because that is one level too low for our purposes.

*Example 11-5. Sample usage of the dictionary object; no need to delve into the guts of the struct, because the interface functions provide all we need (dict_use.c)*

```
#include <stdio.h>
#include "dict.h"

int main(){
    int zero = 0;
    float one = 1.0;
    char two[] = "two";
    dictionary *d = dictionary_new();
    dictionary_add(d, "an int", &zero);
    dictionary_add(d, "a float", &one);
    dictionary_add(d, "a string", &two);
    printf("The integer I recorded was: %i\n", *(int*)dictionary_find(d, "an int"));
    printf("The string was: %s\n", (char*)dictionary_find(d, "a string"));
    dictionary_free(d);
}
```

So writing a struct and its new/copy/free and other associated functions was enough to give us the right level of encapsulation: the dictionary didn't have to care about the internals of the key/value pair, and the application didn't have to worry about dictionary internals.

The boilerplate code is not as bad as it is in some languages, but there is certainly some repetition to the new/copy/free functions. And as the examples continue, you'll see this boilerplate several times more.

At some point, I even wrote myself macros to autogenerate these. For example, the copy functions differ only in dealing with internal pointers, so we could write a macro to automate all the boilerplate not about internal pointers:

```
#define def_object_copy(tname, ...)          \
    void * tname##_copy(tname *in) {          \
        tname *out = malloc(sizeof(tname));  \
        *out = *in;                          \
        __VA_ARGS__;                         \
        return out;                          \
    }
```

```
def_object_copy(keyval) // Expands to the previous declarations of keyval_copy.
```

But the redundancy is nothing to worry about all that much. Despite our mathematical æsthetic of minimizing repetition and text on the page, sometimes having more code really does make the program more readable and robust.

## C, with fewer seams

All the machinery you have in C for inserting new elements into a structure is to wrap it in another structure. Say that we have a type defined via a form such as:

```
typedef struct {
    ...
} list_element_s;
```

which is already packaged and cannot be changed, but we'd like to add a type marker. Then we'll need a new structure:

```
typedef struct {
    list_element_s elmt;
    char typemarker;
} list_element_w_type_s;
```

Pros: this is so stupid easy, and you still get the speed bonus. Cons: Now, every time you want to refer to the name of the element, you'll need to write out the full path, your_typed_list->elmt->name, instead of what you'd get via a C++/Java-like extension: your_typed_list->name. Add a few layers to this and it starts to get annoying. You already saw in "Pointers Without malloc" on page 131 how using aliases can help here.

C11 made structs within structs easier to use by allowing us to include anonymous elements of a structure [C11 §6.7.2.1(13)]. Although this got added to the standard in December 2011, it follows a Microsoft extension from a long time before then. I will show you a strong and weak form; gcc and clang allow the strong form using the the

`--fms-extensions` flag on the command line, while the weak form is supported by these compilers in C11 mode without additional flags.

The syntax for the strong form: include a struct specifier somewhere in the declaration of the new structure, as per the `point` struct in Example 11-6, without a name for the element. The example uses a bare structure name, `struct point`, whereas a named declaration would be something like `struct point elementname`. All of the elements of the referred-to structure are included in the new structure as if they were declared in the wrapping structure.

Example 11-6 extends a 2D point into a 3D point. So far, it is only notable because the `threepoint` struct extends the `point` seamlessly, to the point where users of the `threepoint` won't even know that its definition is based on another struct.

*Example 11-6. An anonymous substructure inside a wrapping structure merges seamlessly into the wrapper (seamlessone.c)*

```
#include <stdio.h>
#include <math.h>

typedef struct point {
    double x, y;
} point;

typedef struct {
    struct point;                                    ❶
    double z;
} threepoint;

double threelength (threepoint p){
    return sqrt(p.x*p.x + p.y*p.y + p.z*p.z);    ❷
}

int main(){
    threepoint p = {.x=3, .y=0, .z=4};              ❸
    printf("p is %g units from the origin\n", threelength(p));
}
```

❶  This is anonymous. The not-anonymous version would have had a name like `struct point twopt`.

❷  The x and y elements of the `point` structure look and behave exactly like the additional z element of the `threepoint`.

❸  Even the declaration gives no hint that x and y were inherited from an existing structure.

The original object, the point, was probably accompanied by several interface functions that are still useful, like a length function measuring the distance between zero and the given point. How are we going to use that function, now that we don't have a name for that subpart of the larger structure?

The solution is to use an anonymous union of a named point and an unnamed point. Being the union of two identical structures, the two structures share absolutely everything, and the only distinction is in the naming: use the named version when you need to call functions that use the original struct as an input, and use the anonymous version for seamless merging into the larger struct. Example 11-7 rewrites Example 11-6 using this form.

*Example 11-7. The point is seamlessly incorporated into a threepoint, and we still have a name for use with functions that operate on a point (seamlesstwo.c)*

```c
#include <stdio.h>
#include <math.h>

typedef struct point {
    double x, y;
} point;

typedef struct {
    union {
        struct point;                    ❶
        point p2;                        ❷
    };
    double z;
} threepoint;

double length (point p){
    return sqrt(p.x*p.x + p.y*p.y);
}

double threelength (threepoint p){
    return sqrt(p.x*p.x + p.y*p.y + p.z*p.z);
}

int main(){
    threepoint p = {.x=3, .y=0, .z=4};    ❸
    printf("p is %g units from the origin\n", threelength(p));
    double xylength = length(p.p2);       ❹
    printf("Its projection onto the XY plane "
            "is %g units from the origin\n", xylength);
}
```

❶  This is an anonymous structure.

**❷** This is a named structure. Being part of a union, it is identical to the anonymous structure, differing only in having a name.

**❸** The `point` structure is still seamlessly included in the `threepoint` structure, but ...

**❹** ... the p2 element is a named element as it always was, so we can use it to call the interface functions written around the original struct.

After the declaration `threepoint p`, we can refer to the $x$ coordinate via `p.x` (because of the anonymous struct) or via `p.p2.x` (because of the named struct). The last line of the example shows the length when projecting onto the $xy$ plane, and does so using `length(p.p2)`. We've successfully extended the structure and can still use all the functions associated with the original.

Inheriting from multiple structures may or may not work: if both structs to be included have an element named x then the compiler will throw an error, and we have no syntax for renaming elements in an existing structure or pulling out only a subset of elements. But if you have a structure in unmodifiable legacy code with ten elements, and you just want to turn that up to eleven so you can address one new requirement, this method will get you there.

 Did you notice this is the first time I've used the `union` keyword in this book? Unions are another one of those things where the explanation is brief—it's like a `struct`, but all the elements occupy the same space—and then the caveats about how to not hang yourself take up several pages. Memory is cheap, and for writing applications, we don't have to care about memory alignment, so sticking to structs will reduce the possibility of errors, even when only one element is used at a time.

The weaker form, which will compile without the `-fms-extensions` flag, does not accept an anonymous struct specifier that refers to the previously-defined structure as above, and requires that the struct be defined in place. Thus, replace the shorter struct specifier `point p2` with the full cut-and-pasted definition of the p2 struct:

```
typedef struct {
    union {
        struct {
            double x, y;
        };
        point p2;
    };
    double z;
} threepoint;
```

In the repository of sample code, you will find `seamlessthree.c`, which uses this form and has different compilation notes, but is otherwise identical to `seamlesstwo.c`.

The weak form may not seem especially useful for the sort of extension discussed here, because now you have to keep the two struct declarations synced. But it can still have utility, depending on your situation:

- Much of this book is about dealing with the immense quantity of legacy C code we have. If the only person who could modify a code base retired in 2003 and everybody else is afraid to touch it, that gives strong indication that the struct you cut and pasted into your extension will not be changed in the legacy code base.

- If the code is under your control, then you have the option of eliminating redundancies via macros. For example:

```
#define pointcontents { \
    double x, y;        \
}

typedef struct pointcontents point;

typedef struct {
    union {
        struct pointcontents;
        point p2;
    };
    double z;
} threepoint;
```

This is not especially convenient, but does achieve the goals of consistency across both the base and extended structs, still compiling given a stricter interpretation of the standard, and retaining the safety of having the compiler check types for you.

## Base Your Code on Pointers to Objects

Most of the techniques presented in Chapter 10 were about data structures, not pointers to data structures, but all the examples in this chapter are about declaring and using pointers to structs.

In fact, if you use a plain struct, the new/copy/free functions write themselves:

*new*

> Use designated initializers on the first line where you need a struct. As an added plus, structures can be declared at compile time, so they are immediately available to users without an initial call to a setup function.

*copy*

> The equals sign does this.

*free*

> Don't bother; it'll go out of scope soon enough.

So we're making things more difficult for ourselves with pointers. Yet from what I've seen, there's consensus on using pointers to objects as the base of our designs.

Pros to using pointers:

- Copying a single pointer is cheaper than copying a full structure, so you save a microsecond on every function call with a struct as an input. Of course, this only adds up after a few billion function calls.

- Data structure libraries (your trees and linked lists, for example) are all written around hooks for a pointer.

- Now that you're filling a tree or a list, having the system automatically free the struct at the end of the scope in which it was created might not be what you want.

- Many of your functions that take in a struct will modify the struct's contents, meaning that you've got to pass a pointer to the struct anyway. Having some functions that take in the struct itself and some that take in a pointer to struct is confusing (I have written an interface like this and I regret it), so you might as well just send a pointer every time.

- If the contents of the struct include a pointer to data elsewhere, then the convenience bonus from using a plain struct evaporates anyway: if you want a deep copy (wherein the data pointed to is copied, not just the pointer) then you need a copy function, and you will probably want a free function to make sure the internal data is eliminated.

There's no one-size-fits-all set of rules for using structs. As struct evolves from being a throwaway to facilitate some logistics to becoming a core of how your data is organized, the benefits to pointers wax and the benefits to nonpointers wane.

# Functions in Your Structs

To this point, every header has presented a struct followed by a set of functions, but a struct can include functions among its member elements as easily as it can hold typical variables, so we could move all but the object_new function into the struct itself:

```
typedef struct keyval{
    char *key;
    void *value;
    keyval *(*keyval_copy)(keyval const *in);
    void (*keyval_free)(keyval *in);
    int (*keyval_matches)(keyval const *in, char const *key);
} keyval;

keyval *keyval_new(char *key, void *value);
```

 Say we have a pointer to a function, *fn*, meaning that *\*fn* is a function and *fn* is its address in memory. Then *(\*fn)(x)* makes sense
as a function call, but what would *fn*(x) mean? In this case, C takes
a do-what-I-mean approach and interprets calling a pointer-to-
function as a simple call to the function. The term for this is *pointer
decay*. This is why I treat functions and pointers-to-functions as
equivalent in the text.

This is, for the most part, a stylistic choice, affecting how we look up functions in the
documentation and how the code looks on the page. The documentation issue, by the
way, is why I prefer the *keyval_copy* naming scheme over the *copy_keyval* scheme:
with the first form, the documentation's index lists all of *keyval_s*'s associated functions in one place.

The real advantage of the element-of-struct form is that you can more easily change
the function associated with every instance of the object. Example 11-8 shows a simple list structure, which is nondescript enough that it could hold an advertisement,
song lyrics, a recipe, or who knows what else. It seems natural to print these different
types of list using different formatting, so we will have several types of print function.

*Example 11-8. A rather generic struct, with a built-in print method (print_typedef.h)*

```
#ifndef textlist_s_h
#define textlist_s_h

typedef struct textlist_s {
    char *title;
    char **items;
    int len;
    void (*print)(struct textlist_s*);
} textlist_s;

#endif
```

Example 11-9 declares and uses two objects with the typedef above. The disparate
print methods are assigned as part of the object definition.

*Example 11-9. Putting the function inside the struct clarifies which function goes with which struct (print_methods.c)*

```c
#include <stdio.h>
#include "print_typedef.h"

static void print_ad(textlist_s *in){
    printf("BUY THIS %s!!!! Features:\n", in->title);
    for (int i=0; i< in->len; i++)
        printf("· %s\n", in->items[i]);
}

static void print_song(textlist_s *in){
    printf("♪ %s ♪\nLyrics:\n\n", in->title);
    for (int i=0; i< in->len; i++)
        printf("\t%s\n", in->items[i]);
}

textlist_s save = {.title="God Save the Queen",
    .len=3, .items=(char*[]){
    "There's no future", "No future", "No future for me."},
    .print=print_song};                                    ❶

textlist_s spend = {.title="Never mind the Bollocks LP",
    .items=(char*[]){"By the Sex Pistols", "Anti-consumption themes"},
    .len=2, .print=print_ad};

#ifndef skip_main
int main(){
    save.print(&save);                                     ❷
    printf("\n-----\n\n");
    spend.print(&spend);
}
#endif
```

❶ So you don't miss it, here is the spot where the function is added to the save struct. A similar thing happens with print_ad in the spend struct a few lines down.

❷ When calling the methods embedded in a struct, they all look the same. You don't have to remember that save is song lyrics and spend an advertisement.

By the last three lines, we are on our way to having a uniform interface to entirely distinct functions. You could picture a function that takes in a textlist_s*, names it t, and calls t->print(&t).

On the minus side, we run risk of once again breaking the rule that things that do different things should look different: if one function in the print slot has subtly different side effects, you have no warning.

Note the use of the `static` keyword, which indicates that outside of this file, no code will be able to call `print_song` or `print_ad` by those names. They will, however, be able to use the names `save.print` and `spend.print` to call them.

There are a few bells and whistles that we'd like to add. First, `save.print(&save)` is a redundant form that repeats `save`. It would be nice to be able to write `save.print()` and let the system just know that the first argument should be the object making the call. The function might see a special variable named `this` or `self`, or we could add a special-case rule that *object.fn(x)* gets reshuffled to *fn(object, x)*.

Sorry, but it's not going to happen in C.

C doesn't define magic variables for you, and it is always honest and transparent about what parameters get sent in to a function. Normally, if we want to futz around with the parameters of a function, we do it with the preprocessor, which will gladly rewrite `f(`*anything*`)` to `f(`*anything else*`)`. However, all the transformations happen to what goes on inside the parens. There's no way to get the preprocessor to transform the text `s.prob(d)` to `s.prob(s, d)`. If you don't want to slavishly imitate C++-type syntax, you can write macros like:

```
#define Print(in) (in).print(&in)
#define Copy(in, ...) (in).copy((in), __VA_ARGS__)
#define Free(in, ...) (in).free((in), __VA_ARGS__)
```

But now you've cluttered up the global namespace with the `Print`, `Copy`, and `Free` symbols. Maybe it's worth it to you (especially given that every function should have associated copy and free functions).

You could keep the namespace organized and prevent name collisions by naming your macros appropriately:

```
#define Typelist_print(in) (in).estimate(&in)
#define Typelist_copy(in, ...) (in).copy((in), __VA_ARGS__)
```

Getting back to the `typelist_s`, we have a way to print songs and advertisements. But what about recipes, or whatever other lists people may dream up? Or, what would happen if somebody writes a list but forgets to add the right function?

We want a default method to fall back on, and one easy way to achieve this is a dispatch function. The function would check the input struct for a `print` method, and use what it finds if it is not `NULL`. Otherwise, it provides a default method. Example 11-10 demonstrates such a dispatch function, which correctly prints a song object with its included `print` method, but because there is no `print` method associated with the recipe for a vegan egg replacer (via Isa Chandra Moskowitz of the Post Punk Kitchen (*http://www.postpunkkitchen.com/veganbaking.html*)), the dispatch function fills in a default.

*Example 11-10. The `recipe` has no `print` method, but the dispatch function prints it anyway (print_dispatch.c)*

```
#define skip_main
#include "print_methods.c"

textlist_s recipe = {.title="1 egg for baking",
    .len=2, .items=(char*[]){"1 Tbsp ground flax seeds", "3 Tbsp water"}};

void textlist_print(textlist_s *in){
    if (in->print){
        in->print(in);
        return;
    }

    printf("Title: %s\n\nItems:\n", in->title);
    for (int i=0; i< in->len; i++)
        printf("\t%s\n", in->items[i]);
}

int main(){
    textlist_print(&save);
    printf("\n-----\n\n");
    textlist_print(&recipe);
}
```

So dispatch functions gave us default routines, solved the annoyance of not having a magic `this` or `self` variable, and did so in a manner that looks similar to the usual interface functions like `textlist_copy` or `textlist_free` (if they were defined).

There are other ways to do it. Earlier, I used designated initializers to set up the functions, so unspecified elements are `NULL` and a dispatch function makes sense. If we required that users always use a `textlist_new` function, then we could set the default functions there. Then eliminating the redundancy of *save*.`print(&save)` can be done by a simple macro, as previously.

Once again, you've got options. We already have more than enough syntactic tools to uniformly call diverse functions for diverse objects. That just leaves the hard part of writing those diverse functions so that calling them in a uniform manner always behaves as expected.

## Vtables

Say that time has passed since the `textlist_s` struct was designed, and we have discovered that we have new needs. We would like to post lists to the World Wide Web, but doing so requires formatting the lists using HTML. How are we going to add a new HTML print function to the existing structure, which has only a print-to-screen function?

You already saw how structs can be extended in "C, with fewer seams" on page 255, and we could use that form to set up a struct with the new functions inside the struct, like the print function.

The alternative presented in this section is to add new functions outside the object's struct. They are recorded in what is called a *virtual table*, where the name is a reference to the virtual functions from the object-oriented lexicon, and the 1990s fashion of calling everything implemented in software *virtual*. A vtable is a hash table, a simple list of key/value pairs. "Implementing a Dictionary" on page 251 showed how to build such a key/value table, but in this section I will use GLib's hash tables.

Given the object(s), generate a hash (the key), and associate a function with the hash. Then, when a user calls the dispatch function for the given operation, the dispatch function will check the hash table for a function, and if it finds one will execute it, else it will execute the default operation.

Here are the ingredients we will need to make this recipe work:

- A hashing function.
- A type-checker. We have to make sure that every function stored in the hash table has the same type signature.
- A key/value table and its accompanying storage and retrieval functions.

### The hash function

A hash function mangles its input into a single number, in a manner such that the odds are close to zero that two inputs are mangled into the same number.

GLib provides a few hashes out of the box, including g_direct_hash, g_int_hash, and g_str_hash. The direct hash is intended for pointers, and simply reads the pointer as a number, in which case there can only be a hash collision if two objects are at the same point in memory.

For more complex situations, we can invent new hashes. Here is a common hash function, attributed to Dan J. Bernstein. For each character in the string (or each byte of a UTF-8 multibyte character), it multiplies the tally so far by 33, then adds the new character (or byte). The value is likely to overflow what an unsigned int can store, but the overflow is just another implicit but deterministic step in the algorithm.

```
static unsigned int string_hash(char const *str){
    unsigned int hash = 5381;
    char c;
    while ((c = *str++)) hash = hash*33 + c;
    return hash;
}
```

Again, GLib offers its `g_str_hash` functions, so there is no need to use the function here, but we could use this as a template to implement alternative hashes. Let us say that we have a list of pointers, then we could use this hash:

```
static unsigned int ptr_list_hash(void const **in){
    unsigned int hash = 5381;
    void *c;
    while ((c = *in++)) hash = hash*33 + (uintptr_t)c;
    return hash;
}
```

For the object-oriented reader, note that we are already most of the way toward implementing multiple dispatch. Give me two distinct objects, and I can hash together one pointer from the first and one from the second, and associate an appropriate function in the key/value table for the pair.

GLib's hash tables will also want an equality check, so GLib provides `g_direct_equal`, `g_int_equal`, and `g_str_equal` to go with the corresponding hashes.

For any hash, there is still some chance of hash collisions, although it is very small for a reasonably written hash. I use hashes like the ones above in my code, and I am aware that there is some small chance that one day somebody will get unlucky and hit on two sets of pointers that cause a hash collision. But when deciding where to allocate my finite time on this Earth, I can always find another bug fix, feature implementation, documentation addition, or personal interaction that will provide a greater benefit for a greater number of users than would eliminating the chance of hash collision. Git relies on hashes to record commits, and users have produced millions (billions?) of commits, and yet eliminating hash collisions also seems very low on the agenda of the Git maintainers.

## Type checking

We are going to allow users to store an arbitrary function in the hash table, and then our dispatch function will at some point retrieve that function and use it via a predefined template. If a user writes a function that takes the wrong types, then your dispatch function will crash, and the user will post snarky comments to various social media about how your code doesn't work.

Normally, when a function call is explicitly written in the code, all the types are checked at compile-time. On the one hand, this is the type safety that we are losing with dynamically selected functions; on the other hand, we can use this to check that a function has the right type.

Let us say that we want our functions to take in a `double*` and an `int` (like a list and its length) and return a struct of type *out_type*. Then we can define its type as:

```
typedef out_type (*object_fn_type)(double *, int);
```

Now define a do-nothing function like this:

```
void object_fn_type_check(object_fn_type in){ };
```

In the example below, this will be wrapped in a macro, to make sure users call it. Calling this function brings us back to type safety: if the user tries to put a function with the wrong arguments into the hash table, then the compiler will throw a type error when attempting to compile the call to the do-nothing function.

### Putting it all together

Example 11-11 is the header needed for the vtable, providing the macro that adds new methods and the dispatch function that does the retrieval.

*Example 11-11. A header for a vtable associating functions with certain objects (print_vtable.h)*

```
#include <glib.h>
#include "print_typedef.h"

extern GHashTable *print_fns;

typedef void (*print_fn_type)(textlist_s*);                    ❶

void check_print_fn(print_fn_type pf);

#define print_hash_add(object, print_fn){                 \    ❷
    check_print_fn(print_fn);                             \
    g_hash_table_insert(print_fns, (object)->print, print_fn);  \
}

void textlist_print_html(textlist_s *in);
```

❶ It's optional, but a good typedef makes life with function pointers much more pleasant.

❷ Admonishing users that they should call the type-checking function is a waste of time—provide a macro that does it for them.

Example 11-12 provides the dispatch function that checks the vtable as its first step. Apart from the doing the lookup in the vtable rather than the input struct itself, it isn't much different from the previous dispatch method.

*Example 11-12. A dispatch function using a virtual table (print_vtable.c)*

```
#include <stdio.h>
#include "print_vtable.h"

GHashTable *print_fns;                                          ❶
```

```
void check_print_fn(print_fn_type pf) { }

void textlist_print_html(textlist_s *in){
    if (!print_fns) print_fns = g_hash_table_new(g_direct_hash, g_direct_equal);    ❷

    print_fn_type ph = g_hash_table_lookup(print_fns, in->print);                   ❸
    if (ph) {
        ph(in);
        return;
    }
    printf("<title>%s</title>\n<ul>", in->title);
    for (int i=0; i < in->len; i++)
        printf("<li>%s</li>\n", in->items[i]);
    printf("</ul>\n");
}
```

❶  Note how the hash table is here in the private implementation, not the public interface. Users never touch it directly.

❷  Initialize GLib's hash tables with the hash and equality functions. Once they are stored in the hash struct, users never need to explicitly refer to them again. This line sets up a hash for the print function, and we could set up as many additional hashes as desired.

❸  The print method of the input struct can be used to identify whether the struct is a song, recipe, or what have you, so we can use that method to retrieve the appropriate HTML print method.

Finally, here is the usage in Example 11-13. Notice that the user uses only the macro to associate a special function with an object, and the dispatch function to do the work.

*Example 11-13. A virtual table associating functions with certain objects (print_vtable_use.c)*

```
#define skip_main
#include "print_methods.c"
#include "print_vtable.h"

static void song_print_html(textlist_s *in){
    printf("<title>♪ %s ♪</title>\n", in->title);
    for (int i=0; i < in->len; i++)
        printf("%s<br>\n", in->items[i]);
}

int main(){
    textlist_print_html(&save);                    ❶
```

```
    printf("\n-----\n\n");

    print_hash_add(&save, song_print_html);     ❷
    textlist_print_html(&save);
}
```

❶ At this point, the hash table is empty, so this call will use the default print method written into the dispatch function

❷ Here, we add the special print method to the hash, so the next call to the dispatch function will find and use it.

Vtables are typically how the officially object-oriented languages implement many features, and they aren't especially difficult to implement. If you count up the lines about vtables in the above examples, I think you'd still be under 10 lines.[2] Even specifying special-case functions for certain combinations of objects works with the setup here, especially given that there was no need to invent an awkward syntax to accommodate it. Vtables do take some setup, but they can often be implemented in later revisions when needed, and in practice there is real benefit to implementing them only for certain operations for certain structures.

# Scope

The *scope* of a variable is the range of code over which it exists and can be used. The rule of thumb for sane programming is to keep the scope of a variable as small as practicable, because doing so limits the number of variables you have to keep in mind at any given point, and means lower risk that a variable will be changed by code you didn't bear in mind.

OK, here goes: all the rules for variable scope in C.

- A variable never has scope in the code before it is declared. That would be silly.
- If a variable is declared somewhere inside a pair of curly braces, then at the closing curly brace, the variable goes out of scope. Semiexception: for loops and

---

2 Because nobody reads footnotes, it is perhaps safe for me to here confess my love for m4, a macro processing language from the 1970s. You probably have m4 on your system right now, because it is a POSIX-standard and Autoconf uses it. Besides being ubiquitous, it has two features that make it relatively unique and useful. First, it is designed to search for macros embedded in a file written for other purposes, like the shell scripts Autoconf produces, or HTML files, or C programs. After macro processing, the output can be a standards-compliant shell/HTML/C file, without any remaining trace of m4. Second, you can write macros that generate other macros. The C preprocessor can't do this. In a project where I knew I would be generating a lot of distinct vtables, I wrote m4 macros that generate the type-checking functions and plain C macros. The code is less redundant for me, and after putting the m4 filtering step in the makefile, I distribute pure C code to others. Anybody who wants to work with the prefiltered source can do so, because m4 is so prevalent.

functions may have variables declared in a set of parens just before their opening curly brace; variables declared within the parens have scope as if they were declared inside the curly braces.

- If a variable isn't inside any curly braces, then it has scope from its declaration to the end of the file.

You're done.

There is no class scope, prototype scope, friend scope, namespace scope, runtime environment rebinding, or special scoping keywords or operators (beyond those curly braces, and arguably the linkage specifiers `static` and `extern`). Does dynamic scoping confuse you? Don't worry about it. If you know where the curly braces are, you can determine which variables can be used where.

Everything else is a simple corollary. For example, if *code.c* has a line that will `#include <header.h>`, then the full text of *header.h* is pasted into *code.c*, and variables therein have scope accordingly.

Functions are just another example of curly-brace scope. Here is a sample function to sum all the integers up to the input number:

```
int sum (int max){
    int total=0;
    for (int i=0; i<= max; i++){
        total += i;
    }
    return total;
}
```

Then `max` and `total` have scope inside the function, by the curly-brace rule and the semiexception about how variables in parens just before the curly brace act as if they are inside the braces. The same holds with the `for` loop, and how `i` is born and dies with the curly braces of the `for` loop. If you have a one-line `for` loop, you don't have to write the curly braces, like `for (int i=0; i <= max; i++) total += i;`, but the scope of `i` is still limited to the loop.

Summary paragraph: C is awesome for having such simple scoping rules, which effectively consist of finding the end of the enclosing curly braces or the end of the file. You can teach the whole scoping system to a novice student in maybe 10 minutes. For the experienced author, the rule is more general than just the curly braces for functions and `for` loops, so you can use them for occasional additional scoping restrictions in exceptional situations, as per the macro examples in "Cultivate Robust and Flourishing Macros" on page 163.

# Private Struct Elements

So we're cathartically throwing out all the additional rules and keywords that support very fine-grained scope control.

Could we implement private struct elements without the extra keywords? In typical OOP usage, "private" data is not encrypted by the compiler or otherwise seriously hidden: if you have the address of the variable (e.g., if you have its offset in the struct), you can point to it, look at it in the debugger, and modify it. To give the data that limited level of opacity, we have the technology.

An object will typically be defined via two files: the .c file with the details and the .h file to be included in other writing that makes use of the object. It is not unreasonable to think of the .c file as the private segment and the .h file as the public. For example, say we are set on keeping some elements of an object private. The public header might be:

```
typedef struct a_box_s {
    int public_size;
    void *private;
} a_box_s;
```

The pointer to `private` is basically useless to other authors, because they don't know what type to cast it to. The private segment, *a_box.c*, would hold the requisite typedef and its uses:

```
typedef struct private_box_s {
    long double how_much_i_hate_my_boss;
    char **coworkers_i_have_a_crush_on;
    double fudge_factor;
} private_box_s;
```

```
//Given the typedef, we have no problem casting the private pointer to
//its desired type and making use here in a_box.c.

a_box_s *box_new(){
    a_box_s *out = malloc(sizeof(a_box_s));
    private_box_s *outp = malloc(sizeof(private_box_s));
    *out = (a_box_s){.public_size=0, .private=outp};
    return out;
}

void box_edit(a_box_s *in){
    private_box_s *pb = in->private;
    //now work with private variables, e.g.:
    pb->fudge_factor *= 2;
}
```

So it's not all that hard to implement a private segment of a C struct, but I rarely see it used in real-world libraries. Few C authors seem to think that there's serious benefit to doing so.

Here's a sample of the much more common means of putting a private element within a public struct:

```
typedef struct {
    int pub_a, pub_b;
    int private_a, private_b; //Private: please do not use these.
} public_s;
```

That is, document when something should not be used, and trust your users to not cheat. If your colleagues won't follow an instruction as simple as this, then chain the coffeemaker to the wall, because you've got problems bigger than a compiler can solve.

Functions are especially easy to make private: don't put their declaration in a header. Optionally, put the `static` keyword in front of the definition so that readers know that the function is private.

## Overload

My impression is that most folks think of integer division—that 3/2==1—as an annoyance. If I type in 3/2, I expect 1.5, darn it, not 1.

Indeed, this is an annoying gotcha to C and other integer-arithmetic languages, and more broadly, it shows us the dangers of *operator overloading*. Operator overloading is when an operator, such as /, does something different depending on the types involved. For two integer types, the slash effectively does a divide-and-truncate operation, and for anything else, it performs the usual division.

Recall the rule from "Pointers Without malloc" on page 131 that things that behave differently should look different. That's the failure of 3/2: integer division and floating-point division behave differently but look identical. Confusion and bugs ensue.

Human language is redundant, which is a good thing, partly because it allows error correction. When Nina Simone says "ne me quitte pas" (which would translate word-for-word as "don't leave me no"), it's OK if you space out at the beginning, because "… me quitte pas" has the *pas* to indicate negation, and it's OK if you space out at the end, because "ne me quitte …" has the *ne* to indicate negation.

Grammatical gender typically doesn't have much real-world meaning, and sometimes objects will change depending on word choice. My favorite example is in Spanish, where *el pene* and *la polla* both refer to the same object, but the first is masculine and the second feminine. The real value to the gender is that it provides redundancy, forcing parts of the sentence to match, and thus adding clarity.

Programming languages avoid redundancy. Negation entirely changes an expression's meaning, yet it is typically expressed with only one character (!). But programming languages do have genders, where they're called types. Generally, your verbs and your nouns need to agree in type (as in Arabic, Hebrew, and Russian, among other languages). With this added redundancy, you'd need `matrix_multiply(a, b)` when you have two matrices, and `complex_multiply(a, b)` when you have two complex numbers.

Operator overloading is about eliminating redundancy: writing `a * b` whether you have a pair of matrices, complex numbers, natural numbers, or sets. Here's a snippet from an excellent essay on the cost of that reduced redundancy: "When you see the code `i = j * 5;` in C you know, at least, that `j` is being multiplied by five and the results stored in `i`. But if you see that same snippet of code in C++, you don't know anything."[3] The problem is that you don't know what `*` means until you look up the type for `j`, look through the inheritance tree for `j`'s type to determine *which version* of `*` you mean, and then you can start over with identifying `i` and how that relates to `=`, given the type of `j * 5`.

Here's my own rule of thumb for overloading, via `_Generic` or whatever other means: *if users forget what the input type is, will they still get the right answer?* For example, the overloading of absolute value for `int`, `float`, and `double` work just fine with this rule. The GNU Scientific Library provides a `gsl_complex` type to represent complex numbers, while standard C allows types like `complex double`; it might make sense to overload functions regarding these types with identical intent.

As you've seen in the examples to this point, the C custom is to closely follow the sort of gender-agreement rules I'd just described; for example:

```
//add two vectors in the GNU Scientific Library
gsl_vector *v1, *v2;
gsl_vector_add(v1, v2);

//Open a GLib I/O channel for reading at a given filename.
GError *e;
GIOChannel *f = g_io_channel_new_file("indata.csv", "r", &e);
```

It's more typing, and when you have 10 lines acting on the same structure, things start to look repetitive, but each line is very clear.

---

3 ""Making Wrong Code Look Wrong" (*http://bit.ly/look-wrong*); reprinted in (Spolsky, 2008; p 192).

# _Generic

C provides limited overloading support via the _Generic keyword. The keyword evaluates to a value based on the type of its input, which lets you write macros that consolidate some types together.

We need type-generic functions when we have a proliferation of types. Some systems provide a voluminous number of precise types, but every new type is another moving part that we have to support. For example, the GNU Scientific Library provides a complex number type, a complex vector type, and a vector type—and then there's the C complex type. One could reasonably multiply any of those four types together, which theoretically means we need 16 functions. Example 11-14 lists several of these functions; if you are not a complex vector aficionado, it would be entirely reasonable to recognize this example as a hairy mess and move on to the part where we clean it up.

*Example 11-14. Where the sausage is made, for those of you with an interest in GSL complex types (complex.c)*

```
#include "cplx.h"              //gsl_cplx_from_c99; see below.
#include <gsl/gsl_blas.h>      //gsl_blas_ddot
#include <gsl/gsl_complex_math.h> //gsl_complex_mul(_real)

gsl_vector_complex *cvec_dot_gslcplx(gsl_vector_complex *v, gsl_complex x){
    gsl_vector_complex *out = gsl_vector_complex_alloc(v->size);
    for (int i=0; i< v->size; i++)
        gsl_vector_complex_set(out, i,
                        gsl_complex_mul(x, gsl_vector_complex_get(v, i)));
    return out;
}

gsl_vector_complex *vec_dot_gslcplx(gsl_vector *v, gsl_complex x){
    gsl_vector_complex *out = gsl_vector_complex_alloc(v->size);
    for (int i=0; i< v->size; i++)
        gsl_vector_complex_set(out, i,
                        gsl_complex_mul_real(x, gsl_vector_get(v, i)));
    return out;
}

gsl_vector_complex *cvec_dot_c(gsl_vector_complex *v, complex double x){
    return cvec_dot_gslcplx(v, gsl_cplx_from_c99(x));
}

gsl_vector_complex *vec_dot_c(gsl_vector *v, complex double x){
    return vec_dot_gslcplx(v, gsl_cplx_from_c99(x));
}

complex double ddot (complex double x, complex double y){return x*y;}  ❶
```

---

```
void gsl_vector_complex_print(gsl_vector_complex *v){
    for (int i=0; i< v->size; i++) {
        gsl_complex x = gsl_vector_complex_get(v, i);
        printf("%4g+%4gi%c", GSL_REAL(x), GSL_IMAG(x), i < v->size-1 ? '\t' : '\n');
    }
}
```

❶  C-native complex numbers are multiplied with a simple *, like real numbers.

The cleanup happens in the header, Example 11-15. It uses _Generic to select one of
the functions from Example 11-14 based on the input types. The first argument (the
*controlling expression*) is not evaluated, but is simply checked for its type, and the
value of the _Generic statement is selected based on that type. We want to select a
function based on two types, so the first macro picks which of the second or third
macros to use.

*Example 11-15. Using _Generic to provide a simple frontend to the mess (cplx.h)*

```
#include <complex.h> //nice names for C's complex types
#include <gsl/gsl_vector.h> //gsl_vector_complex

gsl_vector_complex *cvec_dot_gslcplx(gsl_vector_complex *v, gsl_complex x);
gsl_vector_complex *vec_dot_gslcplx(gsl_vector *v, gsl_complex x);
gsl_vector_complex *cvec_dot_c(gsl_vector_complex *v, complex double x);
gsl_vector_complex *vec_dot_c(gsl_vector *v, complex double x);
void gsl_vector_complex_print(gsl_vector_complex *v);

#define gsl_cplx_from_c99(x) (gsl_complex){.dat= {creal(x), cimag(x)}}   ❶

complex double ddot (complex double x, complex double y);

#define dot(x,y)  _Generic((x),                                   \        ❷
                    gsl_vector*: dot_given_vec(y),                \
                    gsl_vector_complex*: dot_given_cplx_vec(y), \
                    default: ddot)((x),(y))

#define dot_given_vec(y) _Generic((y),                           \
                    gsl_complex: vec_dot_gslcplx,                \
                    default: vec_dot_c)

#define dot_given_cplx_vec(y) _Generic((y),                      \
                    gsl_complex: cvec_dot_gslcplx,               \
                    default: cvec_dot_c)
```

❶  gsl_complex and C99 complex double are both a two-element array consisting
   of real double followed by imaginary double [see the GSL manual and C99 and
   C11 §6.2.5(13)]. All we have to do is build the appropriate struct—and a compound literal is the perfect way to build a struct on the fly.

❷ The first use of x is not actually evaluated, just checked for its type. That means that a call like dot(x++, y) would increment x only once.

In Example 11-16, life is (mostly) easy again: we can use dot to find the product of a gsl_vector times a gsl_complex, a gsl_vector_complex times a C complex, and so on for a great many combinations. Of course, you still need to know the output type, because the return value of a scalar times a scalar is a scalar, not a vector, so the use of the output depends on the input types. The proliferation of types is a fundamental problem, but the _Generic facility at least provides a band-aid.

*Example 11-16. The payoff: we can use dot (almost) regardless of input type (simple_cplx.c)*

```
#include <stdio.h>
#include "cplx.h"

int main(){
    int complex a = 1+2I;                                              ❶
    complex double b = 2+I;
    gsl_complex c = gsl_cplx_from_c99(a);

    gsl_vector *v = gsl_vector_alloc(8);
    for (int i=0; i< v->size; i++) gsl_vector_set(v, i, i/8.);

    complex double adotb = dot(a, b);                                  ❷
    printf("(1+2i) dot (2+i): %g + %gi\n", creal(adotb), cimag(adotb)); ❸

    printf("v dot 2:\n");
    double d = 2;
    gsl_vector_complex_print(dot(v, d));

    printf("v dot (1+2i):\n");
    gsl_vector_complex *vc = dot(v, a);
    gsl_vector_complex_print(vc);

    printf("v dot (1+2i) again:\n");
    gsl_vector_complex_print(dot(v, c));
}
```

❶ Declarations with complex are a bit like declarations with const: both complex int and int complex are valid.

❷ Finally, the payoff: this function will use the dot function four times, each with different input types.

❸ Here are the C-native means of getting the real and imaginary parts of a complex number.

# Count References

The remainder of this chapter shows a few examples of adding a reference counter to the boilerplate new/copy/free functions. Because adding a reference counter is not especially challenging, these are really a chance to provide some extended examples of the form, taking into account more real-world considerations and doing something interesting. Because, after all the interesting extensions and variants presented throughout this chapter, the struct plus accompanying functions is still the workhorse format used by a large chunk of the world's C libraries.

The first example presents a small library that has one structure to speak of, which is intended to read an entire file into a single string. Having all of *Moby Dick* in a single string in memory is not a big deal at all, but having a thousand copies of it floating around starts to be wasteful. So instead of copying the potentially very long data string, we'll have views that just mark different start and end points.

Now that we have several views of the string, we need to free the string exactly once, when the string no longer has any views attached. Thanks to the object framework, it's easy to make this happen.

The second example, an agent-based microsimulation of group formation, has a similar problem: the groups should exist as long as they have members, and need to be freed if and when the last member leaves.

## Example: A Substring Object

The key to managing a lot of objects pointing to the same string is to add a reference-count element to the structure. Modify the four boilerplate elements as follows:

- The type definition includes a pointer-to-integer named refs. It will be set up only once (via the new function), and all copies (made via the copy function) will share the string and this reference counter.
- The new function sets up the refs pointer and sets *refs = 1.
- The copy function copies the original struct into the output copy and increments the reference count.
- The free function decrements the reference count and, if it has hit zero, frees the shared string.

Example 11-17 provides the header for the string manipulation example, *fstr.h*, which introduces the key structure representing a segment of a string and an auxiliary structure representing a list of these string segments.

*Example 11-17. The public tip of the iceberg (fstr.h)*

```
#include <stdio.h>
#include <stdlib.h>
#include <glib.h>

typedef struct {          ❶
    char *data;
    size_t start, end;
    int* refs;
} fstr_s;

fstr_s *fstr_new(char const *filename);
fstr_s *fstr_copy(fstr_s const *in, size_t start, size_t len);
void fstr_show(fstr_s const *fstr);
void fstr_free(fstr_s *in);

typedef struct {          ❷
    fstr_s **strings;
    int count;
} fstr_list;

fstr_list fstr_split (fstr_s const *in, gchar const *start_pattern);
void fstr_list_free(fstr_list in);
```

❶ I hope these typdef/new/copy/free sets are getting dull for you. The fstr_show function will be very useful for debugging.

❷ This is an auxiliary structure that isn't quite a full object. Notice that the fstr_split function returns the list, not a pointer to the list.

Example 11-18 shows the library, *fstr.c*. It uses GLib to read in the text file and for Perl-compatible regular expression parsing. The numbered callouts focus on the steps at the head of this section, so you can follow them to trace the use of the refs element to implement reference counting.

*Example 11-18. An object representing a substring (fstr.c)*

```
#include "fstr.h"
#include "string_utilities.h"

fstr_s *fstr_new(char const *filename){
    fstr_s *out = malloc(sizeof(fstr_s));
    *out = (fstr_s){.start=0, .refs=malloc(sizeof(int))};          ❶
    out->data = string_from_file(filename);
    out->end = out->data ? strlen(out->data): 0;
    *out->refs = 1;
    return out;
}
```

```
fstr_s *fstr_copy(fstr_s const *in, size_t start, size_t len){      ❷
    fstr_s *out = malloc(sizeof(fstr_s));
    *out=*in;
    out->start += start;
    if (in->end > out->start + len)
        out->end = out->start + len;
    (*out->refs)++;                                                 ❸
    return out;
}

void fstr_free(fstr_s *in){                                         ❹
    (*in->refs)--;
    if (!*in->refs) {
        free(in->data);
        free(in->refs);
    }
    free(in);
}

fstr_list fstr_split (fstr_s const *in, gchar const *start_pattern){
    if (!in->data) return (fstr_list){ };

    fstr_s **out=malloc(sizeof(fstr_s*));
    int outlen = 1;
    out[0] = fstr_copy(in, 0, in->end);

    GRegex *start_regex = g_regex_new (start_pattern, 0, 0, NULL);
    gint mstart=0, mend=0;
    fstr_s *remaining = fstr_copy(in, 0, in->end);
    do {                                                            ❺
        GMatchInfo *start_info;
        g_regex_match(start_regex, &remaining->data[remaining->start],
                                0, &start_info);
        g_match_info_fetch_pos(start_info, 0, &mstart, &mend);
        g_match_info_free(start_info);
        if (mend > 0 && mend < remaining->end - remaining->start){  ❻
            out = realloc(out, ++outlen * sizeof(fstr_s*));
            out[outlen-1] = fstr_copy(remaining, mend, remaining->end-mend);
            out[outlen-2]->end = remaining->start + mstart;
            remaining->start += mend;
        } else break;
    } while (1);

    fstr_free(remaining);
    g_regex_unref(start_regex);
    return (fstr_list){.strings=out, .count=outlen};
}

void fstr_list_free(fstr_list in){
    for (int i=0; i< in.count; i++){
        fstr_free(in.strings[i]);
    }
```

```
        free(in.strings);
    }

    void fstr_show(fstr_s const *fstr){
        printf("%.*s", (int)fstr->end-fstr->start, &fstr->data[fstr->start]);
    }
```

❶ For a new `fstr_s`, the owner bit is set to one. Otherwise, the lines to this point are the boilerplate new object function.

❷ The copy function copies the `fstr_s` sent in, and sets the start and end points to the substring given (making sure that the endpoint doesn't go past the endpoint of the input `fstr_s`).

❸ Here's where the owner bit gets set.

❹ Here's where the owner bit gets used, to determine whether the base data should be freed or not.

❺ This function uses GLib's Perl-compatible regular expressions to split the input string at given markers. As discussed in "Parsing Regular Expressions" on page 324, regex matchers gives the location of the segment of the string that matches the input, and we can then use `fstr_copy` to pull that segment. Then, start at the end of that range and try matching again to get the next chunk.

❻ Else, no match or out of bounds.

And finally, an application. To make this work, you'll need a copy of *Moby Dick, or the Whale,* by Herman Melville. If you don't have a copy on your drive, try Example 11-19 to download one from Project Gutenberg.

*Example 11-19. Use curl to get the Project Gutenberg edition of Moby Dick, then use sed to cut the Gutenberg header and footer. You might have to ask your package manger to install curl (find.moby)*

```
if [ ! -e moby ] ; then
 curl http://www.gutenberg.org/cache/epub/2701/pg2701.txt   \
      | sed -e '1,/START OF THIS PROJECT GUTENBERG/d'        \
      | sed -e '/End of Project Gutenberg/,$d'               \
      > moby
fi
```

Now that you have a copy of the book, Example 11-21 splits it into chapters and uses the same splitting function to count the uses of the words *whale(s)* and *I* in each chapter. Notice that the `fstr` structs can be used as opaque objects at this point, using only the new, copy, free, show, and split functions.

---

The program requires GLib, *fstr.c*, and the string utilities from earlier in the book, so the basic makefile is now as in Example 11-20.

*Example 11-20. A sample makefile for the cetology program (cetology.make)*

```
P=cetology
CFLAGS=`pkg-config --cflags glib-2.0` -g -Wall -std=gnu99 -O3
LDLIBS=`pkg-config --libs glib-2.0`
objects=fstr.o string_utilities.o

$(P): $(objects)
```

*Example 11-21. An example, in which a book is split into chapters and characteristics of each chapter counted (cetology.c)*

```
#include "fstr.h"

int main(){
    fstr_s *fstr = fstr_new("moby");
    fstr_list chapters = fstr_split(fstr, "\nCHAPTER");
    for (int i=0; i< chapters.count; i++){
        fstr_list for_the_title=fstr_split(chapters.strings[i],"\\.");
        fstr_show(for_the_title.strings[1]);
        fstr_list me     = fstr_split(chapters.strings[i], "\\WI\\W");
        fstr_list whales = fstr_split(chapters.strings[i], "whale(s|)");
        fstr_list words  = fstr_split(chapters.strings[i], "\\W");
        printf("\nch %i, words: %i.\t Is: %i\twhales: %i\n", i, words.count-1,
                me.count-1, whales.count-1);

        fstr_list_free(for_the_title);
        fstr_list_free(me);
        fstr_list_free(whales);
        fstr_list_free(words);
    }
    fstr_list_free(chapters);
    fstr_free(fstr);
}
```

To give you incentive to try the program, I won't reprint the results in detail. But I will give some notes, which generally point to how hard it would be for Mr. Melville to publish or even blog the book here in the modern day:

- Chapter lengths range by an order of magnitude.

- Whales don't get discussed all that much until around Chapter 30.

- The narrator decidedly has a voice. Even in the famed cetology chapter, he uses the first person singular 60 times, personalizing what would otherwise be an encyclopedia chapter.

- GLib's regex parser is a little slower than I'd hoped it'd be.

## Example: An Agent-Based Model of Group Formation

This example is an agent-based model of group membership. Agents are on a two-dimensional preference space (because we'll plot the groups) in the square between (-1, -1) and (1, 1). At each round, agents will join the group with the best utility to the agent. An agent's utility from a group is -(distance to group's mean position + $M$*number of members). The group's mean position is the mean of the positions of the group's members (excluding the agent querying the group), and $M$ is a constant that scales how much the agents care about being in a large group relative to how much they care about the group's mean position: if $M$ is near zero, then size of group is basically irrelevant, and agents care only about proximity; as $M$ goes to infinity, position becomes irrelevant, and only group size matters.

With some random odds, the agent will originate a new group. However, because agents are picking a new group every period, the agent may abandon that newly originated group in the next period.

The problem of reference counting is similar, and the process is roughly similar for this case:

- The type definition includes an integer named `counter`.
- The `new` function sets `counter = 1`.
- The `copy` function sets `counter++`.
- The free function queries `if(--counter==0)`, and if yes, then `free` all shared data; or else, just leave everything as is, because we know there are still references to the structure.

Again, as long as your changes to the structure are entirely via its interface functions, you don't have to think about memory allocation when using the object at all.

The simulation takes almost 125 lines of code, and because I used CWEB to document it, the code files total almost double that length (where I gave some tips on reading and writing CWEB in "Literate Code with CWEB" on page 64). Given the literate coding style, this should be very readable; even if you're in the habit of skipping big blocks of code, maybe give it a skim. If you have CWEB on hand, you can generate the PDF documentation and try reading it in that format.

The output from this program is intended to be piped to Gnuplot, a plotting program that stands out for being easy to automate. Here is a command-line script that uses a here document to pipe the given text to Gnuplot, including a series of data points (with an `e` to mark the end of the series).

```
cat << "------" | gnuplot --persist
set xlabel "Year"
set ylabel "U.S. Presidential elections"
set yrange [0:5]
set key off
plot '-' with boxes
2000, 1
2001, 0
2002, 0
2003, 0
2004, 1
2005, 0
e
------
```

You can probably already picture producing commands to Gnuplot programmatically, via a `printf` or two for the plot settings, and a `for` loop to output the data set. Further, sending a series of plots to Gnuplot generates an animation sequence.

The simulation below produces an animation like this, so you can run the simulation via `./groups | gnuplot` to display the animation on-screen. It's hard to print an animation, so you'll have to run it yourself. You will see that, even though such behavior was not programmed into the simulation, new groups cause nearby groups to shift, producing an evenly spaced, uniform distribution of group positions. Political scientists have often observed similar behavior in the space of political party positions: when new parties enter, existing parties adjust their positions accordingly.

Now for the header. What I call the join and exit functions might more commonly be read as the copy and free functions. The `group_s` structure has a `size` element, which is the number of group members—the reference count. You can see that I use Apophenia and GLib. Notably, the groups are held in a linked list, private to the *groups.c* file; maintaining that list will require fully two lines of code, including a call to `g_list_append` and `g_list_remove` (Example 11-22).

*Example 11-22. The public portion of the group_s object. (groups.h)*

```
#include <apop.h>
#include <glib.h>

typedef struct {
    gsl_vector *position;
    int id, size;
} group_s;

group_s* group_new(gsl_vector *position);
group_s* group_join(group_s *joinme, gsl_vector *position);
void group_exit(group_s *leaveme, gsl_vector *position);
group_s* group_closest(gsl_vector *position, double mb);
void print_groups();
```

Now for the file defining the details of the group object (shown in Example 11-23).

*Example 11-23. The group_s object. (groups.w)*

```
@ Here in the introductory material, we include the header and specify
the global list of groups that the program makes use of. We'll need
new/copy/free functions for each group.

@c
#include "groups.h"

GList *group_list;
@<new group@>
@<copy group@>
@<free group@>

@ The new group method is boilerplate: we |malloc| some space,
fill the struct using designated initializers, and append the newly formed
group to the list.

@<new group@>=
group_s *group_new(gsl_vector *position){
    static int id=0;
    group_s *out = malloc(sizeof(group_s));
    *out = (group_s) {.position=apop_vector_copy(position), .id=id++, .size=1};
    group_list = g_list_append(group_list, out);
    return out;
}
```

@ When an agent joins a group, the group is `copied' to the agent, but there isn't any memory being copied: the group is simply modified to accommodate the new person. We have to increment the reference count, which is easy enough, and then modify the mean position. If the mean position without the $n$th person is $P_{n-1}$, and the $n$th person is at position $p$, then the new mean position with the person, $P_n$ is the weighted sum.

$$P_n = \left( (n-1)P_{n-1}/n \right) + p/n.$$

We calculate that for each dimension.

```
@<copy group@>=
group_s *group_join(group_s *joinme, gsl_vector *position){
    int n = ++joinme->size;   //increment the reference count
    for (int i=0; i< joinme->position->size; i++){
        joinme->position->data[i] *= (n-1.)/n;
        joinme->position->data[i] += position->data[i]/n;
    }
    return joinme;
}
```

@ The `free' function really only frees the group when the reference count is zero. When it isn't, then we need to run the data-augmenting formula for the mean in reverse to remove a person.

```
@<free group@>=
void group_exit(group_s *leaveme, gsl_vector *position){
    int n = leaveme->size--;   //lower the reference count
    for (int i=0; i< leaveme->position->size; i++){
        leaveme->position->data[i] -= position->data[i]/n;
        leaveme->position->data[i] *= n/(n-1.);
    }
    if (leaveme->size == 0){ //garbage collect?
        gsl_vector_free(leaveme->position);
        group_list= g_list_remove(group_list, leaveme);
        free(leaveme);
    }
}
```

@ I played around a lot with different rules for how exactly people evaluate the distance to the groups. In the end, I wound up using the $L_3$ norm. The standard distance is the $L_2$ norm, aka Euclidian distance, meaning that the distance between $(x_1, y_1)$ and $(x_2, y_2)$ is $\sqrt{(x_1-x_2)^2+(y_1-y_2)^2}$. This is $L_3$, $|\sqrt[3]{(x_1-x_2)^3+(y_1-y_2)^3}|$.
This and the call to |apop_copy| above are the only calls to the Apophenia library; you could write around them if you don't have that library on hand.

```
@<distance@>=
apop_vector_distance(g->position, position, .metric='L', .norm=3)
```

@ By `closest', I mean the group that provides the greatest benefit, by having the smallest distance minus weighted size. Given the utility function represented by the |dist| line, this is just a simple |for| loop to find the smallest distance.

```
@c
group_s *group_closest(gsl_vector *position, double mass_benefit){
    group_s *fave=NULL;
    double smallest_dist=GSL_POSINF;
    for (GList *gl=group_list; gl!= NULL; gl = gl->next){
        group_s *g = gl->data;
        double dist= @<distance@> - mass_benefit*g->size;
        if(dist < smallest_dist){
            smallest_dist = dist;
            fave = g;
        }
    }
    return fave;
}
```

@ Gnuplot is automation-friendly. Here we get an animated simulation with four lines of plotting code. The header |plot '-'| tells the system to plot the data to follow, then we print the $(X, Y)$ positions, one to a line. The final |e| indicates the end of the data set. The main program will set some initial Gnuplot settings.

```
@c
void print_groups(){
    printf("plot '-' with points pointtype 6\n");
    for (GList *gl=group_list; gl!= NULL; gl = gl->next)
        apop_vector_print(((group_s*)gl->data)->position);
    printf("e\n");
}
```

Now that we have a group object and interface functions to add, join, and leave groups, the main program can focus on the simulation procedure: defining the array of persons followed by the main loop of rechecking memberships and printing out (Example 11-24).

*Example 11-24. The agent-based model, making use of the* group_s *object* (groupabm.w)

```
@* Initializations.
```

@ This is the part of the agent-based model with the handlers for the |people| structures and the procedure itself.

At this point all interface with the groups happens via the new/join/exit/print functions from |groups.cweb.c|. Thus, there is zero memory management code in this file--the reference counting guarantees us that when the last member exits a group, the group will be freed.

```
@c
#include "groups.h"

int pop=2000,
    periods=200,
    dimension=2;
```

@ In |main|, we'll initialize a few constants that we can't have as static variables because they require math.

```
@<set up more constants@>=
    double  new_group_odds = 1./pop,
            mass_benefit = .7/pop;
    gsl_rng *r = apop_rng_alloc(1234);

@* The |person_s| structure.
```

@ The people in this simulation are pretty boring: they do not die, and do not move. So the struct that represents them is simple, with just |position| and a pointer to the group of which the agent is currently a member.

```
@c
typedef struct {
```

```
    gsl_vector *position;
    group_s *group;
} person_s;
```

@ The setup routine is also boring, and consists of allocating a uniform
random vector in two dimensions.

```
@c
person_s person_setup(gsl_rng *r){
    gsl_vector *posn = gsl_vector_alloc(dimension);
    for (int i=0; i< dimension; i++)
        gsl_vector_set(posn, i, 2*gsl_rng_uniform(r)-1);
    return (person_s){.position=posn};
}
```

@* Group membership.

@ At the outset of this function, the person leaves its group.
Then, the decision is only whether to form a new group or join an existing one.

```
@c
void check_membership(person_s *p, gsl_rng *r,
                        double mass_benefit, double new_group_odds){
    group_exit(p->group, p->position);
    p->group = (gsl_rng_uniform(r) < new_group_odds)
            ? @<form a new group@>
            : @<join the closest group@>;
}
```

```
@
@<form a new group@>=
group_new(p->position)
```

```
@
@<join the closest group@>=
group_join(group_closest(p->position, mass_benefit), p->position)
```

@* Setting up.

@ The initialization of the population. Using CWEB's macros, it is at this point
self-documenting.

```
@c
void init(person_s *people, int pop, gsl_rng *r){
    @<position everybody@>
    @<start with ten groups@>
    @<everybody joins a group@>
}
```

```
@
@<position everybody@>=
    for (int i=0; i< pop; i++)
```

```
        people[i] = person_setup(r);
```

@ The first ten people in our list form new groups, but because everybody's
position is random, this is assigning the ten groups at random.

```
@<start with ten groups@>=
    for (int i=0; i< 10; i++)
        people[i].group = group_new(people[i].position);
```

```
@
@<everybody joins a group@>=
    for (int i=10; i< pop; i++)
        people[i].group = group_join(people[i%10].group, people[i].position);
```

@* Plotting with Gnuplot.

@ This is the header for Gnuplot. I arrived at it by playing around on
Gnuplot's command line, then writing down my final picks for settings here.

```
@<print the Gnuplot header@>=
printf("unset key;set xrange [-1:1]\nset yrange [-1:1]\n");
```

```
@ Gnuplot animation simply consists of sending a sequence of plot statements.
@<plot one animation frame@>=
print_groups();
```

@* |main|.

@ The |main| routine consists of a few setup steps, and a simple loop:
calculate a new state, then plot it.

```
@c
int main(){
    @<set up more constants@>
    person_s people[pop];
    init(people, pop, r);

    @<print the Gnuplot header@>
    for (int t=0; t< periods; t++){
        for (int i=0; i< pop; i++)
            check_membership(&people[i], r, mass_benefit, new_group_odds);
        @<plot one animation frame@>
    }
}
```

# Conclusion

This section gave several examples of the basic form of an object: a struct with
accompanying new/copy/free elements. I gave so many examples because over the
decades it has proven to be an excellent method for organizing code in thousands of
libraries.

Those parts that weren't giving examples of the basic struct/new/copy/free form demonstrated various ways of extending existing setups. In terms of extending the struct itself, you saw how to extend a struct by anonymous inclusion in a wrapper struct.

With regard to the associated functions, you saw several methods of having one function call take a different action with different struct instances. By including functions inside a struct, you can create dispatch functions that use the struct contained in the object. With vtables, these dispatch functions can be extended even after the struct is written and shipped out. You saw the _Generic keyword, which will select the function to call based on the type of a controlling expression.

Whether these make your code more readable and improve the user interface is up to you. But these additional forms are especially useful for making *other people's* code more readable. You may have a library written perhaps decades ago, and needs that are different from the needs of the original authors. The methods in this chapter become very relevant: you can extend their structs and add new possibilities to their functions.

# CHAPTER 12

# Parallel Threads

*It's 99 revolutions tonight.*
—Green Day, "99 Revolutions"

Just about all the computers sold in the last few years—even many telephones—are multicore. If you are reading this on a keyboard-and-monitor computer, you may be able to find out how many cores your computer has via:

- Linux: `grep cores /proc/cpuinfo`
- Mac: `sysctl hw.logicalcpu`
- Cygwin: `env | grep NUMBER_OF_PROCESSORS`

A single-threaded program doesn't make full use of the resources the hardware manufacturers gave us. Fortunately, it doesn't take much to turn a program into one with concurrent parallel threads—in fact, it often only takes one extra line of code. In this chapter, I will cover:

- A quick overview of the several standards and specifications that exist for writing concurrent C code
- The one line of OpenMP code that will make your for loops multithreaded
- Notes on the compiler flags you'll need to compile with OpenMP or pthreads
- Some considerations of when it's safe to use that one magic line
- Implementing map-reduce, which requires extending that one line by another clause
- The syntax for running a handful of distinct tasks in parallel, like the UI and backend of a GUI-based program

- C's `_Thread_local` keyword, which makes thread-private copies of global static variables

- Critical regions and mutexes

- Atomic variables in OpenMP

- A quick note on sequential consistency and why you want it

- POSIX threads, and how they differ from OpenMP

- Atomic scalar variables via C atoms

- Atomic structs via C atoms

This is another chapter based on what is missing in standard C textbooks. In my survey of the market, I could not find a single general C text that covered OpenMP. So here I will give you enough to get started—maybe even enough that you may never need to refer to the full books on threading theory.

However, there are books dedicated to the topic of concurrent programming, many in C, covering a wealth of details that I don't; see *The Art of Concurrency: A Thread Monkey's Guide to Writing Parallel Applications*; *Multicore Application Programming: for Windows, Linux, and Oracle Solaris*; or *Introduction to Parallel Computing (2nd Edition)*. I will use the default scheduling and the safest form of synchronization throughout, even though cases exist where you can do better by fine-tuning those things; neither will I wade into details of cache optimization, nor give you an exhaustive list of useful OpenMP pragmas (which your Internet search engine will do just fine).

# The Environment

It wasn't until the December 2011 revision that a threading mechanism was a part of standard C. That is late to the party, and others have already provided mechanisms. So you've got several options:

- POSIX threads. The pthreads standard was defined in POSIX v1, circa 1995. The `pthread_create` function works by assigning a function of a certain form to each thread, so you have to write an appropriate function interface, and typically an accompanying struct.

- Windows also has its own threading system, which works like pthreads. For example, the `CreateThread` function takes in a function and a pointer to parameters much like `pthread_create` does.

- OpenMP is a specification that uses `#pragmas` and a handful of library functions to tell the compiler when and how to thread. This is what you can use to turn a serial-running `for` loop into a threaded `for` loop with one line of code. The first OpenMP spec for C came out in 1998.

- The specification for the C standard library now includes headers that define functions for threading and atomic variable operations.

Which to use depends on your target environment, and your own goals and preferences. OpenMP is much easier to write and is therefore much less likely to harbor bugs than the other threading systems. It is supported by almost all major compilers—even Visual Studio—but `clang` support is still in the works as of this writing in late 2014.[1] The compilers and standard libraries that support standard C threading and atoms are not yet universal. If you are unable to rely on OpenMP and its `#pragmas`, then pthreads are available for any POSIX-conformant host (even MinGW).

There are other options, such as the MPI (message passing interface, for talking across networked nodes) or OpenCL (especially useful for GPU processing). On POSIX systems, you can use the `fork` system call to effectively produce two clones of your program that share memory but otherwise operate independently.

## The Ingredients

Our syntactic needs are not great. In all cases, we will need:

- A means of telling the compiler to set off several threads at once. To give an early example, (Nabokov-1962) includes this note on line 404: *[And here time forked.]* The remainder of the section vacillates between two threads.

- A means of marking a point where the new threads cease to exist, and the main thread continues alone. In some cases, like the above early example, the barrier is implicit at the end of the segment, but some of the options will have an explicit gather-the-threads step.

- A means of marking parts of the code that should not be threaded, because they can not be made thread-safe. For example, what would happen if thread one resized an array to size 20 at the same time that thread two is resizing it to size 30? Even though a resize takes a microsecond to us humans, if we could slow down time, we would see that even a simple increment like x++ would be a series of finite-time operations that another thread could conflict with. Using OpenMP pragmas, these unshareable segments will be marked as *critical regions*; in pthread-influenced systems these will be marked via *mutexes* (a crunching-together of *mutual exclusion*).

---

1 Visual Studio supports version 2.0, and OpenMP is at version 4.0, but the basic pragmas covered here are not new.

- Means of dealing with variables that may be simultaneously handled by multiple threads. Strategies include taking a global variable and making a thread-local copy, and syntax to put a mini-mutex around each use of a variable.

# OpenMP

As an example, let us thread a word-counting program. I will borrow some string-handling utilities from Example 11-21 to produce a word-counting function. To get it out of the way of the parts about threading, the function is in its own file; see Example 12-1.

*Example 12-1. A word counter, which works by reading the entire file into memory and then breaking it at nonword characters (wordcount.c)*

```
#include "string_utilities.h"

int wc(char *docname){
    char *doc = string_from_file(docname);              ❶
    if (!doc) return 0;
    char *delimiters = " `~!@#$%^&*()_-+={[]}|\\;:\",<>./?\n";
    ok_array *words = ok_array_new(doc, delimiters);    ❷
    if (!words) return 0;
    double out= words->length;
    ok_array_free(words);
    return out;
}
```

❶ `string_from_file` reads the given document into a string and is borrowed from Example 9-6.

❷ Also borrowed from the string utility library, this function divides a string at the given delimiters. We just want the count from it.

Example 12-2 calls the word-counting function with any list of files given on the command line. In that program, `main` is basically just a for loop calling wc, followed by a step to sum up the individual counts to a grand total.

*Example 12-2. By adding a line of code, we can run chunks of a for loop on different threads (openmp_wc.c)*

```
#include "stopif.h"
#include "wordcount.c"

int main(int argc, char **argv){
    argc--;
    argv++;                                             ❶
```

```
    Stopif(!argc, return 0, "Please give some file names on the command line.");
    int count[argc];

    #pragma omp parallel for                              ❷
    for (int i=0; i< argc; i++){
        count[i] = wc(argv[i]);
        printf("%s:\t%i\n", argv[i], count[i]);
    }

    long int sum=0;
    for (int i=0; i< argc; i++) sum+=count[i];
    printf("Σ:\t%li\n", sum);
}
```

❶  argv[0] is the name of the program, so step the argv pointer past it. The rest of the arguments on the command line are files to be word-counted.

❷  Having added this one line of code, the for loop now runs in parallel threads.

The OpenMP instruction that makes this a threaded program is this line:

```
#pragma omp parallel for
```

indicating that the for loop immediately following should be broken down into segments and run across as many threads as the system running the program deems optimal. In this case, I've lived up to my promise, and turned a not-parallel program into a parallel program with one line of code.

OpenMP works out how many threads your system can run and splits up the work accordingly. In cases where you need to set the number of threads to $N$ manually, you can do so either by setting an environment variable before the program runs:

```
export OMP_NUM_THREADS=N
```

or by using a C function in your program:

```
#include <omp.h>
omp_set_num_threads(N);
```

These facilities are probably most useful for fixing the thread count to $N=1$. If you want to return to the default of requesting as many threads as your computer has processors, use:

```
#include <omp.h>
omp_set_num_threads(omp_get_num_procs());
```

A macro defined via #define can't expand to a #pragma, so what do you do if you want to parallelize a macro? That's what the _Pragma operator is for [C99 and C11 §6.10.9]. The input to the operator is (in the language of the official standard) destringized and used as a pragma. For example:

```
#include <stdio.h>

#define pfor(...) _Pragma("omp parallel for") \
    for(__VA_ARGS__)

int main(){
    pfor(int i=0; i< 1000; i++){
        printf("%i\n", i);
    }
}
```

You can only have a single string inside the parens of the _Pragma( ). The workaround when you need more is to use a sub-macro that treats all its inputs as a string. Here is a preprocessor block that uses this form to define an OMP_critical macro that expands to a header for an OpenMP critical block with the given tag (see below) if _OPENMP is defined, else it is replaced with nothing.

```
#ifdef _OPENMP
    #define PRAGMA(x) _Pragma(#x)
    #define OMP_critical(tag) PRAGMA(omp critical(tag))
#else
    #define OMP_critical(tag)
#endif
```

## Compiling OpenMP, pthreads, and C atoms

For gcc and clang (where clang support for OpenMP is still in progress on some platforms), compiling this requires adding an -fopenmp flag for the compilation. If you need a separate linking step, add -fopenmp to the link flags as well (the compiler will know if any libraries need to be linked and will do what you want). For pthreads, you will need to add a -pthread flag. C atomic support (in gcc, as of this writing) requires linking to the atomic library. So if you were using all three, you might add these lines to your makefile:

```
CFLAGS=-g -Wall -O3 -fopenmp -pthread
LDLIBS=-fopenmp -latomic
```

If you are using Autoconf for your OpenMP project, you will need to add a line to your existing *configure.ac* script:

```
AC_OPENMP
```

which generates an $OPENMP_CFLAGS variable, which you will then need to add to existing flags in *Makefile.am*. For example,

```
AM_CFLAGS = $(OPENMP_CFLAGS) -g -Wall -O3 …
AM_LDFLAGS = $(OPENMP_CFLAGS) $(SQLITE_LDFLAGS) $(MYSQL_LDFLAGS)
```

So that took three lines of code, but now Autoconf will correctly compile your code on every known platform that supports OpenMP.

The OpenMP standard requires that an _OPENMP variable be defined if the compiler accepts OpenMP pragmas. You can use this to put #ifdef _OPENMP blocks into your code as needed.

Once you have the program compiled as threaded_wc, try ./threaded_wc `find ~ -type f` to start a word-count of every file in your home directory. You can open top in another window and see if multiple instances of wc crop up.

## Interference

Now that we have the needed line of syntax to make the program multithreaded, are we guaranteed that it works? For easy cases where you can verify that every iteration of the loop does not interact with any other iteration, yes. But for other cases, we'll need to be more cautious.

To verify whether a team of threads will work, we need to know what happens with each variable, and the effects of any side effects.

- If a variable is private to a thread, then we are guaranteed that it will behave as if in a single-threaded program, without interference. The iterator in the loop, named i in the above example, is made private to each thread (OpenMP 4.0 §2.6). Variables declared inside of the loop are private to the given loop.

- If a variable is being read by a number of threads and is never written by any of them at any point, then you are still safe. This isn't quantum physics: reading a variable never changes its state (and I'm not covering C atomic flags, which actually can't be read without setting them).

- If a variable is written to by one thread and never read by any other thread, there is still no competition—the variable is effectively private.

- If a variable is shared across threads, and it is written to by one thread, and it is read from or written to by any other thread, now you've got real problems, and the rest of this chapter is basically about this case.

The first implication is that, where possible, we should avoid sharing written-to variables. You can go back to the example and see one way of doing this: all the threads use the count array, but iteration i touches only element i in the array, so each array element is effectively thread-private. Further, the count array itself is not resized, freed, or otherwise changed during the loop, and likewise with `argv`. We'll even get rid of the `count` array below.

We don't know what internal variables `printf` uses, but we can check the C standard to verify that all the operations in the standard library that operate on input and output streams (almost everything in `stdio.h`) are thread-safe, so we can call `printf` without worrying about multiple calls stepping on each other (C11 §7.21.2(7) and (8)).

When I wrote this sample, it took some care in writing to make sure that those conditions were met. However, some of the considerations, such as avoiding global variables, are good advice even in the single-threaded world. Also, the post-C99 style of declaring variables at their first use is paying off, because a variable declared inside a segment to be threaded is unambiguously private to that thread.

As an aside, OpenMP's `omp parallel for` pragma understands only simple loops: the iterator is of integer type, it is incremented or decremented by a fixed (loop-invariant) amount every step, and the ending condition compares the iterator to a loop-invariant value or variable. Anything that involves applying the same routine to each element of a fixed array fits this form.

## Map-reduce

The word-count program has a very common form: each thread does some independent task mapping inputs to outputs, but we are really interested in reducing all those individual outputs down to a single aggregate. OpenMP supports this sort of map-reduce workflow via an addendum to the above pragma. Example 12-3 replaces the `count` array with a single variable, `total_wc`, and adds `reduction(+:total_wc)` to the OpenMP pragma. From here, the compiler does the work to efficiently combine each thread's `total_wc` to a grand total.

*Example 12-3. Adapting a for loop to implement a map-reduce workflow requires extending the #pragma omp parallel for line by another clause. (mapreduce_wc.c)*

```
#include "stopif.h"
#include "wordcount.c"

int main(int argc, char **argv){
    argc--;
    argv++;
    Stopif(!argc, return 0, "Please give some file names on the command line.");
    long int total_wc = 0;

    #pragma omp parallel for  \
      reduction(+:total_wc)                        ❶
    for (int i=0; i< argc; i++){
        long int this_count = wc(argv[i]);
```

```
        total_wc += this_count;
        printf("%s:\t%li\n", argv[i], this_count);
    }

    printf("Σ:\t%li\n", total_wc);
}
```

❶ Add a reduction clause to the `pragma omp parallel for` to tell the compiler that this variable holds a sum across all threads.

Again, there are restrictions: the + operator in `reduction(+:variable)` can only be replaced by one of a few a basic arithmetic (+, *, -), bitwise (&, |, ^), or logical (&&, ||) operations. Otherwise, you'll have to go back to something like the `count` array above and write your own post-thread reduction (see Example 12-5 for an example to calculate a maximum). Also, don't forget to initialize the reduction variable before the team of threads runs.

## Multiple Tasks

Instead of having an array and applying the same operation to every array element, you may have two entirely distinct operations, and they are independent and could run in parallel. For example, programs with a user interface often put the UI on one thread and the backend processing on another, so that slowdown in processing doesn't make the UI seize up. Naturally, the pragma for this is the `parallel sec tions` pragma:

```
#pragma omp parallel sections
{
    #pragma omp section
    {
    //Everything in this block happens only in one thread
    UI_starting_fn();
    }

    #pragma omp section
    {
    //Everything in this block happens only in one other thread
    backend_starting_fn();
    }
}
```

Here are a few more features of OpenMP that I didn't cover but that you may enjoy:

*simd*

> Single instruction, multiple data. Some processors have a facility to apply the same operation to every element of a vector. This is not available on all processors, and is distinct from multiple threads, which run on multiple cores. See

`#pragma omp simd`. Also see your compiler manual, because some compilers auto-SIMDify some operations when possible.

#### #pragma omp task

When the number of tasks is not known ahead of time, you can use `#pragma omp task` to set off a new thread. For example, you may be running through a tree structure with a single thread, and at each terminal node, use `#pragma omp task` to start up a new thread to process the leaf.

#### #pragma omp cancel

You may be searching for something with multiple threads, and when one thread finds the goal, there is no point having the other threads continue. Use `#pragma omp cancel` (pthread equivalent: `pthread_cancel`) to call off the other threads.

Also, I must add one more caveat, lest some readers go out and put a `#pragma` over every single for loop in everything: there is overhead to generating a thread. This code:

```
int x = 0;
#pragma omp parallel for reduction(+:x)
for (int i=0; i< 10; i++){
    x++;
}
```

will spend more time generating thread info than incrementing x, and would almost certainly be faster unthreaded. Use threading liberally, but keep an eye on the clock and verify that your changes actually improve performance.

The fact that each thread creation and destruction has some overhead also gives us a rule of thumb that fewer thread creations is better than more. For example, if you have a loop nested inside another loop, it is typically better to parallelize the outer loop rather than the inner loop.

If you have verified that none of your threaded segments write to a shared variable, and all functions called are also thread-safe, then you can stop reading now. Insert `#pragma omp parallel for` or `parallel sections` at the appropriate points, and enjoy your speed gains. The rest of this chapter, and in fact the majority of writing on threading, will be focused on strategies for modifying shared resources.

## Thread Local

Static variables—even those declared inside of your `#pragma omp parallel` region— are shared across all threads by default. You can generate a separate private copy for each thread by adding a `threadprivate` clause to the pragma. For example,

```
static int state;
#pragma omp parallel for threadprivate(state)
```

```
for (int i=0; i< 100; i++)
    ...
```

With some commonsense caveats, the system retains your set of threadprivate variables, so if static_x was 2.7 in thread 4 at the end of one parallel region, it will still be 2.7 in thread 4 at the start of the next parallel region with four threads (OpenMP §2.14.2). There is always a master thread running; outside of the parallel region, the master thread retains its copy of the static variable.

C's _Thread_local keyword splits off static variables in a similar manner. In C, a thread-local static variable's "lifetime is the entire execution of the thread for which it is created, and its stored value is initialized when the thread is started" [C11 §6.2.4(4)]. If we read thread 4 in one parallel region to be the same thread as thread 4 in another parallel region, then this behavior is identical to the OpenMP behavior; if they are read to be separate threads, then the C standard specifies that thread-local storage is re-initialized at every parallel region.

There is still a master thread that exists outside of any parallel regions [it's not stated explicitly, but C11 §5.1.2.4(1) implies this], so a thread-private static variable in the master thread looks a lot like a traditional lifetime-of-the-program static variable.

gcc and clang offer the __thread keyword, which was a gcc extension before the standard added the _Thread_local keyword. Within a function, you can use either of:

```
static __thread int i;       //GCC/clang-specific; works today.
// or
static _Thread_local int i;  //C11, when your compiler implements it.
```

Outside a function, the static keyword is optional, because it is the default. The standard requires a *threads.h* header that defines thread_local as an alias for _Thread_local, much like *stdbool.h* defines bool as an alias for _Bool.

You can check for which to use via a block of preprocessor conditions, like this one, which sets the string threadlocal to the right thing for the given situation.

```
#undef threadlocal
#if __STDC_VERSION__ > 201100L
    #define threadlocal _Thread_local
#elif defined(__APPLE__)
    #define threadlocal              //as of this writing, not yet implemented.
#elif (defined(__GNUC__) || defined(__clang__)) && !defined(threadlocal)
    #define threadlocal __thread
#else
    #define threadlocal
#endif
```

## Localizing Nonstatic Variables

If a variable is to be split into private copies across all threads, we have to establish how the variable is to be initialized in each thread, and what is to be done with it on exit from the threaded region. The `threadprivate()` clause instructs OpenMP to initialize the static variable using the inital value of the variable, and to hold on to the copies on exit from the threaded region for reuse next time the region is entered.

You already saw another such clause: the `reduction(+:var)` clause tells OpenMP to initialize each thread's copy with 0 (or 1 for multiplication), let each thread do its internal additions and subtractions, and then on exit add all the private copies to the original value of *var*.

Nonstatic variables declared outside the parallel region are shared by default. You can make private copies of *localvar* available to each thread by adding a `firstpri vate(localvar)` clause to your `#pragma omp parallel` line. A copy is made for each thread, and initialized with the value of the variable at the start of the thread. At the end they are all destroyed, and the original variable is untouched. Add `lastpri vate(localvar)` to copy the final value of the variable in the last thread (the one with the highest index in a `for` loop, or the last in a list of `sections`) back to the outside-the-region variable. It is not uncommon to have the same variable in both the `first private` and `lastprivate` clauses.

# Shared Resources

To this point, I've stressed the value of using private variables and presented a means of multiplexing a single static variable into a set of thread-local private variables. But sometimes, a resource really does need to be shared, and the *critical region* is the simplest means of protecting it. It marks a segment of code that should only be executed by a single thread at a time. As with most other OpenMP constructs, it operates on the subsequent block:

```
#pragma omp critical (a_private_block)
{
    //interesting code here.
}
```

We are guaranteed that this block will be entered by only one thread at a time. If another thread gets to this point when there is already a thread in the critical region, then the recently arrived thread waits at the head of the region until the thread currently executing the critical region exits the region.

This is called *blocking*, and a blocked thread is inactive for some period of time. This is time-inefficient, but it is far better to have inefficient code than incorrect code.

The (a_private_block), with the parens, is a name that allows you to link together critical regions, such as to protect a single resource used at different points in the code. If you do not want a structure to be read while another thread is writing to the structure, you could use this form:

```
#pragma omp critical (delicate_struct_region)
{
    delicate_struct_update(ds);
}

[other code here]

#pragma omp critical (delicate_struct_region)
{
    delicate_struct_read(ds);
}
```

We are guaranteed that there will be at most one thread in the overall critical region that is the sum of the two segments, and so there will never be a call to `deli cate_struct_update` simultaneous to `delicate_struct_read`. The intermediate code will thread as usual.

The name is technically optional, but all unnamed critical regions are treated as part of the same group. This is a common form for short programs (like sample code you might find on the Internet) but probably not what you want in nontrivial code. By naming every critical region, you can prevent accidentally linking two segments together.

Consider the problem of finding how many factors (prime and nonprime) a number has. For example, the number 18 is evenly divisible by six positive integers: 1, 2, 3, 6, 9, and 18. The number 13 has two factors, 1 and 13, meaning that it is a prime number.

It is easy to find prime numbers—there are 664,579 of them under 10 million. But there are only 446 numbers under 10 million with exactly 3 factors, 6 with exactly 7 factors, and one with exactly 17 factors. Other patterns are easier to find: there are 2,228,418 numbers under 10 million with exactly 8 factors.

Example 12-4 is a program to find those factor counts, threaded via OpenMP. The basic story involves two arrays. The first is a 10-million-element array, `factor_ct`. Initialize it to 2 for all values larger than 1, because every number is divisible by 1 and itself. Then, add 1 to each array element whose index is divisible by 2 (i.e., every even number). Then add 1 to the array elements for indices divisible by 3, and so on, up to 5 million (which would only add a tally to slot 10 million, if it were in the array). At the end of that procedure, we know how many factors every number has. You can insert a for loop to fprintf this array to a file if so desired.

Then, set up another array to tally how many numbers have 1, 2, ... factors. Before doing this, we have to find the maximum factor count, so we know how big an array to set up; then we can go through the factor_ct array and take the tally.

Each step is clearly a candidate for parallelization via #pragma omp parallel for, but conflicts may easily arise. The thread marking multiples of 5 and the thread marking multiples of 7 may both want to increment factor_ct[35] at the same time. To prevent a write conflict, say that we mark the line where we add 1 to the count of factors for item i as a critical region:

```
#pragma omp critical (factor)
factor_ct[i]++;
```

These pragmas operate on the block of code immediately following. Blocks are typically marked by curly braces, but if there are no curly braces, then one line of code is its own block.

When one thread wants to increment factor_ct[30], it needlessly blocks the other thread that wants to increment factor_ct[33]. Critical regions are about certain blocks of code, and they make sense if some blocks are associated with one resource, but we are really trying to protect 10 million separate resources, which brings us to *mutexes* and *atomic variables*.

*Mutex* is short for *mutual exclusion*, and it is used to block threads much like the multipart critical regions above. However, the mutex is a struct like any other, so we can have an array of 10 million of them. Locking mutex i before writing to element i, and releasing mutex i after the write is complete gives us an element i-specific critical region. In code, it would look something like this:

```
omp_lock_t locks[1e7];
for (long int i=0; i< lock_ct; i++)
    omp_init_lock(&locks[i]);

#pragma omp parallel for
for (long int scale=2; scale*i < max; scale++) {
        omp_set_lock(&locks[scale*i]);
        factor_ct[scale*i]++;
        omp_unset_lock(&locks[scale*i]);
    }
```

The omp_set_lock function is really a wait-and-set function: if the mutex is unlocked, then lock it and continue; if the mutex is already locked, block the thread and wait, then continue when the thread that has the lock reaches `omp_unset_lock` and gives the all-clear.

As desired, we have effectively generated 10 million distinct critical regions. The only problem is that the mutex struct itself takes up space, and allocating 10 million of them may be more work than the basic math itself. The solution I present in the code is to use only 128 mutexes and lock mutex `i % 128`. That means any two threads working with two different numbers have about a 1-in-128 chance of needlessly blocking each other. That's not terrible, and on my test boxes is a major speedup from allocating and using 10 million mutexes.

Pragmas are baked into a compiler that understands them, but mutexes are plain C structs, so this example needs to `#include <omp.h>` to get their definition.

Example 12-4 presents the code; the part about finding the largest number of factors is in a separate listing below.

*Example 12-4. Generate an array of factor tallies, find the largest element in that array, then tally how many numbers have 1, 2, ... factors. (openmp_atoms.c)*

```
#include <omp.h>
#include <stdio.h>
#include <stdlib.h> //malloc
#include <string.h> //memset

#include "openmp_getmax.c"                              ❶

int main(){
    long int max = 1e7;
    int *factor_ct = malloc(sizeof(int)*max);

    int lock_ct = 128;
    omp_lock_t locks[lock_ct];
    for (long int i=0; i< lock_ct; i++)
        omp_init_lock(&locks[i]);

    factor_ct[0] = 0;                                   ❷
    factor_ct[1] = 1;
    for (long int i=2; i< max; i++)
        factor_ct[i] = 2;

    #pragma omp parallel for
    for (long int i=2; i<= max/2; i++)
        for (long int scale=2; scale*i < max; scale++) {
                omp_set_lock(&locks[scale*i % lock_ct]);   ❸
                factor_ct[scale*i]++;
                omp_unset_lock(&locks[scale*i % lock_ct]); ❹
            }

    int max_factors = get_max(factor_ct, max);
```

```
    long int tally[max_factors+1];
    memset(tally, 0, sizeof(long int)*(max_factors+1));

    #pragma omp parallel for
    for (long int i=0; i< max; i++){
        int factors = factor_ct[i];
        omp_set_lock(&locks[factors % lock_ct]);          ❺
        tally[factors]++;
        omp_unset_lock(&locks[factors % lock_ct]);
    }

    for (int i=0; i<=max_factors; i++)
        printf("%i\t%li\n", i, tally[i]);
}
```

❶  See next listing.

❷  Initialize. Define 0 and 1 as nonprime.

❸  Lock the mutex just before reading or writing a variable that will be modified.

❹  Unlock the mutex just after reading or writing a variable that will be modified.

❺  I am recycling the set of mutexes to save an initalization step, but this is a distinct mutex use from the one above.

Example 12-5 finds the maximum value within the factor_ct list. Because OpenMP doesn't provide a max reduction, we have to maintain an array of maxes and then find the max among those. The array is omp_get_max_threads() long. A thread can use omp_get_thread_num() to find its own index.

*Example 12-5. Parallelized search for the maximum element in an array (openmp_getmax.c)*

```
int get_max(int *array, long int max){
    int thread_ct = omp_get_max_threads();
    int maxes[thread_ct];
    memset(maxes, 0, sizeof(int)*thread_ct);

    #pragma omp parallel for
    for (long int i=0; i< max; i++){
        int this_thread = omp_get_thread_num();
        if (array[i] > maxes[this_thread])
            maxes[this_thread] = array[i];
    }

    int global_max=0;
    for (int i=0; i< thread_ct; i++)
        if (maxes[i] > global_max)
```

```
        global_max = maxes[i];
    return global_max;
}
```

In the examples here, each mutex wraps a single block of code, but as with the pair of critical regions above, you could use one mutex to protect a resource at several points in a code base.

```
omp_set_lock(&delicate_lock);
delicate_struct_update(ds);
omp_unset_lock(&delicate_lock);

[other code here]

omp_set_lock(&delicate_lock);
delicate_struct_read(ds);
omp_unset_lock(&delicate_lock);
```

## Atoms

An atom is a small, indivisible element.[2] Atomic operations often work via features of the processor, and OpenMP limits them to acting on scalars: almost always an integer or floating-point number, or sometimes a pointer (i.e., a memory address). C will provide atomic structs, but even then you will typically need to use a mutex to protect the struct.

However, the case of simple operations on a scalar is a common one, and in that case we can dispense with mutexes and use atomic operations to effectively put an implicit mutex around every use of a variable.

You'll have to use a pragma that tells OpenMP what you want to do with your atom:

```
#pragma omp atomic read
out = atom;

#pragma omp atomic write seq_cst
atom = out;

#pragma omp atomic update seq_cst
atom ++;        //or atom--

#pragma omp atomic update
//or any binary operation: atom *= x, atom /=x, ...
atom -= x;

#pragma omp atomic capture seq_cst
```

---

2 By the way, the C standard dictates that C atoms have infinite half-life: "Atomic variables shall not decay" [C11 7.17.3(13), footnote].

```
//an update-then-read
out = atom *= 2;
```

The `seq_cst` is optional but recommended (if your compiler supports it); I'll get to it in a moment.

From there, it is up to the compiler to build the right instructions to make sure that a read from an atom in one part of the code is unaffected by a write to an atom in another part of the code.

In the case of the factor-counter, all the resources protected by mutexes are scalars, so we didn't need to use mutexes. Atoms make Example 12-6 shorter and more readable than the mutex version in Example 12-4.

*Example 12-6. Replacing mutexes with atoms (atomic_factors.c)*

```c
#include <omp.h>
#include <stdio.h>
#include <stdlib.h> //malloc
#include <string.h> //memset

#include "openmp_getmax.c"

int main(){
    long int max = 1e7;
    int *factor_ct = malloc(sizeof(int)*max);

    factor_ct[0] = 0;
    factor_ct[1] = 1;
    for (long int i=2; i< max; i++)
        factor_ct[i] = 2;

    #pragma omp parallel for
    for (long int i=2; i<= max/2; i++)
        for (long int scale=2; scale*i < max; scale++) {
            #pragma omp atomic update
            factor_ct[scale*i]++;
        }

    int max_factors = get_max_factors(factor_ct, max);
    long int tally[max_factors+1];
    memset(tally, 0, sizeof(long int)*(max_factors+1));

    #pragma omp parallel for
    for (long int i=0; i< max; i++){
        #pragma omp atomic update
        tally[factor_ct[i]]++;
    }

    for (int i=0; i<=max_factors; i++)
```

```
        printf("%i\t%li\n", i, tally[i]);
}
```

# Sequential consistency

A good compiler will reorder the sequence of operations in a manner that is mathematically equivalent to the code you wrote, but that runs faster. If a variable is initialized on line 10 but first used on line 20, maybe it's faster to do an initialize-and-use on line 20 than to execute two separate steps. Here is a two-threaded example, taken from C11 §7.17.3(15) and reduced to more readable pseudocode:

```
x = y = 0;

// Thread 1:
r1 = load(y);
store(x, r1);

// Thread 2:
r2 = load(x);
store(y, 42);
```

Reading the page, it seems like r2 can't be 42, because 42 is stored in y on the line subsequent to the one where r2 is assigned. If thread 1 executed entirely before thread 2, between the two lines of thread 2, or entirely afterward, then r2 can't be 42. But the compiler could swap the two lines of thread 2, because one line is about r2 and x, and the other is about y, so there is no dependency that requires one to happen before the other. So this sequence is valid:

```
x = y = 0;
store(y, 42);   //thread 2
r1 = load(y);   //thread 1
store(x, r1);   //thread 1
r2 = load(x);   //thread 2
```

Now all of y, x, r1, and r2 are 42.

The C standard goes on with even more perverse cases, even commenting that one of them "is not useful behavior, and implementations should not allow it."

So that's what the seq_cst clause is about: it tells the compiler that atomic operations in a given thread should occur in the order listed in the code file. It was added in OpenMP 4.0, to take advantage of C's sequentially consistent atoms, and your compiler may not support it yet. In the meantime, keep an eye out for the sort of subtleties that could happen when the compiler shuffles your within-a-thread independent lines of code.

# Pthreads

Now let's translate the above example to use pthreads. We have similar elements: a means of dispersing threads and gathering them, and mutexes. Pthreads don't give you atomic variables, but plain C does; see below.

The big difference in the code is that the `pthread_create` function to set a new thread running takes in (among other elements) a single function of the form `void *fn(void *in)`, and because that function takes in one void pointer, we have to write a function-specific struct to take in the data. The function also returns another struct, though if you are defining an ad hoc typedef for a function, it is usually easier to include output elements in the typedef for the input struct than to typedef a special input struct and a special output struct.

Before presenting the full example, let me cut out one of the key sections (meaning some variables will be undefined for now):

```
tally_s thread_info[thread_ct];
for (int i=0; i< thread_ct; i++){
    thread_info[i] = (tally_s){.this_thread=i, .thread_ct=thread_ct,
                               .tally=tally, .max=max, .factor_ct=factor_ct,
                               .mutexes=mutexes, .mutex_ct=mutex_ct};
    pthread_create(&threads[i], NULL, add_tally, &thread_info[i]);
}
for (int t=0; t< thread_ct; t++)
    pthread_join(threads[t], NULL);
```

The first `for` loop generates a fixed number of threads (so it is hard to have pthreads dynamically generate a thread count appropriate to different situations). It first sets up the needed struct, and then it calls `pthread_create` to call the `add_tally` function, sending in the purpose-built struct. At the end of that loop, there are `thread_ct` threads at work.

The next `for` loop is the gather step. The `pthread_join` function blocks until the given thread has concluded its work. Thus, we can't go past this `for` loop until all threads are done, at which point the program is back to the single main thread.

OpenMP mutexes and pthread mutexes behave very much alike. In the limited examples here, changing to pthread mutexes is merely a question of changing names.

Example 12-7 shows the program rewritten with pthreads. Breaking each subroutine into a separate thread, defining a function-specific struct, and the disperse-and-gather routines add a lot of lines of code (and I'm still recycling the OpenMP `get_max` function).

*Example 12-7. The factors example via pthreads (pthread_factors.c)*

```c
#include <omp.h>      //get_max is still OpenMP
#include <pthread.h>
#include <stdio.h>
#include <stdlib.h> //malloc
#include <string.h> //memset

#include "openmp_getmax.c"

typedef struct {
    long int *tally;
    int *factor_ct;
    int max, thread_ct, this_thread, mutex_ct;
    pthread_mutex_t *mutexes;
} tally_s;

void *add_tally(void *vin){
    tally_s *in = vin;                                                    ❶
    for (long int i=in->this_thread; i < in->max; i += in->thread_ct){
        int factors = in->factor_ct[i];
        pthread_mutex_lock(&in->mutexes[factors % in->mutex_ct]);         ❷
        in->tally[factors]++;
        pthread_mutex_unlock(&in->mutexes[factors % in->mutex_ct]);
    }
    return NULL;
}

typedef struct {
    long int i, max, mutex_ct;
    int *factor_ct;
    pthread_mutex_t *mutexes ;
} one_factor_s;

void *mark_factors(void *vin){
    one_factor_s *in = vin;
    long int si = 2*in->i;
    for (long int scale=2; si < in->max; scale++, si=scale*in->i) {
        pthread_mutex_lock(&in->mutexes[si % in->mutex_ct]);
        in->factor_ct[si]++;
        pthread_mutex_unlock(&in->mutexes[si % in->mutex_ct]);
    }
    return NULL;
}

int main(){
    long int max = 1e7;
    int *factor_ct = malloc(sizeof(int)*max);

    int thread_ct = 4, mutex_ct = 128;
    pthread_t threads[thread_ct];
    pthread_mutex_t mutexes[mutex_ct];
```

```
    for (long int i=0; i< mutex_ct; i++)
        pthread_mutex_init(&mutexes[i], NULL);

    factor_ct[0] = 0;
    factor_ct[1] = 1;
    for (long int i=2; i< max; i++)
        factor_ct[i] = 2;

    one_factor_s x[thread_ct];
    for (long int i=2; i<= max/2; i+=thread_ct){
        for (int t=0; t < thread_ct && t+i <= max/2; t++){//extra threads do no harm.
            x[t] = (one_factor_s){.i=i+t, .max=max,
                        .factor_ct=factor_ct, .mutexes=mutexes, .mutex_ct=mutex_ct};
            pthread_create(&threads[t], NULL, mark_factors, &x[t]);    ❸
        }
        for (int t=0; t< thread_ct; t++)
            pthread_join(threads[t], NULL);                            ❹
    }
    FILE *o=fopen("xpt", "w");
    for (long int i=0; i < max; i ++){
        int factors = factor_ct[i];
        fprintf(o, "%i %li\n", factors, i);
    }
    fclose(o);

    int max_factors = get_max(factor_ct, max);
    long int tally[max_factors+1];
    memset(tally, 0, sizeof(long int)*(max_factors+1));

    tally_s thread_info[thread_ct];
    for (int i=0; i< thread_ct; i++){
        thread_info[i] = (tally_s){.this_thread=i, .thread_ct=thread_ct,
                            .tally=tally, .max=max, .factor_ct=factor_ct,
                            .mutexes=mutexes, .mutex_ct=mutex_ct};
        pthread_create(&threads[i], NULL, add_tally, &thread_info[i]);
    }
    for (int t=0; t< thread_ct; t++)
        pthread_join(threads[t], NULL);

    for (int i=0; i<=max_factors; i++)
        printf("%i\t%li\n", i, tally[i]);
}
```

❶ In addition to being required for the pthread_create form, the throwaway type-def, tally_s, adds safety. I still have to be careful to write the inputs and outputs to the pthread system correctly, but the internals of the struct get type-checked, both in main and here in the wrapper function. Next week, when I change tally to an array of plain ints, the compiler will warn me if I don't do the change correctly.

❷ Pthread mutexes and OpenMP mutexes look a lot alike.

❸ Here is the thread-creation step. An array of thread info pointers was declared just before the loop. Then, the loop fills the next thread info pointer, creates a new thread with `pthread_create`, and sends the just-filled thread info pointer to the function the new thread will run. The second argument controls some threading attributes which this intro-level chapter doesn't cover.

❹ This second loop gathers outputs. The second argument to `pthread_join` is an address where we could write the output from the threaded function (`mark_fac tors`).

 The curly brace at the end of a for loop ends the scope, so any locally declared variables are tossed out. Normally, we don't get to the end of scope until all called functions have returned, but the entire point of `pthread_create` is that the main function continues while the thread runs. Thus, this code fails:

```
for (int i=0; i< 10; i++){
    tally_s thread_info = {...};
    pthread_create(&threads[i],
        NULL, add_tally, &thread_info);
}
```

because what is at `&thread_info` will be thrown out by the time `add_tally` gets around to putting it to use. Moving the declaration outside the loop:

```
tally_s thread_info;
for (int i=0; i< 10; i++){
    thread_info = (tally_s) {...};
    pthread_create(&threads[i],
        NULL, add_tally, &thread_info);
}
```

also doesn't work, because what is stored at `thread_info` changes on the second iteration of the loop, even while the first iteration is looking at that location. Thus, the example sets up an array of function inputs, which guarantees that one thread's info will persist and not be changed while the next thread is being set up.

What does pthreads give us for all that extra work? There are more options. For example, the `pthread_rwlock_t` is a mutex that blocks reads or writes if any thread is writing to the thread, but does not block multiple simultaneous reads. The `pthread_cont_t` is a semaphore that can be used to block and unblock multiple threads at once on a signal, and could be used to implement read-write locks or general mutexes. But with great power comes great ways to screw things up. It is easy to write fine-tuned pthreaded code that runs better than OpenMP on the test computer and is all wrong for next year's computer.

The OpenMP spec makes no mention of pthreads, and the POSIX spec makes no mention of OpenMP, so there is no pseudolegal document that requires the meaning of *thread* used by OpenMP to match the meaning of *thread* in POSIX. However, the authors of your compiler had to find some means of implementing OpenMP, POSIX or Windows, and C thread libraries, and they were working too hard by far if they developed distinct threading procedures for each specification. Further, your computer's processor does not have pthread cores and separate OpenMP cores: it has one set of machine instructions to control threads, and it is up to the compiler to reduce the syntax of all the standards and specifications into that single set of instructions. Therefore, it is not unreasonable to mix and match, generating threads via an easy OpenMP #pragma and using pthread mutexes or C atoms to protect resources, or starting with OpenMP and then adopting one segment to pthreads as needed.

# C atoms

The C standard includes two headers, *stdatomic.h* and *threads.h*, which specify functions and types for atomic variables and threads. Here, I will give an example with pthreads to do the threading and C atoms to protect the variables.

There are two reasons why I'm not using C threads. First, I only put sample programs in this book after testing them, and as of this writing, I couldn't get a compiler/standard library pair that implements *threads.h*. This is understandable, because of the second reason: C threads are modeled on C++ threads, which are modeled on a least-common-denominator between Windows and POSIX threads, and so C threads are largely a relabeling without the addition of many especially exciting features. C atoms do bring new things to the table, though.

Given a type my_type, be it a struct, a scalar, or whatever, declare it to be atomic via:

```
_Atomic my_type x;
//or
_Atomic(my_type) x;
```

The first form makes it clearer that _Atomic is a type qualifier, like const. The second is a transitional form that is easier for compiler authors to implement (for example, it could be a macro), and as of this writing it is still easy to run into compilers that support the second but not the first form. For the integer types defined in the standard, you can reduce these to atomic_int x, atomic_bool x, et cetera.

Simply declaring the variable as atomic gives you a few things for free: x++, --x, x *= y, and other simple binary operation/assignment steps work in a thread-safe manner [C11 §6.5.2.4(2) and §6.5.16.2(3)]. These operations, and all the thread-safe operations below, are all seq_cst, as discussed in the context of the OpenMP atoms in

"Sequential consistency" on page 309 (in fact, a note in OpenMP v4.0 §2.12.6 says that OpenMP atoms and C11 atoms should have similar behavior). However, other operations will have to happen via atom-specific functions:

- Initialize with `atomic_init(&your_var, starting_val)`, which sets the starting value "while also initializing any additional state that the implementation might need to carry for the atomic object" [C11 §7.17.2.2(2)]. This is not thread-safe, so do it before you disperse new threads, or wrap it in a mutex or critical region. There is also the `ATOMIC_VAR_INIT` macro that can be used on a declaration line to the same effect, so you can use either:

  ```
  _Atomic int i = ATOMIC_VAR_INIT(12);
  //or
  _Atomic int x;
  atomic_init(&x, 12);
  ```

- Use `atomic_store(&your_var, x)` to assign x to *your_var* thread-safely.

- Use x = `atomic_load(&your_var)` to thread-safely read the value of *your_var* and assign it to *x*.

- Use x = `atomic_exchange(&your_var, y)` to write *y* to *your_var* and copy the previous value to *x*.

- Use x = `atomic_fetch_add(&your_var, 7)` to add 7 to *your_var* and set *x* to the preaddition value; `atomic_fetch_sub` subtracts (but there is no `atomic_fetch_mul` or `atomic_fetch_div`).

There is a lot more to atomic variables, partly because the C committee is hoping that future implementations of threading libraries will use these atomic variables to produce mutexes and other such constructs within standard C. Because I assume that you are not designing your own mutexes, I won't cover those facilities (such as the `atomic_compare_exchange_weak` and `_strong` functions, which implement compare-and-swap operations).

Example 12-8 shows the example rewritten with atomic variables. I use pthreads for the threading, so it is still verbose, but the verbiage about mutexes is eliminated.

*Example 12-8. The factors example via C atomic variables (c_factors.c)*

```
#include <pthread.h>
#include <stdatomic.h>
#include <stdlib.h> //malloc
#include <string.h> //memset
#include <stdio.h>

int get_max_factors(_Atomic(int) *factor_ct, long int max){
    //single-threading to save verbiage.
```

```
    int global_max=0;
    for (long int i=0; i< max; i++){
        if (factor_ct[i] > global_max)
            global_max = factor_ct[i];
    }
    return global_max;
}

typedef struct {
    _Atomic(long int) *tally;
    _Atomic(int) *factor_ct;
    int max, thread_ct, this_thread;
} tally_s;

void *add_tally(void *vin){
    tally_s *in = vin;
    for (long int i=in->this_thread; i < in->max; i += in->thread_ct){
        int factors = in->factor_ct[i];
        in->tally[factors]++;                                    ❶
    }
    return NULL;
}

typedef struct {
    long int i, max;
    _Atomic(int) *factor_ct;
} one_factor_s;

void *mark_factors(void *vin){
    one_factor_s *in = vin;
    long int si = 2*in->i;
    for (long int scale=2; si < in->max; scale++, si=scale*in->i) {
        in->factor_ct[si]++;
    }
    return NULL;
}

int main(){
    long int max = 1e7;
    _Atomic(int) *factor_ct = malloc(sizeof(_Atomic(int))*max);   ❷

    int thread_ct = 4;
    pthread_t threads[thread_ct];

    atomic_init(factor_ct, 0);
    atomic_init(factor_ct+1, 1);
    for (long int i=2; i< max; i++)
        atomic_init(factor_ct+i, 2);

    one_factor_s x[thread_ct];
    for (long int i=2; i<= max/2; i+=thread_ct){
        for (int t=0; t < thread_ct && t+i <= max/2; t++){
```

```
            x[t] = (one_factor_s){.i=i+t, .max=max,
                            .factor_ct=factor_ct};
            pthread_create(&threads[t], NULL, mark_factors, x+t);
        }
        for (int t=0; t< thread_ct && t+i <=max/2; t++)
            pthread_join(threads[t], NULL);
    }

    int max_factors = get_max_factors(factor_ct, max);
    _Atomic(long int) tally[max_factors+1];
    memset(tally, 0, sizeof(long int)*(max_factors+1));

    tally_s thread_info[thread_ct];
    for (int i=0; i< thread_ct; i++){
        thread_info[i] = (tally_s){.this_thread=i, .thread_ct=thread_ct,
                            .tally=tally, .max=max,
                            .factor_ct=factor_ct};
        pthread_create(&threads[i], NULL, add_tally, thread_info+i);
    }
    for (int t=0; t< thread_ct; t++)
        pthread_join(threads[t], NULL);

    for (int i=0; i<max_factors+1; i++)
        printf("%i\t%li\n", i, tally[i]);
}
```

❶ Before, we had a mutex or a #pragma omp atomic preface protecting this line.
Because the elements of the tally array are declared atomic, we are guaranteed
that simple arithmetic like the increment here will be thread-safe by itself.

❷ The _Atomic keyword is a type qualifier, like const. But unlike with const, the
size of an atomic int need not be the same as the size of a plain int [C11
§6.2.5(27)].

## Atomic structs

Structs can be atomic. However, "accessing a member of an atomic structure or
union object results in undefined behavior" [C11 §6.5.2.3(5)] This dictates a certain
procedure for working with them:

1. Copy the shared atomic struct to a not-atomic private struct of the same base
   type: struct_t private_struct = atomic_load(&shared_struct).
2. Mess around with the private copy.
3. Copy the modified private copy back to the atomic struct:
   atomic_store(&shared_struct, private_struct).

If there are two threads that could modify the same struct, you still have no guarantee
that your structs won't change between the read in step 1 and the write in step 3. So

you will probably still need to ensure that only one thread is writing at a time, either by design or with mutexes. But you no longer need a mutex for reading a struct.

Here is a dedicated prime finder. The knock-out method used in the examples to this point (a variant of the Sieve of Eratosthenes) has proven to be much faster for finding primes in my tests, but this version nicely demonstrates an atomic struct.

I want to check that a candidate is not evenly divisible by any number less than itself. But if a candidate number is not divisible by 3 and not divisible by 5, then I know it is not divisible by 15, so I need only check whether a number is divisible by smaller primes. Further, there is no point checking past half of the candidate, because the largest possible factor is the one that satisfies 2 * factor = candidate. So, in pseudo-code:

```
for (candidate in 2 to a million){
    is_prime = true
    for (test in (the primes less than candidate/2))
        if ((candidates/test) has no remainder)
            is_prime = false
}
```

The only problem now is to keep that list of the primes less than candidate/2. We need a size-modifiable list, which means that a realloc will be necessary. I am going to use a raw array with no end-marker, so I also need to keep the length. This is a perfect candidate for an atomic struct, because the array itself and the length must be kept in sync.

In Example 12-9, prime_list is a struct to be shared across all threads. You can see that its address is passed as a function argument a few times, but all other uses are in atomic_init, atomic_store, or atomic_load. The add_a_prime function is the only place where it is modified, and it uses the above workflow of copying to a local struct and working with the local. It is wrapped by a mutex, because simultaneous reallocs would be a disaster.

The test_a_number function has one other notable detail: it waits until the prime_list has primes up to candidate/2 before proceeding, lest some factor be missed. It is a convenient feature of primes that this will work; you can check that this code won't get into a *deadlock*, where every thread is waiting for every other. After that, the algorithm is as per the pseudocode above. Note that there are no mutexes anywhere in this part of the code, because it only uses atomic_load to read the struct.

*Example 12-9. Use an atomic struct to find primes (c_primes.c)*

```
#include <stdio.h>
#include <stdatomic.h>
#include <stdlib.h>   //malloc
#include <stdbool.h>
```

```c
#include <pthread.h>

typedef struct {                                    ❶
    long int *plist;
    long int length;
    long int max;
} prime_s;

int add_a_prime(_Atomic (prime_s) *pin, long int new_prime){
    prime_s p = atomic_load(pin);                   ❷
    p.length++;
    p.plist = realloc(p.plist, sizeof(long int) * p.length);
    if (!p.plist) return 1;
    p.plist[p.length-1] = new_prime;
    if (new_prime > p.max) p.max = new_prime;
    atomic_store(pin, p);
    return 0;
}

typedef struct{
    long int i;
    _Atomic (prime_s) *prime_list;
    pthread_mutex_t *mutex;
} test_s;

void* test_a_number(void *vin){
    test_s *in = vin;
    long int i = in->i;
    prime_s pview;
    do {
        pview = atomic_load(in->prime_list);
    } while (pview.max*2 < i);

    bool is_prime = true;
    for (int j=0; j < pview.length; j++)
        if (!(i % pview.plist[j])){
            is_prime = false;
            break;
        }

    if (is_prime){
        pthread_mutex_lock(in->mutex);              ❸
        int retval = add_a_prime(in->prime_list, i);
        if (retval) {printf("Too many primes.\n"); exit(0);}
        pthread_mutex_unlock(in->mutex);
    }
    return NULL;
}

int main(){
    prime_s inits = {.plist=NULL, .length=0, .max=0};
    _Atomic (prime_s) prime_list = ATOMIC_VAR_INIT(inits);
```

```
pthread_mutex_t m;
pthread_mutex_init(&m, NULL);

int thread_ct = 3;
test_s ts[thread_ct];
pthread_t threads[thread_ct];

add_a_prime(&prime_list, 2);
long int max = 1e6;
for (long int i=3; i< max; i+=thread_ct){
    for (int t=0; t < thread_ct && t+i < max; t++){
        ts[t] = (test_s) {.i = i+t, .prime_list=&prime_list, .mutex=&m};
        pthread_create(threads+t, NULL, test_a_number,  ts+t);
    }
    for (int t=0; t< thread_ct && t+i <max; t++)
        pthread_join(threads[t], NULL);
}

prime_s pview = atomic_load(&prime_list);
for (int j=0; j < pview.length; j++)
    printf("%li\n", pview.plist[j]);
}
```

❶  The list itself and the length of the list must stay consistent across reallocations, so we put them both in a struct and declare only atomic instances of the struct.

❷  This function uses the procedure of loading the atomic struct to a not-atomic local copy, modifying the copy, and then using atomic_store to copy back to the atomic version. It is not thread-safe, so it must be called by one thread at a time.

❸  Because add_a_prime is not thread-safe, wrap its call in a mutex.

This chapter covered some of the many options for running code in parallel. With OpenMP, setting up the code to dispatch and gather threads is as easy as a single annotation. The hard part is tracking all the variables: every variable involved in the part to be threaded must be classified and handled.

The easiest class of variables is read-only variables, followed by those that are generated and destroyed entirely within one thread and thus do not interact with other threads. This advises that we should write functions that do not modify any inputs (i.e., all pointers are marked as const) and do not otherwise have any side effects. We can run such functions in parallel without worry. In a sense, these functions have no concept of time or environment: given a sum function that does what it says, sum(2, 2) always returns 4, no matter when or how often it is called and no matter what is going on elsewhere. In fact, there are some *purely functional* languages that strive to restrict the user to only this type of function.

*State variables* are variables that change over the course of a function's evaluation. Once state variables are included, a function loses its timeless purity. Running a function to return a bank account balance today may show a large balance, but calling the same function in the same manner tomorrow may return a small balance. The philosophy of the purely functional authors reduces to the simple rule that we should avoid state variables. But they are inevitable, because we are writing code to describe a world that is full of states. When reading purely functional authors, it is an amusing exercise to see how far they can get before they mention state. For example, Harold Abelson, et al. get about a third of the way through (to page 217) before confessing that the world is full of stateful situations like bank account balances, pseudorandom number generators, and electric circuits.

Most of this chapter has been about how to deal with state variables in a parallelized environment, after time forks. You have several tools at your disposal to make time coherent again, including atomic operations, mutexes, and critical regions, which force the state to be updated in a sequential manner. Because they can take work to implement, verify, and debug, the easiest way to deal with state variables is to avoid them, and write as much as possible without state before writing the functions that deal with time and environment.

# CHAPTER 13

# Libraries

*And if I really wanted to learn something I'd listen to more records.*
*And I do, we do, you do.*

—The Hives, "Untutored Youth"

This chapter will cover a few libraries that will make your life easier.

My impression is that C libraries have grown less pedantic over the years. Ten years ago, the typical library provided the minimal set of tools necessary for work, and expected you to build convenient and programmer-friendly versions from those basics. The typical library would require you to perform all memory allocation, because it's not the place of a library to grab memory without asking. Conversely, the libraries presented in this chapter all provide an "easy" interface, like curl_easy_... functions for cURL, or SQLite's single function to execute all the gory steps of a database transaction. If they need intermediate workspaces to get the work done, they just do it. They are fun to use.

I'll start with somewhat standard and very general libraries, and move on to a few of my favorite libraries for more specific purposes, including SQLite, the GNU Scientific Library, libxml2, and libcURL. I can't guess what you are using C for, but these are friendly, reliable systems for doing broadly applicable tasks.

## GLib

Given that the standard library left so much to be filled in, it is only natural that a library would eventually evolve to fill in the gaps. GLib implements enough basic computing needs that it will pass the first year of CompSci for you, is ported to just about everywhere (even POSIX-less editions of Windows), and is at this point stable enough to be relied on.

I'm not going to give you sample code for the GLib, because I've already given you several samples:

- The lighting-quick intro to linked lists in Example 2-2
- A test harness, in "Unit Testing" on page 52
- Unicode tools, in "Unicode" on page 199
- Hashes, in "Generic Structures" on page 241
- Reading a text file into memory and using Perl-compatible regular expressions, in "Count References" on page 277

And over the next few pages, I'll mention GLib's contributions for wrapping mmap for both POSIX and Windows, in "Using mmap for Gigantic Data Sets" on page 329.

There's more: if you are writing a mouse-and-window program, then you will need an event loop to catch and dispatch mouse and keyboard events; GLib provides this. There are file utilities that do the right thing on POSIX and non-POSIX (i.e., Windows) systems. There's a simple parser for configuration files, and a lightweight lexical scanner for more complex processes. Et cetera.

# POSIX

The POSIX standard adds several useful functions to the standard C library. Given how prevalent POSIX is, they are worth getting to know. Here, I'll give some usage notes on two parts that stand out as especially useful: regular expression parsing and mapping a file to memory.

## Parsing Regular Expressions

*Regular expressions* are a means of expressing a pattern in text, like (a number followed by one or more letters) or (number-comma-space-number, with nothing else on the line); in basic regex-ese, these could be expressed as [0-9]\+[[:alpha:]]\+ and ^[0-9]\+, [0-9]\+\$. The POSIX standard specifies a set of C functions to parse the regular expressions whose grammar it defines, and those functions have been wrapped by hundreds of tools. I think it is literally true that I use them every day, either at the command line via POSIX-standard tools like sed, awk, and grep, or to deal with little text-parsing details in code. Maybe I need to find somebody's name in a file, or somebody sent me date ranges in single strings like "04Apr2009-12Jun2010" and I want to break that down into six usable fields, or I have a fictionalized treatise on cetology and need to find the chapter markers.

If you want to break a string down into tokens demarcated with a single-character delimiter, strtok will work for you. See "A Pæan to strtok" on page 194.

However, I resolved to not include a regular expression tutorial in this book. My Internet search for *"regular expression tutorial"* gives me 12,900 hits. On a Linux box, man 7 regex should give you a rundown, and if you have Perl installed, you have man perlre summarizing Perl-compatible regular expressions (PCREs). (Friedl, 2002) gives an excellent book-length discussion of the topic. Here, I will cover how they work in POSIX's C library.

There are three major types of regular expression:

- Basic regular expressions (BREs) were the first draft, with only a few of the more common symbols having special meaning, like the * meaning zero or more of the previous atom, as in [0-9]* to represent an optional integer. Additional features required a backslash to indicate a special character: *one or more digits* is expressed via \+, so an integer preceded by a plus sign would be +[0-9]\+.

- Extended regular expressions (EREs) were the second draft, mostly taking special characters to be special without the backslashes, and plain text with a backslash. Now an integer preceded by a plus sign is \+[0-9]+.

- Perl has regular expressions at the core of the language, and its authors made several significant additions to the regex grammar, including a lookahead/lookbehind feature, nongreedy quantifiers that match the smallest possible match, and in-regex comments.

The first two types of regular expression are implemented via a small set of functions defined in the POSIX standard. They are probably part of your standard library. PCREs are available via libpcre, which you can download from online or via your package manager. See man pcreapi for details of its functions. GLib provides a convenient, higher-level wrapper for libpcre, as shown in Example 11-18.

Given that regexes are such a fundamental part of POSIX, the sample of regex use in this segment, Example 13-2, compiles on Linux and Mac without any compiler flags beyond the usual necessities:

```
CFLAGS="-g -Wall -O3 --std=gnu11" make regex
```

The POSIX and PCRE interfaces have a common four-step procedure:

1. Compile the regex via regcomp or pcre_compile
2. Run a string through the compiled regex via regexec or pcre_exec.

3. If you marked substrings in the regular expression to pull out (see below), copy them from the base string using the offsets returned by the regexec or pcre_exec function.
4. Free the internal memory used by the compiled regex.

The first two steps and the last step can be executed with a single line of code each, so if your question is only whether a string matches a given regular expression, then life is easy. I won't go into great detail about the flags and details of usage of regcomp, regexec, and regfree here, because the page of the POSIX standard about them is reprinted in the Linux and BSD manpages (try man regexec), and there are *many* websites devoted to reprinting those manpages.

If you need to pull substrings, things get more complicated. Parens in a regex indicate that the parser should retrieve the match for the subpattern within the parens (even if it only matches the null string). Thus, the ERE pattern "(.*)o" matches the string "hello", and as a side effect, stores the largest possible match for the .*, which is hell. The third argument to the regexec function is the number of parenthesized subexpressions in the pattern; I call it matchcount in the example below. The fourth argument to regexec is an array of matchcount+1 regmatch_t elements. The regmatch_t has two elements: rm_so, marking the start of the match, and rm_eo, marking the end. The zeroth element of the array will have the start and end of the match of the entire regex (imagine parens around the entire pattern), and subsequent elements have the start and end of each parenthesized subexpression, ordered by where their open-parens are in the pattern.

By way of foreshadowing, Example 13-1 displays a header describing the two utility functions provided by the sample code at the end of this segment. The regex_match function + macro + struct allows named and optional arguments, as per "Optional and Named Arguments" on page 228. It takes in a string and a regex and produces an array of substrings.

*Example 13-1. The header for a few regex utilities (regex_fns.h)*

```
typedef struct {
    const char *string;
    const char *regex;
    char ***substrings;
    _Bool use_case;
} regex_fn_s;

#define regex_match(...) regex_match_base((regex_fn_s){__VA_ARGS__})

int regex_match_base(regex_fn_s in);
char * search_and_replace(char const *base, char const*search, char const *replace);
```

We need a separate search-and-replace function because POSIX doesn't provide one. Unless the replacement is exactly the same length as what it is replacing, the operation requires reallocating the original string. But we already have the tools to break a string into substrings, so `search_and_replace` uses parenthesized substrings to break down a function into substrings, and then rebuilds a new string, inserting the replacement part at the appropriate point.

It returns `NULL` on no match, so you could do a global search and replace via:

```
char *s2;
while((s2 = search_and_replace(long_string, pattern))){
    char *tmp = long_string;
    long_string = s2;
    free(tmp);
}
```

There are inefficiencies here: the `regex_match` function recompiles the string every time, and the global search-and-replace would be more efficient if it used the fact that everything up to `result[1].rm_eo` does not need to be re-searched. In this case, we can use C as a prototyping language for C: write the easy version, and if the profiler shows that these inefficiencies are a problem, replace them with more efficient code.

Example 13-2 provides the code. The lines where key events in the above discussion occur are marked, with some additional notes at the end. The test function at the end shows some simple uses of the provided functions.

*Example 13-2. A few utilities for regular expression parsing (regex.c)*

```
#define _GNU_SOURCE //cause stdio.h to include asprintf
#include "stopif.h"
#include <regex.h>
#include "regex_fns.h"
#include <string.h> //strlen
#include <stdlib.h> //malloc, memcpy

static int count_parens(const char *string){                    ❶
    int out = 0;
    int last_was_backslash = 0;
    for(const char *step=string; *step !='\0'; step++){
        if (*step == '\\' && !last_was_backslash){
            last_was_backslash = 1;
            continue;
        }
        if (*step == ')' && !last_was_backslash)
            out++;
        last_was_backslash = 0;
    }
    return out;
}
```

```
int regex_match_base(regex_fn_s in){
    Stopif(!in.string, return -1, "NULL string input");
    Stopif(!in.regex, return -2, "NULL regex input");

    regex_t re;
    int matchcount = 0;
    if (in.substrings) matchcount = count_parens(in.regex);
    regmatch_t result[matchcount+1];
    int compiled_ok = !regcomp(&re, in.regex, REG_EXTENDED        ❷
                                        + (in.use_case ? 0 : REG_ICASE)
                                        + (in.substrings ? 0 : REG_NOSUB) );
    Stopif(!compiled_ok, return -3, "This regular expression didn't "
                                "compile: \"%s\"", in.regex);

    int found = !regexec(&re, in.string, matchcount+1, result, 0);   ❸
    if (!found) return 0;
    if (in.substrings){
        *in.substrings = malloc(sizeof(char*) * matchcount);
        char **substrings = *in.substrings;
        //match zero is the whole string; ignore it.
        for (int i=0; i< matchcount; i++){
            if (result[i+1].rm_eo > 0){//GNU peculiarity: match-to-empty marked with -1.
                int length_of_match = result[i+1].rm_eo - result[i+1].rm_so;
                substrings[i] = malloc(strlen(in.string)+1);
                memcpy(substrings[i], in.string + result[i+1].rm_so,
                        length_of_match);
                substrings[i][length_of_match] = '\0';
            } else { //empty match
                substrings[i] = malloc(1);
                substrings[i][0] = '\0';
            }
        }
        in.string += result[0].rm_eo; //end of whole match;
    }
    regfree(&re);                                                    ❹
    return matchcount;
}

char * search_and_replace(char const *base, char const*search, char const *replace){
    char *regex, *out;
    asprintf(&regex, "(.*)(%s)(.*)", search);                        ❺
    char **substrings;
    int match_ct = regex_match(base, regex, &substrings);
    if(match_ct < 3) return NULL;
    asprintf(&out, "%s%s%s", substrings[0], replace, substrings[2]);
    for (int i=0; i< match_ct; i++)
        free(substrings[i]);
    free(substrings);
    return out;
}

#ifdef test_regexes
```

```
int main(){
    char **substrings;

    int match_ct = regex_match("Hedonism by the alps, savory foods at every meal.",
            "([He]*)do.*a(.*)s, (.*)or.* ([em]*)al", &substrings);
    printf("%i matches:\n", match_ct);
    for (int i=0; i< match_ct; i++){
        printf("[%s] ", substrings[i]);
        free(substrings[i]);
    }
    free(substrings);
    printf("\n\n");

    match_ct = regex_match("", "([[:alpha:]]+) ([[:alpha:]]+)", &substrings);
    Stopif(match_ct != 0, return 1, "Error: matched a blank");

    printf("Without the L, Plants are: %s",
            search_and_replace("Plants\n", "l", ""));
}
#endif
```

❶ You need to send regexec an allocated array to hold substring matches and its length, meaning that you need to know how many substrings there will be. This function takes in an ERE and counts open-parens that aren't escaped by a backslash.

❷ Here we compile the regex to a regex_t. The function would be inefficient in repeated use, because the regex gets recompiled every time. It is left as an exercise to the reader to cache already-compiled regular expressions.

❸ Here is the regexec use. If you just want to know whether there is a match or not, you can send NULL and 0 as the list of matches and its length.

❹ Don't forget to free the internal memory used by the regex_t.

❺ The search-and-replace works by breaking down the input string into (everything before the match)(the match)(everything after the match). This is the regex representing that.

## Using mmap for Gigantic Data Sets

I've mentioned the three types of memory (static, manual, and automatic), and here's a fourth: disk-based. With this type, we take a file on the hard drive and map it to a location in memory using mmap.

This is often how shared libraries work: the system finds *libwhatever.so*, assigns a memory address to the segment of the file representing a needed function, and there you go: you've loaded a function into memory.

Or, we could share data across processes by having them both mmap the same file.

Or, we could use this to save data structures to memory. mmap a file to memory, use memmove to copy your in-memory data structure to the mapped memory, and it's stored for next time. Problems come up when your data structure has a pointer to another data structure; converting a series of pointed-to data structures to something savable is the *serialization* problem, which I won't cover here.

And, of course, there's dealing with data sets too large to fit in memory. The size of an mmaped array is constrained by the size of your disk, not memory.

Example 13-3 presents sample code. The load_mmap routine does most of the work. If used as a malloc, then it needs to create the file and stretch it to the right size; if you are opening an already-existing file, it just has to be opened and mmaped.

*Example 13-3. A file on disk can be mapped transparently to memory (mmap.c)*

```
#include <stdio.h>
#include <unistd.h> //lseek, write, close
#include <stdlib.h> //exit
#include <fcntl.h>  //open
#include <sys/mman.h>
#include "stopif.h"

#define Mapmalloc(number, type, filename, fd) \                      ❶
        load_mmap((filename), &(fd), (number)*sizeof(type), 'y')
#define Mapload(number, type, filename, fd)   \
        load_mmap((filename), &(fd), (number)*sizeof(type), 'n')
#define Mapfree(number, type, fd, pointer)    \
        releasemmap((pointer), (number)*sizeof(type), (fd))

void *load_mmap(char const *filename, int *fd, size_t size, char make_room){  ❷
    *fd=open(filename,
            make_room=='y' ?  O_RDWR | O_CREAT | O_TRUNC : O_RDWR,
            (mode_t)0600);
    Stopif(*fd==-1, return NULL, "Error opening file");

    if (make_room=='y'){ // Stretch the file size to the size of the (mmapped) array
        int result=lseek(*fd, size-1, SEEK_SET);
        Stopif(result==-1, close(*fd); return NULL,
            "Error stretching file with lseek");

        result=write(*fd, "", 1);
        Stopif(result!=1, close(*fd); return NULL,
            "Error writing last byte of the file");
    }
```

```
    void *map=mmap(0, size, PROT_READ | PROT_WRITE, MAP_SHARED, *fd, 0);
    Stopif(map==MAP_FAILED, return NULL, "Error mmapping the file");
    return map;
}

int releasemmap(void *map, size_t size, int fd){                            ❸
    Stopif(munmap(map, size) == -1, return -1, "Error un-mmapping the file");
    close(fd);
    return 0;
}

int main(int argc, char *argv[]) {
    int fd;
    long int N=1e5+6;
    int *map = Mapmalloc(N, int, "mmapped.bin", fd);

    for (long int i = 0; i <N; ++i) map[i] = i;                             ❹

    Mapfree(N, int, fd, map);

    //Now reopen and do some counting.
    int *readme = Mapload(N, int, "mmapped.bin", fd);

    long long int oddsum=0;
    for (long int i = 0; i <N; ++i) if (readme[i]%2) oddsum += i;
    printf("The sum of odd numbers up to %li: %lli\n", N, oddsum);

    Mapfree(N, int, fd, readme);
}
```

❶  I wrapped the functions that follow in macros so you don't have to type sizeof
   every time, and you won't have to remember how to call load_mmap when allocating, as opposed to when loading.

❷  The macros hide that this function gets called two different ways. If only reopen-
   ing existing data, the file gets opened, mmap gets called, the results are checked,
   and that's all. If called as an allocate function, we need to stretch the file to the
   right length.

❸  Releasing the mapping requires using munmap, which is akin to malloc's friend
   free, and closing the file handle. The data is left on the hard drive, so when you
   come back tomorrow you can reopen it and continue where you left off. If you
   want to remove the file entirely, use unlink("filename").

❹  The payoff: you can't tell map is on disk and not in the usual memory.

Final details: the mmap function is POSIX-standard, so it is available everywhere but Windows boxes and some embedded devices. In Windows, you can do the identical thing but with different function names and flags; see CreateFileMapping and Map ViewOfFile. GLib wraps both mmap and the Windows functions in an *if POSIX ... else if Windows ...* construct and names the whole thing g_mapped_file_new.

# The GNU Scientific Library

If you ever read a question that starts "I'm trying to implement something from Numerical Recipes in C ..." (Press, 1992), the correct response is almost certainly "Download the The GNU Scientific Library (GSL), because they already did it for you" (Gough, 2003).

Some means of numerically integrating a function are better than others, and as hinted in "Deprecate Float" on page 155, some seemingly sensible numeric algorithms will give you answers that are too imprecise to be considered anywhere near correct. So especially in this range of computing, it pays to use existing libraries where possible.

At the least, the GSL provides a reliable random-number generator (the C-standard RNG may be different on different machines, which makes it inappropriate for reproducible inquiry), and vector and matrix structures that are easy to subset and otherwise manipulate. The standard linear algebra routines, function minimizers, basic statistics (means and variances), and permutation structure may be of use to you even if you aren't spending all day crunching numbers.

And if you know what an Eigenvector, Bessel function, or Fast Fourier Transform are, here's where you can get routines for them.

You saw one example using the GSL's vectors and complex numbers in Example 11-14. I give another example of the GSL's use in Example 13-4, though you'll notice that the string gsl_ only appears once or twice in the example. The GSL is a fine example of an old-school library that provides the minimal tools needed and then expects you to build the rest from there. For example, the GSL manual will show you the page of boilerplate you will need to use the provided optimization routines to productive effect. It felt like something the library should do for us, so I wrote a set of wrapper functions for portions of the GSL, which became Apophenia, a library aimed at modeling with data. For example, the apop_data struct binds together raw GSL matrices and GSL vectors with row and column names and an array of text data, which brings the basic numeric-processing structs closer to what real-world data looks like. The library's calling conventions look like the modernized forms in Chapter 10.

An optimizer has a setup much like the routines in "The Void Pointer and the Structures It Points To" on page 236, where routines took in any function and used the provided function as a black box. The optimizer tries an input to the given function and uses the output value to improve its next guess for an input that will produce a larger output; with a sufficiently intelligent search algorithm, the sequence of guesses will converge to the function-maximizing input. Using an optimization routine is then a problem of writing a function to be optimized in the appropriate form and sending it and the right settings to the optimizer.

To give an example, say that we are given a list of data points $x_1$, $x_2$, $x_3$, ... in some space (in the example, $\mathbb{R}^2$), and we want the point $y$ that minimizes the total distance to each of those points. That is, given a distance function $D$, we want the value of $y$ that minimizes $D(y, x_1) + D(y, x_2) + D(y, x_3) + ...$ .

The optimizer will need a function that takes in those data points and a candidate point, and calcuates $D(y, x_i)$ for each $x_i$. This sounds a lot like a map-reduce operation like those discussed in "Map-reduce" on page 298, and apop_map_sum facilitates this (it even parallelizes the process using OpenMP). The apop_data struct offers a consistent means of providing the set of $x$s against which the optimization will occur. Also, physicists and the GSL usually prefer to minimize; economists and Apophenia maximize. This difference is easily surmounted by adding a minus sign: instead of minimizing the total distance, maximize the negation of the total distance.

An optimization procedure is relatively complex (over how many dimensions is the optimizer searching? Where can the optimizer find the reference data set? Which search procedure should the optimizer use?), so the apop_estimate function takes in an apop_model struct with hooks for the function and the relevant additional information. It may seem odd to call this distance-minimzer a model, but many of the things we recognize as statistical models (linear regressions, support vector machines, simulations, etc.) are estimated via exactly this form of taking in data, finding the optimum given some objective function, and reporting the optimum as the most likely parameter set for the model given the data.

Example 13-4 goes through the full procedure of writing down a distance function, wrapping it and all the relevant metatdata into an apop_model, and the one-line call to apop_estimate that does the actual optimization, and spits out a model struct with its parameters set to the point that minimizes total distance to the input data points.

*Example 13-4. Finding the point that minimizes the sum of distances to a set of input points (gsl_distance.c)*

```
#include <apop.h>

double one_dist(gsl_vector *v1, void *v2){
    return apop_vector_distance(v1, v2);
}

long double distance(apop_data *data, apop_model *model){
```

```
        gsl_vector *target = model->parameters->vector;
        return -apop_map_sum(data, .fn_vp=one_dist, .param=target);        ❶
}

apop_model *min_distance= &(apop_model){
    .name="Minimum distance to a set of input points.", .p=distance, .vsize=-1};  ❷

int main(){
    apop_data *locations = apop_data_falloc((5, 2),                        ❸
                          1.1, 2.2,
                          4.8, 7.4,
                          2.9, 8.6,
                          -1.3, 3.7,
                          2.9, 1.1);
    Apop_model_add_group(min_distance, apop_mle, .method="NM simplex",     ❹
                                        .tolerance=1e-5);
    apop_model *est=apop_estimate(locations, min_distance);                ❺
    apop_model_show(est);
}
```

❶ Apply the one_dist function to every row of the input data set. The negation is because we are using a maximization system to find a minimum distance.

❷ The .vsize element is a hint that apop_estimate does a lot under the hood. It will allocate the model's parameters element, and setting this element to -1 indicates that the parameter count should equal the number of columns in the data set.

❸ The first argument to apop_data_falloc is a list of dimensions; then fill the grid of the given dimensions with five 2D points. See "Multiple Lists" on page 212.

❹ This line appends a group of settings to the model regarding how optimization should be done: use the Nelder-Mead simplex algorithm, and keep trying until the algorithm's error measure is less than 1e-5. Add .verbose='y' for some information about each iteration of the optimization search.

❺ OK, everything is now in place, so run the optimization engine in one last line of code: search for the point that minimizes the min_distance function given the locations data.

# SQLite

Structured Query Language (SQL) is a roughly human-readable means of interacting with a database. Because the database is typically on disk, it can be as large as desired. An SQL database has two especial strengths for these large data sets: taking subsets of a data set and joining together data sets.

---

I won't go into great detail about SQL, because there are voluminous tutorials available. If I may cite myself, *Modeling with Data: Tools and Techniques for Statisical Computing* has a chapter on SQL and using it from C, or just type `sql tutorial` into your favorite search engine. The basics are pretty simple. Here, I will focus on getting you started with the SQLite library itself.

SQLite provides a database via a single C file plus a single header. That file includes the parser for SQL queries, the various internal structures and functions to talk to a file on disk, and a few dozen interface functions for our use in interacting with the database. Download the file, unzip it into your project directory, add *sqlite3.o* to the `objects` line of your makefile, and you've got a complete SQL database engine on hand.

There are only a few functions that you will need to interact with, to open the database, close the database, send a query, and get rows of data from the database.

Here are some serviceable database-opening and -closing functions:

```
sqlite3 *db=NULL;  //The global database handle.

int db_open(char *filename){
    if (filename)  sqlite3_open(filename, &db);
    else           sqlite3_open(":memory:", &db);
    if (!db) {printf("The database didn't open.\n"); return 1;}
    return 0;
}

//The database closing function is easy:
sqlite3_close(db);
```

I prefer to have a single global database handle. If I need to open multiple databases, then I use the SQL `attach` command to open another database. The SQL to use a table in such an attached database might look like:

```
attach "diskdata.db" as diskdb;
create index diskdb.index1 on diskdb.tab1(col1);
select * from diskdb.tab1 where col1=27;
```

If the first database handle is in memory, and all on-disk databases are attached, then you will need to be explicit about which new tables or indices are being written to disk; anything you don't specify will be taken to be a temporary table in faster, throwaway memory. If you forget and write a table to memory, you can always write it to disk later using a form like `create table diskdb.saved_table as select * from table_in_memory`.

# The Queries

Here is a macro for sending SQL that doesn't return a value to the database engine. For example, the `attach` and `create index` queries tell the database to take an action but return no data.

```
#define ERRCHECK {if (err!=NULL) {printf("%s\n",err);   return 0;}}

#define query(...){char *query; asprintf(&query, __VA_ARGS__);  \
                    char *err=NULL;                              \
                    sqlite3_exec(db, query, NULL,NULL, &err);    \
                    ERRCHECK                                     \
                    free(query); free(err);}
```

The `ERRCHECK` macro is straight out of the SQLite manual. I wrap the call to `sqlite3_exec` in a macro so that you can write things like:

```
for (int i=0; i< col_ct; i++)
    query("create index idx%i on data(col%i)", i, i);
```

Building queries via `printf`-style string construction is the norm for SQL-via-C, and you can expect that more of your queries will be built on the fly than will be verbatim from the source code. This format has one pitfall: SQL `like` clauses and `printf` bicker over the % sign, so `query("select * from data where col1 like 'p%%nts'")` will fail, as `printf` thinks the %% was meant for it. Instead, `query("%s", "select * from data where col1 like 'p%%nts'")` works. Nonetheless, building queries on the fly is so common that it's worth the inconvenience of an extra %s for fixed queries.

Getting data back from SQLite requires a callback function, as per "Functions with Generic Inputs" on page 237. Here is an example that prints to the screen.

```
int the_callback(void *ignore_this, int argc, char **argv, char **column){
    for (int i=0; i< argc; i++)
        printf("%s,\t", argv[i]);
    printf("\n");
    return 0;
}

#define query_to_screen(...){                                      \
    char *query; asprintf(&query, __VA_ARGS__);                    \
    char *err=NULL;                                                \
    sqlite3_exec(db, query, the_callback, NULL, &err);  \
    ERRCHECK                                                       \
    free(query); free(err);}
```

The inputs to the callback look a lot like the inputs to `main`: you get an `argv`, which is a list of text elements of length `argc`. The column names (also a text list of length `argc`) are in `column`. Printing to screen means that I treat all the strings as such, which is easy enough. So is a function that fills an array, for example:

```
typedef {
    double *data;
    int rows, cols;
} array_w_size;

int the_callback(void *array_in, int argc, char **argv, char **column){
    array_w_size *array = array_in;
    *array = realloc(&array->data,  sizeof(double)*(++(array->rows))*argc);
    array->cols=argc;
    for (int i=0; i< argc; i++)
        array->data[(array->rows-1)*argc + i] = atof(argv[i]);
}

#define query_to_array(a, ...){\
    char *query; asprintf(&query, __VA_ARGS__);      \
    char *err=NULL;                                  \
    sqlite3_exec(db, query, the_callback, a, &err); \
    ERRCHECK                                         \
    free(query); free(err);}
```

*//sample usage:*
```
array_w_size untrustworthy;
query_to_array(&untrustworthy, "select * from people where age > %i", 30);
```

The trouble comes in when we have mixed numeric and string data. Implementing something to handle a case of mixed numeric and text data took me about page or two in the previously mentioned Apophenia library.

Nonetheless, let us delight in how the given snippets of code, along with the two SQLite files themselves and a tweak to the objects line of the makefile, are enough to provide full SQL database functionality to your program.

# libxml and cURL

The cURL library is a C library that handles a long list of Internet protocols, including HTTP, HTTPS, POP3, Telnet, SCP, and of course Gopher. If you need to talk to a server, you can probably use libcURL to do it. As you will see in the following example, the library provides an easy interface that requires only that you specify a few variables, and then run the connection.

While we're on the Internet, where markup languages like XML and HTML are so common, it makes sense to introduce libxml2 at the same time.

Extensible Markup Language (XML) is used to describe the formatting for plain text files, but it is really the definition of a tree structure. The first half of Figure 13-1 is a typical barely readable slurry of XML data; the second half displays the tree structure formed by the text. Handling a well-tagged tree is a relatively easy affair: we could start at the root node (via xmlDocGetRootElement) and do a recursive traversal to check all elements, or we could get all elements with the tag par, or we could get all elements with the tag `title` that are children of the second chapter, and so on. In the following sample code, `//item/title` indicates all `title` elements whose parent is an `item`, anywhere in the tree.

libxml2 therefore speaks the language of tagged trees, with its focal objects being representations of the document, nodes, and lists of nodes.

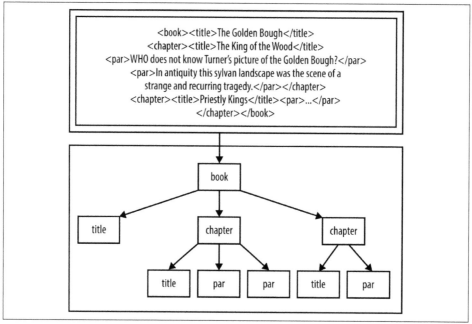

*Figure 13-1. An XML document and the tree structure encoded therein*

Example 13-5 presents a full example. I documented it via Doxygen (see "Interweaving Documentation" on page 62), which is why it looks so long, but the code explains itself. Again, if you're in the habit of skipping long blocks of code, do try it out and see if it's readable. If you have Doxygen on hand, you can try generating the documentation and viewing it in your browser.

*Example 13-5. Parse the NYT Headline feed to a simpler format (nyt_feed.c)*

```
/** \file

 A program to read in the NYT's headline feed and produce a simple
 HTML page from the headlines. */
#include <stdio.h>
#include <curl/curl.h>
#include <libxml2/libxml/xpath.h>
#include "stopif.h"
```

```
/** \mainpage
The front page of the Grey Lady's web site is as gaudy as can be, including
several headlines and sections trying to get your attention, various formatting
schemes, and even photographs--in <em>color</em>.

This program reads in the NYT Headlines RSS feed, and writes a simple list in
plain HTML. You can then click through to the headline that modestly piques
your attention.

For notes on compilation, see the \ref compilation page.
*/

/** \page compilation Compiling the program

Save the following code to \c makefile.

Notice that cURL has a program, \c curl-config, that behaves like \c pkg-config,
but is cURL-specific.

\code
CFLAGS =-g -Wall -O3 `curl-config --cflags` -I/usr/include/libxml2
LDLIBS=`curl-config --libs ` -lxml2 -lpthread
CC=c99

nyt_feed:
\endcode

Having saved your makefile, use <tt>make nyt_feed</tt> to compile.

Of course, you have to have the development packages for libcurl and libxml2
installed for this to work.
*/

//These have in-line Doxygen documentation. The < points to the prior text
//being documented.
char *rss_url = "http://rss.nytimes.com/services/xml/rss/nyt/HomePage.xml";
                                  /**< The URL for an NYT RSS feed. */
char *rssfile = "nytimes_feeds.rss";  /**< A local file to write the RSS to.*/
char *outfile = "now.html";       /**< The output file to open in your browser.*/

/** Print a list of headlines in HTML format to the outfile, which is overwritten.

\param urls The list of urls. This should have been tested for non-NULLness
\param titles The list of titles, also pre-tested to be non-NULL. If the length
      of the \c urls list or the \c titles list is \c NULL, this will crash.
*/
void print_to_html(xmlXPathObjectPtr urls, xmlXPathObjectPtr titles){
    FILE *f = fopen(outfile, "w");
    for (int i=0; i< titles->nodesetval->nodeNr; i++)
        fprintf(f, "<a href=\"%s\">%s</a><br>\n"
                , xmlNodeGetContent(urls->nodesetval->nodeTab[i])
                , xmlNodeGetContent(titles->nodesetval->nodeTab[i]));
```

```
        fclose(f);
}

/** Parse an RSS feed on the hard drive. This will parse the XML, then find
all nodes matching the XPath for the title elements and all nodes matching
the XPath for the links. Then, it will write those to the outfile.

  \param infile The RSS file in.
*/
int parse(char const *infile){
    const xmlChar *titlepath= (xmlChar*)"//item/title";
    const xmlChar *linkpath= (xmlChar*)"//item/link";

    xmlDocPtr doc = xmlParseFile(infile);
    Stopif(!doc, return -1, "Error: unable to parse file \"%s\"\n", infile);

    xmlXPathContextPtr context = xmlXPathNewContext(doc);
    Stopif(!context, return -2, "Error: unable to create new XPath context\n");

    xmlXPathObjectPtr titles = xmlXPathEvalExpression(titlepath, context);
    xmlXPathObjectPtr urls = xmlXPathEvalExpression(linkpath, context);
    Stopif(!titles || !urls, return -3, "either the Xpath '//item/title' "
                            "or '//item/link' failed.");

    print_to_html(urls, titles);

    xmlXPathFreeObject(titles);
    xmlXPathFreeObject(urls);
    xmlXPathFreeContext(context);
    xmlFreeDoc(doc);
    return 0;
}

/** Use cURL's easy interface to download the current RSS feed.

\param url The URL of the NY Times RSS feed. Any of the ones listed at
          \url http://www.nytimes.com/services/xml/rss/nyt/ should work.

\param outfile The headline file to write to your hard drive. First save
the RSS feed to this location, then overwrite it with the short list of links.

  \return 1==OK, 0==failure.
 */
int get_rss(char const *url, char const *outfile){
    FILE *feedfile = fopen(outfile, "w");
    if (!feedfile) return -1;

    CURL *curl = curl_easy_init();
    if(!curl) return -1;
    curl_easy_setopt(curl, CURLOPT_URL, url);
    curl_easy_setopt(curl, CURLOPT_WRITEDATA, feedfile);
    CURLcode res = curl_easy_perform(curl);
```

```
    if (res) return -1;

    curl_easy_cleanup(curl);
    fclose(feedfile);
    return 0;
}

int main(void) {
    Stopif(get_rss(rss_url, rssfile), return 1, "failed to download %s to %s.\n",
                                                    rss_url, rssfile);

    parse(rssfile);
    printf("Wrote headlines to %s. Have a look at it in your browser.\n", outfile);
}
```

# Epilogue

*Strike another match, go start anew—*
—Bob Dylan, closing out his 1965 Newport Folk Festival
set, "It's All Over Now Baby Blue"

*Wait!,* you exclaim. *You said that I can use libraries to make my work easier, but I'm an expert in my field, I've searched everywhere, and I still can't find a library to suit my needs!*

If that's you, then it's time for me to reveal my secret agenda in writing this book: as a C user, I want more people writing good libraries that I can use. If you've read this far, you know how to write modern code based on other libraries, how to write a suite of functions around a few simple objects, how to make the interface user-friendly, how to document it so others can use it, what tools are available so you can test it, how to use a Git repository so that others can contribute, and how to package it for use by the general public using Autotools. C is the foundation of modern computing, so when you solve your problem in C, then the solution is available for all sorts of platforms everywhere.

Punk rock is a do-it-yourself art form. It is the collective realization that music is made by people like us, and that you don't need permission from a corporate review committee to write something new and distribute it to the world. In fact, we already have all the tools we need to make it happen.

# C 101

This appendix covers the basics of the language. It's not for everyone.

- If you already have experience writing code in a common scripting language, like Python, Ruby, or Visual Basic, this appendix will be at your level. I don't have to explain to you what variables, functions, loops, or other basic building blocks are, so the main headings of this appendix are about the big differences between C and typical scripting languages.
- If you learned C a long time ago and are feeling rusty, skimming this tutorial should remind you of the quirks that make C different and unique.
- If you already work with C on a regular basis, don't bother reading this appendix. You may also want to skip or skim the early parts of Part II as well, which are aimed at common errors and misunderstandings about the core of the language.

Don't expect to be an expert in C by the end of this tutorial—there's no substitute for real experience with the language. But you will be in a position to get started with Part II of this book and find out about the nuances and useful customs of the language.

## The Structure

I'll kick off the tutorial the way Kernighan & Ritchie did in their 1978 blockbuster book: with a program to say hello.

```
//tutorial/hello.c
#include <stdio.h>

int main(){
    printf("Hello, world.\n");
}
```

The double slashes on the first line indicate a comment that the compiler will ignore. All of the code samples in this appendix marked with a file name like this are available online at: *https://github.com/b-k/21st-Century-Examples*.

Even this much reveals a few key points about C. Structurally, almost everything in a C program is:

- A preprocesser directive, like `#include <stdio.h>`
- A declaration of a variable or a type (though this program has none)
- A function block, like `main`, containing expressions to evaluate (like `printf`)

But before going into detail about the definition and use of preprocessor directives, declarations, blocks, and expressions, we have to work out how to run this program so the computer can greet us.

## C requires a compilation step, which consists of running a single command

A scripting language comes with a program that parses the text of your scripts; C has a compiler that takes in your program text and produces a program directly executed by the operating system. Using the compiler is something of a pain, so there are programs to run the compiler for you. Your integrated development environments (IDEs) typically have a compile-and-run button, and on the command line, a POSIX-standard program named `make` will run the compiler for you.

If you don't have a compiler and `make`, then go to "Use a Package Manager" on page 4 and read about how to obtain them. The short version: ask your package manager to install `gcc` or `clang`, and `make`.

With a compiler and `make` installed, if you saved the above program as *hello.c* then you can use `make` to run the compiler via this command:

```
make hello
```

This produces the `hello` program, which you can run from the command line or click on in your file browser to verify that it prints what we expect it to.

The sample code repository includes a makefile, which instructs `make` to send some compilation flags to the compiler. The workings of `make` and the contents of the makefile are discussed at length in "Using Makefiles" on page 17. For now, I'll mention one flag: `-Wall`. This flag asks the compiler to list all warnings about parts of your program that are technically correct, but may not be what you meant. This is known as *static analysis*, and modern C compilers are very good at it. You can thus think of the compilation step not as a useless formality, but as a chance to submit your code to a team of the world's foremost experts in C before running the program.

If you have a Mac that doesn't like the -Wall flag, see the warning in "A Few of My Favorite Flags" on page 12 on how to re-alias gcc.

A lot of bloggers see the compilation step as a big deal. On the command line, if typing make *yourprogram* before running via *./yourprogram* is just too much effort, you can write an alias or shell script to do it. In the POSIX shell, you could define:

```
function crun { make $1 && ./$1; }
```

and then use

```
crun hello
```

to compile and, if the compilation worked, run.

## There's a standard library, and it's part of your operating system

Programs in the present day are typically not completely standalone, but link to libraries of common functions possibly used by more than one program. The library path is a list of directories on your hard drive that the compiler searches for such libraries; see "Paths" on page 13 for details. Key among these libraries is the C standard library, defined in the ISO C standard and about as close to universally available as computer code can be. This is where the printf function is defined.

## There's a preprocessor

The libraries are in binary format, executable by the computer but illegible to humans. Unless you have binary-reading superpowers, you can't look at the compiled library to verify that you are using printf correctly. So there are companion files to a library, *header files*, that list plain-text declarations for the utilities in the library, giving the inputs that each function expects and the outputs they produce. If you include the appropriate header in your program, then the compiler can do consistency checks to verify that your use of a function, variable, or type is consistent with what the binary code in the library expects.

The primary activity of the preprocessor is to substitute the text of preprocessor directives (which all begin with a #) with other text. There are many other uses (see "The Preprocessor" on page 168), but the only use I'll cover in this appendix is including other files. When the preprocessor sees

```
#include <stdio.h>
```

it will substitute the full text of *stdio.h* at this point. The angle brackets in <stdio.h> indicate that the library is on the include path, which is distinct from the library path (and is also discussed in detail in "Paths" on page 13). If a file is in the working directory for the project, use #include "myfile.h".

The *.h* ending indicates that the file is a header file. Header files are plain code, and the compiler doesn't know a header from other code files, but the custom is to put only declarations in header files.

After the preprocessor has done its work, almost everything in the file will either be a declaration of a variable or type, or the definition of a function.

## There are two types of comment

```
/* Multiline comments run between a slash-star
    and a star-slash.  */

//Single-line comments run from a double-slash to the end of the line.
```

## There is no print keyword

The `printf` function from the standard library prints text to the screen. It has its own sublanguage for precisely expressing how variables are printed. I won't give you a detailed explanation of its working because there are comprehensive descriptions of the `printf` sublanguage everywhere (try `man 3 printf` from your command line), and because you'll see examples throughout this tutorial and throughout the book. The sublanguage consists of plain text interspersed with *insert variable here* markers and codes for invisible characters like tabs and newlines. Here are the six elements that will get you by as you read examples of `printf`-family functions in the rest of the tutorial:

\n   A newline

\t   A tab

%i   Insert an integer value here

%g   Insert a real number in general format here

%s   Insert a string of text here

%%   Insert a plain percent sign here

# Variable Declarations

Declarations are a big difference between C and a lot of scripting languages that infer the type of a variable—and even its existence—via the first use. Above, I suggested that the compilation step is really a chance to do prerun checks to verify that your code has some chance of doing what you promised it does; declaring the type of each variable gives the compiler much more of an opportunity to check that your writing is coherent. There is also a declaration syntax for functions and new types.

## Variables have to be declared

The hello program didn't have any variables, but here is a program that declares a few variables and demonstrates the use of printf. Notice how the first argument to printf (the *format specifier*) has three *insert variable here* markers, so it is followed by the three variables to insert.

```
//tutorial/ten_pi.c
#include <stdio.h>

int main(){
    double pi= 3.14159265; //POSIX defines the constant M_PI in math.h, by the way.
    int count= 10;
    printf("%g times %i = %g.\n", pi, count, pi*count);
}
```

This program outputs:

```
3.14159 times 10 = 31.4159.
```

There are three basic types that I use throughout the book: int, double, and char, which are short for integer, double-precision floating-point real number, and character.

There are bloggers who characterize the work of declaring a variable as a fate worse than death, but as in the example above, the only work required is often just putting a type name before the first use of the variable. And when reading unfamiliar code, having every variable's type and having a marker for its first use are nice guideposts.

If you have multiple variables of the same type, you can even declare them all on one line, like replacing the above declaration with:

```
int count=10, count2, count3=30; //count2 is uninitialized.
```

## Even functions have to be declared or defined

The definition of a function describes the full working of the function, like this trivial function:

```
int add_two_ints(int a, int b){
    return a+b;
}
```

This function takes in two integers, which the function will refer to as a and b, and return a single integer, which is the sum of a and b.

We can also split off the declaration as its own statement, which gives the name, the input types (in parens) and the output type (in front):

```
int add_two_ints(int a, int b);
```

This doesn't tell us what `add_two_ints` actually does, but it is sufficient for the compiler to consistency-check every use of the function, verifying that every use sends in two integers, and uses the result as an integer. As with all declarations, this might be in a code file as-is, or it might be in a header file inserted via a line like `#include "mydeclarations.h"`.

A *block* is a unit of code to be treated as a unit, surrounded by curly braces. Thus, a function definition is a declaration immediately followed by a single block of code to be executed when the function runs.

If the full definition of the function is in your code before the use of the function, then the compiler has what it needs to do consistency checks, and you don't need to bother with a separate declaration. Because of this, a lot of C code is written and read in a bottom-up style, with `main` as the last thing in the file, and above that the definition of functions called by `main`, and above those the definitions of functions called by those functions, and so on up to the headers at the top of the file declaring all the library functions used.

By the way, your functions can have `void` type, meaning that they return nothing. This is useful for functions that don't output or change variables but have other effects. For example, here is a program largely consisting of a function to write error messages to a file (which will be created on your hard drive) in a fixed format, using the `FILE` type and related functions all declared in *stdio.h*. You'll see why `char*` is the type that specifies a string of text below:

```
//tutorial/error_print.c
#include <stdio.h>

void error_print(FILE *ef, int error_code, char *msg){
    fprintf(ef, "Error #%i occurred: %s.\n", error_code, msg);
}

int main(){
    FILE *error_file = fopen("example_error_file", "w"); //open for writing
    error_print(error_file, 37, "Out of karma");
}
```

## Basic types can be aggregated into arrays and structs

How can one get any work done with only three basic types? By compounding them into arrays of homogeneous types, and structures of heterogeneous types.

An array is a list of identically typed elements. Here is a program that declares a list of 10 integers and a 20-character string, and uses part of both:

```
//tutorial/item_seven.c
#include <stdio.h>
```

```
    int intlist[10];

    int main(){
        int len=20;
        char string[len];

        intlist[7] = 7;
        snprintf(string, len, "Item seven is %i.", intlist[7]);
        printf("string says: <<%s>>\n", string);
    }
```

The `snprintf` function prints to a string whose maximum length you provide, using the same syntax that plain `printf` used to write to the screen. More on handling strings of characters, and why `intlist` could be declared outside of a function but `string` had to be declared inside one, below.

The index is an *offset* from the first element. The first element is zero steps from the head of the array, so it is `intlist[0]`; the last element of the 10-item array is `intlist[9]`. This is another cause of panic and flame wars, but it has its own sense.

You can find a zeroth symphony from various composers (Bruckner, Schnittke). But in most situations, we use counting words like *first, second, seventh* that clash with offset numbering: the seventh item in the array is `intlist[6]`. I try to stick with language like *element 6 of the array*.

For reasons that will become clear, the type of an array can also be written with a star, like:

```
    int *intlist;
```

You saw an example above, where a sequence of characters was declared via `char *msg`.

## New structure types can be defined

Heterogeneous types can be combined into a structured list (herein a *struct*) that can then be treated as a unit. Here is an example which declares and makes use of a `ratio_s` type, describing a fraction with a numerator, denominator, and decimal value. The type definition is basically a list of declarations inside curly braces.

When using the defined struct, you'll see that there are a lot of dots: given a `ratio_s` struct r, `r.numerator` is the numerator element of that struct. The expression (double)den is a type cast, converting the integer den to a double (for reasons explained below). The means of setting up a new struct outside a declaration line looks like a type cast, with a type name in parens, followed by the dotted elements in curly braces. There are other more terse (i.e., less legible) ways to initialize a struct.

```
    //tutorial/ratio_s.c
    #include <stdio.h>
```

```
typedef struct {
    int numerator, denominator;
    double value;
} ratio_s;

ratio_s new_ratio(int num, int den){
    return (ratio_s){.numerator=num, .denominator=den, .value=num/(double)den};
}

void print_ratio(ratio_s r){
    printf("%i/%i = %g\n", r.numerator, r.denominator, r.value);
}

ratio_s ratio_add(ratio_s left, ratio_s right){
    return (ratio_s){
        .numerator=left.numerator*right.denominator
                    + right.numerator*left.denominator,
        .denominator=left.denominator * right.denominator,
        .value=left.value + right.value
        };
}

int main(){
    ratio_s twothirds= new_ratio(2, 3);
    ratio_s aquarter= new_ratio(1, 4);
    print_ratio(twothirds);
    print_ratio(aquarter);
    print_ratio(ratio_add(twothirds, aquarter));
}
```

## You can find out how much space a type takes

The sizeof operator can take a type name, and will tell you how much memory is required to write down an instance of that type. This is sometimes handy.

This short program compares the size of two ints and a double to the size of the ratio_s defined above. The %zu format specifier for printf exists solely for the type of output produced by sizeof.

```
//tutorial/sizeof.c
#include <stdio.h>

typedef struct {
    int numerator, denominator;
    double value;
} ratio_s;

int main(){
    printf("size of two ints: %zu\n", 2*sizeof(int));
    printf("size of two ints: %zu\n", sizeof(int[2]));
    printf("size of a double: %zu\n", sizeof(double));
```

```
    printf("size of a ratio_s struct: %zu\n", sizeof(ratio_s));
}
```

## There is no special string type

Both the integer 5100 and the integer 51 take up sizeof(int) space. But "Hi" and
"Hello" are strings of different numbers of characters. Scripting languages typically
have a dedicated string type, which manages lists of an indeterminate number of
characters for you. A string in C is an array of chars, pure and simple.

The end of a string is marked with a NUL character, '\0', though it is never printed
and is usually taken care of for you. (Note that single characters are given single-ticks,
like 'x', while strings are given double-ticks, like "xx" or the one-character string
"x".) The function strlen(*mystring*) will count the number of characters up to (but
not including) that NUL character. How much space was allocated for the string is
another matter entirely: you could easily declare char pants[1000] = "trousers",
though you are wasting 991 bytes after the NUL character.

Some things are surprisingly easy thanks to the array nature of strings. Given

```
char str[]="Hello";
```

you can turn a Hello into Hell by inserting a NUL character:

```
str[4]='\0';
```

But most of what you want to do with a string involves calling a library function to do
the byte-twiddling for you. Here are a few favorites:

```
#include <string.h>
char *str1 = "hello", str2[100];
strlen(str1);              //get the length up to but excluding the '\0'
strncpy(str2, str1, 100); //copy at most 100 bytes from str1 to str2
strncat(str2, str1, 100); //append at most 100 bytes from str1 onto str2
strcmp(str1, str2);        //are str1 and str2 different? zero=no, nonzero=yes
snprintf(str2,  100, "str1 says: %s", str1); //write to a string, as above.
```

In Chapter 9, I discuss a few other functions for making life easier with strings,
because with enough intelligent functions, string handling can be pleasant again.

# Expressions

A program that does nothing but declare types, functions, and variables would just be
a list of nouns, so it is time to move on to some verbs making use of our nouns. C's
mechanism for executing any sort of action is evaluation of an expression, and
expressions are always grouped into functions.

# The scoping rules for C are very simple

The *scope* of a variable is the range of the program over which it can be used.

If a variable is declared outside of a function, then it can be used by any expression from the declaration until the end of the file. Any function in that range can make use of that variable. Such variables are initialized at the start of the program and persist until the program terminates. They are referred to as static variables, perhaps because they sit in one place for the entire program.

If a variable is declared inside a block (including the block defining a function), then the variable is created at the declaration line and destroyed at the closing curly brace of the block.

See "Persistent State Variables" on page 130 for further notes on static variables, including how we can have long-lived variables inside a function.

# The main function is special

When a program runs, the first thing that happens is the setup of the file-global variables as above. No math happens yet, so they can be assigned either a given constant value (if declared like `int gv=24;`), or the default value of zero (if declared like `int gv;`).

Scripting languages usually allow some instructions to be inside functions, and some loose in the main body of the script. Any C expression that needs to be evaluated is in the body of a function, and the evaluations start with the `main` function. In the `snprintf` example above, the array with length `len` had to be inside of `main`, because getting the value of `len` is already too much math for the startup phase of the program.

Because the `main` function is effectively called by the operating system, its declaration must have one of two forms that the OS knows how to use: either

```
int main(void)
//which can be written as
int main()
```

or

```
int main(int, char**)
//where the two inputs are customarily named:
int main(int argc, char** argv)
```

You have already seen examples of the first version, where nothing comes in but a single integer comes out. That integer is generally treated as an error code, interpreted to indicate trouble if it is nonzero, and OK execution (reaching the end of `main` and exiting normally) if it is zero. This is such an ingrained custom that the C standard specifies that there is an implied `return 0;` at the end of `main` (see "Don't Bother Explicitly Returning from main" on page 143 for discussion). For a simple example of the second form, see Example 8-6.

## Most of what a C program actually does is evaluate expressions

So the global variables have been set up, the operating system has prepared the inputs to `main`, and the program is starting to actually execute code in the `main` function block.

From here on out, everything will be the declaration of a local variable, flow control (branching on an `if-else`, looping through a `while` loop), or the evaluation of an expression.

To borrow from an earlier example, consider what the system has to do to evaluate this sequence:

```
int a1, two_times;
a1 = (2+3)*7;
two_times = add_two_ints(a1, a1);
```

After the declarations, the line `a1=(2+3)*7` requires first evaluating the expression `(2+3)`, which can be replaced with 5, then evaluating the expression `5*7`, which can be replaced with 35. This is exactly how we humans do it when facing an expression like this, but C carries this evaluate-and-substitute principle further.

In the evaluation of the expression `a1=35`, two things occur. The first is the replacement of the expression with its value: 35. The second is a side effect that a state has changed: the value of the variable `a1` is changed to 35. There are languages that strive to be more pure in evaluation, but C allows evaluations to have side effects that change state. You saw another example several times above: in the evaluation of `printf("hello\n")`, the expression is replaced by a zero on success, but the evaluation is useful for the side effect of changing the state of the screen.

After all those substitutions, we'd be left with only `35;` on the line. With nothing left to evaluate, the system moves on to the next line.

## Functions are evaluated using copies of the inputs

That line of the above snippet, `two_times = add_two_ints(a1, a1)` first requires evaluating `a1` twice, then evaluating `add_two_ints` with the evaluated inputs, 35 and 35. So a *copy* of the value of `a1` is handed to the function, not `a1` itself. That means that the function has no way to modify the value of `a1` itself. If you have function code that looks like it is modyfing an input, it is really modifying a copy of the input's value. A workaround for when we want to modify the variables sent to a function call will be presented below.

## Expressions are delimited by semicolons

Yes, C uses semicolons to delimit expressions. This is a contentious stylistic choice, but it does allow you to put newlines, extra spaces, and tabs anywhere they would improve readability.

## There are many shortcuts for incrementing or scaling a variable

C has a few pleasant shorthand expressions for arithmetic to modify a variable. We can shorten x=x+3 to x+=3 and x=x/3 to x/=3, respectively. Incrementing a variable by one is so common that there are two ways of doing it. Both x++ and ++x have the side effect of incrementing x, but the evaluation of x++ replaces the expression with the preincrement value of x, while the evaluation of ++x replaces the expression with the postincrement value of x+1.

```
x++; //increment x. Evaluates to x.
++x; //increment x. Evaluates to x+1.

x--; //decrement x. Evaluates to x.
--x; //decrement x. Evaluates to x-1.

x+=3; //add three to x.
x-=7; //subtract seven from x.
x*=2; //multiply x by two.
x/=2; //divide x by two.
x%=2; //replace x with x modulo 2
```

## C has an expansive definition of truth

We will sometimes need to know whether an expression is true or false, such as deciding which branch to choose in an if-else construction. There are no true and false keywords in C, though they are commonly defined as in "True and False" on page 185. Instead, if the expression is zero (or the NUL character '\0', or a NULL pointer), then the expression is taken to be false; if it is anything else at all, it is taken to be true.

Conversely, all of these expressions evaluate to either zero or one:

```
!x              //not x
x==y            //x equals y
x != y          //x is not equal to y
x < y           //x is less than y
x <= y          //x is less than or equal to y
x || y          //x or y
x && y          //x and y
x > y || y >= z //x is greater than y or y is greater than or equal to z
```

For example, if x is any nonzero value, then !x evaluates to zero, and !!x evaluates to one.

The && and || are lazy, and will evaluate only as much of the expression as is necessary to establish the truth or falsehood of the whole. For example, consider the expression (a < 0 || sqrt(a) < 10). The square root of an int or double -1 is an error (but see "_Generic" on page 274 for discussion of C support of imaginary numbers). But if a==-1, then we know that (a < 0 || sqrt(a) < 10) evaluates to true without even looking at the second half of the expression. So sqrt(a) < 10 is left ignored and unevaluated, and disaster is averted.

## Dividing two integers always produces an integer

Many authors prefer to avoid floating-point real numbers to the greatest extent possible, because integers are processed faster and without roundoff errors. C facilitates this by having three distinct operators: real division, integer division, and modulo. The first two happen to look identical.

```
//tutorial/divisions.c
#include <stdio.h>

int main(){
    printf("13./5=%g\n", 13./5);
    printf("13/5=%i\n", 13/5);
    printf("13%%5=%i\n", 13%5);
}
```

Here's the output:

```
13./5=2.6
13/5=2
13%5=3
```

The expression 13. is a floating-point real number, and if there is a real number in the numerator or denominator, then floating-point division happens, producing a floating-point result. If both numerator and denominator are integers, then the result is the integer you would get from doing the division with real numbers and then rounding toward zero to an integer. The modulo operator, %, gives the remainder.

The difference between floating-point and integer division is why the new_ratio example above typecast the denominator via num/(double)den. For further discussion, see "Cast Less" on page 147.

## C has a trinary conditional operator

The expression

```
x ? a : b
```

evaluates to a if x is true, and to b if x is false.

I used to think this was illegible, and few scripting languages have such an operator, but it has grown on me for its great utility. Being just another expression, we can put it anywhere; for example:

```
//tutorial/sqrt.c
#include <math.h>    //The square root function is declared here.
#include <stdio.h>

int main(){
    double x = 49;
    printf("The truncated square root of x is %g.\n",
                            x > 0 ? sqrt(x) : 0);
}
```

The trinary conditional operator has the same short-circuit behavior as && and || above: if x<=0, then sqrt(x) is never evaluated.

## Branching and looping expressions are not very different from any other language

Probably the only unique point about if-else statements in C is that there is no then keyword. Parens mark the condition to be evaluated, and then the following expression or block is run through if the condition is true. A few sample uses:

```
//tutorial/if_else.c
#include <stdio.h>

int main(){
    if (6 == 9)
        printf("Six is nine.\n");

    int x=3;
    if (x==1)
        printf("I found x; it is one.\n");
    else if (x==2)
        printf("x is definitely two.\n");
    else
        printf("x is neither one nor two.\n");
}
```

The while loop repeats a block until the given condition is false. For example, this program regreets the user 10 times:

```
//tutorial/while.c
#include <stdio.h>

int main(){
    int i=0;
    while (i < 10){
        printf("Hello #%i\n", i);
        i++;
```

```
    }
}
```

If the controlling condition in parens after the `while` keyword is false on the first try, then the body of the `while` loop will be skipped entirely. But the do-while loop is guaranteed to run at least once:

```c
//tutorial/do_while.c
#include <stdio.h>

void loops(int max){
    int i=0;
    do {
        printf("Hello #%i\n", i);
        i++;
    } while (i < max);      //Note the semicolon.
}

int main(){
    loops(3); //prints three greetings
    loops(0); //prints one greeting
}
```

## The for loop is just a compact version of the while loop

Traffic control for the `while` loop had three parts:

- The initializer (`int i=0`);
- The test condition (`i < 10`);
- The stepper (`i++`).

The `for` loop encapsulates all of these into one place. This `for` loop is otherwise equivalent to the `while` loop above:

```c
//tutorial/for_loop.c
#include <stdio.h>

int main(){
    for (int i=0; i < 10; i++){
        printf("Hello #%i\n", i);
    }
}
```

Because this block is one line, even the curly braces are optional, and we could get away with:

```c
//tutorial/for_loop2.c
#include <stdio.h>

int main(){
```

```
    for (int i=0; i < 10; i++) printf("Hello #%i\n", i);
}
```

People often worry about fencepost errors, wherein they want 10 steps and get 9 or 11. The form above (start at i=0, test i< 10) correctly counts 10 steps, and is the standard boilerplate for stepping through an array. For example:

```
int len=10;
double array[len];
for (int i=0; i< len; i++) array[i] = 1./(i+1);
```

There is no additional special syntax for counting through a sequence or applying an operation to every element of an array (though such syntax would be easy to write via macros or functions), which means that you'll be seeing this sort of (int i=0; i< len; i++) boilerplate a lot.

On the other hand, this form is easy to modify for different situations. If you need to step by two, you want for (int i=0; i< len; i+=2). If you need to step until you hit a zero array element, you want for (int i=0; array[i]!=0; i++). You can leave any of the elements blank, so if you are not initializing a new variable, you might wind up with something like for ( ; array[i]!=0; i++).

# Pointers

Pointers to variables are sometimes called aliases, references, or labels (though C has unrelated things called labels, which are rarely used; I discuss them in "Labels, gotos, switches, and breaks" on page 150).

A pointer or alias to a double does not itself hold a double, but it points to some location that does. Now you have two names for the same thing. If the thing is changed, then both versions see the change. This is in contrast to a full copy of a thing, where a change to the original after the copy was made does not affect the copy.

## You can directly request a block of memory

The malloc function allocates memory for use by the program. For example, we might allocate enough space for 3,000 integers via:

```
malloc(3000*sizeof(int));
```

This is the first mention of memory allocation in this tutorial because the declarations above, like int list[100], auto-allocate memory. When the scope in which the declaration was made comes to a close, auto-allocated memory is auto-deallocated. Conversely, memory you manually allocated via malloc exists until you manually free it (or the end of the program). This sort of longevity is sometimes desirable. Also, an array cannot be resized after it is initialized, whereas manually allocated memory can be. Other differences between manually and automatically allocated memory are discussed in "Automatic, Static, and Manual Memory" on page 125.

Now that we've allocated this space, how do we refer to it? This is where pointers come in, because we can assign an alias to the `malloc`ed space:

```
int *intspace = malloc(3000*sizeof(int));
```

The star on the declaration (`int *`) indicates that we are declaring a pointer to a location.

Memory is a finite resource, so indiscriminate use will eventually cause the sort of out-of-memory errors that have bothered us all at one time or another. Free memory back to the system via the `free` function; e.g., `free(intspace)`. Or just wait until the end of the program, when the operating system deallocates all memory used by your program for you.

## Arrays are just blocks of memory; any block of memory can be used like an array

In Chapter 6, I discuss exactly how arrays and pointers are and are not identical, but they certainly have a lot in common.

In memory, an array is a contiguous span set aside for one data type. If you request element 6 of an array declared as `int list[100]`, the system would start at wherever the list is located, then step `6*sizeof(int)` bytes down.

So the square-bracket notation like `list[6]` is really just a notation about offsetting from the position pointed to by the named variable, and this happens to be a common operation when working with arrays. But if we have a pointer to any contiguous span of memory, the same operations of finding the location and stepping forward could be done with the pointer.

Here is an example that fills a manually allocated array and then prints it to a file. This example could more easily be done using an automatically allocated array, but for demonstration purposes, here it is:

```
//tutorial/manual_memory.c
#include <stdlib.h> //malloc and free
#include <stdio.h>

int main(){
    int *intspace = malloc(3000*sizeof(int));
    for (int i=0; i < 3000; i++)
        intspace[i] = i;

    FILE *cf = fopen("counter_file", "w");
    for (int i=0; i < 3000; i++)
        fprintf(cf, "%i\n", intspace[i]);
```

```
    free(intspace);
    fclose(cf);
}
```

Memory reserved via `malloc` can be reliably used by the program, but it is not initialized and so may contain any sort of unknown junk. Allocate and clear to all zeros with:

```
int *intspace = calloc(3000, sizeof(int));
```

Notice that this takes two numbers as input, while `malloc` takes one.

## A pointer to a scalar is really just a one-item array

Say that we have a pointer named i to a single integer. It is an array of length 1, and if you request i[0], finding the location pointed to by i and stepping forward 0 steps works exactly as it did for longer arrays.

But we humans don't really think of single values as arrays of length 1, so there is a notational convenience for the common case of a one-item array: outside of a declaration line, i[0] and *i are equivalent. This can be confusing, because on the declaration line, the star seems to mean something different. There are rationales for why this makes sense (see "The Fault Is in Our Stars" on page 137), but for now remember that a star on a declaration line indicates a new pointer; a star on any other line indicates the value being pointed to.

Here is a block of code that sets the first value of the `list` array to 7. The last line checks this, and halts the program with an error if I'm wrong.

```
//tutorial/assert.c
#include <assert.h>

int main(){
    int list[100];
    int *list2 = list;    //Declares list2 as a pointer-to-int,
                          //pointing to the same block of memory list points to.

    *list2 = 7;           //list2 is a pointer-to-int, so *list2 is an int.

    assert(list[0] == 7);
}
```

## There is a special notation for elements of pointed-to structs

Given the declaration

```
ratio_s *pr;
```

we know that `pr` is a pointer to a `ratio_s`, not a `ratio_s` itself. The size of `pr` in memory is exactly as much as is required to hold a single pointer, not a full `ratio_s` structure.

One could get the numerator at the pointed-to struct via `(*pr).numerator`, because `(*pr)` is a plain `ratio_s`, and the dot notation gets a subelement. There is an arrow notation that saves the trouble of the parens-and-star combination. For example:

```
ratio_s *pr = malloc(sizeof(ratio_s));
pr->numerator = 3;
```

The two forms `pr->numerator` and `(*pr).numerator` are exactly identical, but the first is generally preferred as more legible.

## Pointers let you modify function inputs

Recall that copies of input variables are sent to a function, not the variables themselves. When the function exits, the copies are destroyed, and the original function inputs are entirely unmodified.

Now say that a pointer is sent in to a function. The copy of a pointer refers to the same space that the original pointer refers to. Here is a simple program using this strategy to modify what the input refers to:

```
//tutorial/pointer_in.c
#include <stdlib.h>
#include <stdio.h>

void double_in(int *in){
    *in *= 2;
}

int main(){
    int x[1]; // declare a one-item array, for demonstration purposes
    *x= 10;
    double_in(x);
    printf("x now points to %i.\n", *x);
}
```

The `double_in` function doesn't change `in`, but it does double the value pointed to by `in`, `*in`. Therefore, the value `x` points to has been doubled by the `double_in` function.

This workaround is common, so you will find many functions that take in a pointer, not a plain value. But sometimes you will want to use those functions to operate on a plain value. In these cases, you can use the ampersand (&) to get the address of the variable. That is, if `x` is a variable, `&x` is a pointer to that variable. This simplifies the above sample code:

```
//tutorial/address_in.c
#include <stdlib.h>
```

```
#include <stdio.h>

void double_in(int *in){
    *in *= 2;
}

int main(){
    int x= 10;
    double_in(&x);
    printf("x is now %i.\n", x);
}
```

## Everything is somewhere, so everything can be pointed to

You can't send a function to another function, and you can't have arrays of functions. But you can send a pointer to a function to a function, and you can have arrays of pointers to functions. I won't go into details of the syntax here, but see "Typedef as a teaching tool" on page 141.

Functions that don't really care what data is present, but only handle pointers to data, are surprisingly common. For example, a function that builds a linked list doesn't care what data it is linking together, only where it is located. To give another example, we can pass pointers to functions, so you could have a function whose sole purpose is to run other functions, and the inputs to those called functions can be pointed to without regard to their content. In these cases, C provides an out from the type system, the void pointer. Given the declaration

```
void *x;
```

the pointer x can be pointing to a function, a struct, an integer, or anything else. See "The Void Pointer and the Structures It Points To" on page 236 for examples of how void pointers can be used for all sorts of purposes.

# Glossary

alignment

A requirement that data elements begin at certain boundaries in memory. For example, given an 8-bit alignment requirement, a struct holding a 1-bit char followed by an 8-bit int might need 7 bits of padding after the char so that the int starts on an 8-bit boundary.

ASCII

American Standard Code for Information Interchange. A standard mapping from the naïve English character set to the numbers 0–127. Tip: on many systems, man ascii will print the table of codes.

automatic allocation

For an automatically allocated variable, its space in memory is allocated by the system at the point of the variable's declaration, then removed at the end of the given scope.

Autotools

A set of programs from GNU that simplify automatic compilation on any system, including Autoconf, Automake, and Libtool.

Benford's law

Leading digits in a wide range of data sets tend to have a log-like distribution: *1* has about 30% frequency, *2* about 17.5%, ... *9* about 4.5%.

Boolean

True/false. Named after George Boole, an English mathematician living in the early-to-mid 1800s.

BSD

Berkeley Software Distribution. An implementation of POSIX.

callback function

A function (A) that is sent as an input to another function (B) so that function B can call function A over the course of its operation. For example, generalized sort functions typically take as input a function to compare two elements.

call graph

A box-and-arrow diagram showing which functions call and are called by which other functions.

cetology

The study of whales.

compiler

Formally, the program that converts the (human-readable) text of a program into (human-illegible) machine instructions. Often used to refer to the preprocessor + compiler + linker.

debugger

A program for interactive execution of a compiled program, allowing users to pause the program, check and modify variable values, et cetera. Often useful for understanding bugs.

deep copy

A copy of a structure containing pointers, which follows all pointers and makes copies of the pointed-to data.

encoding

The means by which human-language characters are converted into numeric codes for processing by the computer. See also *ASCII*, *multibyte encoding*, and *wide-character encoding*.

environment variable

A variable present in the environment of a program, set by the parent program (typically the shell).

external pointer

See *opaque pointer*.

floating point

A representation of a number akin to scientific notation, like *2.3×10^4*, with an exponent part (in this example, 4) and a mantissa (here, 2.3). After writing down the mantissa, think of the exponent allowing the decimal point to float to its correct position.

frame

The space in the stack in which function information (such as inputs and automatic variables) is stored.

GDB

GNU debugger.

global

A variable is global when its scope is the entire program. C doesn't really have global scope, but if a variable is in a header that can reasonably be expected to be included in every code file in a program, then it is reasonable to call it a global variable.

glyph

A symbol used for written communication.

GNU

Gnu's Not Unix.

GSL

GNU Scientific Library.

heap

The space of memory from which manually allocated memory is taken. Compare with the *stack*.

IDE

Integrated development environment. Typically a program with a graphical interface based around a text editor, with facilities for compilation, debugging, and other programmer-friendly features.

integration test

A test that executes a sequence of steps that involve several segments of a code base (each of which should have its own unit test).

library

Basically, a program that has no main function, and is therefore a set of functions, typedefs, and variables available for use by other programs.

linker

The program that joins together disparate portions of a program (such as separate object files and libraries) and thus reconciles references to external-to-one-object-file functions or variables.

Linux

Technically, an operating system kernel, but generally used to refer to a full suite of BSD/GNU/Internet Systems Consortium/Linux/Xorg/… utilities bundled as a unified package.

macro

A (typically) short blob of text for which a (typically) longer blob is substituted.

manual allocation

Allocation of a variable on the heap at the programmer's request, using malloc or calloc, and freed at the user's request via free.

**multibyte encoding**

An encoding of text that uses a variable number of chars to represent a single human-language character. Contrast with *wide-character encoding.*

**mutex**

Short for mutual exclusion, a structure that can be used to ensure that only one thread is using a resource at a time.

**NaN**

Not-a-Number. The IEEE 754 (floating-point) standard defines this as the outcome of mathematical impossibilities like 0/0 or log(-1). Often used as a flag for missing or bad data.

**object**

A data structure and the associated functions that act on the data structure. Ideally, the object encapsulates a concept, providing a limited set of entry points for other code to interact with the object.

**object file**

A file containing machine-readable instructions. Typically the result of running a compiler on a source code file.

**opaque pointer**

A pointer to data in a format that can't be read by the function handling the pointer, but that can be passed on to other functions that can read the data. A function in a scripting language might call one C function that returns an opaque pointer to C-side data, and then a later function in the scripting language would use that pointer to act on the same C-side data.

**POSIX**

The Portable Operating System Interface. An IEEE standard to which UNIX-like operating systems conform, describing a set of C functions, the shell, and some basic utilities.

**preprocessor**

Conceptually, a program that runs just before the compiler, executing directives

such as #include and #define. In practice, typically a part of the compiler.

**process**

A running program.

**profiler**

A program that reports where your program is spending its time, so you know where to focus your efforts at speedup.

**pthread**

POSIX thread. A thread generated using the C threading interface defined in the POSIX standard.

**RNG**

Random number generator, where *random* basically means that one can reasonably expect that a sequence of random numbers is not systematically related to any other sequence.

**RTFM**

Read the manual.

**Sapir-Whorf Hypothesis**

The claim that the language we speak determines the thoughts we are capable of having. Its weakest form, that we often think in words, is obvious; its strongest form, that we are incapable of thoughts that our language lacks words or constructions for, is clearly false.

**scope**

The portion of the code base over which a variable is declared and accessible. Good coding style depends on keeping the scope of variables small.

**segfault**

Segmentation fault.

**segmentation fault**

Touching an incorrect segment of memory. Causes the operating system to halt the program immediately, and so often used metonymically to refer to any program-halting error.

**SHA**

Secure Hash Algorithm.

**shell**

A program that allows users to interact with an operating system, either at a command line or via scripts.

**SQL**

Structured Query Language. A standardized means of interacting with databases.

**stack**

The space in memory where function execution occurs. Notably, automatic variables are placed here. Each function gets a frame, and every time a subfunction is called, its frame is conceptually stacked on top of the calling function's frame.

**static allocation**

The method by which variables with file scope and variables inside functions declared as `static` are allocated. Allocation occurs before the program starts, and the variable continues to exist until the end of the program.

**test harness**

A system for running a sequence of unit tests and integration tests. Provides easy setup and teardown of auxiliary structures, and allows for checking of failures that may (correctly) halt the main program.

**thread**

A sequence of instructions that a computer executes independently of any other thread.

**token**

A set of characters to be treated as a semantic unit, such as a variable name, a keyword, or an operator like `*` or `+`. The first step in parsing text is to break it down into tokens; `strtok_r` and `strtok_s` are designed for this.

**type punning**

Casting a variable of one type to a second type, thus forcing the compiler to treat the variable as data of the second type. For example, given `struct {int a; char *b:}` astruct, then `(int)` astruct is an integer (but for a safer alternative, see "C, with fewer seams" on page 255). Frequently not portable; always bad form.

**type qualifier**

A descriptor of how the compiler may handle a variable. Is unrelated to the type of the variable (`int`, `float`, et cetera). C's only type qualifiers are `const`, `restrict`, `volatile`, and `_Atomic`.

**union**

A single block of memory that can be interpreted as one of several types.

**unit test**

A block of code to test a small piece of a code base. Compare with *integration test.*

**UI**

User interface. For a C library, this includes the typedefs, macro definitions, and function declarations that users are expected to be comfortable with when using the library.

**UTF**

Unicode Transformation Format.

**variadic function**

A function that takes in a variable number of inputs (e.g., `printf`).

**wide-character encoding**

An encoding of text where each human-language character is given a fixed number of chars. For example, UTF-32 guarantees that each Unicode character is expressed in exactly 4 bytes. Contrast this definition with *multibyte encoding.*

**XML**

Extensible Markup Language.

# References

Abelson, H., G. J. Sussman, and J. Sussman (1996). *Structure and Interpretation of Computer Programs*. The MIT Press.

Breshears, C. (2009). *The Art of Concurrency: A Thread Monkey's Guide to Writing Parallel Applications*. O'Reilly Media.

Calcote, J. (2010). *Autotools: A Practioner's Guide to GNU Autoconf, Automake, and Libtool*. No Starch Press.

Deitel, P. and H. Deitel (2013). *C for Programmers with an Introduction to C11 (Deitel Developer Series)*. Prentice Hall.

Dijkstra, E. (1968, March). Go to statement considered harmful. *Communications of the ACM 11*(3), 147–148.

Friedl, J. E. F. (2002). *Mastering Regular Expressions*. O'Reilly Media.

Goldberg, D. (1991). What every computer scientist should know about floating-point arithmetic. *ACM Computing Surveys 23*(1), 5–48.

Goodliffe, P. (2006). *Code Craft: The Practice of Writing Excellent Code*. No Starch Press.

Gough, B. (Ed.) (2003). *GNU Scientific Library Reference Manual* (2nd ed.). Network Theory, Ltd.

Gove, D. (2010). *Multicore Application Programming: for Windows, Linux, and Oracle Solaris (Developer's Library)*. Addison-Wesley Professional.

Grama, A., G. Karypis, V. Kumar, and A. Gupta (2003). *Introduction to Parallel Computing (2nd Edition)*. Addison-Wesley.

Griffiths, D. and D. Griffiths (2012). *Head First C*. O'Reilly Media.

Hanson, D. R. (1996). *C Interfaces and Implementations: Techniques for Creating Reusable Software*. Addison-Wesley Professional.

Harbison, S. P. and G. L. Steele Jr. (1991). *C: A Reference Manual* (3rd ed.). Prentice Hall.

Kernighan, B. W. and D. M. Ritchie (1978). *The C Programming Language* (1st ed.). Prentice Hall.

Kernighan, B. W. and D. M. Ritchie (1988). *The C Programming Language* (2nd ed.). Prentice Hall.

Klemens, B. (2008). *Modeling with Data: Tools and Techniques for Statistical Computing*. Princeton University Press.

Kochan, S. G. (2004). *Programming in C* (3rd ed.). Sams.

van der Linden, P. (1994). *Expert C Programming: Deep C Secrets*. Prentice Hall.

Meyers, S. (2000, February). How non-member functions improve encapsulation. *C/C++ Users Journal*.

Meyers, S. (2005). *Effective C++: 55 Specific Ways to Improve Your Programs and Designs* (3rd ed.). Addison-Wesley Professional.

Nabokov, V. (1962). *Pale Fire*. G P Putnams's Sons.

Norman, D. A. (2002). *The Design of Everyday Things*. Basic Books.

Oliveira, S. and D. E. Stewart (2006). *Writing Scientific Software: A Guide to Good Style*. Cambridge University Press.

Oram, A. and Talbott, T (1991). *Managing Projects with Make*. O'Reilly Media.

Oualline, S. (1997). *Practical C Programming* (3rd ed.). O'Reilly Media.

Page, A., K. Johnston, and B. Rollison (2008). *How We Test Software at Microsoft*. Microsoft Press.

Perry, G. (1994). *Absolute Beginner's Guide to C* (2nd ed.). Sams.

Prata, S. (2004). *The Waite Group's C Primer Plus* (5th ed.). Waite Group Press.

Press, W. H., B. P. Flannery, S. A. Teukolsky, and W. T. Vetterling (1988). *Numerical Recipes in C: The Art of Scientific Computing*. Cambridge University Press.

Press, W. H., B. P. Flannery, S. A. Teukolsky, and W. T. Vetterling (1992). *Numerical Recipes in C: The Art of Scientific Computing* (2nd ed.). Cambridge University Press.

Prinz, P. and T. Crawford (2005). *C in a Nutshell*. O'Reilly Media.

Spolsky, J. (2008). *More Joel on Software: Further Thoughts on Diverse and Occasionally Related Matters That Will Prove of Interest to Software Developers, Designers, and to Those Who, Whether by Good Fortune or Ill Luck, Work with Them in Some Capacity*. Apress.

Stallman, R. M., R. Pesch, and S. Shebs (2002). *Debugging with GDB: The GNU Source-Level Debugger*. Free Software Foundation.

Stroustrup, B. (1986). *The C++ Programming Language*. Addison-Wesley.

Ullman, L. and M. Liyanage (2004). *C Programming*. Peachpit Press.

# Index

automatic allocation, 365
automatic memory management, 126
Autotools
    contingency hooks in, 119
    Distutils, 120
    interfacing with, 116, 118
    packaging with
        benefits of, 79
        configure.ac shell script, 89
        content variables, 85
        example run, 81
        flowchart for, 83
        form variables, 84
        makefile bits, 88
        testing, 87
    using libraries from source with, 24

## B

backtraces, 35, 38, 51
basic environment setup
    compiling via here document
        benefits of, 29
        compilation pattern, 27
        compiling from stdin, 30
        including header files, 27
        unified headers, 28
    compiling with Windows
        POSIX for Windows, 6
        with POSIX, 8
        without POSIX, 9
    libraries
        compiler flags, 12
        compiler warnings, 13
        generating shared, 23
        locating, 14
        paths, 13
        private root directory for, 25
        runtime linking, 16
        using, 10
        using from source, 24
    makefiles
        benefits of, 17
        built-in variables, 20
        environment variables, 19
        rules for, 20
        setting variables, 17
    overview of, 3
    package manager, 4

Basic Linear Algebra Subprograms (BLAS)
    library, 15
basic regular expressions (BREs), 325
Benford's law, 365
blank tokens, 196
block scope variables, 177
blocking, 302
blocks, 350
Boolean arguments, 185, 365
Bourne shell, 17
BSD (Berkeley Software Distribution), xvi, 365
BSD License, xvii

## C

C language
    basic packages for development, 4
    Boolean arguments and, 185
    comparing unsigned integers, 158
    concurrent C code (see parallel threads)
    const keyword
        as type qualifier, 179
        char const** issue, 182
        depth of, 181
        noun-adjective form of, 180
        tension created by, 181
    declarations in, 144
    double vs. float, 155
    easier text handling in (see text handling)
    enums and strings, 149
    explicitly returning from main, 143
    externally linked variables in header files,
        177
    goto function, 151
    inessential concepts in, 143
    linkage with static and extern, 176
    macros in
        arguments and, 171
        basic principle, 167
        commenting out code, 175
        commonly defined, 172
        cultivating robust, 163
        debugging, 167
        do-while loops, 166
        header guards, 174
        preprocessor tricks, 168
        syntax rules, 164
        test macros, 172
        text substitutions with, 164
        types of, 164

ISO C99 standard, xiv
ISO/IEC 8859 format, 200

# K

K & R standard, xiii
Kernighan, Brian, xiii
keyboarding skills, 65

# L

lambda calculus, 249
Lesser GPL (LGPL), xvii
libiconv function, 202
libraries
  commonly used C libraries, 6
  compiler flags, 12
  compiler warnings, 13
  cURL, 337
  definition of, 366
  distribution licenses, xvi
  dynamic loading of, 109
  generating shared, 23
  GLib, 323
  GNU C, 26
  GNU Scientific Library (GSL), 332
  improvements in, 323
  libxml, 337
  locating, 14
  paths, 13
  POSIX
    gigantic data sets and mmap, 329
    parsing regular expressions with, 324
  private root directory for, 25
  runtime linking, 16
  standard, 347
  static vs. shared, 16
  Structured Query Language (SQL), 334
  typical format for, 247
  using, 10
  using from source, 24
Libtool, 23, 81, 88
  (see also Autoconf; Automake)
Libxml
  tagged trees in, 337
  UTF-8 encoding in, 202
licenses, xvi
linker flags, 23
linking, 116, 118, 176
list command, 36
lists

multiple, 212
returning multiple values with, 222
safely terminated, 211
vs. block-of-memory, 250
literate programming, 64
LLDB Debugger
  common commands in, 42
  popularity of, 34
  printing structures from, 49
  sample run of, 36
LoadLibrary function, 109
long double function, 155

# M

macros
  # (octothorps) and, 168
  arguments and, 171
  basic principle of, 167
  commenting out code, 175
  commonly defined, 172
  cultivating robust, 163
  debugging, 167
  definition of, 366
  do-while loops in, 166
  header guards, 174
  preprocessor tricks, 168
  SQL query, 336
  syntax rules, 164
  test macros, 172
  text substitutions with, 164
  types of, 164
  variable-length arguments, 210
main function, 35, 143, 354
makefiles
  benefits of, 17
  built-in variables, 20
  environment variables, 19
  Makefile.am
    content variables, 85
    form variables, 84
    makefile bits, 88
  rules for, 20
  setting variables, 17
  vs. shell scripts for packaging, 77
malloc
  avoiding bugs related to, 136
  location of memory allocated via, 127
  reasons to use, 136
  void pointer in, 147

## T

tab completion feature, 68
technical documentation, 63
tentative definitions, 178
terminal multiplexers, 74
test harnesses, 52, 368
TeX documentation system, 64
text files, retrieving, 109
text handling
  asprintf function
    constant strings, 191
    extending strings with, 193
    sensitive information and, 190
    string allocation with, 187
  drawbacks of C for, 187
  string-handling utilities, 197
  strtok function
    basic working of, 195
    tasks possible with, 194
  translations, 205
  Unicode
    display of, 200
    encoding for C code, 201
    premise of, 199
    programming caveats, 200
    sample program, 204
    Unicode libraries, 202
    UTF encoding, 199
threads (see parallel threads)
tmux multiplexer, 74
tokenization, 194, 368
translations, 205
tuples, 223
Turing, Alan, 249
two-dimensional arrays, 140
type checking, 266
type punning, 368
type qualifier, 179, 368
type-casting, 148
typedef, 141, 174, 219
types
  aggregating, 350
  defining, 351
  determining size of, 352

## U

U. S. copyright laws, xvi
Unicode
  display of, 200

encoding for C code, 201
libraries for, 202
premise of, 199
programming caveats, 200
sample program, 204
UTF encoding, 199
union keyword, 258
unit testing
  test coverage, 57
  test harnesses, 52
  using programs as libraries, 55
Unix standard, xv
unsigned integers, 158
UTF encoding, 199, 201

## V

Valgrind, 50
variables
  atomic, 314
  automatic management of, 126
  block scope, 177
  built-in, 20
  content variables, 85
  convenience variables, 45
  creating auxilary with preprocessor, 169
  declarations, 348
  environment, 19, 69, 366
  externally linked in header files, 177
  file scope variables, 176
  for GDB (GNU Debugger), 45
  form variables, 84
  global, 366
  in macros, 165
  in memory management, 128
  incrementing/scaling, 356
  localizing nonstatic, 302
  private copies of, 300
  scope, 269, 354
  setting, 17
  shell variables, 69
  state, 321
  static, 126, 130, 300
  undefined, 218
variadic functions, 225
variadic macros, 210
version control, 95
virtual tables (vtables)
  adding new functions with, 264
  benefits of, 269

hash function, 265
    macro for, 267
    type checking, 266
Visual Studio, 8
vsnprintf function, 187

## W

while keyword, 150
whitespace, preprocessors and, 168
wide character types, 203, 368
Windows

    compilation with, 6-10
    UTF encoding in, 200, 203
wrapper function, 113

## X

XML libraries, 247

## Z

Z shell, 75

## About the Author

**Ben Klemens** has been doing statistical analysis and computationally intensive modeling of populations ever since getting his Ph.D. in Social Sciences from Caltech. He is of the opinion that writing code should be fun, and has had a grand time writing analyses and models (mostly in C) for the Brookings Institution, the World Bank, National Institute of Mental Health, et al. As a nonresident fellow at Brookings and with the Free Software Foundation, he has done work on ensuring that creative authors retain the right to use the software they write. He currently works for the United States Federal Government.

## Colophon

The animal on the cover of *21st Century C* is the common spotted cuscus (*Spilocuscus maculatus*), a marsupial that lives in the rainforests and mangroves of Australia, New Guinea, and nearby smaller islands. It has a round head, small hidden ears, thick fur, and a prehensile tail to aid in climbing. The curled tail is a distinctive characteristic; the upper part of the tail closest to the body is covered in fur, while the lower half is covered in rough scales on the inside surface to grip branches. Its eyes range in color from yellows and oranges to reds, and are slit much like a snake's.

The common spotted cuscus is typically very shy, so it is rarely seen by humans. It is nocturnal, hunting and feeding at night and sleeping during the day on self-made platforms in tree branches. It is slow moving and somewhat sluggish—sometimes mistaken for sloths, other possums, or even monkeys.

Cuscuses are typically solitary creatures, feeding and nesting alone. Interactions with others, especially between competing males, can be aggressive and confrontational. Male cuscuses scent-mark their territory to warn off other males, emitting a penetrating musk odor both from their bodies and scent gland excretions. They distribute saliva on branches and twigs of trees to inform others of their territory and mediate social interactions. If they encounter another male in their area, they make barking, snarling, and hissing noises, and stand upright to defend their territory.

The common spotted cuscus has an unspecialized dentition, allowing it to eat a wide variety of plant products. It is also known to eat flowers, small animals, and occasionally eggs. Predators of the common spotted cuscus include pythons and some birds of prey.

The cover image is from Wood's *Animate Creation*. The cover fonts are URW Typewriter and Guardian Sans. The text font is Adobe Minion Pro; the heading font is Adobe Myriad Condensed; and the code font is Dalton Maag's Ubuntu Mono.

# Get even more for your money.

## Join the O'Reilly Community, and register the O'Reilly books you own. It's free, and you'll get:

- $4.99 ebook upgrade offer
- 40% upgrade offer on O'Reilly print books
- Membership discounts on books and events
- Free lifetime updates to ebooks and videos
- Multiple ebook formats, DRM FREE
- Participation in the O'Reilly community
- Newsletters
- Account management
- 100% Satisfaction Guarantee

### Signing up is easy:

1. Go to: oreilly.com/go/register
2. Create an O'Reilly login.
3. Provide your address.
4. Register your books.

Note: English-language books only

To order books online:
oreilly.com/store

For questions about products or an order:
orders@oreilly.com

To sign up to get topic-specific email announcements and/or news about upcoming books, conferences, special offers, and new technologies:
elists@oreilly.com

For technical questions about book content:
booktech@oreilly.com

To submit new book proposals to our editors:
proposals@oreilly.com

O'Reilly books are available in multiple DRM-free ebook formats. For more information:
oreilly.com/ebooks

O'REILLY®

Milton Keynes UK
Ingram Content Group UK Ltd.
UKHW050113240424
441577UK00003B/11